Business Plans Handbook

Business Plans

A COMPILATION
OF BUSINESS
PLANS DEVELOPED
BY INDIVIDUALS
THROUGHOUT
NORTH AMERICA

Plans

Handbook

VOLUME

20

Lynn M. Pearce,
Project Editor

GALE
CENGAGE Learning

Detroit • New York • San Francisco • New Haven, Conn • Waterville, Maine • London

GALE
CENGAGE Learning™

Business Plans Handbook, Volume 20

Project Editor: Lynn M. Pearce

Product Manager: Jenai Drouillard

Product Design: Jennifer Wahi

Composition and Electronic Prepress: Evi Seoud

Manufacturing: Rita Wimberley

Gale, a part of Cengage Learning
27500 Drake Rd.
Farmington Hills, MI 48331-3535

ISBN-13: 978-14144-6832-7
1084-4473

Printed in Mexico
1 2 3 4 5 6 7 13 12 11

Contents

BUSINESS PLANS

CONTENTS

Highlights

Business Plans Handbook, Volume 20 (BPH-20) is a collection of business plans compiled by entrepreneurs seeking funding for small businesses throughout North America. For those looking for examples of how to approach, structure, and compose their own business plans, *BPH-20* presents 20 sample plans, including plans for the following businesses:

- Ambulance Service
- Apartment Complex
- Barbershop
- Elder Care
- Human Resources Consultant
- Landscaping Service
- Marketing Consultant
- Montessori School
- Non-Medical Assistance
- Organic Food Store
- Pet Sitting Business
- Pet Waste Removal Business
- Retail Clothing
- Specialty Bakery
- Steak House
- Teacher Continuing Education
- Tutoring Service
- Used Furniture Business
- Virtual Assistance
- Wedding Planning Service

FEATURES AND BENEFITS

BPH-20 offers many features not provided by other business planning references including:

- Twenty business plans, each of which represent an attempt at clarifying (for themselves and others) the reasons that the business should exist or expand and why a lender should fund the enterprise.
- Two fictional plans that are used by business counselors at a prominent small business development organization as examples for their clients. (You will find these in the Business Plan Template Appendix.)
- A directory section that includes: listings for venture capital and finance companies, which specialize in funding start-up and second-stage small business ventures, and a comprehensive

listing of Service Corps of Retired Executives (SCORE) offices. In addition, the Appendix also contains updated listings of all Small Business Development Centers (SBDCs); associations of interest to entrepreneurs; Small Business Administration (SBA) Regional Offices; and consultants specializing in small business planning and advice. It is strongly advised that you consult supporting organizations while planning your business, as they can provide a wealth of useful information.

- A Small Business Term Glossary to help you decipher the sometimes confusing terminology used by lenders and others in the financial and small business communities.

- A cumulative index, outlining each plan profiled in the complete *Business Plans Handbook* series.

- A Business Plan Template which serves as a model to help you construct your own business plan. This generic outline lists all the essential elements of a complete business plan and their components, including the Summary, Business History and Industry Outlook, Market Examination, Competition, Marketing, Administration and Management, Financial Information, and other key sections. Use this guide as a starting point for compiling your plan.

- Extensive financial documentation required to solicit funding from small business lenders. You will find examples of: Cash Flows, Balance Sheets, Income Projections, and other financial information included with the textual portions of the plan.

Introduction

Perhaps the most important aspect of business planning is simply doing it. More and more business owners are beginning to compile business plans even if they don't need a bank loan. Others discover the value of planning when they must provide a business plan for the bank. The sheer act of putting thoughts on paper seems to clarify priorities and provide focus. Sometimes business owners completely change strategies when compiling their plan, deciding on a different product mix or advertising scheme after finding that their assumptions were incorrect. This kind of healthy thinking and re-thinking via business planning is becoming the norm. The editors of *Business Plans Handbook, Volume 20 (BPH-20)* sincerely hope that this latest addition to the series is a helpful tool in the successful completion of your business plan, no matter what the reason for creating it.

This twentieth volume, like each volume in the series, offers business plans used and created by real people. *BPH-20* provides 20 business plans. The business and personal names and addresses and general locations have been changed to protect the privacy of the plan authors.

NEW BUSINESS OPPORTUNITIES

As in other volumes in the series, *BPH-20* finds entrepreneurs engaged in a wide variety of creative endeavors. Examples include a proposal for an ambulance service, a barbershop, and a landscaping service. In addition, several other plans are provided, including a Montessori school, an organic food store, a specialty bakery, and a teacher continuing education service, among others.

Comprehensive financial documentation has become increasingly important as today's entrepreneurs compete for the finite resources of business lenders. Our plans illustrate the financial data generally required of loan applicants, including Income Statements, Financial Projections, Cash Flows, and Balance Sheets.

ENHANCED APPENDIXES

In an effort to provide the most relevant and valuable information for our readers, we have updated the coverage of small business resources. For instance, you will find: a directory section, which includes listings of all of the Service Corps of Retired Executives (SCORE) offices; an informative glossary, which includes small business terms; and a cumulative index, outlining each plan profiled in the complete *Business Plans Handbook* series. In addition we have updated the list of Small Business Development Centers (SBDCs); Small Business Administration Regional Offices; venture capital and finance companies, which specialize in funding start-up and second-stage small business enterprises; associations of interest to entrepreneurs; and consultants, specializing in small business advice and planning. For your reference, we have also reprinted the business plan template, which provides a comprehensive overview of the essential components of a business plan and two fictional plans used by small business counselors.

SERIES INFORMATION

If you already have the first nineteen volumes of *BPH*, with this twentieth volume, you will now have a collection of over 415 business plans (not including the updated plans); contact information for hundreds of organizations and agencies offering business expertise; a helpful business plan template; more than 1,500 citations to valuable small business development material; and a comprehensive glossary of terms to help the business planner navigate the sometimes confusing language of entrepreneurship.

ACKNOWLEDGEMENTS

The Editors wish to sincerely thank the contributors to *BPH-20*, including:

- BizPlanDB.com
- Heidi Denler
- Hannah Dust
- Christina Garcia
- Paul Greenland
- Michael Holthaus
- Kari Lucke
- Samuel Maguire
- Jintong Tang, Saint Louis University

COMMENTS WELCOME

Your comments on *Business Plans Handbook* are appreciated. Please direct all correspondence, suggestions for future volumes of *BPH*, and other recommendations to the following:

Managing Editor, Business Product
Business Plans Handbook
Gale, a part of Cengage Learning
27500 Drake Rd.
Farmington Hills, MI 48331-3535
Phone: (248)699-4253
Fax: (248)699-8052
Toll-Free: 800-347-GALE
E-mail: BusinessProducts@gale.com

Ambulance Service

CareOne Ambulance Service

9981 Main St.
Flushing, NY 11355

BizPlanDB.com

CareOne Ambulance Service, Inc. is a New York-based corporation that will provide emergency and non-emergency medical transportation services to people in its targeted market.

1.0 EXECUTIVE SUMMARY

The purpose of this business plan is to raise $250,000 for the development of an ambulance service while showcasing the expected financials and operations over the next three years. CareOne Ambulance Service, Inc. is a New York-based corporation that will provide emergency and non-emergency medical transportation services to people in its targeted market. The Company was founded by Andrew McNally.

1.1 The Services

As mentioned above, the business intends to provide emergency and non-emergency transportation of people to hospitals, physicians, physical therapy clinics, and outpatient centers. The Company will be able to attend to both 911 calls and traditional medical ambulatory needs.

The business will receive a majority of its income from publicly funded healthcare systems and private insurance companies.

The third section of the business plan will further describe the services offered by CareOne Ambulance Service.

1.2 Financing

Mr. McNally is seeking to raise $250,000 from a bank loan. The interest rate and loan agreement are to be further discussed during negotiation. This business plan assumes that the business will receive a 10-year loan with a 9% fixed interest rate. The financing will be used for the following:

- Development of the dispatch location.

- Financing for the first six months of operation.

- Capital to purchase two ambulances with medical equipment.

Mr. McNally will contribute $50,000 to the venture.

1.3 Mission Statement

CareOne Ambulance Service's mission is to become the recognized premier provider of ambulatory services within its target market.

1.4 Management Team

The Company was founded by Andrew McNally. Mr. McNally has more than 10 years of experience as an emergency medical technician. Through his expertise, he will be able to bring the operations of the business to profitability within its first year of operations.

1.5 Sales Forecasts

Mr. McNally expects a strong rate of growth at the start of operations. Below are the expected financials over the next three years.

Proforma profit and loss (yearly)

Year	1	2	3
Sales	$806,778	$968,134	$1,132,716
Operating costs	$499,867	$522,203	$ 545,631
EBITDA	$226,233	$349,117	$ 473,813
Taxes, interest, and depreciation	$125,491	$162,947	$ 209,303
Net profit	$100,742	$186,170	$ 264,510

Sales, operating costs, and profit forecast

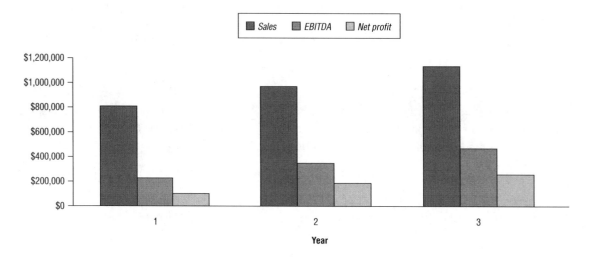

1.6 Expansion Plan

Mr. McNally expects that the business will aggressively expand during the first three years of operation. He intends to implement marketing campaigns that will effectively target individuals within the target market.

2.0 COMPANY AND FINANCING SUMMARY

2.1 Registered Name and Corporate Structure

CareOne Ambulance Service, Inc. is registered as a corporation in the State of New York.

2.2 Required Funds

At this time, CareOne Ambulance Service requires $250,000 of debt funds. Below is a breakdown of how these funds will be used:

Projected startup costs

Initial lease payments and deposits	$ 10,000
Working capital	$ 45,000
FF&E	$ 20,000
Leasehold improvements	$ 5,000
Security deposits	$ 5,000
Insurance	$ 2,500
Ambulances with equipment	$200,000
Marketing budget	$ 7,500
Miscellaneous and unforeseen costs	$ 5,000
Total startup costs	**$300,000**

Use of funds

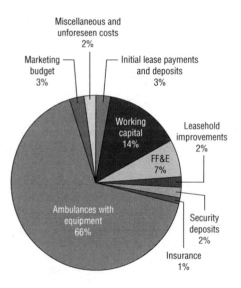

2.3 Investor Equity

Mr. McNally is not seeking an investment from a third party at this time.

2.4 Management Equity

Andrew McNally owns 100% of CareOne Ambulance Service, Inc.

2.5 Exit Strategy

If the business is very successful, Mr. McNally may seek to sell the business to a third party for a significant earnings multiple. Most likely, the Company will hire a qualified business broker to sell the business. Based on historical numbers, the business could fetch a sales premium of up to 3 to 6 times earnings.

3.0 CAREONE AMBULANCE SERVICES

CareOne Ambulance Service is an emergency medical services transportation company that will be licensed by the State of New York. The Company will provide basic and advanced life support ground transport in an emergency and non–emergency setting, 24 hours a day, seven days a week. The Company will make both local and out–of–town services available.

Management will remain focused on providing prompt, high–quality patient care at the Advanced and Basic Life Support levels. Employees will work diligently to achieve goals while maintaining the highest standards of care. This is imperative as patients will depend on CareOne Ambulance Service for all medical transportation needs.

4.0 STRATEGIC AND MARKET ANALYSIS

4.1 Economic Outlook

This section of the analysis will detail the economic climate, the ambulatory service industry, the customer profile, and the competition that the business will face as it progresses through its business operations.

Currently, the economic market condition in the United States is in recession. This slowdown in the economy has also greatly impacted real estate sales, which has halted to historical lows. Many economists expect that this recession will continue for a prolonged period of time, at which point the economy will begin a prolonged recovery period. Among medical businesses, there are very few risks beyond standard operating procedural risks. The demand for medical services (including ambulatory transportation) remains high regardless of the overall economic environment.

4.2 Industry Analysis

Within the United States, there are 4,000 companies that provide emergency and non-emergency ambulatory care services to the general public. Approximately 30% of these businesses operate in a not-for-profit capacity. Each year, these businesses generate more than $6.6 billion dollars a year while providing jobs to more than 111,000 people. Aggregate payrolls in each of the last five years have exceeded $2.7 billion dollars.

4.3 Customer Profile

The average patient of CareOne Ambulance Service, Inc. will be a person living within Company's target service area. The demographics that the Company will use when advertising and marketing its services are:

- Aged 15 to 80

- Has a family household income of $25,000 to $80,000 per year

- Is in need of emergency or non-emergency ambulatory medical services.

As anyone in need of emergency medical assistance could become a potential patient of CareOne Ambulance Service, it is difficult to determine the exact demographics of individuals that will use the Company for their emergency medical needs. However, Management anticipates that the majority of people using the Company's ambulatory services will be over the age of 65. Based on demographic information regarding the New York metropolitan area, there are more than 400,000 people in the targeted market that may require emergency or non-emergency ambulatory care.

4.4 Competition

Within the greater New York metropolitan area there are approximately 200 independent ambulatory service companies that provide both emergency and non-emergency care to patients. The business will compete among these businesses for when emergencies arise. However, Management intends to develop ongoing relationships with New York area hospitals and doctors that will call CareOne Ambulance Service when their patients are in need of transportation to medical facilities.

5.0 MARKETING PLAN

The CareOne Ambulance Service intends to maintain an extensive marketing campaign that will ensure maximum visibility for the business in its targeted market. Below is an overview of the marketing strategies and objectives of the Company.

5.1 Marketing Objectives

- Establish relationships with hospitals and 911 call centers within the targeted market.

- Develop relationships with nursing homes, outpatient facilities, assisted living facilities, and other healthcare businesses that have non-emergency ambulatory transportation needs.

5.2 Marketing Strategies

Management intends on using a number of marketing strategies that will allow the business to generate revenue from its ambulatory services at the onset of operations. Prior to commencing business, Mr. McNally will develop relationships with physicians, hospitals, outpatient facilities, and physical therapy clinics. Mr. McNally intends to develop an expansive brochure regarding the Company's services that will showcase the licensure and cost effectiveness of the Company's services.

The business will also develop relationships with municipal governments that maintain 911 call centers so that pick ups are dispatched to the Company.

It is important to note that once these relationships are solidified, the Company will be able to maintain a regular (if not daily) stream of referrals to the business. As such, the marketing expenditures of the business will decline once CareOne Ambulance Service has developed these ongoing relationships.

5.3 Pricing

For each emergency ambulatory service provided, Management anticipates that the business will generate approximately $500 of revenue. For non-emergency ambulatory care, Management anticipates that each patient will pay (via their insurance/Medicare) $50 for transportation to a medical facility.

6.0 ORGANIZATIONAL PLAN AND PERSONNEL SUMMARY

6.1 Corporate Organization

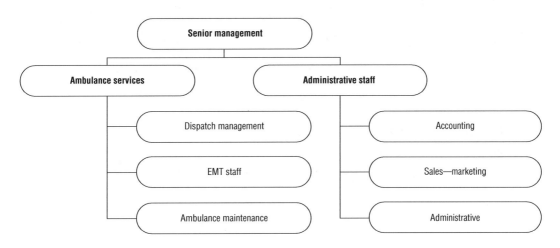

6.2 Organizational Budget

Personnel plan—yearly

Year	2009	2010	2011
Owner	$ 50,000	$ 51,500	$ 53,045
Dispatch manager	$ 47,500	$ 48,925	$ 50,393
EMT staff	$150,000	$154,500	$159,135
Bookkeeper (P/T)	$ 12,500	$ 12,875	$ 13,261
Administrative	$ 46,000	$ 47,380	$ 48,801
Total	**$306,000**	**$315,180**	**$324,635**

Numbers of personnel

Owner	1	1	1
Dispatch manager	1	1	1
EMT staff	4	4	4
Bookkeeper (P/T)	1	1	1
Administrative	2	2	2
Totals	**9**	**9**	**9**

Personnel expense breakdown

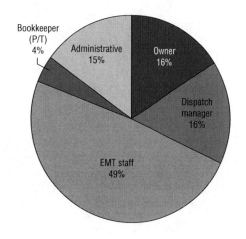

7.0 FINANCIAL PLAN

7.1 Underlying Assumptions

The Company has based its proforma financial statements on the following:

• CareOne Ambulance Service will have an annual revenue growth rate of 11% per year.

• The Owner will acquire $250,000 of debt funds to develop the business.

• The loan will have a 10 year term with a 9% interest rate.

7.2 Sensitivity Analysis

The Company's revenues are not sensitive to changes in the general economy. Emergency medical services, including ambulatory services, are required despite deleterious changes in the general economy. Additionally, the Company will receive its revenues directly from private insurance companies and publicly funded health systems, which will ensure the Company's profitability and cash flow on a monthly basis.

7.3 Source of Funds

Financing

Equity contributions

Management investment	$ 50,000.00
Total equity financing	**$ 50,000.00**

Banks and lenders

Banks and lenders	$ 250,000.00
Total debt financing	**$ 250,000.00**
Total financing	**$ 300,000.00**

7.4 General Assumptions

General assumptions

Year	1	2	3
Short term interest rate	9.5%	9.5%	9.5%
Long term interest rate	10.0%	10.0%	10.0%
Federal tax rate	33.0%	33.0%	33.0%
State tax rate	5.0%	5.0%	5.0%
Personnel taxes	15.0%	15.0%	15.0%

7.5 Profit and Loss Statements

Proforma profit and loss (yearly)

Year	1	2	3
Sales	**$806,778**	**$968,134**	**$1,132,716**
Cost of goods sold	$ 80,678	$ 96,813	$ 113,272
Gross margin	90.00%	90.00%	90.00%
Operating income	**$726,100**	**$871,320**	**$1,019,445**
Expenses			
Payroll	$306,000	$315,180	$ 324,635
General and administrative	$ 25,200	$ 26,208	$ 27,256
Marketing expenses	$ 4,034	$ 4,841	$ 5,664
Professional fees and licensure	$ 15,219	$ 15,676	$ 16,146
Insurance costs	$ 21,987	$ 23,086	$ 24,241
Fuel and maintenance costs	$ 57,596	$ 63,356	$ 69,691
Rent and utilities	$ 14,250	$ 14,963	$ 15,711
Miscellaneous costs	$ 9,681	$ 11,618	$ 13,593
Payroll taxes	$ 45,900	$ 47,277	$ 48,695
Total operating costs	**$499,867**	**$522,203**	**$ 545,631**
EBITDA	**$226,233**	**$349,117**	**$ 473,813**
Federal income tax	$ 74,657	$108,500	$ 150,197
State income tax	$ 11,312	$ 16,439	$ 22,757
Interest expense	$ 21,844	$ 20,328	$ 18,671
Depreciation expenses	$ 17,679	$ 17,679	$ 17,679
Net profit	**$100,742**	**$186,170**	**$ 264,510**
Profit margin	**12.49%**	**19.23%**	**23.35%**

Sales, operating costs, and profit forecast

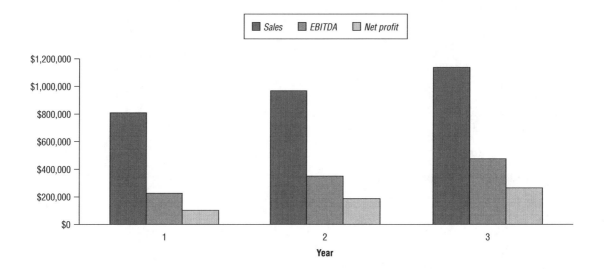

7.6 Cash Flow Analysis

Proforma cash flow analysis—yearly

Year	1	2	3
Cash from operations	$118,420	$203,849	$282,188
Cash from receivables	$ 0	$ 0	$ 0
Operating cash inflow	**$118,420**	**$203,849**	**$282,188**
Other cash inflows			
Equity investment	$ 50,000	$ 0	$ 0
Increased borrowings	$250,000	$ 0	$ 0
Sales of business assets	$ 0	$ 0	$ 0
A/P increases	$ 37,902	$ 43,587	$ 50,125
Total other cash inflows	**$337,902**	**$ 43,587**	**$ 50,125**
Total cash inflow	**$456,322**	**$247,436**	**$332,314**
Cash outflows			
Repayment of principal	$ 16,158	$ 17,674	$ 19,332
A/P decreases	$ 24,897	$ 29,876	$ 35,852
A/R increases	$ 0	$ 0	$ 0
Asset purchases	$247,500	$ 50,962	$ 70,547
Dividends	$ 82,894	$142,694	$197,532
Total cash outflows	**$371,450**	**$241,207**	**$323,263**
Net cash flow	**$ 84,873**	**$ 6,229**	**$ 9,051**
Cash balance	**$ 84,873**	**$ 91,102**	**$100,153**

Proforma cash flow (yearly)

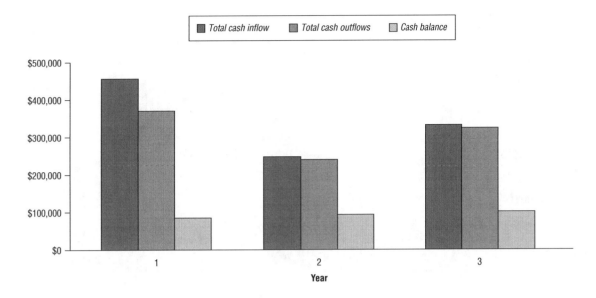

7.7 Balance Sheet

Proforma balance sheet—yearly

Year	1	2	3
Assets			
Cash	$ 84,873	$ 91,102	$100,153
Amortized development/expansion costs	$ 27,500	$ 32,596	$ 39,651
Ambulances and equipment	$ 200,000	$225,481	$260,755
FF&E	$ 20,000	$ 40,385	$ 68,604
Accumulated depreciation	($ 17,679)	($ 35,357)	($ 53,036)
Total assets	**$314,694**	**$354,207**	**$416,126**
Liabilities and equity			
Accounts payable	$ 13,005	$ 26,716	$ 40,990
Long term liabilities	$233,842	$216,167	$198,493
Other liabilities	$ 0	$ 0	$ 0
Total liabilities	**$246,847**	**$242,883**	**$239,483**
Net worth	**$ 67,847**	**$111,324**	**$176,644**
Total liabilities and equity	**$314,694**	**$354,207**	**$416,126**

Proforma balance sheet

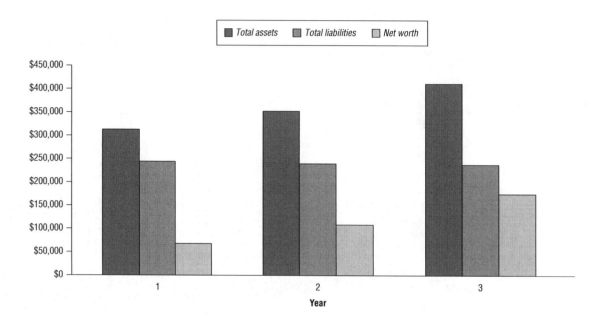

7.8 Breakeven Analysis

Monthly break even analysis

Year	1	2	3
Monthly revenue	$ 46,284	$ 48,352	$ 50,521
Yearly revenue	$555,408	$580,226	$606,257

Break even analysis

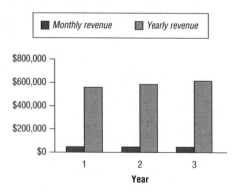

7.9 Business Ratios

Business ratios—yearly

Year	1	2	3
Sales			
Sales growth	0.00%	20.00%	17.00%
Gross margin	90.00%	90.00%	90.00%
Financials			
Profit margin	12.49%	19.23%	23.35%
Assets to liabilities	1.27	1.46	1.74
Equity to liabilities	0.27	0.46	0.74
Assets to equity	4.64	3.18	2.36
Liquidity			
Acid test	0.34	0.38	0.42
Cash to assets	0.27	0.26	0.24

7.10 Three Year Profit and Loss Statement

Profit and loss statement (first year)

Months	1	2	3	4	5	6	7
Sales	$66,500	$66,633	$66,766	$66,899	$67,032	$67,165	$67,298
Cost of goods sold	$ 6,650	$ 6,663	$ 6,677	$ 6,690	$ 6,703	$ 6,717	$ 6,730
Gross margin	90.0%	90.0%	90.0%	90.0%	90.0%	90.0%	90.0%
Operating income	$59,850	$59,970	$60,089	$60,209	$60,329	$60,449	$60,568
Expenses							
Payroll	$25,500	$25,500	$ 25,500	$25,500	$25,500	$25,500	$25,500
General and administrative	$ 2,100	$ 2,100	$ 2,100	$ 2,100	$ 2,100	$ 2,100	$ 2,100
Marketing expenses	$ 336	$ 336	$ 336	$ 336	$ 336	$ 336	$ 336
Professional fees and licensure	$ 1,268	$ 1,268	$ 1,268	$ 1,268	$ 1,268	$ 1,268	$ 1,268
Insurance costs	$ 1,832	$ 1,832	$ 1,832	$ 1,832	$ 1,832	$ 1,832	$ 1,832
Fuel and maintenance costs	$ 4,800	$ 4,800	$ 4,800	$ 4,800	$ 4,800	$ 4,800	$ 4,800
Rent and utilities	$ 1,188	$ 1,188	$ 1,188	$ 1,188	$ 1,188	$ 1,188	$ 1,188
Miscellaneous costs	$ 807	$ 807	$ 807	$ 807	$ 807	$ 807	$ 807
Payroll taxes	$ 3,825	$ 3,825	$ 3,825	$ 3,825	$ 3,825	$ 3,825	$ 3,825
Total operating costs	$41,656	$41,656	$ 41,656	$41,656	$41,656	$41,656	$41,656
EBITDA	$18,194	$18,314	$ 18,434	$18,553	$18,673	$18,793	$18,913
Federal income tax	$ 6,154	$ 6,166	$ 6,178	$ 6,191	$ 6,203	$ 6,215	$ 6,228
State income tax	$ 932	$ 934	$ 936	$ 938	$ 940	$ 942	$ 944
Interest expense	$ 1,875	$ 1,865	$ 1,856	$ 1,846	$ 1,836	$ 1,826	$ 1,816
Depreciation expense	$ 1,473	$ 1,473	$ 1,473	$ 1,473	$ 1,473	$ 1,473	$ 1,473
Net profit	$ 7,760	$ 7,875	$ 7,991	$ 8,106	$ 8,221	$ 8,337	$ 8,452

Profit and loss statement (first year cont.)

Month	8	9	10	11	12	1
Sales	**$67,431**	**$67,564**	**$67,697**	**$67,830**	**$67,963**	**$806,778**
Cost of goods sold	$ 6,743	$ 6,756	$ 6,770	$ 6,783	$ 6,796	$ 80,678
Gross margin	90.0%	90.0%	90.0%	90.0%	90.0%	90.0%
Operating income	**$60,688**	**$60,808**	**$60,927**	**$61,047**	**$61,167**	**$726,100**
Expenses						
Payroll	$25,500	$25,500	$25,500	$25,500	$25,500	$306,000
General and administrative	$ 2,100	$ 2,100	$ 2,100	$ 2,100	$ 2,100	$ 25,200
Marketing expenses	$ 336	$ 336	$ 336	$ 336	$ 336	$ 4,034
Professional fees and licensure	$ 1,268	$ 1,268	$ 1,268	$ 1,268	$ 1,268	$ 15,219
Insurance costs	$ 1,832	$ 1,832	$ 1,832	$ 1,832	$ 1,832	$ 21,987
Fuel and maintenance costs	$ 4,800	$ 4,800	$ 4,800	$ 4,800	$ 4,800	$ 57,596
Rent and utilities	$ 1,188	$ 1,188	$ 1,188	$ 1,188	$ 1,188	$ 14,250
Miscellaneous costs	$ 807	$ 807	$ 807	$ 807	$ 807	$ 9,681
Payroll taxes	$ 3,825	$ 3,825	$ 3,825	$ 3,825	$ 3,825	$ 45,900
Total operating costs	**$41,656**	**$41,656**	**$41,656**	**$41,656**	**$41,656**	**$499,867**
EBITDA	**$19,032**	**$19,152**	**$19,272**	**$19,391**	**$19,511**	**$226,233**
Federal income tax	$ 6,240	$ 6,252	$ 6,264	$ 6,277	$ 6,289	$ 74,657
State income tax	$ 945	$ 947	$ 949	$ 951	$ 953	$ 11,312
Interest expense	$ 1,806	$ 1,795	$ 1,785	$ 1,775	$ 1,764	$ 21,844
Depreciation expense	$ 1,473	$ 1,473	$ 1,473	$ 1,473	$ 1,473	$ 17,679
Net profit	**$ 8,568**	**$ 8,684**	**$ 8,800**	**$ 8,916**	**$ 9,032**	**$100,742**

Profit and loss statement (second year)

Quarter	Q1	2 Q2	Q3	Q4	2
Sales	**$193,627**	**$242,033**	**$261,396**	**$271,077**	**$968,134**
Cost of goods sold	$ 19,363	$ 24,203	$ 26,140	$ 27,108	$ 96,813
Gross margin	90.0%	90.0%	90.0%	90.0%	90.0%
Operating income	**$174,264**	**$217,830**	**$235,256**	**$243,970**	**$871,320**
Expenses					
Payroll	$ 63,036	$ 78,795	$ 85,099	$ 88,250	$315,180
General and administrative	$ 5,242	$ 6,552	$ 7,076	$ 7,338	$ 26,208
Marketing expenses	$ 968	$ 1,210	$ 1,307	$ 1,355	$ 4,841
Professional fees and licensure	$ 3,135	$ 3,919	$ 4,232	$ 4,389	$ 15,676
Insurance costs	$ 4,617	$ 5,772	$ 6,233	$ 6,464	$ 23,086
Fuel and maintenance costs	$ 12,671	$ 15,839	$ 17,106	$ 17,740	$ 63,356
Rent and utilities	$ 2,993	$ 3,741	$ 4,040	$ 4,190	$ 14,963
Miscellaneous costs	$ 2,324	$ 2,904	$ 3,137	$ 3,253	$ 11,618
Payroll taxes	$ 9,455	$ 11,819	$ 12,765	$ 13,238	$ 47,277
Total operating costs	**$104,441**	**$130,551**	**$140,995**	**$146,217**	**$522,203**
EBITDA	**$ 69,823**	**$ 87,279**	**$ 94,262**	**$ 97,753**	**$349,117**
Federal income tax	$ 21,700	$ 27,125	$ 29,295	$ 30,380	$108,500
State income tax	$ 3,288	$ 4,110	$ 4,439	$ 4,603	$ 16,439
Interest expense	$ 5,230	$ 5,133	$ 5,034	$ 4,932	$ 20,328
Depreciation expense	$ 4,420	$ 4,420	$ 4,420	$ 4,420	$ 17,679
Net profit	**$ 35,186**	**$ 46,492**	**$ 51,075**	**$ 53,418**	**$186,170**

Profit and loss statement (third year)

Quarter	Q1	3 Q2	Q3	Q4	3
Sales	**$226,543**	**$283,179**	**$305,833**	**$317,161**	**$1,132,716**
Cost of goods sold	$ 22,654	$ 28,318	$ 30,583	$ 31,716	$ 113,272
Gross margin	90.0%	90.0%	90.0%	90.0%	90.0%
Operating income	**$203,889**	**$254,861**	**$275,250**	**$285,445**	**$1,019,445**
Expenses					
Payroll	$ 64,927	$ 81,159	$ 87,652	$ 90,898	$ 324,635
General and administrative	$ 5,451	$ 6,814	$ 7,359	$ 7,632	$ 27,256
Marketing expenses	$ 1,133	$ 1,416	$ 1,529	$ 1,586	$ 5,664
Professional fees and licensure	$ 3,229	$ 4,036	$ 4,359	$ 4,521	$ 16,146
Insurance costs	$ 4,848	$ 6,060	$ 6,545	$ 6,787	$ 24,241
Fuel and maintenance costs	$ 13,938	$ 17,423	$ 18,817	$ 19,514	$ 69,691
Rent and utilities	$ 3,142	$ 3,928	$ 4,242	$ 4,399	$ 15,711
Miscellaneous costs	$ 2,719	$ 3,398	$ 3,670	$ 3,806	$ 13,593
Payroll taxes	$ 9,739	$ 12,174	$ 13,148	$ 13,635	$ 48,695
Total operating costs	**$109,126**	**$136,408**	**$147,321**	**$152,777**	**$ 545,631**
EBITDA	**$ 94,763**	**$118,453**	**$127,930**	**$132,668**	**$ 473,813**
Federal income tax	$ 30,039	$ 37,549	$ 40,553	$ 42,055	$ 150,197
State income tax	$ 4,551	$ 5,689	$ 6,144	$ 6,372	$ 22,757
Interest expense	$ 4,829	$ 4,723	$ 4,615	$ 4,504	$ 18,671
Depreciation expense	$ 4,420	$ 4,420	$ 4,420	$ 4,420	$ 17,679
Net profit	**$ 50,923**	**$ 66,072**	**$ 72,198**	**$ 75,317**	**$ 264,510**

7.11 Three Year Cash Flow Analysis

Cash flow analysis (first year)

Month	1	2	3	4	5	6	7	8
Cash from operations	$ 9,233	$ 9,349	$ 9,464	$ 9,579	$ 9,695	$ 9,810	$ 9,926	$ 10,041
Cash from receivables	$ 0	$ 0	$ 0	$ 0	$ 0	$ 0	$ 0	$ 0
Operating cash inflow	**$ 9,233**	**$ 9,349**	**$ 9,464**	**$ 9,579**	**$ 9,695**	**$ 9,810**	**$ 9,926**	**$ 10,041**
Other cash inflows								
Equity investment	$ 50,000	$ 0	$ 0	$ 0	$ 0	$ 0	$ 0	$ 0
Increased borrowings	$250,000	$ 0	$ 0	$ 0	$ 0	$ 0	$ 0	$ 0
Sales of business assets	$ 0	$ 0	$ 0	$ 0	$ 0	$ 0	$ 0	$ 0
A/P increases	$ 3,159	$ 3,159	$ 3,159	$ 3,159	$ 3,159	$ 3,159	$ 3,159	$ 3,159
Total other cash inflows	**$303,159**	**$ 3,159**	**$ 3,159**	**$ 3,159**	**$ 3,159**	**$ 3,159**	**$ 3,159**	**$ 3,159**
Total cash inflow	**$312,392**	**$12,507**	**$12,622**	**$12,738**	**$12,853**	**$ 12,969**	**$ 13,084**	**$ 13,200**
Cash outflows								
Repayment of principal	$ 1,292	$ 1,302	$ 1,311	$ 1,321	$ 1,331	$ 1,341	$ 1,351	$ 1,361
A/P decreases	$ 2,075	$ 2,075	$ 2,075	$ 2,075	$ 2,075	$ 2,075	$ 2,075	$ 2,075
A/R increases	$ 0	$ 0	$ 0	$ 0	$ 0	$ 0	$ 0	$ 0
Asset purchases	$247,500	$ 0	$ 0	$ 0	$ 0	$ 0	$ 0	$ 0
Dividends	$ 0	$ 0	$ 0	$ 0	$ 0	$ 0	$ 0	$ 0
Total cash outflows	**$250,867**	**$ 3,376**	**$ 3,386**	**$ 3,396**	**$ 3,406**	**$ 3,416**	**$ 3,426**	**$ 3,436**
Net cash flow	**$ 61,525**	**$ 9,131**	**$ 9,236**	**$ 9,342**	**$ 9,447**	**$ 9,553**	**$ 9,658**	**$ 9,764**
Cash balance	**$ 61,525**	**$70,656**	**$79,892**	**$89,234**	**$98,681**	**$108,234**	**$117,892**	**$127,656**

Cash flow analysis (first year cont.)

Month	9	10	11	12	1
Cash from operations	$ 10,157	$ 10,273	$ 10,389	$10,505	$118,420
Cash from receivables	$ 0	$ 0	$ 0	$ 0	$ 0
Operating cash inflow	**$ 10,157**	**$ 10,273**	**$ 10,389**	**$10,505**	**$118,420**
Other cash inflows					
Equity investment	$ 0	$ 0	$ 0	$ 0	$ 50,000
Increased borrowings	$ 0	$ 0	$ 0	$ 0	$250,000
Sales of business assets	$ 0	$ 0	$ 0	$ 0	$ 0
A/P increases	$ 3,159	$ 3,159	$ 3,159	$ 3,159	$ 37,902
Total other cash inflows	**$ 3,159**	**$ 3,159**	**$ 3,159**	**$ 3,159**	**$337,902**
Total cash inflow	**$ 13,316**	**$ 13,431**	**$ 13,547**	**$13,663**	**$456,322**
Cash outflows					
Repayment of principal	$ 1,371	$ 1,382	$ 1,392	$ 1,403	$ 16,158
A/P decreases	$ 2,075	$ 2,075	$ 2,075	$ 2,075	$ 24,897
A/R increases	$ 0	$ 0	$ 0	$ 0	$ 0
Asset purchases	$ 0	$ 0	$ 0	$ 0	$247,500
Dividends	$ 0	$ 0	$ 0	$82,894	$ 82,894
Total cash outflows	**$ 3,446**	**$ 3,457**	**$ 3,467**	**$86,371**	**$371,450**
Net cash flow	**$ 9,869**	**$ 9,975**	**$ 10,080**	**−$72,708**	**$ 84,873**
Cash balance	**$137,525**	**$147,500**	**$157,581**	**$84,873**	**$ 84,873**

Cash flow analysis (second year)

Quarter	Q1	2 Q2	Q3	Q4	2
Cash from operations	$40,770	$50,962	$55,039	$57,078	$203,849
Cash from receivables	$ 0	$ 0	$ 0	$ 0	$ 0
Operating cash inflow	**$40,770**	**$50,962**	**$55,039**	**$57,078**	**$203,849**
Other cash inflows					
Equity investment	$ 0	$ 0	$ 0	$ 0	$ 0
Increased borrowings	$ 0	$ 0	$ 0	$ 0	$ 0
Sales of business assets	$ 0	$ 0	$ 0	$ 0	$ 0
A/P increases	$ 8,717	$10,897	$11,769	$12,204	$ 43,587
Total other cash inflows	**$ 8,717**	**$10,897**	**$11,769**	**$12,204**	**$ 43,587**
Total cash inflow	**$49,487**	**$61,859**	**$66,808**	**$69,282**	**$247,436**
Cash outflows					
Repayment of principal	$ 4,271	$ 4,368	$ 4,467	$ 4,568	$ 17,674
A/P decreases	$ 5,975	$ 7,469	$ 8,067	$ 8,365	$ 29,876
A/R increases	$ 0	$ 0	$ 0	$ 0	$ 0
Asset purchases	$10,192	$12,741	$13,760	$14,269	$ 50,962
Dividends	$28,539	$35,674	$38,527	$39,954	$142,694
Total cash outflows	**$48,978**	**$60,251**	**$64,821**	**$67,157**	**$241,207**
Net cash flow	**$ 510**	**$ 1,608**	**$ 1,987**	**$ 2,125**	**$ 6,229**
Cash balance	**$85,382**	**$86,990**	**$88,977**	**$91,102**	**$ 91,102**

Cash flow analysis (third year)

Quarter	Q1	3 Q2	Q3	Q4	3
Cash from operations	$56,438	$70,547	$76,191	$ 79,013	$282,188
Cash from receivables	$ 0	$ 0	$ 0	$ 0	$ 0
Operating cash inflow	**$56,438**	**$70,547**	**$76,191**	**$ 79,013**	**$282,188**
Other cash inflows					
Equity investment	$ 0	$ 0	$ 0	$ 0	$ 0
Increased borrowings	$ 0	$ 0	$ 0	$ 0	$ 0
Sales of business assets	$ 0	$ 0	$ 0	$ 0	$ 0
A/P increases	$10,025	$12,531	$13,534	$ 14,035	$ 50,125
Total other cash inflows	**$10,025**	**$12,531**	**$13,534**	**$ 14,035**	**$ 50,125**
Total cash inflow	**$66,463**	**$83,078**	**$89,725**	**$ 93,048**	**$332,314**
Cash outflows					
Repayment of principal	$ 4,672	$ 4,778	$ 4,886	$ 4,997	$ 19,332
A/P decreases	$ 7,170	$ 8,963	$ 9,680	$ 10,038	$ 35,852
A/R increases	$ 0	$ 0	$ 0	$ 0	$ 0
Asset purchases	$14,109	$17,637	$19,048	$ 19,753	$ 70,547
Dividends	$39,506	$49,383	$53,334	$ 55,309	$197,532
Total cash outflows	**$65,458**	**$80,760**	**$86,947**	**$ 90,097**	**$323,263**
Net cash flow	**$ 1,005**	**$ 2,318**	**$ 2,777**	**$ 2,951**	**$ 9,051**
Cash balance	**$92,107**	**$94,425**	**$97,202**	**$100,153**	**$100,153**

Apartment Complex

Olde Towne Apartments

7777 W. River Place
Philadelphia, PA 19103

BizPlanDB.com

Olde Towne Apartments is a Philadelphia-based corporation that will provide rental services to customers in its targeted market. The Company was founded by Sally Barnes.

1.0 EXECUTIVE SUMMARY

The purpose of this business plan is to raise $1,000,000 for the acquisition of a 20-unit apartment complex while showcasing the expected financials and operations over the next three years. Olde Towne Apartments is a Philadelphia-based corporation that will provide rental services to customers in its targeted market. The Company was founded by Sally Barnes.

1.1 The Services

The primary revenue center for the business is acquiring apartment complex properties with the intent to rent the properties to the general public. The business will generate profits from both the ongoing rental income paid to Olde Towne Apartments while generating capital appreciation from the long-term holding of these properties. Now that the real estate market has hit its bottom, Management expects that the market will have a future growth rate of 5% to 6% per year.

The third section of the business plan will further document the residential rental services offered by the business.

1.2 Financing

Mrs. Barnes is seeking to raise $1,000,000 from an investor. The terms, dividend payouts, and aspects of the deal are to be determined at negotiation. This business plan assumes that an investor will receive 50% of the Company's stock, a regular stream of dividends, and a seat on the board of directors. The financing will be used for the following:

- Financing to acquire the initial property.

- Financing for the first six months of operation.

- Capital to purchase a company vehicle.

Mrs. Barnes will contribute $10,000 to the venture.

17

1.3 Mission Statement

Mrs. Barnes' mission is to develop Olde Towne Apartments into a premier regional real estate investment firm that will acquire apartment complexes and rent properties profitably.

1.4 Management Team

The Company was founded by Sally Barnes. Mrs. Barnes has more than 10 years of experience in the real estate industry. Through her expertise, she will be able to bring the operations of the business to profitability within its first year of operations.

1.5 Sales Forecasts

Mrs. Barnes expects a strong rate of growth at the start of operations. Below are the expected financials over the next three years.

Proforma profit and loss (yearly)

Year	1	2	3
Sales	$240,000	$288,000	$336,960
Operating costs	$ 93,277	$ 97,412	$101,738
EBITDA	$134,723	$176,188	$218,374
Taxes, interest, and depreciation	$125,266	$141,023	$157,054
Net profit	$ 9,457	$ 35,165	$ 61,320

Sales, operating costs, and profit forecast

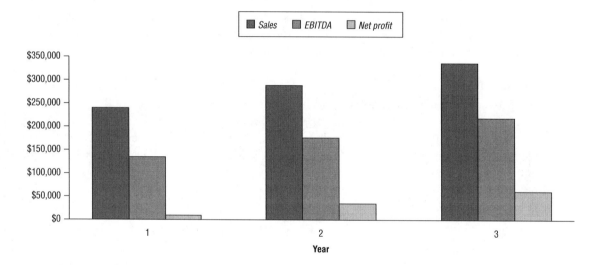

1.6 Expansion Plan

The Founder expects that the business will aggressively expand during the first three years of operation. As the real estate market returns to normal conditions, Olde Towne Apartments will be an excellent position to recognize profits from the sale of properties. In the future, the business may seek to acquire additional capital for the acquisition of additional apartment complex-type properties.

2.0 COMPANY AND FINANCING SUMMARY

2.1 Registered Name and Corporate Structure

Olde Towne Apartments is registered as a corporation in the State of Pennsylvania.

2.2 Required Funds

At this time, Olde Towne Apartments requires $1,000,000 of investor funds. Below is a breakdown of how these funds will be used:

Projected startup costs

Working capital	$ 15,000
FF&E	$ 10,000
Leasehold improvements	$ 5,000
Security deposits	$ 5,000
Insurance	$ 2,500
Apartment complex acquisition	$ 950,000
Marketing budget	$ 7,500
Miscellaneous and unforeseen costs	$ 5,000
Total startup costs	**$1,000,000**

2.3 Investor Equity

Sally Barnes intends to sell 50% of Olde Towne Apartments in exchange for the capital.

2.4 Management Equity

Sally Barnes will retain 50% of the business once the capital is raised.

2.5 Exit Strategy

If the business is very successful, Mrs. Barnes may seek to sell the business to a third party for a significant earnings multiple or divest Olde Towne Apartments property or properties individually. Most likely, the Company will hire a qualified real estate broker to sell the properties on behalf of Olde Towne Apartments, Inc.

2.6 Investor Divestiture

This will be discussed during negotiations.

3.0 REAL ESTATE SERVICES

Below is a description of the real estate services offered by Olde Towne Apartments.

3.1 Rental of Acquired Olde Towne Apartments Property

The direct finance and purchase of apartment complex properties is the primary business of Olde Towne Apartments. Residential real estate will provide a continuous stream of rental income that the Management will use for reinvestment and profit stability for the Company. Mrs. Barnes has already sourced a 20 unit apartment complex that will be the initial property acquired by the business.

Management is developing a complex economic pricing strategy that will determine the fair market rate of a property based on its capitalization rate in conjunction with the market values of residential property. Residential real estate is the least risky form of real estate investing because the service offered is a necessity.

4.0 STRATEGIC AND MARKET ANALYSIS

4.1 Economic Outlook

Management is developing a very complex pricing method to ensure that the Company can continue to provide its units at profit despite possible drawbacks in the overall economic market. The Company's two-prong approach to real estate will allow the business to grow successfully in the rapidly changing real estate market.

More importantly, this strategy will allow the Company to offset the risks from each business unit so that there is a diversified balance in the Company's real estate portfolio. This is especially important as the business uses leverage to finance the acquisition of its properties.

4.2 Real Estate Strategies

Olde Towne Apartments plans to actively pursue a real estate acquisition program that will focus on the purchase of multiunit apartment buildings and apartment complexes with the intent of creating a recurring stream of income. Management will use reasonable leverage to purchase these properties so that a positive cash flow is generated after debt service has been paid.

The recurring streams of revenue generated from the rental of multi-unit residential property will allow the Company to continually recognize revenue despite drawbacks in the real estate market. As these properties increase in value through capital appreciation, the Company will divest of these properties to reap its capital gain profits.

The Company will divest its properties once Management feels that its real estate holdings have become overvalued. Mrs. Barnes has worked diligently to create a pricing model that will allow the business to understand when the properties have become overvalued. This model will examine the capitalization rates of the income producing properties for a determination of true asset value.

There are tremendous tax benefits for the Company as it engages its real estate investments. As the business makes its real estate divestitures, the Company will recognize capital gain income rather than income on its properties. These windfall gains will be taxed at a rate that is significantly lower than the federal regular income tax levels. This assumes that the business will divest its properties after one year's time.

4.3 Customer Profile

As the Company intends to operate among several different investment and operating units, it is hard to characterize any specific tenant that will occupy the Company's apartment complex property. However, Management will enact strict tenant quality and credit review procedures to ensure the Company's revenues will not be interrupted by tenant default.

4.4 Competition

Since real estate is effectually one of the most free market-oriented businesses in the country, competition can not be accurately categorized. Olde Towne Apartments anticipates that there will be a sizable amount of competition from both single owner investment firms to large construction companies throughout the Philadelphia metropolitan area.

5.0 MARKETING PLAN

Olde Towne Apartments intends to maintain an extensive marketing campaign that will ensure maximum visibility for the acquired units in its targeted market. Below is an overview of the marketing strategies and objectives of the Company.

5.1 Marketing Objectives

- Develop an online presence by acquiring accounts for major online real estate portals.

- Implement a local campaign with the Company's targeted market via the use of flyers, local newspaper advertisements, and word of mouth.

- Establish relationships with other real estate brokers and agents within the targeted market.

5.2 Marketing Strategies

Property renter marketing will be the most difficult portion of the marketing strategy. This task will be accomplished through the business's broad marketing campaign throughout its targeted market. Primarily, Mrs. Barnes intends to use local real estate brokerage firms to place tenants with the Company's Olde Towne Apartments. In addition to using a real estate broker, Mrs. Barnes intends to develop her own marketing strategies that will further increase the visibility of the business's units. This is especially important with the current real estate market environment.

Olde Towne Apartments will also use an internet-based strategy. This is very important as many people seeking real estate for purchase or rent use the Internet to conduct their preliminary searches. Mrs. Barnes will register Olde Towne Apartments and subsequent properties with these online portals so that potential renters can easily reach the business. The Company will also develop its own online website.

The Company will maintain a sizable amount of print and traditional advertising methods within local markets to promote the apartment complex property.

5.3 Pricing

Management anticipates that each unit rented by the business will generate approximately $600 of monthly revenue for the business.

6.0 ORGANIZATIONAL PLAN AND PERSONNEL SUMMARY

6.1 Corporate Organization

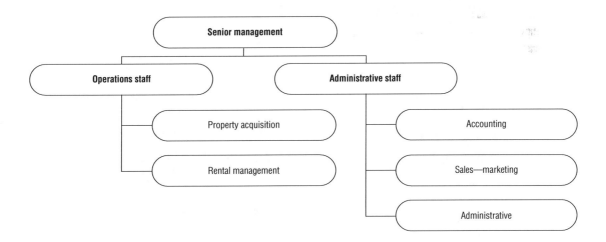

6.2 Organizational Budget

Personnel plan—yearly

Year	1	2	3
Property manager	$35,000	$36,050	$37,132
Administrative staff (P/T)	$12,500	$12,875	$13,261
Total	**$47,500**	**$48,925**	**$50,393**

Numbers of personnel

Property manager	1	1	1
Administrative staff (P/T)	1	1	1
Totals	**2**	**2**	**2**

Personnel expense breakdown

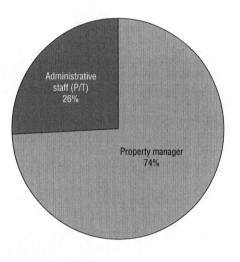

7.0 FINANCIAL PLAN

7.1 Underlying Assumptions

The Company has based its proforma financial statements on the following:

- Olde Towne Apartments will have an annual revenue growth rate of 6% per year.

- The Owner will acquire $1,000,000 of investor funds to develop the business.

- The Company will not seek debt financing in the first three years of operations.

7.2 Sensitivity Analysis

The Company's revenues can change depending on the general economic climate of the real estate industry. In times of economic recession, the Company may have issues with its top line income and rental income may decrease. However, the highly recurring nature of Olde Towne Apartments's rental income streams will ensure that the business is able to maintain profitability and a positive cash flow at all times.

7.3 Source of Funds

Financing

Equity contributions

Investor(s)	$ 1,000,000.00
Total equity financing	**$1,000,000.00**

Banks and lenders

Bank loan	$ 0.00
Total debt financing	**$ 0.00**
Total financing	**$1,000,000.00**

7.4 General Assumptions

General assumptions

Year	1	2	3
Short term interest rate	9.5%	9.5%	9.5%
Long term interest rate	10.0%	10.0%	10.0%
Federal tax rate	33.0%	33.0%	33.0%
State tax rate	5.0%	5.0%	5.0%
Personnel taxes	15.0%	15.0%	15.0%

7.5 Profit and Loss Statements

Proforma profit and loss (yearly)

Year	1	2	3
Sales	**$240,000**	**$288,000**	**$336,960**
Cost of goods sold	$ 12,000	$ 14,400	$ 16,848
Gross margin	95.00%	95.00%	95.00%
Operating income	**$228,000**	**$273,600**	**$320,112**
Expenses			
Payroll	$ 47,500	$ 48,925	$ 50,393
General and administrative	$ 7,200	$ 7,488	$ 7,788
Marketing expenses	$ 1,200	$ 1,440	$ 1,685
Professional fees and licensure	$ 5,219	$ 5,376	$ 5,537
Insurance costs	$ 1,987	$ 2,086	$ 2,191
Travel and vehicle costs	$ 7,596	$ 8,356	$ 9,191
Property maintenance cost	$ 14,250	$ 14,963	$ 15,711
Miscellaneous costs	$ 1,200	$ 1,440	$ 1,685
Payroll taxes	$ 7,125	$ 7,339	$ 7,559
Total operating costs	**$ 93,277**	**$ 97,412**	**$101,738**
EBITDA	**$134,723**	**$176,188**	**$218,374**
Federal income tax	$ 44,459	$ 58,142	$ 72,063
State income tax	$ 6,736	$ 8,809	$ 10,919
Interest expense	$ 0	$ 0	$ 0
Depreciation expenses	$ 74,071	$ 74,071	$ 74,071
Net profit	**$ 9,457**	**$ 35,165**	**$ 61,320**
Profit margin	**3.94%**	**12.21%**	**18.20%**

Sales, operating costs, and profit forecast

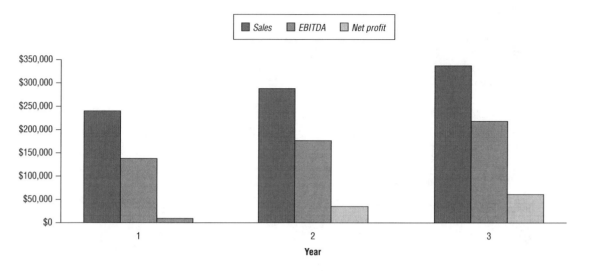

7.6 Cash Flow Analysis

Proforma cash flow analysis—yearly

Year	1	2	3
Cash from operations	$ 83,528	$109,237	$135,392
Cash from receivables	$ 0	$ 0	$ 0
Operating cash inflow	**$ 83,528**	**$109,237**	**$135,392**
Other cash inflows			
Equity investment	$ 1,000,000	$ 0	$ 0
Increased borrowings	$ 0	$ 0	$ 0
Sales of business assets	$ 0	$ 0	$ 0
A/P increases	$ 37,902	$ 43,587	$ 50,125
Total other cash inflows	**$1,037,902**	**$ 43,587**	**$ 50,125**
Total cash inflow	**$1,121,430**	**$152,824**	**$185,517**
Cash outflows			
Repayment of principal	$ 0	$ 0	$ 0
A/P decreases	$ 24,897	$ 29,876	$ 35,852
A/R increases	$ 0	$ 0	$ 0
Asset purchases	$ 950,000	$ 27,309	$ 33,848
Dividends	$ 58,470	$ 76,466	$ 94,774
Total cash outflows	**$1,033,367**	**$133,651**	**$164,474**
Net cash flow	**$ 88,063**	**$ 19,173**	**$ 21,043**
Cash balance	**$ 88,063**	**$107,236**	**$128,280**

Proforma cash flow (yearly)

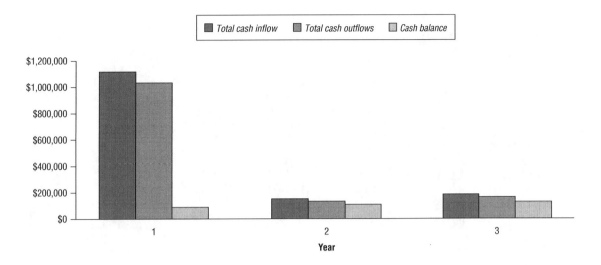

7.7 Balance Sheet

Proforma balance sheet—yearly

Year	1	2	3
Assets			
Cash	$ 88,063	$ 107,236	$ 128,280
Amortized development/expansion costs	$ 15,000	$ 17,731	$ 21,116
Apartment complex	$1,007,000	$1,089,131	$1,181,388
FF&E	$ 15,000	$ 19,096	$ 24,174
Accumulated depreciation	($ 74,071)	($ 148,143)	($ 222,214)
Total assets	**$1,050,992**	**$1,085,051**	**$1,132,742**
Liabilities and equity			
Accounts payable	$ 13,005	$ 26,716	$ 40,990
Long term liabilities	$ 0	$ 0	$ 0
Other liabilities	$ 0	$ 0	$ 0
Total liabilities	**$ 13,005**	**$ 26,716**	**$ 40,990**
Net worth	**$1,037,987**	**$1,058,336**	**$1,091,753**
Total liabilities and equity	**$1,050,992**	**$1,085,051**	**$1,132,742**

Proforma balance sheet

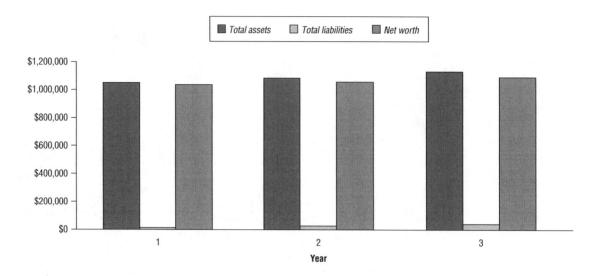

7.8 Breakeven Analysis

Monthly break even analysis

Year	1	2	3
Monthly revenue	$ 8,182	$ 8,545	$ 8,924
Yearly revenue	$98,186	$102,539	$107,093

Break even analysis

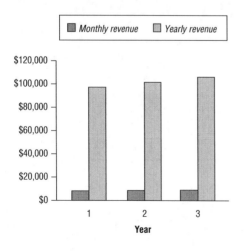

7.9 Business Ratios

Business ratios—yearly

Year	1	2	3
Sales			
Sales growth	0.00%	20.00%	17.00%
Gross margin	95.00%	95.00%	95.00%
Financials			
Profit margin	3.94%	12.21%	18.20%
Assets to liabilities	80.81	40.61	27.63
Equity to liabilities	79.81	39.61	26.63
Assets to equity	1.01	1.03	1.04
Liquidity			
Acid test	6.77	4.01	3.13
Cash to assets	0.08	0.10	0.11

7.10 Three Year Profit and Loss Statement

Profit and loss statement (first year)

Months	1	2	3	4	5	6	7
Sales	$20,000	$20,000	$20,000	$20,000	$20,000	$20,000	$20,000
Cost of goods sold	$ 1,000	$ 1,000	$ 1,000	$ 1,000	$ 1,000	$ 1,000	$ 1,000
Gross margin	95.0%	95.0%	95.0%	95.0%	95.0%	95.0%	95.0%
Operating income	$19,000	$19,000	$19,000	$19,000	$19,000	$19,000	$19,000
Expenses							
Payroll	$ 3,958	$ 3,958	$ 3,958	$ 3,958	$ 3,958	$ 3,958	$ 3,958
General and administrative	$ 600	$ 600	$ 600	$ 600	$ 600	$ 600	$ 600
Marketing expenses	$ 100	$ 100	$ 100	$ 100	$ 100	$ 100	$ 100
Professional fees and licensure	$ 435	$ 435	$ 435	$ 435	$ 435	$ 435	$ 435
Insurance costs	$ 166	$ 166	$ 166	$ 166	$ 166	$ 166	$ 166
Travel and vehicle costs	$ 633	$ 633	$ 633	$ 633	$ 633	$ 633	$ 633
Property maintenance costs	$ 1,188	$ 1,188	$ 1,188	$ 1,188	$ 1,188	$ 1,188	$ 1,188
Miscellaneous costs	$ 100	$ 100	$ 100	$ 100	$ 100	$ 100	$ 100
Payroll taxes	$ 594	$ 594	$ 594	$ 594	$ 594	$ 594	$ 594
Total operating costs	$ 7,773	$ 7,773	$ 7,773	$ 7,773	$ 7,773	$ 7,773	$ 7,773
EBITDA	$11,227	$11,227	$11,227	$11,227	$11,227	$11,227	$11,227
Federal income tax	$ 3,705	$ 3,705	$ 3,705	$ 3,705	$ 3,705	$ 3,705	$ 3,705
State income tax	$ 561	$ 561	$ 561	$ 561	$ 561	$ 561	$ 561
Interest expense	$ 0	$ 0	$ 0	$ 0	$ 0	$ 0	$ 0
Depreciation expense	$ 6,173	$ 6,173	$ 6,173	$ 6,173	$ 6,173	$ 6,173	$ 6,173
Net profit	$ 788	$ 788	$ 788	$ 788	$ 788	$ 788	$ 788

Profit and loss statement (first year cont.)

Months	8	9	10	11	12	1
Sales	**$20,000**	**$20,000**	**$20,000**	**$20,000**	**$20,000**	**$240,000**
Cost of goods sold	$ 1,000	$ 1,000	$ 1,000	$ 1,000	$ 1,000	$ 12,000
Gross margin	95.0%	95.0%	95.0%	95.0%	95.0%	95.0%
Operating income	**$19,000**	**$19,000**	**$19,000**	**$19,000**	**$19,000**	**$228,000**
Expenses						
Payroll	$ 3,958	$ 3,958	$ 3,958	$ 3,958	$ 3,958	$ 47,500
General and administrative	$ 600	$ 600	$ 600	$ 600	$ 600	$ 7,200
Marketing expenses	$ 100	$ 100	$ 100	$ 100	$ 100	$ 1,200
Professional fees and licensure	$ 435	$ 435	$ 435	$ 435	$ 435	$ 5,219
Insurance costs	$ 166	$ 166	$ 166	$ 166	$ 166	$ 1,987
Travel and vehicle costs	$ 633	$ 633	$ 633	$ 633	$ 633	$ 7,596
Property maintenance costs	$ 1,188	$ 1,188	$ 1,188	$ 1,188	$ 1,188	$ 14,250
Miscellaneous costs	$ 100	$ 100	$ 100	$ 100	$ 100	$ 1,200
Payroll taxes	$ 594	$ 594	$ 594	$ 594	$ 594	$ 7,125
Total operating costs	**$ 7,773**	**$ 7,773**	**$ 7,773**	**$ 7,773**	**$ 7,773**	**$ 93,277**
EBITDA	**$11,227**	**$11,227**	**$11,227**	**$11,227**	**$11,227**	**$134,723**
Federal income tax	$ 3,705	$ 3,705	$ 3,705	$ 3,705	$ 3,705	$ 44,459
State income tax	$ 561	$ 561	$ 561	$ 561	$ 561	$ 6,736
Interest expense	$ 0	$ 0	$0	$ 0	$ 0	$ 0
Depreciation expense	$ 6,173	$ 6,173	$ 6,173	$ 6,173	$ 6,173	$ 74,071
Net profit	**$ 788**	**$ 788**	**$ 788**	**$ 788**	**$ 788**	**$ 9,457**

Profit and loss statement (second year)

Quarter	Q1	2 Q2	Q3	Q4	2
Sales	**$57,600**	**$72,000**	**$77,760**	**$80,640**	**$288,000**
Cost of goods sold	$ 2,880	$ 3,600	$ 3,888	$ 4,032	$ 14,400
Gross margin	95.0%	95.0%	95.0%	95.0%	95.0%
Operating income	**$54,720**	**$68,400**	**$73,872**	**$76,608**	**$273,600**
Expenses					
Payroll	$ 9,785	$12,231	$13,210	$13,699	$ 48,925
General and administrative	$ 1,498	$ 1,872	$ 2,022	$ 2,097	$ 7,488
Marketing expenses	$ 288	$ 360	$ 389	$ 403	$ 1,440
Professional fees and licensure	$ 1,075	$ 1,344	$ 1,451	$ 1,505	$ 5,376
Insurance costs	$ 417	$ 522	$ 563	$ 584	$ 2,086
Travel and vehicle costs	$ 1,671	$ 2,089	$ 2,256	$ 2,340	$ 8,356
Property maintenance costs	$ 2,993	$ 3,741	$ 4,040	$ 4,190	$ 14,963
Miscellaneous costs	$ 288	$ 360	$ 389	$ 403	$ 1,440
Payroll taxes	$ 1,468	$ 1,835	$ 1,981	$ 2,055	$ 7,339
Total operating costs	**$19,482**	**$24,353**	**$26,301**	**$27,275**	**$ 97,412**
EBITDA	**$35,238**	**$44,047**	**$47,571**	**$49,333**	**$176,188**
Federal income tax	$11,628	$14,536	$15,698	$16,280	$ 58,142
State income tax	$ 1,762	$ 2,202	$ 2,379	$ 2,467	$ 8,809
Interest expense	$ 0	$ 0	$ 0	$ 0	$ 0
Depreciation expense	$18,518	$18,518	$18,518	$18,518	$ 74,071
Net profit	**$ 3,329**	**$ 8,791**	**$10,976**	**$12,068**	**$ 35,165**

Profit and loss statement (third year)

Quarter	Q1	Q2	Q3	Q4	3
Sales	$67,392	$84,240	$90,979	$94,349	$336,960
Cost of goods sold	$ 3,370	$ 4,212	$ 4,549	$ 4,717	$ 16,848
Gross margin	95.0%	95.0%	95.0%	95.0%	95.0%
Operating income	$64,022	$80,028	$86,430	$89,631	$320,112
Expenses					
Payroll	$10,079	$12,598	$13,606	$14,110	$ 50,393
General and administrative	$ 1,558	$ 1,947	$ 2,103	$ 2,181	$ 7,788
Marketing expenses	$ 337	$ 421	$ 455	$ 472	$ 1,685
Professional fees and licensure	$ 1,107	$ 1,384	$ 1,495	$ 1,550	$ 5,537
Insurance costs	$ 438	$ 548	$ 591	$ 613	$ 2,191
Travel and vehicle costs	$ 1,838	$ 2,298	$ 2,482	$ 2,574	$ 9,191
Property maintenance costs	$ 3,142	$ 3,928	$ 4,242	$ 4,399	$ 15,711
Miscellaneous costs	$ 337	$ 421	$ 455	$ 472	$ 1,685
Payroll taxes	$ 1,512	$ 1,890	$ 2,041	$ 2,116	$ 7,559
Total operating costs	$20,348	$25,435	$27,469	$28,487	$101,738
EBITDA	$43,675	$54,593	$58,961	$61,145	$218,374
Federal income tax	$14,413	$18,016	$19,457	$20,178	$ 72,063
State income tax	$ 2,184	$ 2,730	$ 2,948	$ 3,057	$ 10,919
Interest expense	$ 0	$ 0	$ 0	$ 0	$ 0
Depreciation expense	$18,518	$18,518	$18,518	$18,518	$ 74,071
Net profit	$ 8,561	$15,330	$18,038	$19,392	$ 61,320

7.11 Three Year Cash Flow Analysis

Cash flow analysis (first year)

Month	1	2	3	4	5	6	7	8
Cash from operations	$ 6,961	$ 6,961	$ 6,961	$ 6,961	$ 6,961	$ 6,961	$ 6,961	$ 6,961
Cash from receivables	$ 0	$ 0	$ 0	$ 0	$ 0	$ 0	$ 0	$ 0
Operating cash inflow	$ 6,961	$ 6,961	$ 6,961	$ 6,961	$ 6,961	$ 6,961	$ 6,961	$ 6,961
Other cash inflows								
Equity investment	$1,000,000	$ 0	$ 0	$ 0	$ 0	$ 0	$ 0	$ 0
Increased borrowings	$ 0	$ 0	$ 0	$ 0	$ 0	$ 0	$ 0	$ 0
Sales of business assets	$ 0	$ 0	$ 0	$ 0	$ 0	$ 0	$ 0	$ 0
A/P increases	$ 3,159	$ 3,159	$ 3,159	$ 3,159	$ 3,159	$ 3,159	$ 3,159	$ 3,159
Total other cash inflows	$1,003,159	$ 3,159	$ 3,159	$ 3,159	$ 3,159	$ 3,159	$ 3,159	$ 3,159
Total cash inflow	$1,010,119	$10,119	$10,119	$10,119	$10,119	$10,119	$ 10,119	$ 10,119
Cash outflows								
Repayment of principal	$ 0	$ 0	$ 0	$ 0	$ 0	$ 0	$ 0	$ 0
A/P decreases	$ 2,075	$ 2,075	$ 2,075	$ 2,075	$ 2,075	$ 2,075	$ 2,075	$ 2,075
A/R increases	$ 0	$ 0	$ 0	$ 0	$ 0	$ 0	$ 0	$ 0
Asset purchases	$ 950,000	$ 0	$ 0	$ 0	$ 0	$ 0	$ 0	$ 0
Dividends	$ 0	$ 0	$ 0	$ 0	$ 0	$ 0	$ 0	$ 0
Total cash outflows	$ 952,075	$ 2,075	$ 2,075	$ 2,075	$ 2,075	$ 2,075	$ 2,075	$ 2,075
Net cash flow	$ 58,044	$ 8,044	$ 8,044	$ 8,044	$ 8,044	$ 8,044	$ 8,044	$ 8,044
Cash balance	$ 58,044	$66,089	$74,133	$82,178	$90,222	$98,267	$106,311	$114,356

Cash flow analysis (first year cont.)

Month	9	10	11	12	1
Cash from operations	$ 6,962	$ 6,961	$ 6,961	$ 6,961	$ 83,528
Cash from receivables	$ 0	$ 0	$ 0	$ 0	$ 0
Operating cash inflow	**$ 6,962**	**$ 6,961**	**$ 6,961**	**$ 6,961**	**$ 83,528**
Other cash inflows					
Equity investment	$ 0	$ 0	$ 0	$ 0	$1,000,000
Increased borrowings	$ 0	$ 0	$ 0	$ 0	$ 0
Sales of business assets	$ 0	$ 0	$ 0	$ 0	$ 0
A/P increases	$ 3,159	$ 3,159	$ 3,159	$ 3,159	$ 37,902
Total other cash inflows	**$ 3,159**	**$ 3,159**	**$ 3,159**	**$ 3,159**	**$1,037,902**
Total cash inflow	**$ 10,120**	**$ 10,119**	**$ 10,119**	**$10,119**	**$1,121,430**
Cash outflows					
Repayment of principal	$ 0	$ 0	$ 0	$ 0	$ 0
A/P decreases	$ 2,075	$ 2,075	$ 2,075	$ 2,075	$ 24,897
A/P increases	$ 0	$ 0	$ 0	$ 0	$ 0
Asset purchases	$ 0	$ 0	$ 0	$ 0	$ 950,000
Dividends	$ 0	$ 0	$ 0	$58,470	$ 58,470
Total cash outflows	**$ 2,075**	**$ 2,075**	**$ 2,075**	**$60,545**	**$1,033,367**
Net cash flow	**$ 8,045**	**$ 8,044**	**$ 8,044**	**−$50,426**	**$ 88,063**
Cash balance	**$122,401**	**$130,445**	**$138,490**	**$88,064**	**$ 88,063**

Cash flow analysis (second year)

| Quarter | Q1 | 2 | | | |
		Q2	Q3	Q4	2
Cash from operations	$21,847	$27,309	$ 29,494	$ 30,586	$109,237
Cash from receivables	$ 0	$ 0	$ 0	$ 0	$ 0
Operating cash inflow	**$21,847**	**$27,309**	**$ 29,494**	**$ 30,586**	**$109,237**
Other cash inflows					
Equity investment	$ 0	$ 0	$ 0	$ 0	$ 0
Increased borrowings	$ 0	$ 0	$ 0	$ 0	$ 0
Sales of business assets	$ 0	$ 0	$ 0	$ 0	$ 0
A/P increases	$ 8,717	$10,897	$ 11,769	$ 12,204	$ 43,587
Total other cash inflows	**$ 8,717**	**$10,897**	**$ 11,769**	**$ 12,204**	**$ 43,587**
Total cash inflow	**$30,565**	**$38,206**	**$ 41,262**	**$ 42,791**	**$152,824**
Cash outflows					
Repayment of principal	$ 0	$ 0	$ 0	$ 0	$ 0
A/P decreases	$ 5,975	$ 7,469	$ 8,067	$ 8,365	$ 29,876
A/R increases	$ 0	$ 0	$ 0	$ 0	$ 0
Asset purchases	$ 5,462	$ 6,827	$ 7,373	$ 7,647	$ 27,309
Dividends	$15,293	$19,116	$ 20,646	$ 21,410	$ 76,466
Total cash outflows	**$26,730**	**$33,413**	**$ 36,086**	**$ 37,422**	**$133,651**
Net cash flow	**$ 3,835**	**$ 4,793**	**$ 5,177**	**$ 5,368**	**$ 19,173**
Cash balance	**$91,898**	**$96,691**	**$101,868**	**$107,236**	**$107,236**

Cash flow analysis (third year)

		3			
Quarter	Q1	Q2	Q3	Q4	3
Cash from operations	$ 27,078	$ 33,848	$ 36,556	$ 37,910	$135,392
Cash from receivables	$ 0	$ 0	$ 0	$ 0	$ 0
Operating cash inflow	**$ 27,078**	**$ 33,848**	**$ 36,556**	**$ 37,910**	**$135,392**
Other cash inflows					
Equity investment	$ 0	$ 0	$ 0	$ 0	$ 0
Increased borrowings	$ 0	$ 0	$ 0	$ 0	$ 0
Sales of business assets	$ 0	$ 0	$ 0	$ 0	$ 0
A/P increases	$ 10,025	$ 12,531	$ 13,534	$ 14,035	$ 50,125
Total other cash inflows	**$ 10,025**	**$ 12,531**	**$ 13,534**	**$ 14,035**	**$ 50,125**
Total cash inflow	**$ 37,103**	**$ 46,379**	**$ 50,090**	**$ 51,945**	**$185,517**
Cash outflows					
Repayment of principal	$ 0	$ 0	$ 0	$ 0	$ 0
A/P decreases	$ 7,170	$ 8,963	$ 9,680	$ 10,038	$ 35,852
A/R increases	$ 0	$ 0	$ 0	$ 0	$ 0
Asset purchases	$ 6,770	$ 8,462	$ 9,139	$ 9,477	$ 33,848
Dividends	$ 18,955	$ 23,694	$ 25,589	$ 26,537	$ 94,774
Total cash outflows	**$ 32,895**	**$ 41,118**	**$ 44,408**	**$ 46,053**	**$164,474**
Net cash flow	**$ 4,209**	**$ 5,261**	**$ 5,682**	**$ 5,892**	**$ 21,043**
Cash balance	**$111,445**	**$116,706**	**$122,387**	**$128,280**	**$128,280**

Barbershop

D'Angelo's Choice Cut Barbershop Inc.

67158 Charleston St.
Indianapolis, IN 46222

Paul Greenland

Choice Cut Barbers combines old-school barbershop service with new styles and amenities for today's modern man.

EXECUTIVE SUMMARY

Business Overview

When Tom D'Angelo decided to cut hair for a living, he was following in his father's footsteps...sort of. His father, Antonio D'Angelo, established Indianapolis-based D'Angelo's Barbershop in 1968 at the age of 24. Tom pursued a slightly different path, earning a degree in cosmetology and eventually working in popular salons in Chicago and New York.

After a long and successful career, Antonio decided to retire in 2010 and put his well-known barbershop up for sale. At the age of 40, Tom has decided to move back home and buy the family business. "This is a chance for me to be closer to my family, and continue the good work my father started more than 40 years ago," Tom told a local business writer for the *Indianapolis Tribune-Herald*. "As unisex hair salons and national haircutting chains have grown in popularity, traditional barbershops are fading from the scene."

Bucking a national trend, Tom D'Angelo will continue, and build upon, the tradition of D'Angelo's Barbershop by upgrading and rebranding the family business, which will become D'Angelo's Choice Cut Barbershop. Choice Cut combines old-school barbershop service with new styles and amenities for today's modern man.

MARKET ANALYSIS

Overview

According to the research firm OnTarget, Indianapolis' population included 810,043 people in 2009. This figure was projected to reach 847,862 by 2014 (a 4.7% increase). Of the population total, males comprised 48.8 percent of the total in 2009 (395,260). This figure was expected to increase at about the same rate (5.2%) as the overall population through 2014, reaching 416,003.

Choice Cut will primarily cater to men between the ages of 35 and 64. The segment of the Indianapolis population between the ages of 35 and 44 was expected to fall by 3.1 percent between 2009 and 2014.

However, a 3.6 percent increase was expected among those between the ages of 45 and 54. Finally, those between the ages of 55 and 64 were expected to increase 22.2 percent.

Although Choice Cut provides basic haircuts and services for all men, we will concentrate our marketing efforts on households with annual incomes of $50,000 and up. Households earning between $50,000 and $74,999 are projected to increase 7.5 percent by 2014, reaching 70,704. Those households with incomes between $75,000 and $99,999 were projected to increase 7.7 percent, reaching 45,253. A substantial increase was projected for households with incomes between $100,000 and $149,999, which were expected to increase 24.3 percent, reaching 47,267. Finally, the strongest growth was expected among households with incomes of more than $150,000, which were expected to increase 29.7 percent, reaching 27,304.

Choice Cut is located in a busy, high-traffic area located near several large office buildings, a large chain bookstore, a popular sports bar, and the area's largest health club. Geographically speaking, we are in a prime location to reach prospective customers who fit the above criteria.

Competition

According to an analysis conducted by University Research Associates LLC, the greater Indianapolis area was home to approximately 965 beauty and barbershops in 2009. On average, these establishments employed four people. A great number of our would-be competitors are "mom and pop" hairstyling businesses. Many of these are home-based businesses. In addition, we face competition from traditional barbershops and unisex salons, as well as national haircutting chains like Cost Cutters. Choice Cut will differentiate itself from the competition by becoming a destination for area men. Beyond hairstyling and grooming services, we will offer amenities that our competitors do not, and personal service that is quickly becoming a thing of the past.

INDUSTRY ANALYSIS

According to the U.S. Bureau of Labor Statistics' *2010-11 Occupational Outlook Handbook*, some 821,900 barbers, cosmetologists, and other personal appearance workers were employed in 2008. Barbers accounted for a relatively small segment of the industry overall (53,500). While the larger industry is projected to grow 20 percent by 2018, the employment of barbers also is projected to increase, rising 12 percent to 59,700. For the industry overall, 44 percent of workers are self-employed. On average, barbers earned median hourly wages of $11.56 in 2008. However, those in the upper 10 percent earned hourly wages of $19.51. Industry professionals are required to obtain the appropriate licensure in all 50 states.

PERSONNEL

Tom D'Angelo (Owner)—Tom graduated from Smith's Barber College at the age of 19, with a plan of working in his father's barbershop. However, the lure of the big city brought him to New York, where he pursued additional training at the Brookfield Beauty Institute and earned a cosmetology degree. Tom then worked for several well-known salons in New York, and later Chicago. At the age of 40, Tom has decided to move back home and buy the family business, in order to be closer to his family and carry on the tradition his father began more than 40 years ago.

Antonio D'Angelo (advisor)—Antonio established Indianapolis-based D'Angelo's Barbershop in 1968 at the age of 24. Over the course of four decades, he has built a thriving barbershop business and made personal connections with hundreds of customers. In 2010 Antonio decided to retire after a long and successful career, and sell his barbershop to Tom. However, he will remain with the business on an as-needed basis, providing back up when Tom needs to focus on business operations, and helping to maintain and develop customer relationships.

In addition to the owner's chair, Choice Cut also has five additional chairs that it rents out to barbers. Three chairs have been rented for many years to the same barbers:

- Joe Cacciatore (30 years)

- Stan Falstaff (22 years)

- Warren Johnson (15 years)

Two chairs are currently open, due to recent retirements. Tom D'Angelo plans to immediately rent these chairs out to younger barbers who are more knowledgeable about contemporary hairstyles.

In addition, Choice Cut receives professional and advisory support in a number of key areas. The business is a long-term customer of City National Bank, where it has established a business banking account, as well as a merchant account for accepting credit card payments. Legal services are provided by the firm of Tripani & O'Neill, and tax advisory services are provided by Bottom Line Tax & Accounting LLC.

GROWTH STRATEGY

The rebranding of D'Angelo's Barbershop as D'Angelo's Choice Cut Barbershop will be accompanied by significant changes to the business, which will appeal to the target market.

The barbershop currently is located on the lower level of a building (owned by the D'Angelo family) that is subdivided into two storefronts, one of which is currently unoccupied. The upper level includes four 750-square-foot apartments which are currently occupied by tenants. Tom D'Angelo plans to remove the wall dividing the two storefronts on the main level, creating one large open space. New hardwood-like laminate flooring will be installed throughout, and the area will be repainted in a contemporary color scheme.

The area currently occupied by the six barber chairs (as well as an office/storage area in the rear) will remain as-as, with the exception of reupholstered barber chairs and the addition of two large-screen TVs. The unoccupied storefront space will be converted into a large lounge area, with comfortable furniture, a bar (selling coffee and non-alcoholic beverages), and four big-screen TVs that will carry sports and outdoor-related programming. The additional space also will include an area devoted to the sale of personal care products, as well as cigars and related accessories (e.g., lighters, cigar cutters, cigar cases, etc.).

Tom D'Angelo will add two additional barbers, as well a shoe shine services during year one. During year two, a 5 percent price increase on haircuts will be introduced. Finally, a number of spa-like services will be introduced during year three, including:

- Swedish Massage

- Foot Massage

- Scalp Massage

- Neckline Wax

- Back Wax

- Chest Wax

- Brow Wax

- Facial

SERVICES

Choice Cut initially will offer the following services:

- Adult Haircut and Style
- Kids Haircut
- Hot Lather Shave
- Beard Trim
- Mustache Trim
- Scalp Treatments
- Shampoo
- Hair Coloring/Highlighting
- Ear Candling (ear wax removal)

MARKETING & SALES

Choice Cut has developed a marketing plan that involves the following primary tactics:

1. Radio advertising promoting our business as a *destination* for men; not just a place to get a haircut. Tom D'Angelo has met with a local media buyer to determine the best AM/FM stations for reaching the business' target markets.

2. A glossy, four-color flier describing our business that offers a 15 percent discount coupon for first-time customers. Initially, we will distribute these to male members of two area health clubs, as well as players on a men's softball league.

3. A Yellow Page listing.

4. A Web site with complete details about our business and the services we offer.

5. A presence on Facebook and other social media sites.

6. A customer loyalty program that provides a 10 percent discount to those referring a friend or family member to our business.

7. Active membership in the local Chamber of Commerce.

OPERATIONS

Hours of Operation

Monday through Friday: 8 AM to 6 PM

Saturday: 8 AM to 5 PM

Closed on Sunday

Prices

- Adult Haircut & Style—$19 (seniors $16)
- Kids Haircut—$13
- Hot Lather Shave—$22

- Beard Trim—$8

- Mustache Trim—$5

- Scalp Treatments—$35

- Shampoo—$10

- Hair Coloring/Highlighting—$15 to $30

- Ear Candling (ear wax removal) —$30

- Shoe Shine—$5

Regulatory

Choice Cut's barbers all hold the appropriate state licensure. Per the Indiana's State Board of Barber Examiners, barbers are required to sit for an examination ($50) and pay a license fee ($40).

FINANCIAL ANALYSIS

General Information

Antonio D'Angelo has agreed to transition ownership of the family barbershop business to Tom for $1. Antonio owns the building in which the barbershop is located. The rental income from this real estate (the lower-level commercial space and the upstairs apartments) represents a major portion of his retirement income. Based on the local commercial real estate market, the expanded space occupied by the barbershop can be leased for $.83 per square foot per month, or $2,490. Because Tom plans to make $21,850 in improvements to the building (from his personal savings), Antonio has agreed to waive this amount from the first year's rent, after which Tom will lease the space for $2,490 per month.

The profit and loss statement included with this plan reflects an arrangement in which barbers rent their chairs from Choice Cut in exchange for 25 percent of service charges. Tom D'Angelo will contribute all of his service revenues to the business and draw a salary, while the other barbers will serve as self-employed independent contractors. A substantial revenue increase is projected for year three due to the addition of spa-like services.

Tom D'Angelo plans to use profits from the business to eventually purchase the building (commercial space and apartments) from his father.

Remodeling Expenses

Tom D'Angelo will invest $21,850 from his personal savings to remodel and expand the barbershop.

- Main level wall removal: $1,000

- Laminate Flooring Installation: $9,500 (materials & installation)

- Painting: $1,850

- Reupholstering: $1,000

- Two Large-Screen TVs (Barber Area): $1,500

- Four Big-Screen TVs (Lounge Area): $3,000

- Lounge Area Furniture: $2,000

- Retail Area Fixtures: $500

- Bar: $1,500

Three-year pro forma profit and loss

	Year 1	Year 2	Year 3
Sales			
Barber services	$192,960	$202,608	$253,260
Personal care products	$ 7,500	$ 7,650	$ 7,803
Beverages	$ 19,200	$ 19,584	$ 19,976
Tobacco	$ 3,250	$ 3,315	$ 3,381
Gross sales	**$222,910**	**$233,157**	**$284,420**
Cost of goods sold	**$ 11,300**	**$ 11,527**	**$ 11,757**
Net sales	**$211,610**	**$221,630**	**$272,663**
Operating expenses			
Barbershop supplies	$ 28,944	$ 30,391	$ 37,989
Maintenance	$ 350	$ 350	$ 350
Owner's salary	$ 60,000	$ 70,000	$ 80,000
Advertising	$ 7,000	$ 5,000	$ 5,000
Equipment	$ 3,500	$ 3,500	$ 3,500
Accounting and legal	$ 1,200	$ 1,200	$ 1,200
Rent	$ 8,030	$ 29,880	$ 29,880
Telephone	$ 1,000	$ 1,000	$ 1,000
Utilities	$ 5,500	$ 5,750	$ 6,000
Insurance	$ 3,500	$ 3,500	$ 3,500
Cable Television/Internet	$ 1,800	$ 1,800	$ 1,800
Total	**$120,824**	**$152,371**	**$170,219**
Net income	**$ 90,786**	**$ 69,259**	**$102,444**

Elder Care

Summer Gardens Residential Care Facility for the Ambulatory Elderly

472 Gull Flight Ave.
Freemont Hills, CA 56789

Summer Gardens is a living facility providing food preparation, laundry, housekeeping, and personal care services to its senior residents. Run by a professional nurse, the facility will provide an alternative to traditional nursing homes.

This plan originally appeared in Business Plans Handbook, Volume 1; it has been updated for this volume.

PRODUCT PROFILE

With the aging of the population, companies offering alternatives to the nursing home are in strong demand. Residential Care Facilities for the Elderly (RCFE) are a recognized, cost-effective alternative to the nursing home. Summer Gardens Residential Care Facility for the Ambulatory Elderly will be a community-based living and care giving facility established to serve the needs of our rapidly increasing elderly population.

Residential care facilities have existed in various forms for decades. Over the past several decades years, most states have developed licensure requirements as a means of standardizing the quality of these facilities. RCFEs operating in the state of California must be licensed and must operate under the comprehensive Code of California Regulations.

Summer Gardens will comply with all licensure and Title 22 requirements. The facility will focus on providing services that promote independence in a safe and pleasant environment. As the elderly struggle to stay out of nursing homes and hospitals, they seek help with food preparation, laundry, and housekeeping. As an alternative to nursing home placement, Summer Gardens will provide housing and assistance to its residents, including meal preparation (general and special diets), laundry, linen, housekeeping, and personal care. Appropriate staff will assist in recreational activities. Staff will also arrange physician appointments and coordinate transportation.

Elderly men and women frequently express a desire for basic companionship or the need for assistance, but prefer not to impose on family members. Concerned family members may be forced to acknowledge that it has become increasingly difficult for loved ones to take care of themselves and their homes. Summer Gardens will provide needed services to adults 60 years of age and older who require assistance to remain safely independent. Summer Gardens will be able to accommodate eight residents, 24 hours a day, seven days a week. The facility will be staffed 24 hours a day with qualified employees who are trained to respect the individuality and promote the dignity of every resident.

While there are other residential care facilities in the area, Summer Gardens is the only one owned and operated by a Masters-prepared Registered Professional Nurse. My fifteen years of nursing experience include the start-up and management of a Medicare-certified home health agency, and the management of a private home health services branch office. Additionally, I have been on the staff of Andrews Hospice as an on-call advisory nurse for two years. Both relatives and residents will feel confident that the appropriate level of care will be provided, along with monitoring and supervision. As a professional nurse, I am a credible and competent link to the physician. I am qualified to make nursing assessments and able to communicate findings to physicians as appropriate.

The elderly population in this country is increasing. In Aaron County, the population aged 75 and older increased 27.2% between 1990 and 2000 alone. The elderly are living longer and requiring alternative living arrangements. RCFEs are fulfilling a need. Qualified owner/administrators of care facilities are in demand. A loan in the amount of $40,000 will facilitate the acquisition of property to house this community-based RCFE. The loan will also provide beginning capital for lease deposit, leasehold improvements, insurance, and furniture.

MARKET

The residents at Summer Gardens and their families will live in the San Francisco Bay area; most will live in Aaron County. The Aaron County location chosen for Summer Gardens is important because the elderly will want to continue to live in an area that is familiar to them, and families will want their loved ones close enough to visit regularly.

The primary users of residential care services are men and women who cannot live safely in their own homes, but do not require the full-time skilled nursing care provided by convalescent hospitals. The targeted client market for the services provided at Summer Gardens RCFE is comprised of people who are 65 years of age and older. Of the 167,958 people in Aaron county aged 65 and older, 76,520 are over the age of 75. Many of these elderly adults are single or widowed individuals who may have outlived other relatives and friends. If they are left alone at home, confusion or forgetfulness may render them unsafe and may affect their ability to care for themselves. However, with supervision and minimal assistance, these elderly will be able to maintain dignity, remain safe and independent, and conserve needed funds for future medical care. In addition, state and federal funds need not be used to provide care for these elderly at a level much higher and much more costly than they require.

According to a 2009 report from Archer Research Associates LLC, 77.7% of household heads in Aaron County between the ages of 65 and 74 had an annual income of $25,000 or more. Specifically, 21.6% had incomes between $25,000 and $49,999; 29% had incomes between $50,000 and $99,999; and 27.1% had household incomes of more than $100,000. Only 12.6% of household heads had an annual income of less than $15,000.

Among household heads over age 75, 67.2% had annual incomes of $25,000 or more. Specifically, 22.6% had incomes between $25,000 and $49,999; 23.4% had incomes between $50,000 and $99,999; and 21.2% had household incomes of more than $100,000. Compared to the 65-74 age group, a greater percentage of household heads in this age range have annual incomes of less than $15,000 (26.6%).

Of the market targeted as potential residents of Summer Gardens, the majority will be able to afford the services offered and a very small percentage will be dependent solely on SSI (see Addendum B).

The cost of a semi-private room at Summer Gardens will be $3,300 per month, or $106 per day (less than the cost of a hotel room). Future residents and families who investigate available options will find that the cost of the average semiprivate room in a convalescent or nursing home in Aaron County is roughly $5,000 per month ($165 per day), and the cost to hire 24-hour unskilled home care is much higher (see Addendum C).

Residents and families who choose Summer Gardens will do so because of:

- The nursing experience and expertise of the owner

- The high quality of care provided

- The safe, comfortable, and home-like environment

- The locality, which makes visitation easy

- The peace of mind, which comes from keeping loved ones out of nursing homes

Presently, the existing residential care facilities located in the Aaron County area cannot meet the needs of that portion of the 167,958 elderly residents over the age of 65 who are in need of some degree of assistance. There are waiting lists at most of these facilities. Reports from the County Conservator, Rehabilitation Hospital, and Acute Care Hospital discharge planners show that there are not enough residential options for people who are unable to live alone but not ready for convalescent home care.

LOCATION

Summer Gardens RCFE will be located in Freemont Hills, California. It is important that the facility be located in Aaron County because of its reputation for beauty, relative safety, affluence, and proximity to desired clients and their families. The city of Freemont Hills was chosen because property is less expensive than any other city in Aaron County and has less restrictions (e.g., use of water).

Summer Gardens will be located in a large home in a quiet residential area of the city. Residents will be able to sit safely on the patio or take short walks in the neighborhood. The house itself will be built on one level. It will be large enough to accommodate 8 adults comfortably and will be brought into compliance with all state and local safety regulations. (See Floor Plan).

COMPETITION

There are six (6) other RCFE's located in Freemont Hills. Five (5) are of similar size and offer similar services. According to the California Code of Regulations, RCFE facilities cannot be located within 300 feet of another RCFE. The names and locations of the RCFE facilities located in Freemont Hills are:

Riverview Terrace
Administrator: Lee Smith
123 Bay St.
Freemont Hills, CA 56789

Seaside Residential Care
Administrator: Donna Jones
234 Mason Ave.
Freemont Hills, CA 56780

Pine Acres
Administrator: Thomas Beech
345 Pollyanna
Freemont Hills, CA 56789

Lyle B. Morton Care Facility
Administrator: Andrea Morton
4567 J St.
Freemont Hills, CA 56789

Shady Arbor
Administrator: Diane Brown
56789 Irving Lane
Freemont Hills, CA 56780

The similarities between RCFE facilities is due to the California Code of Regulations, Title 22, Division 6, Chapter 8. All facilities offering services to the elderly are strictly supervised and mandated by this Code. Despite the inherent similarities, I do not expect to need to take clients away from my competitors because of the growing elderly population. These businesses are very profitable and many owners (e.g., Andrea Morton) subsequently opened second and third facilities. Once eight residents are found, it may be 1-5 years before an opening exists for another resident.

DISTRIBUTION

I intend to contact individuals who will use my facility through professionals in the community who find appropriate accommodations for the elderly. These referral sources include the county conservators, hospital discharge planners, rehabilitation center discharge planners, day care centers, senior citizen centers, home care agencies, and independent case managers. I plan to mail a brochure describing Summer Gardens along with a cover letter announcing the opening of the new facility. I will follow up with a phone call and a request for referrals. I plan to place a continuous ad in the local "senior" newspaper and advertise in the yellow pages. I will gain access to many referral sources by taking advantage of the contacts made when I was in an administrative position at Miller Health Care Services, which was located in Aaron County.

SALES

I plan to open with one resident in January 2011, and expect to increase to three residents by February, six residents by March, and a full census of eight residents in April. Based on these projections, end of the year assets will be $119,646.

I have considered what could go wrong with this plan. The condition of the economy could affect the ability of the elderly to pay for their care with private funds. Regardless of the economy, there will be an elderly population. If funds run out and the elderly are placed on SSI, or if I would need to admit some residents whose only source of income was SSI, I would be guaranteed some payment from the state. In the unlikely event that this would occur to some of my clients, it would decrease the amount of profit, but would not result in a negative income.

KEY PERSONNEL

As the owner of Summer Gardens, I will be in charge of the business operations (See Resume for qualifications). I will have three employee care givers: two regular employees and one on-call or back-up person to handle sick calls, vacations, and holidays. Tracy Stevens and Samuel Jackson will be regular employees and Lucy Johnson will be on-call as needed.

Tracy Stevens is a Registered Nurse with five years experience in home care, hospice, and rehabilitation hospitals. Samuel Jackson is a Certified Home Health Care Aide with six years experience in acute care hospitals, convalescent hospitals, rehabilitation hospitals, and home care. Lucy Johnson is a Nurse Assistant with six years experience working with the elderly in their own homes. She has also worked in acute care hospitals and convalescent hospitals.

Employees will be responsible for providing personal care and related services for residents, providing companionship, and promoting mental alertness and physical well being. Please contact Marian Currey, the owner, for complete descriptions of employee qualifications and comprehensive job descriptions.

ORGANIZATION

This organization will be a sole proprietorship owned by Marian Currey. My short-term goals are: l) to open Summer Gardens in January 2011, 2) to have 8 residents by April 2011, and 3) to show a small profit by March 2011.

My long-term goals are to purchase the leased property in January 2012 and to begin the process of opening a second RCFE in 2013.

REFERENCE LIST

Anand, Preet. "Affordable Housing for Seniors." *San Diego Business Journal*, August 20, 2007.

Coburn, Linda. "Aging Population Excites Senior Housing Developers." *San Fernando Valley Business Journal*, Dec 8, 2008.

Encyclopedia of Private Equity & Venture Capital. VC Experts, Inc., 2010. Available from: http://vcexperts.com/vce/library/encyclopedia.

Ford, Brian R., Borenstein, Jay M., and Patrick T. Pruitt. *The Ernst & Young Business Plan Guide.* Hoboken, N.J.: John Wiley & Sons Sons, Inc., 2007.

Hansen, Norman N., and Gregory J. Almquist. "The Development of Senior Housing in the United States." *Real Estate Review*, Fall 2009.

Johnson, Emma. "Senior Class: An Aging Population and Increasing Senior Housing Options Will Likely Lead to a Senior Housing Boom." *Journal of Property Management*, Sept.–Oct. 2007.

"No Place like Home; Care for the Aged." *The Economist*, Feb 20, 2010.

Scott, Mike. "Solving the Retirement Home Puzzle; Flexible Plans, Negotiations Help Seniors Find the Most Appropriated Living Situations." *Crain's Detroit Business*, June 9, 2008.

"They've Fallen, but They Can Get Up." Kopin Tan, *Barron's*, March 10, 2008.

Timmins, Nicholas. "Beyond the Bleak Houses of the Elderly: Residential Care: As Older People Lead Healthier, More Active Lives, Is the Traditional Model of the Care Home under Threat?" *The Financial Times*, May 25, 2004.

ADDENDUM A

Census of Aaron County

Age	2009	2014	Change
65–74	91,438	120,845	32.20%
75+	76,520	77,882	1.80%
Total population	1,477,082	1,508,540	2.10%

ADDENDUM B

Annual income of Aaron County 2009

Income bracket	Percent of total
Population age 65–74	
$0 to $9,999	8.10%
$10,000 to $14,999	4.50%
$15,000 to $19,999	5.10%
$20,000 to $24,999	4.80%
$25,000 to $29,999	4.50%
$30,000 to $34,999	4.40%
$35,000 to $39,999	4.00%
$40,000 to $49,999	8.70%
$50,000 to $59,999	7.60%
$60,000 to $74,999	9.60%
$75,000 to $99,999	11.80%
$100,000 to $124,999	8.60%
$125,000 to $149,999	5.80%
$150,000 to $199,999	5.50%
$200,000 or more	7.20%
Population age 75+	
$0 to $9,999	11.00%
$10,000 to $14,999	7.60%
$15,000 to $19,999	8.00%
$20,000 to $24,999	6.30%
$25,000 to $29,999	5.20%
$30,000 to $34,999	4.60%
$35,000 to $39,999	4.30%
$40,000 to $49,999	8.50%
$50,000 to $59,999	6.20%
$60,000 to $74,999	7.80%
$75,000 to $99,999	9.40%
$100,000 to $124,999	7.10%
$125,000 to $149,999	3.90%
$150,000 to $199,999	4.00%
$200,000 or more	6.20%

ADDENDUM C

Daily rates

Convalescent hospital/ nursing home	Private	Semiprivate
Murphy Convalescent Hospital	$200	$170
Rosewood Convalescent Hospital	$180–$200	$175
Ellworth Convalescent Hospital	$235	$180
Ivy Terrace Convalescent Hospital	$205	$160
St. Mary's Convalescent Hospital	$200	$165

Daily rates

24-hour live-in

Jenson Home Care	$290
Alert Nursing Service	$260–$270
Guardian	$250–$275
Desmond Home Care	$265–$285
Martin Critical Care	$270–$280
Certified Home Care	$260–$270

FLOOR PLAN

A floor plan of the Summer Gardens facility is available through Simon Architecture, Inc., 100 Diamond Ave., Fremont Hills, CA 56780.

CASH FLOW STATEMENT

The Tribunal Accounting Firm has developed a spreadsheet to illustrate cash flow for Summer Gardens during the first year of operation. The statement includes data on cash receipts, investments, capital expenditures, operating expenses, loan payments, taxes, sales, and administrative tasks.

RESUME

A personal resume and references are available upon request.

Human Resources Consultant

Anders Johnson LLC

56090 Thistle Trail
Mountainview, OH 41041

Paul Greenland

Anders Johnson LLC is an independent human resources consultant who focuses on helping emerging small and mid-sized companies deal with organizational change and develop more efficient human resources systems and programs.

EXECUTIVE SUMMARY

Business Overview

By 2010 companies of all sizes had been impacted by difficult economic conditions. Downsizing, reorganization, restructuring, and consolidation were familiar themes in virtually every industry. This resulted in rapid change for many organizations. Human resources professionals were tasked with managing this change in numerous ways.

Established in 2010, Anders Johnson LLC is an independent human resources consultant concentrates his practice on change management and several other related areas:

- Process Reengineering

- Strategic Development

- Executive Coaching

- Human Resources Information Systems (HRIS)

Using 25 years of industry experience, Anders' objective is to help emerging small and mid-sized companies manage rapid change as effectively as possible, and develop more efficient human resources systems and programs.

Prior to becoming an independent consultant, Anders served as director of corporate human resources for GLS Aerospace, and was responsible for overseeing human resources functions at all five of the company's divisions which are located in seven states. At the corporate level Anders oversaw substantial improvements in a number of areas, including staffing, HR administration, regional benefits administration support, and training/development. As a result of his leadership in these areas, the company achieved annual savings of several million dollars, and the HR function became more of a strategic asset for GLS Aerospace.

Anders has a Masters degree in Human Resources Management from Greater Pennsylvania University and has pursued additional graduate studies in change management and human resources information systems (HRIS). He holds professional accreditation as a Professional in Human Resources (PHR) from the Society for Human Resources Management, and is a seasoned and highly capable human resources executive.

MARKET ANALYSIS

Although Anders will work with companies in any industry, he will concentrate his new business development efforts on technology-oriented firms. Specifically, he will aggressively pursue new clients in these specific sectors:

- Aerospace
- Alternative Energy
- Aviation & Airport Security
- Biometrics
- Biotechnology
- e-Commerce
- Fiber Optics
- Green Manufacturing
- Information Security
- Nanotechnology
- Pharmaceuticals
- Radio Frequency Identification
- Robotics & Industrial Automation

INDUSTRY ANALYSIS

According to the U.S. Department of Labor's *Career Guide to Industries, 2010-11 Edition*, the management, scientific, and technical consulting services industry employed approximately 1 million wage and salary workers during the late 2000s. Although the consulting industry is dominated by a number of large players with thousands of employees, the majority of industry establishments are small firms, most of which have less than five employees. In addition, the industry includes many self-employed consultants like Anders.

Approximately 5 percent of industry establishments are devoted to human resources and executive search consulting. By employment, 7.7 percent of consultants work in this field. Wage and salary workers in the management, scientific, and technical consulting services field are projected to experience growth of 82.8 percent from 2008 to 2018, according to the U.S. Department of Labor. Specifically, those working in the employment, recruitment, and placement specialist field are projected to experience growth of 46.9 percent during the same timeframe. Despite these lofty growth projections, competition for work will remain highly competitive.

The primary professional organizations within the human resources consulting field include the Society for Human Resource Management, the American Society for Training and Development, the International Foundation of Employee Benefit Plans, the Association of Executive Search Consultants, and the Association of Management Consulting Firms.

PERSONNEL

A native of Philadelphia, Anders Johnson graduated from Central State University in 1985 with a BA in Industrial Psychology and Business Administration, and went on to earn a Masters degree in Human Resources Management from Greater Pennsylvania University.

Anders began his career with Rexfield Specialty Fasteners, where he held several corporate human resources positions of increasing responsibility. Beginning as a human resources generalist, he eventually was promoted to compensation manager, and finally human resources manager.

In 1995 Anders was named human resources director at GLS Wakefield, a division of GLS Aerospace Technology, which manufactures a wide range of components for the aerospace industry. At GLS Wakefield, Anders significantly improved many departmental processes. In addition, he oversaw the implementation of several human resources information systems (HRIS). Together, his efforts resulted in a dramatic improvement in operational efficiency. New employment and interdepartmental transfer applications were processed faster, internal communications were improved, employee turnover was reduced significantly, and employee benefits were enhanced at a minimal cost to the organization.

Anders' work at GLS Wakefield was quickly noticed at the corporate level, and his department became a model for the company's other divisions. In 2000 Anders was promoted to director of corporate human resources, which involved oversight of human resources functions at all five of GLS Aerospace's divisions, which are located in seven states. At the corporate level Anders oversaw substantial improvements in a number of areas, including staffing, HR administration, regional benefits administration support, and training/development. As a result of his leadership in these areas, the company achieved annual savings of several million dollars, and the HR function became more of a strategic asset for GLS Aerospace.

Anders has pursued additional graduate studies in the areas of change management and HRIS. He holds professional accreditation as a Professional in Human Resources (PHR) from the Society for Human Resources Management, and is a seasoned and highly capable human resources executive.

When GLS Aerospace was acquired by another company in 2010, Anders' position was eliminated as part of the restructuring that followed. Rather than seeking another executive position, he has decided to work as an independent consultant.

Professional & Advisory Support

Anders realizes that his consulting work will often involve complicated legal matters. Although he has secured appropriate liability insurance, Anders will rely on the law firm of Mitchum & Farrell, which has specialized expertise in employment law, in the event that counsel is needed. In addition, he has established a business banking account with Mountainview Community Bank, as well as a merchant account for accepting credit card payments. Tax advisement will be provided by Peterson, Smith & Green Accountants, a local firm in Mountainview.

GROWTH STRATEGY

Considering the challenging economic climate, and that it will take time to become accustomed to working as a consultant, Anders Johnson plans to grow his practice at a steady, measured pace. During his first year of business, Anders' objective is to average 20 hours of billable consulting time per week. He expects to increase this target to 30 weekly hours of billable consulting time during year two, and 40 hours during year three. He acknowledges that additional non-billable hours will be required to manage administrative aspects of his business (e.g., billing, record keeping, project estimating, etc.).

Throughout his career, Anders has written a number of white papers on change management and authored several expert articles for leading trade magazines. He has now begun work on a new book about successful change management strategies. Jim Williamson, a noted authority in the field, as agreed to co-author the book with Anders. A publishing agreement has been signed with BusinessPoint Publishing, and a national speaker's bureau has agreed to promote the authors' availability to speak at business conferences. In addition to royalties from book sales, the co-authors expect the book will lead to new consulting contracts (potentially lucrative joint assignments) for both of them.

SERVICES

Generally speaking, Anders will provide organizations with technical human resources expertise and/or tools that they do not possess internally, or that is intended to complement or enhance existing resources. For example, an organization may possess the internal expertise necessary to complete a particular project, but cannot spare the time.

When necessary, Anders has the ability to advise clients regarding general human resources matters, such as:

- Compensation
- Policy Development
- Workforce Assessment
- Benefits
- Job Analysis
- Employment/Placement
- Training & Development
- Employee Relations

However, he will offer specialized consulting services in the following areas:

- Change Management
- Process Reengineering
- Strategic Development
- Executive Coaching
- Human Resources Information Systems (HRIS)

When working with clients, his objectives will vary depending on the organization's needs, but may include:

- Identifying/Defining Human Resources Challenges/Problems
- Identifying/Implementing Solutions
- Increasing Efficiency
- Improving Productivity
- Reducing Turnover
- Enhancing Organizational Performance
- Implementing More Effective Systems

MARKETING & SALES

In order to promote his consulting services, Anders Johnson has developed a marketing plan that involves the following primary tactics:

1. Printed collateral describing his consulting philosophy, as well as the services he offers. A four-color brochure will be developed, which includes general information about the consulting practice. The brochure will include a pocket, which can accommodate one or more specific panel card inserts that go into more detail about specific services (e.g., executive coaching, change management, HRIS, etc.).

2. Advertisements in the print and online edition of human resources management professional directories.

3. A Web site with complete details about Anders' practice and services offered.

4. A blog, through which Anders will provide observations regarding various business issues and industry trends.

5. A monthly e-mail newsletter for human resources professionals that provides case studies, tips, and insight from prior experiences.

6. The use of social media channels, including LinkedIn, to network with potential customers, as well as industry colleagues.

7. Direct mailings to human resources professionals at companies that meet specific criteria (e.g., company size, industry, revenue, etc.). Arrangements have been made with several reputable list brokers, as well as a local mail house, in order to schedule an ongoing direct mail effort and generate a steady stream of inquiries.

8. Writing expert columns for human resources management trade publications, as well as specialized trade publications serving the technology-oriented target markets identified in this business plan.

9. A media relations strategy that involves the submission of case studies/success stories to appropriate business and trade magazines.

10. Presentations at industry conferences attended by human resources professionals. When cost allows, advertisements will be placed in conference-related publications.

11. Publication of a book about change management in partnership with a recognized authority in the field. Following publication, Anders will work with the publisher's publicity department to identify key publications that should receive review copies (e.g., to generate book reviews, interviews, etc.).

OPERATIONS

Anders Johnson will operate his consulting practice from an existing home office, in order to keep overhead low. He already is equipped with a laptop computer, as well as an Internet-enabled cell phone, which will enable him to check e-mail and stay in touch with customers at all times.

When business travel is required, Johnson's home is located near the interstate, providing quick access to Cincinnati, as well as the Cincinnati/Northern Kentucky International Airport.

Anders will need to make several capital purchases in order to operate his consulting practice, including a portable projector for presentations, as well as a high-quality Web cam for video/Web conferencing.

Fees

In speaking with contacts throughout the industry, one mistake that beginning consultants often make is setting their fees too low, in an effort to out-price the competition and gain new business. This can be problematic later on, when attempting to increase fees with existing customers. In addition, when working with new consultants, Anders has learned that many clients are more comfortable with an hourly rate, versus a project rate.

According to data from Rockwell & Associates, entry-level management consultants often charge as much as $175 per hour for their services. Fees generally are higher in coastal regions, and lower in the central states. With this in mind, Anders will set his hourly consulting rate at $125. He will require clients to pay for a minimum, pre-determined/agreed-upon number of service hours.

FINANCIAL ANALYSIS

Following is Anders Johnson's projected balance sheet for 2011. Revenue calculations are conservative, and are based upon 20 hours of billable consulting time per week in 2011. Anders anticipates that his net income will increase significantly in 2012 and 2013 as he increases his average weekly billable consulting hours to 30 and 40 hours, respectively. In addition, additional income will result from speaking engagements and royalties from his new change management book.

2011 balance sheet

Revenue

Consulting	$125,000
Public speaking	$ 15,000
Royalty income	$ 2,450
Total revenue	**$142,450**

Expenses

Salary	$ 95,000
Home office	$ 875
Insurance	$ 2,540
Office supplies	$ 570
Equipment	$ 5,200
Marketing and advertising	$ 5,500
Telecommunications and internet	$ 1,500
Professional development	$ 7,500
Travel and entertainment	$ 15,275
Subscriptions and dues	$ 2,650
Miscellaneous	$ 500
Total expenses	**$137,110**
Net income	**$ 5,340**

Landscaping Service

G & D Landscaping

352 Denby St.
Romeo, MI 48065

Heidi Denler

G & D Landscaping will offer lawn care for suburban upper middle class and middle class homeowners. The company's target customer will be those who are unable to manage their own lawns, whether because of size (too large), no time to care for their lawn, and those with no interest in maintaining their lawn. Other customers will be those unable to do their own lawn care because of age or physical challenge.

COMPANY SUMMARY

G & D Landscaping will offer lawn care for suburban upper middle class and middle class homeowners. The company's target customer will be those who are unable to manage their own lawns, whether because of size (too large), no time to care for their lawn, and those with no interest in maintaining their lawn. Other customers will be those unable to do their own lawn care because of age or physical challenge. The partners have been cutting lawns for several years, but have decided to formalize their business into an actual limited liability company (LLC) to allow them to hire additional help more easily.

MANAGEMENT SUMMARY

Robert Guillermo and Frank Delgado have been friends since high school. Guillermo began cutting lawns during summer vacations in high school, and Frank Delgado helped on as-needed basis when Guillermo was away on vacation or needed help to catch up on lawn care because of weather delays. The two decided to form a partnership when they were freshmen in college with the goal of formalizing the business as an LLC with the two sharing responsibility equally. Guillermo and Delgado have built a reputation for quality work done professionally at competitive prices. Guillermo is majoring in landscaping with a minor in environmental science, which enables him to put his newly-acquired knowledge to work immediately on his customers' lawns. Delgado is an education major with a concentration in math and science. The owners will hire part-time help as their business grows. Robert Guillermo's mother is an accountant currently working in a small office and will assist with bookkeeping and other financial paperwork, such as payroll and payment of taxes.

MISSION STATEMENT

G & D Landscaping will meet and surpass customer needs and expectations, providing 100 percent satisfaction in lawn care, including mowing, edging, trimming, and clean-up.

VISION STATEMENT

Robert Guillermo & Frank Delgado will maintain the current 20 contracts and grow 5 percent per year, hiring additional crew as needed to maintain profitability and a living income for both owners. G & D will build its reputation and target their own neighbors and their current customer base to avoid driving between job sites.

VALUES STATEMENT

G & D Landscaping brings experience, a commitment to quality, and a professional approach to every service and customer.

BUSINESS PHILOSOPHY

The owners' goal is 100 percent customer satisfaction. This will be achieved by building on the reputation of their informal business. G & D Landscaping will continue to provide reliable, affordable landscaping to its customers. Their experience has shown that by remaining a small, service-oriented business they can maintain personal interaction with every customer and address concerns immediately. Recognizing that landscaping is seasonal, Robert Guillermo and Frank Delgado will expand their business to include spring and fall clean-up services, as well as snow removal in winter months.

ORGANIZATION STRUCTURE

G & D Landscaping will be a limited liability partnership owned by Robert Guillermo and Frank Delgado, who will share the responsibilities of the business. Both will canvass their immediate neighborhoods to increase their current customer base slowly.

Part-time employees will be hired as the business expands in order to maintain high-quality, individualized services. Within six months G & D expects to hire a master gardener to handle landscape design and implementation.

ADVERTISING AND PROMOTION

Robert Guillermo and Frank Delgado will promote G & D Landscaping initially by talking directly with their current customers and providing them with a rate sheet that will reflect their continuing services, as well as new services being offered. They will discuss individual lawn care needs and provide customers with a personalized plan for lawn care and landscaping needs. The owners will then spend a minimum of four evenings a week talking to their immediate neighbors about their landscaping services, encouraging them to become customers. As neighbors, they know Guillermo and Delgado and are likely to trust them with their landscaping needs.

In addition, Guillermo and Delgado will scout problem lawns and prepare plans of action that they can present to the homeowner, showing what can be done to make their lawn beautiful and addressing perceived landscaping needs.

Flyers and brochures will be printed for distribution to prospective customers. Flyers will be placed on community bulletin boards at local garden centers and hardware stores. They will include bullet points of services offered by G & D Landscaping, one or two testimonials from current customers, and contact information. Brochures will be given to prospective customers, detailing services, flat rate costs, and testimonials, along with photos of current customers' lawns and landscaping.

Small advertisements will be placed in local weekly newspapers that serve the community once the business is established and the company has identified potential employees who share the owners' work ethic and dedication to quality service.

CUSTOMER BASE

G & D Landscaping will build on its current customer base slowly to enable the company to continue to provide quality, personalized landscaping needs to every customer. Upper middle class and middle class suburban homeowners are the target market for the company.

The partners will build on this base in the immediate neighborhoods of current customers. The plan is to increase the company's customer base slowly, adding part-time help as needed and as services are expanded to meet the year-round development of landscaping, clean-up, and snow removal offerings.

PRODUCTS AND SERVICES

G & D Landscaping will offer basic lawn care service, landscaping care, design, and implementation; spring and fall clean-up; and snow removal service. Robert Guillermo and Frank Delgado will work with customers and potential customers to determine the frequency of any and all services and to personalize the needs for every lawn.

Basic residential lawn care will include:

- Lawn mowing
- Trimming
- Edging
- Removal of clippings

Extended residential lawn care will include:

- Hedge trimming
- Small tree trimming
- Weeding of garden areas
- Fertilizing

Landscaping design and implementation will include:

- Consultation with customer to determine needs and viability of those needs (for example, soil testing to determine any additional services to improve the soil for desired plantings)
- Computer-based illustrations of proposed landscape design for approval by customer (including making any changes requested by customer)
- Purchase of required shrubbery and plantings
- Planting of shrubbery and other plantings
- Maintenance of shrubbery and plantings

Spring clean-up will include:

- Raking

- Aeration

- Preparation of garden beds

Fall clean-up will include:

- Leaf removal

- Weeding

- Application of organic weed-killers in garden beds

Snow removal will include:

- Snowblowing of driveways and all requested walkways

- Shoveling of areas too small for snowblower

- Application of lawn-safe ice-melting pellets on driveways and walkways

Pricing will be affordable and competitive with local companies offering similar services.

PERSONNEL REQUIREMENTS

Initially, Robert Guillermo and Frank Delgado will continue to care for the customers they have served for the last three years. As they add customers, they will add two part-time employees. Each owner will train one of those part-time employees, taking them with them as they work on customers' lawns. As the company continues to grow, those part-time employees will be offered full-time positions and new part-time employees will be hired.

Guillermo and Delgado will make decisions as a team, supervising employees and having direct contact with customers to ensure quality standards are met by G & D Landscaping.

Robert Guillermo's mother, who is a bookkeeper and office manager in a small office, will handle G & D Landscaping's books, including payroll, taxes, and insurance, as well as accounts payable and receivable.

LOCATION

Initially, G & D Landscaping will continue to house their pick-up truck and equipment in Robert Guillermo's garage. As the company grows and services expand, the owners plan to rent a garage to house their truck and equipment. Within two years they will move record-keeping and bookkeeping activities into a small office in the garage.

STORE DESIGN AND EQUIPMENT

G & D Landscaping will not require a store-front office, but will use Frank Delgado's laptop to maintain databases of customers and prospective customers, as well as landscape designs. The laptop will also have any necessary financial software, so information can be transferred via e-mail and/or flash drive storage from Mrs. Guillermo's computer. The office will require an all-in-one printer for printing customer invoices, proposals, and even flyers. A four-drawer filing cabinet will be housed in the garage at Guillermo's house for hard copies of data saved on computers as needed. The owners will have pager-style cell phones.

The truck with trailer currently being used by the owners will continue to serve G & D Landscaping, with the addition of commercial magnets on the driver and passenger doors, advertising the name of the company , phone number, and e-mail address. The company will continue to use its two commercial mowers, trimmers, edgers, blowers, hedge trimming equipment, safety equipment (steel-toed shoes, goggles, gloves), and tools for simple repairs to equipment. Future employees will be required to have their own cell phones to remain in contact with their employers.

FINANCIAL

Start-up costs are expected to be minimal because the owners already have two commercial lawn mowers, two edgers, multiple trimmers and blowers, rakes, and gasoline containers to hold the special mixtures required by each piece of gas-powered equipment. The company will incur legal costs related to filing the company name, forming the LLC structure, and reviewing liability and workers' compensation policies.

Within a year, Robert Guillermo and Frank Delgado plan to rent a garage to house their truck and equipment, which will add to their overhead. In addition, they will be purchasing snow removal equipment, along with such landscaping tools as shovels and, eventually, a Bobcat to move larger amounts of dirt as the landscaping offerings are expanded to include design and implementation.

Guillermo and Delgado will purchase payroll and landscaping software for the company's laptop computer. They will invest in a professional all-in-one printer that will enable them to print personalized landscaping plans and estimates for potential customers.

Ongoing expenses will include gas for transportation and equipment; maintenance of equipment, such as blade sharpening; payroll for bookkeeping and part time help; printing of flyers and brochures; and miscellaneous office supplies. Cell phones for the owners will also incur ongoing costs.

Revenues are expected to be the highest in late spring through early fall, which will help support slower winter months. These revenues will allow the partners time to build their spring and fall growth, as well as the introduction of landscape design and implementation and snow removal services.

G & D Landscaping will also incur costs for the printing of flyers, brochures, business cards, and business stationary. In addition, they will require liability insurance, workers' compensation insurance, and property/casualty insurance.

PROFESSIONAL AND ADVISORY SUPPORT

Robert Guillermo and Frank Delgado have begun to work with an attorney to file the necessary paperwork with the state of Michigan to become an LLC, including "doing business as" (DBA) paperwork. They will continue to work with their attorney to ensure compliance with all federal, state, and local laws and regulations for a small business. The attorney will also handle any paperwork involved with future lease arrangements for the proposed garage/office.

Guillermo's mother will handle all financial aspects of the G & D Landscaping, consulting fellow CPAs as the need arises.

The owners will join local small business organizations in the area to promote their business, as well as to network with other small business owners. This will potentially serve as an additional way to identify potential customers for G & D Landscaping.

BUSINESS AND GROWTH STRATEGY

G & D Landscaping will build on the informal business established in their community over the last three years. Robert Guillermo and Frank Delgado will maintain their reputation of quality, timely work and depend on face-to-face meetings with their own neighbors, as well as neighbors of the current customers. They will expand slowly, using flyers, brochures, and referrals to inform potential customers of their work and work ethic. G & D Landscaping will advertise that they treat every lawn and garden as if it was their own. They will return calls promptly, be on time, and take breaks only when not in view of customers' homes.

Personal contact with current and prospective customers will be an integral part of the owners' and employees' work ethic. Part-time employees will have at least two years experience in landscape and lawn care and will be trained personally by the owners.

As the company grows, Guillermo and Delgado will add a landscape designer/master gardener to the company's staff to build the business. Additional employees will be hired as needed to implement design plans.

COMPETITION

Robert Guillermo and Frank Delgado recognize that there is a great deal of competition in the area, including several small, private landscapers and many large, commercial companies, as well as local high school and college students looking to make a "quick buck" over their summer vacations.

However, because G & D Landscaping will be building on its owners' current customer base, they can turn their reputation to an advantage, especially for customer referrals. They will continue to provide high-quality work and maintain professionalism and a good work ethic. They realize that landscaping could be considered a luxury and is vulnerable to recession, but they have weathered the economic downturn of the latter half of the first decade of the twenty-first century and even have added customers during that downturn. They are confident that their reputation will help them succeed in the face of tough economic times and when dealing with their competition.

WEB SITE

Because the owners want to build the business slowly and remain local, an Internet presence is not an immediate requirement. Robert Guillermo and Frank Delgado will build a company Web site, but will not launch it until year-round service has been implemented and the owners have identified and retained reliable part-time help.

The Web site will provide information about services the company offers and the target neighborhoods served by G & D Landscaping. It will also include contact information and testimonials of current customers.

CONCLUSION

Robert Guillermo and Frank Delgado, as the owners of G & D Landscaping, look forward to building their business by maintaining their reputation for high-quality lawn care and by adding landscape design, spring and fall clean up services, and snow removal. This will move them from an informal lawn service to a small, competitive, growing business. The owners will bring their experience not only for lawn care, but also for customer service. As an LLC, G & D Landscaping will continue to grow, expanding its services from summer lawn care to year-round landscaping and maintenance. Careful planning, slow growth, and a solid reputation for high-quality work will ensure continued profitability for the company and its owners.

Marketing Consultant

TargetPoint Consulting LLC

49 Willowbrook St.
Houston, TX 77001

Paul Greenland

TargetPoint Consulting guides businesses through a strategic approach to marketing planning.

EXECUTIVE SUMMARY

Business Overview

Marketing is critical to a company's success. An organization can offer the best product or service in the world, but fail miserably due to a lack of awareness. After all, if potential customers do not know about a particular product or service, they cannot buy it.

Today, marketing is arguably more challenging than ever. At virtually every turn, consumers are bombarded with marketing messages. Beyond the obvious print advertisements, radio spots, and television commercials, marketing messages are delivered via floor graphics, vehicle wraps, kiosks, digital billboards, mobile phones, social networks, backlit displays, word-of-mouth, and more. With so many choices, deciding which tactics are the most effective and appropriate for a given product or service can be overwhelming.

Those with limited or no experience often take a reactive approach to marketing. A decline in sales or an advertising campaign from a competitor may cause a state of panic. Even if business is going well, low levels of marketing activity (actual or perceived) can produce anxiety among management and board members. At the other end of the spectrum, excessive promotion may lead to more customer inquiries or demand than a business can support operationally, causing internal frustration and dissatisfaction in the marketplace.

Established by John Kendall, TargetPoint Consulting guides businesses through a strategic approach to marketing. We help clients define their specific situation and position by identifying strengths, weaknesses, opportunities, and threats; evaluate the competition; develop measurable objectives; choose the most effective tactics to reach their target markets; calculate an appropriate budget; and outline a process for evaluation and adjustment. Once a strong marketing plan is in place, we will work with clients to develop a marketing mindset throughout the organization and build a marketing-focused culture.

John Kendall, who holds an MBA from Central Texas University, most recently served as a vice president and account supervisor at Jasper Wyatt Marketing in Houston. He continues to blend marketing theory with real-life industry experience by serving as an adjunct professor at Ripley Fellowes University. It was Kendall's teaching experience that led him to reconsider his own career choice and decide to pursue work as an independent consultant.

MARKET ANALYSIS

TargetPoint Consulting will concentrate on securing consulting projects from mid-sized businesses that (1) have between 20 and 250 employees and (2) are preparing for significant expansion (organic or via acquisitions). According to data from Geo Research LLC, Houston was home to 114,889 business establishments in 2010. Among these establishments, 11,153 firms fall within TargetPoint's defined size target:

- 20-49 Employees: 6,812

- 50-99 Employees: 2,638

- 100-249 Employees: 1,703

By industry, we will concentrate our efforts on companies in the retail, services, and transportation/communications fields. According to data from the aforementioned research firm, 78,793 Houston-area businesses are classified in these three industries:

- Retail Trade (21,509)

- Services (52,560)

- Transportation and Communications (4,724)

John Kendall estimates that, when filtering results for both industry and number of employees, the total universe of prospective clients will total approximately 5,000 establishments. He is in the process of conducting further analysis to obtain an exact count. In addition, Kendall will then analyze this smaller universe of prospects to identify (1) companies with the highest industry sales (based on actual or estimated figures from Dun & Bradstreet Inc.) and (2) companies with the most significant year-to-year sales growth.

INDUSTRY ANALYSIS

According to the U.S. Department of Labor's *Career Guide to Industries, 2010-11 Edition*, the management, scientific, and technical consulting services industry employed approximately 1 million wage and salary workers during the late 2000s. Although the consulting industry is dominated by a few large players with thousands of employees, the majority of industry establishments are small firms, most of which have less than five employees. In addition, the industry includes many self-employed consultants.

Second only to administrative management and general management consultants, marketing consultants accounted for 15.5 percent of industry establishments, according to the Department of Labor. By employment, 15.1 percent of consultants work in this field. Wage and salary workers in the management, scientific, and technical consulting services field are projected to experience growth of 82.8 percent from 2008 to 2018.

Specifically, market research analysts are projected to grow at a rate of 84 percent during this same time period. Although these growth projections are encouraging, it is important to note that competition for projects will be very competitive—especially because of weak economic conditions and heightened competition for a smaller pool of consulting projects.

The primary professional organization within the marketing consulting field is the American Marketing Association (AMA). Offering networking opportunities and comprehensive education, the association "assists marketers in deepening their marketing expertise, elevating their careers and ultimately, achieving better results." Other relevant associations include the Association of Management Consulting Firms and the Institute of Management Consultants.

PERSONNEL

John Kendall's love for marketing was evident at an early age. In high school, he began paying close attention to television commercials, radio commercials, billboards, catalogs, and even "junk mail" that his parents intended for the circular file. However, his affinity for marketing went beyond mere appreciation for innovative and clever tactics. Before long he was preoccupied with branding, and the factors that motivate people to buy products and services and become loyal customers.

Kendall honed his marketing mindset by earning an undergraduate degree in business administration, followed by an MBA, from Central Texas University. After beginning his career with Holland & Fremont as an account coordinator, Kendall was promoted to the role of account executive. Within seven years he had been named vice president and account supervisor at Jasper Wyatt Marketing in Houston.

For the past five years Kendall has been able to blend marketing theory with real-life industry experience by serving as an adjunct professor at Ripley Fellowes University. While challenging students to engage in self discovery, Kendall began thinking about his own career and discovered that, professionally, he often felt as if he were "going through the motions." What Kendall missed the most was the often intense interaction with clients that was a more integral part of his career during the early years.

Professional & Advisory Support

TargetPoint Consulting has secured business liability insurance through Stone Fortress Insurance. A business banking relationship has been established with Houston Federal Savings Bank, where Kendall has opened a business checking account, as well as a merchant account for accepting credit card payments. Tax and accounting services will be provided by the firm of Gagliano, Richter & Peters.

BUSINESS STRATEGY

During the early 2010s, some industry observers noted that many companies were beginning to move away from traditional "agency of record" relationships with advertising and marketing agencies, and moving toward more project-based relationships. This presents independent consultants with additional opportunities. Although some may argue that this scenario is less advantageous, Kendall feels that it is a matter of perspective. Successful consultants will be able to cross-sell and up-sell services to their clients, and present projects in potential phases. This strategy sets the stage for additional work if the customer is pleased with the consultant's initial performance.

Despite the general trend toward more project-based relationships between companies and marketing agencies, John Kendall will put an emphasis on learning about his clients' industries, corporate cultures, histories, and challenges. In the long run, he feels this will make him a more valuable, informed strategic partner when working on projects.

SERVICES

Generally speaking, TargetPoint will provide marketing-related consulting services.

The American Marketing Association (AMA) defines marketing as "the activity, set of institutions, and processes for creating, communicating, delivering, and exchanging offerings that have value for customers, clients, partners, and society at large."

Our consulting firm also will provide marketing research, which the AMA defines as "the function that links the consumer, customer, and public to the marketer through information—information used to identify and define marketing opportunities and problems; generate, refine, and evaluate marketing actions; monitor marketing performance; and improve understanding of marketing as a process. Marketing research specifies the information required to address these issues, designs the method for collecting information, manages and implements the data collection process, analyzes the results, and communicates the findings and their implications."

Specifically, the services we offer will include, but are not limited to:

- Branding

- Product Development

- New Business Development

- SWOT Analyses

- Marketing Research

- Competitive Analysis & Benchmarking

- Marketing New Products

- Product Pricing

- Sales Forecasting

- Marketing Strategy Development

- Customer Service Improvement/Enhancement

- Image Management

- Presentation Development

MARKETING & SALES

In order to promote TargetPoint's consulting services, John Kendall has developed a marketing plan that involves the following primary tactics:

1. Printed collateral describing his consulting philosophy, as well as the services he offers. A four-color brochure will be developed, which includes general information about the consulting practice. The brochure will include a pocket, which can accommodate one or more specific panel card inserts that go into more detail about specific services (e.g., Branding; Marketing Research; Competitive Analysis & Benchmarking, etc.). In addition, the brochure will include a die cut for his business card.

2. A Web site with complete details about TargetPoint.

3. A blog, through which John Kendall will provide observations regarding various business issues and industry trends.

4. A monthly e-mail newsletter for marketing managers, directors, and vice presidents that provides case studies, tips, and insight from prior experiences.

5. The use of social media channels, including LinkedIn, to network with potential customers, as well as industry colleagues.

6. Direct mailings to marketing executives at companies that match the criteria mentioned in the Market Analysis section of this business plan. Several reputable list brokers have been identified for this purpose, and arrangements have been made with a local mail house to handle an ongoing campaign.

7. Cold calls to key prospects that receive direct mailings from TargetPoint. Phone calls to prospects will be made approximately 10 business days after direct-mail drops.

8. Occasional expert columns for regional and national business/marketing trade publications. Reprints will be used during direct-mail campaigns, and as "leave behinds" following sales presentations to prospective clients.

9. A media relations strategy involving the submission of case studies/success stories to appropriate business and trade magazines.

10. Presentations at industry conferences attended by marketing executives. When cost allows, advertisements will be placed in conference-related publications.

OPERATIONS

John Kendall will operate his consulting practice from an existing home office, in order to keep overhead low. He is already equipped with a laptop computer, as well as an Internet-enabled cell phone, which will enable him to check e-mail and stay in touch with customers at all times.

Fees

TargetPoint will bill clients a flat fee of $130 per hour for consulting services. According to data from Webster Research, entry-level management consultants often charge as much as $175 per hour for their services. Fees generally are higher in coastal regions, and lower in the central states. Considering this, as well as his level of experience and conditions in the Houston market, Kendall feels that TargetPoint's rates are appropriate. New clients will be asked to pay for a minimum, pre-determined number of service hours in advance. Fees for writing trade articles and presenting at conferences will be negotiated on an individual basis.

FINANCIAL ANALYSIS

Following is TargetPoint's projected balance sheet for 2011. Revenue calculations are based on 25 hours of billable consulting time per week in 2011 (240 business days, or 48 weeks). Kendall anticipates that his net income will increase gradually in 2012 and 2013 as he increases his average weekly billable consulting hours to 30 and 35 hours, respectively.

2011 balance sheet

Revenue	
Consulting	$156,000
Public speaking	$ 2,500
Trade article contributions	$ 1,250
Total revenue	**$159,750**
Expenses	
Salary	$135,000
Home office	$ 950
Insurance	$ 2,125
Office supplies	$ 470
Equipment	$ 1,200
Marketing and advertising	$ 7,000
Telecommunications and internet	$ 1,375
Professional development	$ 1,500
Travel and entertainment	$ 4,275
Subscriptions and dues	$ 1,250
Miscellaneous	$ 500
Total expenses	**$155,645**
Net income	**$ 4,105**

Montessori School

Edison Park Montessori

1234 N. Nina Ave.
Chicago, IL 60631

BizPlanDB.com

Edison Park Montessori is a Chicago-based school that will provide early childhood education to customers in its targeted market using the Montessori system. The Company was founded by Jimm Kelley.

1.0 EXECUTIVE SUMMARY

The purpose of this business plan is to raise $100,000 for the development of a Montessori School while showcasing the expected financials and operations over the next three years. Edison Park Montessori is a Chicago-based school that will provide early childhood education to customers in its targeted market using the Montessori system. The Company was founded by Jimm Kelley.

1.1 The Services

Edison Park Montessori will provide students (age 3 through 5th grade) with a specialized form of education that was developed by Dr. Montessori. Unlike traditional teaching methods, this style provides students with an interactive approach to learning that focuses on independent problem solving, self-discovery, and nature intensive learning. This teaching method has become extremely popular over the last one hundred years and has proliferated worldwide. There are approximately 7,000 Montessori schools operating worldwide.

The third section of the business plan will further describe the services offered by Edison Park Montessori.

1.2 Financing

Mr. Kelley is seeking to raise $100,000 from as a bank loan. The interest rate and loan agreement are to be further discussed during negotiation. This business plan assumes that the business will receive a 10 year loan with a 9% fixed interest rate. The financing will be used for the following:

- Development of the school's location.

- Financing for the first six months of operation.

- Capital to purchase FF&E.

Mr. Kelley will contribute $10,000 to the venture.

1.3 Mission Statement

Edison Park Montessori provides a quality Montessori educational background that influences and supports life long learning for children in the Chicago area.

1.4 Management Team

The Company was founded by Jimm Kelley. Mr. Kelley has more than 10 years of experience in the early childhood education industry. Through his expertise, he will be able to bring the operations of the business to profitability within its first year of operations.

1.5 Sales Forecasts

Mr. Kelley expects a strong rate of growth at the start of operations. Below are the expected financials over the next three years.

Proforma profit and loss (yearly)

Year	1	2	3
Sales	$416,460	$449,777	$485,759
Operating costs	$302,832	$313,494	$324,590
EBITDA	$ 71,982	$ 91,305	$112,593
Taxes, interest, and depreciation	$ 40,198	$ 43,844	$ 51,523
Net profit	$ 31,784	$ 47,460	$ 61,070

Sales, operating costs, and profit forecast

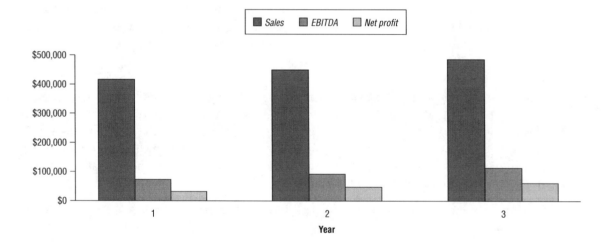

1.6 Expansion Plan

The Founder expects that the business will aggressively expand during the first three years of operation. Mr. Kelley intends to implement marketing campaigns that will effectively target individuals with children within the target market.

2.0 COMPANY AND FINANCING SUMMARY

2.1 Registered Name and Corporate Structure

Edison Park Montessori is registered as a corporation in the State of Illinois.

2.2 Required Funds

At this time, Edison Park Montessori requires $100,000 of debt funds. Below is a breakdown of how these funds will be used:

Projected startup costs

Initial lease payments and deposits	$ 10,000
Working capital	$ 35,000
FF&E	$ 23,000
Leasehold improvements	$ 5,000
Security deposits	$ 5,000
Insurance	$ 2,500
Classroom equipment	$ 17,000
Marketing budget	$ 7,500
Miscellaneous and unforeseen costs	$ 5,000
Total startup costs	**$110,000**

Use of funds

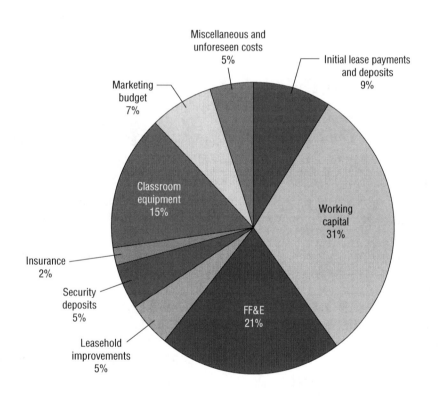

2.3 Investor Equity

Mr. Kelley is not seeking an investment from a third party at this time.

2.4 Management Equity

Jimm Kelley owns 100% of Edison Park Montessori.

2.5 Exit Strategy

If the business is very successful, Mr. Kelley may seek to sell the business to a third party for a significant earnings multiple. Based on historical numbers, the business could fetch a sales premium of up to 6 times earnings.

3.0 PRODUCTS AND SERVICES

Below is a description of the services offered by Edison Park Montessori.

3.1 Montessori School Services

The Company provides students with an alternative style of education developed by Maria Montessori, MD. This unique methodology of teaching focuses specifically on the development of the child, and provides them with an atmosphere where they can learn through both traditional teaching and self-directed learning.

This style of teaching was developed by the Italian educator and physician, Dr. Maria Montessori in the early 1900s. Over the last one hundred years, her unique methods have led to the creation of more than 7,000 schools worldwide (4,000 in the US) that use her philosophy to educate students. Almost 98% of these schools are private entities.

The primary goal of a Montessori education is to provide children with a stimulating environment where students are freer to explore subjects and appreciate learning during the course of their tutelage. The philosophy of Dr. Montessori seeks to instill a love of learning that does not end when a child's education is completed.

4.0 STRATEGIC AND MARKET ANALYSIS

4.1 Economic Outlook

This section of the analysis will detail the economic climate, the education industry, the customer profile, and the competition that the business will face as it progresses through its business operations.

Currently, the economy is coming out of a difficult economic period. The job picture has improved and lending has resumed to small businesses. As such, the demand for private schooling services has increased. Additionally, parents that work will always require schooling services and as such the business will be able to remain profitable and cash flow positive at all times.

4.2 Industry Analysis

In the United States, there are approximately 4,000 Montessori schools that operate within the country. A vast majority of these programs are operated as not-for-profit entities. Approximately 200 schools within North America are publicly funded on the municipal level. Worldwide, there are 7,000 institutions that provide a Montessori elementary and/or secondary school education.

The tremendous popularity of this alternative teaching method has allowed these institutions to grow steadily over the last twenty years. Schools that specialize in providing Montessori education make up 4% of the aggregate private elementary and secondary school market. Typically a Montessori school charges tuition based on the age of the student. In the United States, the average yearly tuition charged for this type of schooling is $6,900 per year for full-time student enrollment. These fees can vary significantly depending on the per capita income of the school's specific market.

4.3 Customer Profile

Edison Park Montessori's average client will be a middle to upper middle class man or woman living in the Company's target market. Common traits among clients will include:

- Annual household income exceeding $50,000

- Lives or works no more than 15 miles from the Company's location.

- Will spend up to $700 per month on private school services.

There is a strong demand among parents that want to provide their children with a Montessori focused education during their elementary school years. These parents are willing to pay significant tuition fees for these services. Based on the demographics of the Company's targeted demographic in the Chicago metropolitan area, there are approximately 100,000 families that would be interested in enrolling their children in Edison Park Montessori.

4.4 Competition

In the greater Chicago metropolitan area, there are approximately 200 Montessori educational institutions that are in direct competition with the business. Management intends to maintain a competitive advantage over these other competitors by operating a low operating overhead business that will provide low tuition costs that are normally associated with Chicago based Montessori educational institutions.

5.0 MARKETING PLAN

Edison Park Montessori intends to maintain an extensive marketing campaign that will ensure maximum visibility for the business in its targeted market. Below is an overview of the marketing strategies and objectives of Edison Park Montessori.

5.1 Marketing Objectives

- Continue to maintain a strong relationship with the Chicago community.

- Develop new marketing strategies for generating additional enrollment.

- Continually enroll in state and federal programs to provide educational grants to Edison Park Montessori on a monthly/yearly basis.

5.2 Marketing Strategies

The Company will maintain a reasonable print advertisement campaign in Chicago area publications and newspapers to generate visibility for parents seeking to enroll their students in a Montessori program. Mr. Kelley's intention is to build the school as one of the premier Montessori educational facilities in the Chicago area, which will lead to significant word of mouth referrals during the first three years of operation.

As stated earlier, the Montessori style of education and teaching is a prominent alternative to a traditional public or private school education. Parents that are specifically seeking this type of service will actively search for Montessori schools in their area. As such, the Company will primarily market itself as a Montessori school and provides prospective parents of students with an abundance of literature regarding the school's commitment to this style of teaching.

5.3 Pricing

Management anticipates that Edison Park Montessori will charge $7,000 per year per student for providing a Montessori education to children that are of elementary school age.

6.0 ORGANIZATIONAL PLAN AND PERSONNEL SUMMARY

6.1 Corporate Organization

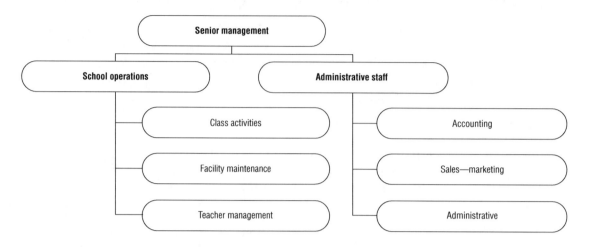

6.2 Organizational Budget

Personnel plan—Yearly

Year	1	2	3
Owner	$ 40,000	$ 41,200	$ 42,436
Director	$ 35,000	$ 36,050	$ 37,132
Teachers	$ 97,500	$100,425	$103,438
Bookkeeper (P/T)	$ 12,500	$ 12,875	$ 13,261
Administrative	$ 20,000	$ 20,600	$ 21,218
Total	**$205,000**	**$211,150**	**$217,485**

Numbers of personnel

Owner	1	1	1
Director	1	1	1
Teachers	3	3	3
Bookkeeper (P/T)	1	1	1
Administrative	1	1	1
Totals	**7**	**7**	**7**

Personnel expense breakdown

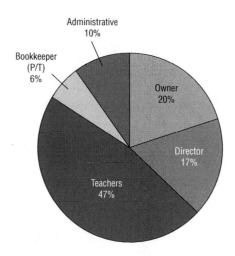

7.0 FINANCIAL PLAN

7.1 Underlying Assumptions

The Company has based its proforma financial statements on the following:

- Edison Park Montessori will have an annual revenue growth rate of 16% per year.

- The Owner will acquire $100,000 of debt funds to develop the business.

- The loan will have a 10 year term with a 9% interest rate.

7.2 Sensitivity Analysis

In the event of an economic downturn, the business may have a decline in its revenues. However, the demand for parents that want to enroll their children in Montessori Schools is increasing steadily. As such, Edison Park Montessori will be able to remain profitable and cash flow positive at all times despite certain drawbacks in the economy.

7.3 Source of Funds

Financing

Equity contributions	
Management investment	$ 10,000.00
Total equity financing	**$ 10,000.00**
Banks and lenders	
Banks and lenders	$ 100,000.00
Total debt financing	**$100,000.00**
Total financing	**$110,000.00**

7.4 General Assumptions

General assumptions

Year	1	2	3
Short term interest rate	9.5%	9.5%	9.5%
Long term interest rate	10.0%	10.0%	10.0%
Federal tax rate	33.0%	33.0%	33.0%
State tax rate	5.0%	5.0%	5.0%
Personnel taxes	15.0%	15.0%	15.0%

7.5 Profit and Loss Statements

Proforma profit and loss (yearly)

Year	1	2	3
Sales	**$416,460**	**$449,777**	**$485,759**
Cost of goods sold	$ 41,646	$ 44,978	$ 48,576
Gross margin	90.00%	90.00%	90.00%
Operating income	**$374,814**	**$404,799**	**$437,183**
Expenses			
Payroll	$205,000	$211,150	$217,485
General and administrative	$ 25,200	$ 26,208	$ 27,256
Marketing expenses	$ 2,082	$ 2,249	$ 2,429
Professional fees and licensure	$ 5,219	$ 5,376	$ 5,537
Insurance costs	$ 1,987	$ 2,086	$ 2,191
Travel and vehicle costs	$ 7,596	$ 8,356	$ 9,191
Rent and utilities	$ 20,000	$ 21,000	$ 22,050
Miscellaneous costs	$ 4,998	$ 5,397	$ 5,829
Payroll taxes	$ 30,750	$ 31,673	$ 32,623
Total operating costs	**$302,832**	**$313,494**	**$324,590**
EBITDA	**$ 71,982**	**$ 91,305**	**$112,593**
Federal income tax	$ 23,754	$ 27,447	$ 34,691
State income tax	$ 3,599	$ 4,159	$ 5,256
Interest expense	$ 8,738	$ 8,131	$ 7,468
Depreciation expenses	$ 4,107	$ 4,107	$ 4,107
Net profit	**$ 31,784**	**$ 47,460**	**$ 61,070**
Profit margin	**7.63%**	**10.55%**	**12.57%**

Sales, operating costs, and profit forecast

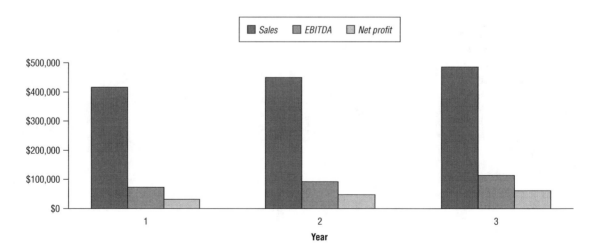

7.6 Cash Flow Analysis

Proforma cash flow analysis—yearly

Year	1	2	3
Cash from operations	$ 35,891	$51,568	$ 65,177
Cash from receivables	$ 0	$ 0	$ 0
Operating cash inflow	**$ 35,891**	**$51,568**	**$ 65,177**
Other cash inflows			
Equity investment	$ 10,000	$ 0	$ 0
Increased borrowings	$100,000	$ 0	$ 0
Sales of business assets	$ 0	$ 0	$ 0
A/P increases	$ 37,902	$43,587	$ 50,125
Total other cash inflows	**$147,902**	**$43,587**	**$ 50,125**
Total cash inflow	**$183,793**	**$95,155**	**$115,303**
Cash outflows			
Repayment of principal	$ 6,463	$ 7,070	$ 7,733
A/P decreases	$ 24,897	$29,876	$ 35,852
A/R increases	$ 0	$ 0	$ 0
Asset purchases	$ 57,500	$ 7,735	$ 9,777
Dividends	$ 28,713	$41,254	$ 52,142
Total cash outflows	**$117,573**	**$85,935**	**$105,503**
Net cash flow	**$ 66,220**	**$ 9,220**	**$ 9,800**
Cash balance	**$ 66,220**	**$75,439**	**$ 85,239**

Proforma cash flow (yearly)

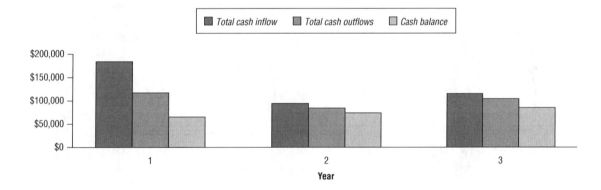

7.7 Balance Sheet

Proforma balance sheet—yearly

Year	1	2	3
Assets			
Cash	$ 66,220	$ 75,439	$ 85,239
Amortized development/expansion costs	$ 17,500	$ 18,274	$ 19,251
Classroom equipment	$ 17,000	$ 22,801	$ 30,134
FF&E	$ 23,000	$ 24,160	$ 25,627
Accumulated depreciation	($ 4,107)	($ 8,214)	($ 12,321)
Total assets	**$119,613**	**$132,460**	**$147,929**
Liabilities and equity			
Accounts payable	$ 13,005	$ 26,716	$ 40,990
Long term liabilities	$ 93,537	$ 86,467	$ 79,397
Other liabilities	$ 0	$ 0	$ 0
Total liabilities	**$106,542**	**$113,183**	**$120,387**
Net worth	**$ 13,071**	**$ 19,277**	**$ 27,543**
Total liabilities and equity	**$119,613**	**$132,460**	**$147,929**

Proforma balance sheet

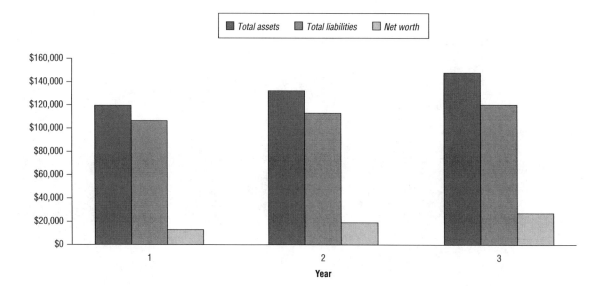

7.8 Breakeven Analysis

Monthly break even analysis

Year	1	2	3
Monthly revenue	$ 28,040	$ 29,027	$ 30,055
Yearly revenue	$336,480	$348,327	$360,656

Break even analysis

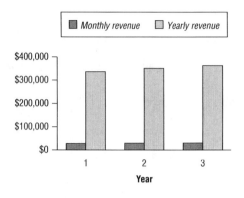

7.9 Business Ratios

Business ratios—yearly

Year	1	2	3
Sales			
Sales growth	0.00%	8.00%	8.00%
Gross margin	90.00%	90.00%	90.00%
Financials			
Profit margin	7.63%	10.55%	12.57%
Assets to liabilities	1.12	1.17	1.23
Equity to liabilities	0.12	0.17	0.23
Assets to equity	9.15	6.87	5.37
Liquidity			
Acid test	0.62	0.67	0.71
Cash to assets	0.55	0.57	0.58

7.10 Three Year Profit and Loss Statement

Profit and loss statement (first year)

Months	1	2	3	4	5	6	7
Sales	$34,100	$34,210	$34,320	$34,430	$34,540	$34,650	$34,760
Cost of goods sold	$ 3,410	$ 3,421	$ 3,432	$ 3,443	$ 3,454	$ 3,465	$ 3,476
Gross margin	90.0%	90.0%	90.0%	90.0%	90.0%	90.0%	90.0%
Operating income	$30,690	$30,789	$30,888	$30,987	$31,086	$31,185	$31,284
Expenses							
Payroll	$17,083	$17,083	$17,083	$17,083	$17,083	$17,083	$17,083
General and administrative	$ 2,100	$ 2,100	$ 2,100	$ 2,100	$ 2,100	$ 2,100	$ 2,100
Marketing expenses	$ 174	$ 174	$ 174	$ 174	$ 174	$ 174	$ 174
Professional fees and licensure	$ 435	$ 435	$ 435	$ 435	$ 435	$ 435	$ 435
Insurance costs	$ 166	$ 166	$ 166	$ 166	$ 166	$ 166	$ 166
Travel and vehicle costs	$ 633	$ 633	$ 633	$ 633	$ 633	$ 633	$ 633
Rent and utilities	$ 1,667	$ 1,667	$ 1,667	$ 1,667	$ 1,667	$ 1,667	$ 1,667
Miscellaneous costs	$ 416	$ 416	$ 416	$ 416	$ 416	$ 416	$ 416
Payroll taxes	$ 2,563	$ 2,563	$ 2,563	$ 2,563	$ 2,563	$ 2,563	$ 2,563
Total operating costs	$25,236	$25,236	$25,236	$25,236	$25,236	$25,236	$25,236
EBITDA	$ 5,454	$ 5,553	$ 5,652	$ 5,751	$ 5,850	$ 5,949	$ 6,048
Federal income tax	$ 1,945	$ 1,951	$ 1,958	$ 1,964	$ 1,970	$ 1,976	$ 1,983
State income tax	$ 295	$ 296	$ 297	$ 298	$ 298	$ 299	$ 300
Interest expense	$ 750	$ 746	$ 742	$ 738	$ 734	$ 730	$ 726
Depreciation expense	$ 342	$ 342	$ 342	$ 342	$ 342	$ 342	$ 342
Net profit	$ 2,122	$ 2,218	$ 2,313	$ 2,409	$ 2,505	$ 2,601	$ 2,696

Profit and loss statement (first year cont.)

Month	8	9	10	11	12	1
Sales	$34,870	$34,980	$35,090	$35,200	$35,310	$416,460
Cost of goods sold	$ 3,487	$ 3,498	$ 3,509	$ 3,520	$ 3,531	$ 41,646
Gross margin	90.0%	90.0%	90.0%	90.0%	90.0%	90.0%
Operating income	$31,383	$31,482	$31,581	$31,680	$31,779	$374,814
Expenses						
Payroll	$17,083	$17,083	$17,083	$17,083	$17,083	$205,000
General and administrative	$ 2,100	$ 2,100	$ 2,100	$ 2,100	$ 2,100	$ 25,200
Marketing expenses	$ 174	$ 174	$ 174	$ 174	$ 174	$ 2,082
Professional fees and licensure	$ 435	$ 435	$ 435	$ 435	$ 435	$ 5,219
Insurance costs	$ 166	$ 166	$ 166	$ 166	$ 166	$ 1,987
Travel and vehicle costs	$ 633	$ 633	$ 633	$ 633	$ 633	$ 7,596
Rent and utilities	$ 1,667	$ 1,667	$ 1,667	$ 1,667	$ 1,667	$ 20,000
Miscellaneous costs	$ 416	$ 416	$ 416	$ 416	$ 416	$ 4,998
Payroll taxes	$ 2,563	$ 2,563	$ 2,563	$ 2,563	$ 2,563	$ 30,750
Total operating costs	$25,236	$25,236	$25,236	$25,236	$25,236	$302,832
EBITDA	$ 6,147	$ 6,246	$ 6,345	$ 6,444	$ 6,543	$ 71,982
Federal income tax	$ 1,989	$ 1,995	$ 2,001	$ 2,008	$ 2,014	$ 23,754
State income tax	$ 301	$ 302	$ 303	$ 304	$ 305	$ 3,599
Interest expense	$ 722	$ 718	$ 714	$ 710	$ 706	$ 8,738
Depreciation expense	$ 342	$ 342	$ 342	$ 342	$ 342	$ 4,107
Net profit	$ 2,792	$ 2,888	$ 2,984	$ 3,080	$ 3,176	$ 31,784

Profit and loss statement (second year)

Quarter	Q1	2 Q2	Q3	Q4	2
Sales	$89,955	$112,444	$121,440	$125,938	$449,777
Cost of goods sold	$ 8,996	$ 11,244	$ 12,144	$ 12,594	$ 44,978
Gross margin	90.0%	90.0%	90.0%	90.0%	90.0%
Operating income	$80,960	$101,200	$109,296	$113,344	$404,799
Expenses					
Payroll	$42,230	$ 52,788	$ 57,011	$ 59,122	$211,150
General and administrative	$ 5,242	$ 6,552	$ 7,076	$ 7,338	$ 26,208
Marketing expenses	$ 450	$ 562	$ 607	$ 630	$ 2,249
Professional fees and licensure	$ 1,075	$ 1,344	$ 1,451	$ 1,505	$ 5,376
Insurance costs	$ 417	$ 522	$ 563	$ 584	$ 2,086
Travel and vehicle costs	$ 1,671	$ 2,089	$ 2,256	$ 2,340	$ 8,356
Rent and utilities	$ 4,200	$ 5,250	$ 5,670	$ 5,880	$ 21,000
Miscellaneous costs	$ 1,079	$ 1,349	$ 1,457	$ 1,511	$ 5,397
Payroll taxes	$ 6,335	$ 7,918	$ 8,552	$ 8,868	$ 31,673
Total operating costs	$62,699	$ 78,374	$ 84,643	$ 87,778	$313,494
EBITDA	$18,261	$ 22,826	$ 24,652	$ 25,565	$ 91,305
Federal income tax	$ 5,489	$ 6,862	$ 7,411	$ 7,685	$ 27,447
State income tax	$ 832	$ 1,040	$ 1,123	$ 1,164	$ 4,159
Interest expense	$ 2,092	$ 2,053	$ 2,013	$ 1,973	$ 8,131
Depreciation expense	$ 1,027	$ 1,027	$ 1,027	$ 1,027	$ 4,107
Net profit	$ 8,821	$ 11,845	$ 13,078	$ 13,716	$ 47,460

Profit and loss statement (third year)

Quarter	Q1	3 Q2	Q3	Q4	3
Sales	**$97,152**	**$121,440**	**$131,155**	**$136,013**	**$485,759**
Cost of goods sold	$ 9,715	$ 12,144	$ 13,115	$ 13,601	$ 48,576
Gross margin	90.0%	90.0%	90.0%	90.0%	90.0%
Operating income	**$87,437**	**$109,296**	**$118,039**	**$122,411**	**$437,183**
Expenses					
Payroll	$43,497	$ 54,371	$ 58,721	$ 60,896	$217,485
General and administrative	$ 5,451	$ 6,814	$ 7,359	$ 7,632	$ 27,256
Marketing expenses	$ 486	$ 607	$ 656	$ 680	$ 2,429
Professional fees and licensure	$ 1,107	$ 1,384	$ 1,495	$ 1,550	$ 5,537
Insurance costs	$ 438	$ 548	$ 591	$ 613	$ 2,191
Travel and vehicle costs	$ 1,838	$ 2,298	$ 2,482	$ 2,574	$ 9,191
Rent and utilities	$ 4,410	$ 5,513	$ 5,954	$ 6,174	$ 22,050
Miscellaneous costs	$ 1,166	$ 1,457	$ 1,574	$ 1,632	$ 5,829
Payroll taxes	$ 6,525	$ 8,156	$ 8,808	$ 9,134	$ 32,623
Total operating costs	**$64,918**	**$ 81,148**	**$ 87,639**	**$ 90,885**	**$324,590**
EBITDA	**$22,519**	**$ 28,148**	**$ 30,400**	**$ 31,526**	**$112,593**
Federal income tax	$ 6,938	$ 8,673	$ 9,367	$ 9,714	$ 34,691
State income tax	$ 1,051	$ 1,314	$ 1,419	$ 1,472	$ 5,256
Interest expense	$ 1,932	$ 1,889	$ 1,846	$ 1,802	$ 7,468
Depreciation expense	$ 1,027	$ 1,027	$ 1,027	$ 1,027	$ 4,107
Net profit	**$11,571**	**$ 15,245**	**$ 16,742**	**$ 17,512**	**$ 61,070**

7.11 Three Year Cash Flow Analysis

Cash flow analysis (first year)

Month	1	2	3	4	5	6	7	8
Cash from operations	$ 2,464	$ 2,560	$ 2,656	$ 2,751	$ 2,847	$ 2,943	$ 3,039	$ 3,134
Cash from receivables	$ 0	$ 0	$ 0	$ 0	$ 0	$ 0	$ 0	$ 0
Operating cash inflow	**$ 2,464**	**$ 2,560**	**$ 2,656**	**$ 2,751**	**$ 2,847**	**$ 2,943**	**$ 3,039**	**$ 3,134**
Other cash inflows								
Equity investment	$ 10,000	$ 0	$ 0	$ 0	$ 0	$ 0	$ 0	$ 0
Increased borrowings	$100,000	$ 0	$ 0	$ 0	$ 0	$ 0	$ 0	$ 0
Sales of business assets	$ 0	$ 0	$ 0	$ 0	$ 0	$ 0	$ 0	$ 0
A/P increases	$ 3,159	$ 3,159	$ 3,159	$ 3,159	$ 3,159	$ 3,159	$ 3,159	$ 3,159
Total other cash inflows	**$113,159**	**$ 3,159**	**$ 3,159**	**$ 3,159**	**$ 3,159**	**$ 3,159**	**$ 3,159**	**$ 3,159**
Total cash inflow	**$115,623**	**$ 5,718**	**$ 5,814**	**$ 5,910**	**$ 6,006**	**$ 6,101**	**$ 6,197**	**$ 6,293**
Cash outflows								
Repayment of principal	$ 517	$ 521	$ 525	$ 528	$ 532	$ 536	$ 540	$ 545
A/P decreases	$ 2,075	$ 2,075	$ 2,075	$ 2,075	$ 2,075	$ 2,075	$ 2,075	$ 2,075
A/R increases	$ 0	$ 0	$ 0	$ 0	$ 0	$ 0	$ 0	$ 0
Asset purchases	$ 57,500	$ 0	$ 0	$ 0	$ 0	$ 0	$ 0	$ 0
Dividends	$ 0	$ 0	$ 0	$ 0	$ 0	$ 0	$ 0	$ 0
Total cash outflows	**$ 60,092**	**$ 2,595**	**$ 2,599**	**$ 2,603**	**$ 2,607**	**$ 2,611**	**$ 2,615**	**$ 2,619**
Net cash flow	**$ 55,531**	**$ 3,123**	**$ 3,215**	**$ 3,307**	**$ 3,398**	**$ 3,490**	**$ 3,582**	**$ 3,674**
Cash balance	**$ 55,531**	**$58,654**	**$61,869**	**$65,176**	**$68,574**	**$72,064**	**$75,646**	**$79,320**

Cash flow analysis (first year cont.)

Month	9	10	11	12	1
Cash from operations	$ 3,230	$ 3,326	$ 3,422	$ 3,518	$ 35,891
Cash from receivables	$ 0	$ 0	$ 0	$ 0	$ 0
Operating cash inflow	**$ 3,230**	**$ 3,326**	**$ 3,422**	**$ 3,518**	**$ 35,891**
Other cash inflows					
Equity investment	$ 0	$ 0	$ 0	$ 0	$ 10,000
Increased borrowings	$ 0	$ 0	$ 0	$ 0	$100,000
Sales of business assets	$ 0	$ 0	$ 0	$ 0	$ 0
A/P increases	$ 3,159	$ 3,159	$ 3,159	$ 3,159	$ 37,902
Total other cash inflows	**$ 3,159**	**$ 3,159**	**$ 3,159**	**$ 3,159**	**$147,902**
Total cash inflow	**$ 6,389**	**$ 6,485**	**$ 6,581**	**$ 6,677**	**$183,793**
Cash outflows					
Repayment of principal	$ 549	$ 553	$ 557	$ 561	$ 6,463
A/P decreases	$ 2,075	$ 2,075	$ 2,075	$ 2,075	$ 24,897
A/R increases	$ 0	$ 0	$ 0	$ 0	$ 0
Asset purchases	$ 0	$ 0	$ 0	$ 0	$ 57,500
Dividends	$ 0	$ 0	$ 0	$28,713	$ 28,713
Total cash outflows	**$ 2,623**	**$ 2,627**	**$ 2,632**	**$31,349**	**$117,573**
Net cash flow	**$ 3,766**	**$ 3,857**	**$ 3,949**	**−$24,672**	**$ 66,220**
Cash balance	**$83,086**	**$86,943**	**$90,892**	**$66,220**	**$ 66,220**

Cash flow analysis (second year)

Quarter	Q1	2 Q2	Q3	Q4	2
Cash from operations	$10,314	$12,892	$13,923	$14,439	$51,568
Cash from receivables	$ 0	$ 0	$ 0	$ 0	$ 0
Operating cash inflow	**$10,314**	**$12,892**	**$13,923**	**$14,439**	**$51,568**
Other cash inflows					
Equity investment	$ 0	$ 0	$ 0	$ 0	$ 0
Increased borrowings	$ 0	$ 0	$ 0	$ 0	$ 0
Sales of business assets	$ 0	$ 0	$ 0	$ 0	$ 0
A/P increases	$ 8,717	$10,897	$11,769	$12,204	$43,587
Total other cash inflows	**$ 8,717**	**$10,897**	**$11,769**	**$12,204**	**$43,587**
Total cash inflow	**$19,031**	**$23,789**	**$25,692**	**$26,643**	**$95,155**
Cash outflows					
Repayment of principal	$ 1,708	$ 1,747	$ 1,787	$ 1,827	$ 7,070
A/P decreases	$ 5,975	$ 7,469	$ 8,067	$ 8,365	$29,876
A/R increases	$ 0	$ 0	$ 0	$ 0	$ 0
Asset purchases	$ 1,547	$ 1,934	$ 2,088	$ 2,166	$ 7,735
Dividends	$ 8,251	$10,314	$11,139	$11,551	$41,254
Total cash outflows	**$17,482**	**$21,464**	**$23,080**	**$23,910**	**$85,935**
Net cash flow	**$ 1,549**	**$ 2,325**	**$ 2,611**	**$ 2,734**	**$ 9,220**
Cash balance	**$67,769**	**$70,094**	**$72,706**	**$75,439**	**$75,439**

Cash flow analysis (third year)

Quarter	Q1	3 Q2	Q3	Q4	3
Cash from operations	$13,035	$16,294	$17,598	$18,250	$ 65,177
Cash from receivables	$ 0	$ 0	$ 0	$ 0	$ 0
Operating cash inflow	**$13,035**	**$16,294**	**$17,598**	**$18,250**	**$ 65,177**
Other cash inflows					
Equity investment	$ 0	$ 0	$ 0	$ 0	$ 0
Increased borrowings	$ 0	$ 0	$ 0	$ 0	$ 0
Sales of business assets	$ 0	$ 0	$ 0	$ 0	$ 0
A/P increases	$10,025	$12,531	$13,534	$14,035	$ 50,125
Total other cash inflows	**$10,025**	**$12,531**	**$13,534**	**$14,035**	**$ 50,125**
Total cash inflow	**$23,061**	**$28,826**	**$31,132**	**$32,285**	**$115,303**
Cash outflows					
Repayment of principal	$ 1,869	$ 1,911	$ 1,954	$ 1,999	$ 7,733
A/P decreases	$ 7,170	$ 8,963	$ 9,680	$10,038	$ 35,852
A/R increases	$ 0	$ 0	$ 0	$ 0	$ 0
Asset purchases	$ 1,955	$ 2,444	$ 2,640	$ 2,737	$ 9,777
Dividends	$10,428	$13,035	$14,078	$14,600	$ 52,142
Total cash outflows	**$21,423**	**$26,354**	**$28,352**	**$29,374**	**$105,503**
Net cash flow	**$ 1,638**	**$ 2,472**	**$ 2,779**	**$ 2,910**	**$ 9,800**
Cash balance	**$77,077**	**$79,549**	**$82,329**	**$85,239**	**$ 85,239**

Non-Medical Assistance

Helping Hands Companion Service

1212 W. 13 Mile Rd.
Royal Oak, MI 48073

Heidi Denler

Helping Hands will offer non-medical, in-home companion care services in the Metropolitan Detroit community for seniors and those individuals who are physically challenged, recovering from illness or surgery, or suffering with a chronic illness. Clients may choose from short-term service or long-term care, which will allow them to remain in the comfortable surroundings of their own home rather than be moved to a "step-down" nursing facility or assisted living arrangement.

COMPANY SUMMARY

Helping Hands will offer non-medical, in-home companion care services in the Metropolitan Detroit community for seniors and those individuals who are physically challenged, recovering from illness or surgery, or suffering with a chronic illness. Clients may choose from short-term service or long-term care, which will allow them to remain in the comfortable surroundings of their own home rather than be moved to a "step-down" nursing facility or assisted living arrangement. Jennifer Klein and Ava Jones will form a partnership to run the company. Klein and Jones have determined that as baby boomers reach retirement age in increasing numbers, the need will arise for non-medical assistants to enable those boomers to stay in their homes when they have a chronic illness or want to recuperate from surgery or injury. Patients will be referred by physicians, insurance companies, and health care facilities, as well as by social workers at hospitals. The partners have an extensive professional network and can boast excellent reputations in their fields in Metropolitan Detroit, which will provide a basis for starting and building their company.

MANAGEMENT SUMMARY

Jennifer Klein holds M.S. degrees in gerontology and sociology. She brings 20 years of experience working in nursing homes, assisted living facilities, and, most recently, in private home care. Ava Jones holds an M.B.A. and has 22 years experience as an accountant and is currently the assistant treasurer of a large, franchised multi-level senior center. Their skills will complement each other, allowing for a successful, growing, service-oriented business partnership.

MISSION STATEMENT

Helping Hands will provide non-medical services—including rides to the doctor, light cleaning, food preparation, and companionship—for anyone who is homebound for any reason or length of time.

VISION STATEMENT

Helping Hands will build its clientele by providing non-medical, companion services to seniors or those recuperating, who wish to remain in the comfort of their own homes. The company will expand slowly, opening a second office outside a 60-mile radius of the home office, and eventually via franchising.

VALUES STATEMENT

Whether a client requires short-term, hourly assistance, long-term assistance, or occasional help with errands or household chores, Helping Hands will provide quality, nurturing care equivalent to what a family member or life-long friend would provide.

BUSINESS PHILOSOPHY

Customer satisfaction, reliability, networking with other health care professionals, increased client numbers, and a solid bottom line are the goals of Jennifer Klein and Ava Jones as they start Helping Hands. Providing affordable, friendly, professional services to every client is the goal of Helping Hands. Employees will be well-trained and will meet state and federal standards.

ORGANIZATION STRUCTURE

Helping Hands will be run as a partnership owned and operated by Jennifer Klein and Ava Jones. Klein will act as clinical director, overseeing employees in the field, who will provide companion care to the company's clients. She will also handle the in-home assessments and create the specific care plan for each client. Jones will serve as administrative director, and will handle the business aspects of the company. This will include payroll, insurance needs, and any office responsibilities. Jones will oversee an administrative assistant, who will answer phones and help with paperwork and filing, as well as monitor updates of client files.

Field representatives of Helping Hands will interact directly with clients and their families and will make daily updates regarding care given and client status. In-home caregivers will be responsible for following the specific program of care created following the in-home assessment. They will report directly to Jennifer Klein.

Occupational therapists, physical therapists, and speech therapists will be employed part-time to provide services to clients who require such rehabilitation.

A social worker will be hired full-time to coordinate client needs with local agencies and associations that offer additional support and services not provided by Helping Hands. As the client base increases, Klein and Jones expect to hire a second social worker to assist their client base.

ADVERTISING AND PROMOTION

Jennifer Klein and Ava Jones have created a database of former and current colleagues in the medical field who have indicated an interest in working with them to provide referrals and recommendations for their client base.

Each partner in Helping Hands will make personal presentations to service groups, such as Services for Older Citizens, United Way, Gilda's Club. They will also work in concert with assisted living facilities to identify potential clients who are not quite ready to move from their homes or who have been placed on a waiting list to move to a facility.

Advertisements will be placed in local papers, and press releases will be given to explain the types of services offered by Helping Hands.

Klein and Jones plan to place brochures in waiting rooms of doctors, physical therapy facilities, gyms (and other places where people might suffer an injury), and in local offices of associations who serve those with such chronic diseases as multiple sclerosis, Alzheimer's disease, and Parkinson's disease. They will also work with caregiver respite groups for those who require long-term breaks not offered by the respite group.

The partners of Helping Hands recognize that marketing their services is about the quality of care and relationships built between the caregiver and the client and will exploit the offering of that relationship in their marketing efforts.

CUSTOMER BASE

The initial customer base for Helping Hands will come from referrals from Klein's and Jones's former clients and former and current colleagues at medical offices and health care facilities. Their services will enable those who have been injured, are recovering from surgery, are suffering from a chronic illness, and the elderly. All of these people deserve the right to stay in their own homes as long as possible rather than moving to a health care facility.

In addition, Helping Hands will build referrals from local chapters of associations, such as the Alzheimers Association, the American Society on Aging, the Arthritis Foundation, Meals on Wheels, National Area Agencies on Aging, United Way, and the Veterans' Administration. These agencies are constantly seeking to assist their own clients and patients with affordable assistance that will allow them to remain in their own homes.

PRODUCTS AND SERVICES

Helping Hands will offer non-medical services based on an in-home assessment conducted by Clkinical Manager Jennifer Klein. A personalized plan will be created to fill the needs and wants of every client as Klein works with the company's social worker, occupational therapist, and physical therapist. The in-home assessment will include a home safety review, discussion of the client/family requirements, and billing requirements.

Basic services will include:

- Assessment and planning, including referral to medical services as deemed necessary
- Transportation to appointments, club meetings, shopping, restaurants, plays/concerts, etc.
- Transportation for errands and shopping with client
- Running errands and completing shopping if client is unable to leave his/her home

- Light housekeeping (making bed, trash removal, dusting/vacuuming)
- Laundry
- Meal preparation to ensure proper nutrition
- Personal care (bathing/grooming, medication reminders)
- Companionship (conversation/socialization, reading to client, discussion, playing games, going for walks, making appointments, helping with bill payment)
- Hospital/step-down facility discharge & follow-up (help getting home from facility and getting settled at home)

For Alzheimers and dementia clients, Helping Hands offers:

- Companionship
- Meal preparation and assistance eating
- Games to encourage cognitive abilities
- Exercise (walking, PT exercises prescribed by doctor)
- Safety (monitor client remaining in home)

Cancer patients can expect Helping Hands to assist with:

- Companionship
- Running errands
- Help with personal hygiene
- Medication reminders
- Transportation to doctor
- Reduction of stress when patient is frustrated by inability to be independent

Helping Hands can assist families with a loved one in hospice care by offering:

- Comfort
- Meal preparation
- Help with personal hygiene
- Turning a bedridden client to avoid bedsores
- Call to family/hospice as necessary

For those clients in rehabilitation programs, Helping Hands will provide:

- Transportation to doctor appointments
- Transportation to physical therapy clinic
- Follow-up at home with PT exercises under the direction of a Helping Hands physical therapist
- Medication assistance
- Meal preparation
- Assistance with dressing, grooming, etc.

When family members/caregivers require a break or have to be at work, Helping Hands will offer loving, nurturing care of loved ones. Clients will be able to remain independent by making their own decisions about how they live and making choices about how to get things done.

Affordable pricing will be based on estimated or requested time. Helping Hands will offer 24-hour care for those who require or request it, but can be hired for as few as two hours per day once per week and anything in between.

Client files will be updated following each visit, or in the case of 24-hour care, on a daily basis.

PERSONNEL REQUIREMENTS

The partners will hold managing director positions within the firm and share decision-making in regard to all office and field personnel, as well as future expansion of the business. Jennifer Klein will serve as clinical director. She will manage Helping Hands employees who will meet the needs of the company's clients in the field, including initial interviews of potential employees. Klein will also conduct in-home assessments and create individualized plans to meet each client's particular needs.

Ava Jones will put her business expertise to use, overseeing all business aspects of the company, including finance, insurance, and legal matters. A part-time administrative assistant will help her with paperwork, filing, and updating client reports daily.

Other employees will include a social worker, who will assist clients who might require services from such local and national organizations as United Way, the American Cancer Society, Services for Older Citizens, and the Agency for Aging. Occupational and physical therapists will be retained for part-time work for individual cases, as will a speech therapist for clients whose injury or illness has caused loss of speech (for example, following a closed head injury or stroke). Proof of active state licensing will be required for this group of employees.

Field employees are those who will actually serve as an in-home companion to the client. They will undergo extensive background screening and mandatory random drug testing. In addition they must provide multiple work references as well as personal references. A valid driver's license is another requirement for Helping Hands companions. Potential companion employees will be selected from social workers and graduate students in occupational and physical therapy programs, as well as from nurses and medical employees who have "burned out" in a hospital, clinic, or medical office, but are highly qualified to provide basic companion care to Helping Hands' clients. All must be bonded and insured.

LOCATION

Klein and Jones are working with a realtor to locate an office in a central location in the Metropolitan Detroit area. They are focusing on the Royal Oak, Michigan, community, which allows easy access to area freeways to allow employees limited driving time to client homes. The area is growing rapidly, and Baby Boomers (the typical prospective client for Helping Hands) are embracing the development in the county in particular.

STORE DESIGN AND EQUIPMENT

Limited office space will be required by Helping Hands because most work will be in client homes. A small office will be necessary to house:

- Offices for Klein and Jones, with a desk and chair, bookshelves, and filing cabinet(s)

- An office to be shared by field employees that will have two or three desks with chairs, a filing cabinet, a work table and chairs, printer

- A large conference room with a table and chairs for 6 with a white board

- Bookshelves for employee handbooks and books, magazines, and newspapers that might be read to clients

- A small break room with a refrigerator, microwave, sink and counter space where all employees, as well as the owners, can eat lunch or a quick snack, relax, and interact

- A unisex bathroom

Helping Hands will also require a fleet of cars for caregivers to use to transport clients. Klein and Jones have determined that at least one vehicle will be a van equipped to handle wheelchair-bound clients. Each vehicle will be customized with the company name/logo, phone number, and e-mail address/Web site URL.

FINANCIAL

Start up costs will be moderate and will include state licensing and attorney fees, as well as furnishing the office space. Costs will include:

- Office supplies (paper, staplers, paper clips, pencils, pens, stationary, brochures, and business cards for all employees)

- Insurance (professional liability, workers' compensation, property/casualty, key man, car, and health insurance for full-time employees)

- Rental (office space and cars)

- Utilities (landline phone, mobile phones for all employees, pagers, gas, electric, water)

- Technology (computers for each partner and two in the office for employees to make updates to client files, one all-in-one printer and one regular printer, billing software, payroll and tax software)

- Miscellaneous office expenses (rent; such kitchen supplies as paper toweling, soap, plates, silverware, cups/glasses; such bathroom supplies as toilet paper, soap; alarm system)

- Cleaning service to maintain the office once or twice a week

- Office furnishings (desks, desk chairs, conference table and chairs, filing cabinets, Wi-Fi Internet access, refrigerator, microwave)

PROFESSIONAL AND ADVISORY SUPPORT

Klein and Jones will work with the state licensing boards to ensure compliance with all laws related to home care in the state of Michigan. Legal counsel will be retained to handle all paperwork incurred with the start-up of a new business and the state, as well as leases for the company's office and for the rental cars for employees to provide transportation to and from client homes and to drive clients to appointments and on errands.

Jones will put her M.B.A. to use handling taxes, payroll, and any financial matters for Helping Hands, which will avoid CPA costs.

The partners are working with PNC Bank to establish a loan and line of credit to cover start-up costs and such initial expenses as payroll and advertising. They expect to show a modest profit within three months that will become a strong profit by the end of the first year of operation.

BUSINESS AND GROWTH STRATEGY

Jennifer Klein and Ava Jones plan to build their business by building their client base. They intend to start with 50 clients and build to 100 by the end of the first year in operation. They are looking for 10 to 20 percent growth annually thereafter.

Clients will be lost from a variety of reasons, including returning to health and death. However, this will be offset by ongoing referrals from Klein's and Jones's networking database of professionals, as well as from word-of-mouth referrals from satisfied clients and their family members.

Slow growth will be mandated for Helping Hands in order to avoid the pitfall of loss of quality in care and management. However, within five years, Klein and Jones expect to open at least one additional office that will serve the central part of the state near Lansing.

COMPETITION

Helping Hands will fill a niche for those individuals who prefer staying in their own homes rather than moving to a rehabilitation facility or an assisted living facility, but require non-medical assistance to do so. Most agencies in Metropolitan Detroit offer skilled nursing care, whether the patient client requires nursing or not. There are limited options available for those who simply need someone to be a companion, take them to appointments or shopping, do light housework and laundry, or give family members acting as caregivers for those with such chronic illnesses as Alzheimers or ALS a break from their responsibilities for a few hours or a few days.

Because of the limited competition, Klein and Jones expect to be successful immediately and show at least a modest profit within three months of beginning operation.

WEB SITE

Helping Hands will have an Internet presence with a professionally constructed Web site. Contact information, hours, and testimonials will be available, along with credentials of the managing partners and companion staff.

Pages of the Web site will be dedicated to services offered, from simple companionship for a couple of hours an afternoon, to 24-hour services to help Alzheimer patients stay in familiar surroundings as long as possible.

CONCLUSION

Individuals who require non-medical assistance to remain in their own homes and maintain a sense of independence will benefit from the services offered by Helping Hands. Basic companionship, meal preparation, light housekeeping, and transportation provided by nurturing caregivers who are bonded and insured will be the signature for the company. Jennifer Klein and Ava Jones bring years of experience in their respective fields of home health care and business management to Helping Hands, creating an environment for success. Costs will be carefully discussed with the client and their family members to ensure affordability. Most importantly, clients will be treated like a member of the family, with love and concern for their well-being.

Organic Food Store

Earth's Bounty Organic Foods

11 Dover Center Road
Bay Village, OH 44140

BizPlanDB.com

Earth's Bounty Organic Foods will sell organic food and grocery items from its moderate-sized retail location to customers in its targeted market of Cuyahoga County, Ohio. The Company was founded by Marcie Hill.

1.0 EXECUTIVE SUMMARY

The purpose of this business plan is to raise $250,000 for the development of an organic food store while showcasing the expected financials and operations over the next three years. Earth's Bounty Organic Foods is an Ohio-based corporation that will sell organic food and grocery items from its moderate sized retail location to customers in its targeted market. The Company was founded by Marcie Hill.

1.1 The Products

Earth's Bounty Organic Foods will offer the general public a number of products that are found throughout supermarkets. The business will carry thousands of items across many organic brand names. The business will maintain the following divisions within the market:

- General Organic Grocery

- Organic Deli and Packaged Meats

- Organic Produce

- General Merchandise

- Specialty organic food kiosks

1.2 Financing

Ms. Hill is seeking to raise $250,000 from as a bank loan. The interest rate and loan agreement are to be further discussed during negotiation. This business plan assumes that the business will receive a 10-year loan with a 9% fixed interest rate. The financing will be used for the following:

- Development of the retail location.

- Financing for the first six months of operation.

- Capital to purchase inventory.

Ms. Hill will contribute $50,000 to the venture.

1.3 Mission Statement

The mission of Earth's Bounty Organic Foods is to become the recognized leader in its targeted market of Cuyahoga County, Ohio for providing organic grocery items at a reasonable cost.

1.4 Management Team

Earth's Bounty Organic Foods was founded by Marcie Hill. Ms. Hill has more than 10 years of experience in the retail management industry. Through her expertise, she will be able to bring the operations of the business to profitability within its first year of operations.

1.5 Sales Forecasts

Ms. Hill expects a strong rate of growth at the start of operations. Below are the expected financials over the next three years.

Proforma profit and loss (yearly)

Year	1	2	3
Sales	$777,000	$831,390	$889,587
Operating costs	$340,428	$353,237	$366,606
EBITDA	$203,472	$228,736	$256,105
Taxes, interest, and depreciation	$114,699	$115,059	$124,431
Net profit	$ 88,773	$113,677	$131,674

Sales, operating costs, and profit forecast

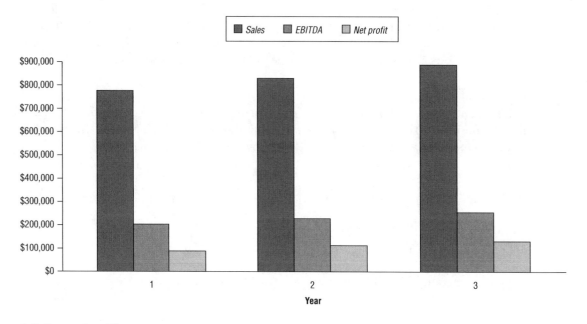

1.6 Expansion Plan

The Founder expects that the business will aggressively expand during the first three years of operation. Ms. Hill intends to implement marketing campaigns that will effectively target individuals within the target market.

2.0 COMPANY AND FINANCING SUMMARY

2.1 Registered Name and Corporate Structure

Earth's Bounty Organic Foods is registered as a corporation in the State of Ohio.

2.2 Required Funds

At this time, Earth's Bounty Organic Foods requires $250,000 of debt funds. Below is a breakdown of how these funds will be used:

Projected startup costs

Initial lease payments and deposits	$ 25,000
Working capital	$ 65,000
FF&E	$ 40,000
Leasehold improvements	$ 30,000
Security deposits	$ 15,000
Insurance	$ 2,500
Initial inventory	$100,000
Marketing budget	$ 17,500
Miscellaneous and unforeseen costs	$ 5,000
Total startup costs	**$300,000**

Use of funds

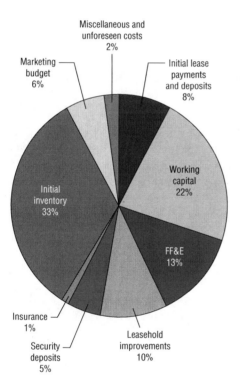

2.3 Investor Equity

Ms. Hill is not seeking an investment from a third party at this time.

2.4 Management Equity

Marcie Hill owns 100% of Earth's Bounty Organic Foods, Inc.

2.5 Exit Strategy

If the business is very successful, Ms. Hill may seek to sell the business to a third party for a significant earnings multiple. Most likely, the Company will hire a qualified business broker to sell the business. Based on historical numbers, the business could fetch a sales premium of up to 4 times earnings.

3.0 GROCERY STORE PRODUCTS

3.1 General Organic Grocery

The primary business unit of Earth's Bounty Organic Foods will be the general grocery section, where the business will feature a number of prepackaged organic products including cereals, breads, pastas, cookies/candies, pet food supplies, ethnic foods, and a number of other staple goods. The business will carry these products under several brand names.

3.2 Packaged and Deli Meats

The business will also maintain an extensive organic deli that will serve a variety of beef, pork, and seafood products. The business will always have a butcher on staff, and all meat (both fresh and packaged) will meet all regulations regarding the sale of organic meat products.

Management expects that sales of deli and packaged meat products will account for almost 20% of the Company's transactions.

3.3 Produce

The business will also have a large organic produce section that will provide a wide variety of fresh fruits and vegetables that are purchased from local and exporting growers. Produce is an especially important division for the business.

At all times, the Company will maintain the freshness of the produce by continually spraying and maintaining clean inventories.

3.4 General Merchandise

The last aspect to the operations is the sale of general merchandise which will include a limited selection of household goods, cleaning suppliers, mops, brooms, pots, pans, and other assorted products that are used for general and light home maintenance. This will be the smallest division of the business.

4.0 STRATEGIC AND MARKET ANALYSIS

4.1 Economic Outlook

This section of the analysis will detail the economic climate, the grocery store industry, the customer profile, and the competition that the business will face as it progresses through its business operations.

Currently, the economic market condition in the United States is recessed. The meltdown of the sub prime mortgage market coupled with increasing gas prices has led many people to believe that the US is on the cusp of a double dip economic recession. This slowdown in the economy has also greatly impacted real estate sales, which has halted to historical lows. However, grocery stores tend to operate with great economic stability as people will continue to purchase grocery goods in any economic climate.

4.2 Industry Analysis

Within the United States, three are approximately 95,000 grocery stores in operation. Approximately 10% of all food stores now operate solely in an organic manner. Each year, these businesses aggregately generate more than $500 billion of revenues while providing jobs for more than 2.9 million people. In each of the last five years, annual payrolls have exceeded $50 billion.

This is a mature industry, and the anticipated future growth rate will remain in line with that of the general economy.

4.3 Customer Profile

The Company expects that the average customer of Earth's Bounty Organic Foods will have the following demographics:

- Household/family income of $50,000 per year or more.

- Will regularly use the store once a quality rapport has been developed.

- Is concerned about the quality of food, produce, and meat they are purchasing.

Through these demographics, the Company will structure its advertising and marketing campaigns to appeal to the above demographics. Based on information provided by the US Census, there are approximately 200,000 people within the target market of Cuyahoga County, Ohio that could become regular customers of Earth's Bounty Organic Foods.

5.0 MARKETING PLAN

The Organic Food Store intends to maintain an extensive marketing campaign that will ensure maximum visibility for the business in its targeted market. Below is an overview of the marketing strategies and objectives of the Company.

5.1 Marketing Objectives

- Develop an online presence by developing a website and placing the Company's name and contact information with online directories.

- Implement a local campaign with the Company's targeted market of Cuyahoga County, Ohio via the use of flyers, local newspaper advertisements, and word of mouth advertising.

- Establish relationships with organic food wholesalers within the regional market.

5.2 Marketing Strategies

Retail marketing will be the most difficult portion of the marketing strategy. This is because one of the essential elements to reaching a retail audience is building a brand affinity with the customer. Management fully expects to enlist the help of a local marketing firm to reach the Company's targeted organic conscious consumer. The grocery store industry is an extremely competitive market, and as such, the Management of Earth's Bounty Organic Foods will need to develop a marketing program that creates a branded image edge over its competition.

The Company will maintain a moderate level of traditional print and media advertising, which will be exclusively geared towards current and potential consumers. These traditional advertisements include billboards and distribution of flyers/circulars in controlled circulation publications. This will ensure that the target audience is continually aware of Earth's Bounty Organic Foods' grand opening and regular discount promotions.

Finally, the business will develop a small online platform (registered with several online directories) so that people can easily find the store's location by searching (via sites like Google, Yahoo, etc.) for organic food and organic grocery stores.

5.3 Pricing

Earth's Bounty Organic Foods will carry thousands of grocery and household items. As such, it is difficult to determine the pricing of each product offered by the business. However, a full preliminary pricing matrix is available upon request. The anticipated gross margins generated by the business will be 70% per dollar of revenue.

6.0 ORGANIZATIONAL PLAN AND PERSONNEL SUMMARY

6.1 Corporate Organization

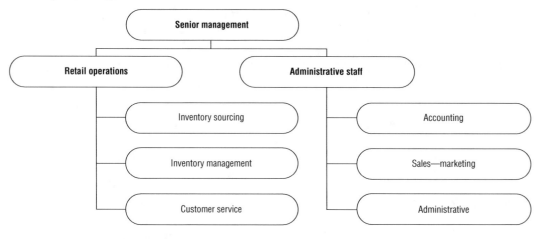

6.2 Organizational Budget

Personnel plan—yearly

Year	1	2	3
Owner	$ 40,000	$ 41,200	$ 42,436
Store manager	$ 35,000	$ 36,050	$ 37,132
Store employees	$ 85,000	$ 87,550	$ 90,177
Bookkeeper	$ 23,000	$ 23,690	$ 24,401
Administrative	$ 25,000	$ 25,750	$ 26,523
Total	**$208,000**	**$214,240**	**$220,667**

Numbers of personnel

Owner	1	1	1
Store manager	1	1	1
Store employees	5	5	5
Bookkeeper	1	1	1
Administrative	1	1	1
Totals	**9**	**9**	**9**

Personnel expense breakdown

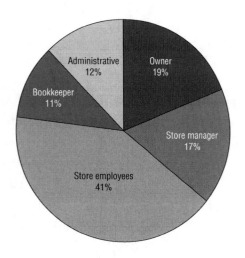

7.0 FINANCIAL PLAN

7.1 Underlying Assumptions

The Company has based its proforma financial statements on the following:

- Earth's Bounty will have an annual revenue growth rate of 7% per year.

- The Owner will acquire $250,000 of debt funds to develop the business.

- The loan will have a 10 year term with a 9% interest rate.

7.2 Sensitivity Analysis

Revenues are not sensitive to changes in the general economy. People demand certain grocery store items as a necessity, and the business only expects that an economic catastrophe could result in decreases in revenue. The Company's programs for general merchandise will ensure that Earth's Bounty Organic Foods continues to thrive despite deleterious changes in the general economy.

7.3 Source of Funds

Financing

Equity contributions	
Management investment	$ 50,000.00
Total equity financing	**$ 50,000.00**
Banks and lenders	
Banks and lenders	$ 250,000.00
Total debt financing	$ 250,000.00
Total financing	**$300,000.00**

7.4 General Assumptions

General assumptions

Year	1	2	3
Short term interest rate	9.5%	9.5%	9.5%
Long term interest rate	10.0%	10.0%	10.0%
Federal tax rate	33.0%	33.0%	33.0%
State tax rate	5.0%	5.0%	5.0%
Personnel taxes	15.0%	15.0%	15.0%

7.5 Profit and Loss Statements

Proforma profit and loss (yearly)

Year	1	2	3
Sales	**$777,000**	**$831,390**	**$889,587**
Cost of goods sold	$233,100	$249,417	$266,876
Gross margin	70.00%	70.00%	70.00%
Operating income	**$543,900**	**$581,973**	**$622,711**
Expenses			
Payroll	$208,000	$214,240	$220,667
General and administrative	$ 25,200	$ 26,208	$ 27,256
Marketing expenses	$ 23,310	$ 24,942	$ 26,688
Professional fees and licensure	$ 5,000	$ 5,150	$ 5,305
Insurance costs	$ 11,987	$ 12,586	$ 13,216
Travel and vehicle costs	$ 7,596	$ 8,356	$ 9,191
Rent and utilities	$ 24,250	$ 25,463	$ 26,736
Miscellaneous costs	$ 3,885	$ 4,157	$ 4,448
Payroll taxes	$ 31,200	$ 32,136	$ 33,100
Total operating costs	**$340,428**	**$353,237**	**$366,606**
EBITDA	**$203,472**	**$228,736**	**$256,105**
Federal income tax	$ 67,146	$ 68,774	$ 78,353
State income tax	$ 10,174	$ 10,420	$ 11,872
Interest expense	$ 21,844	$ 20,328	$ 18,671
Depreciation expenses	$ 15,536	$ 15,536	$ 15,536
Net profit	**$ 88,773**	**$113,677**	**$131,674**
Profit margin	**11.43%**	**13.67%**	**14.80%**

Sales, operating costs, and profit forecast

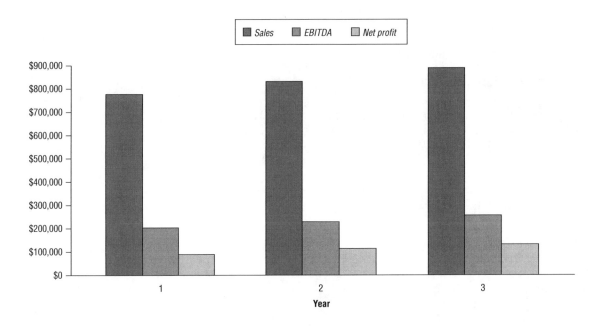

7.6 Cash Flow Analysis

Proforma cash flow analysis—yearly

Year	1	2	3
Cash from operations	$104,308	$129,213	$147,209
Cash from receivables	$ 0	$ 0	$ 0
Operating cash inflow	**$104,308**	**$129,213**	**$147,209**
Other cash inflows			
Equity investment	$ 50,000	$ 0	$ 0
Increased borrowings	$250,000	$ 0	$ 0
Sales of business assets	$ 0	$ 0	$ 0
A/P increases	$ 37,902	$ 43,587	$ 50,125
Total other cash inflows	**$337,902**	**$ 43,587**	**$ 50,125**
Total cash inflow	**$442,210**	**$172,800**	**$197,335**
Cash outflows			
Repayment of principal	$ 16,158	$ 17,674	$ 19,332
A/P decreases	$ 24,897	$ 29,876	$ 35,852
A/R increases	$ 0	$ 0	$ 0
Asset purchases	$217,500	$ 32,303	$ 36,802
Dividends	$ 73,016	$ 90,449	$103,047
Total cash outflows	**$331,571**	**$170,303**	**$195,033**
Net cash flow	**$110,639**	**$ 2,497**	**$ 2,302**
Cash balance	**$110,639**	**$113,136**	**$115,438**

Proforma cash flow (yearly)

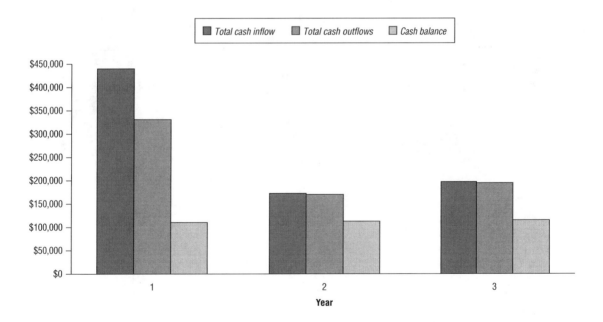

7.7 Balance Sheet

Proforma balance sheet—yearly

Year	1	2	3
Assets			
Cash	$110,639	$113,136	$115,438
Amortized development/expansion costs	$ 77,500	$ 80,730	$ 84,411
Inventory	$100,000	$116,152	$134,553
FF&E	$ 40,000	$ 52,921	$ 67,642
Accumulated depreciation	($ 15,536)	($ 31,071)	($ 46,607)
Total assets	**$312,603**	**$331,868**	**$355,437**
Liabilities and equity			
Accounts payable	$ 13,005	$ 26,716	$ 40,990
Long term liabilities	$233,842	$216,167	$198,493
Other liabilities	$ 0	$ 0	$ 0
Total liabilities	**$246,847**	**$242,883**	**$239,483**
Net worth	**$ 65,757**	**$ 88,985**	**$115,954**
Total liabilities and equity	**$312,603**	**$331,868**	**$355,437**

Proforma balance sheet

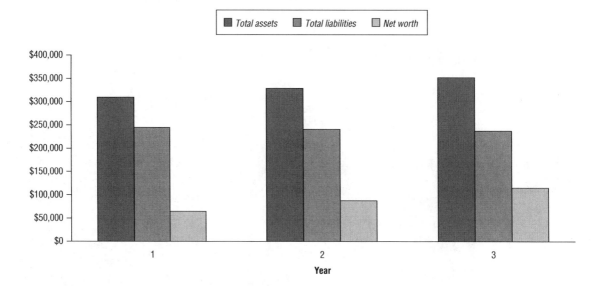

7.8 Breakeven Analysis

Monthly break even analysis

Year	1	2	3
Monthly revenue	$ 40,527	$ 42,052	$ 43,644
Yearly revenue	$486,326	$504,624	$523,723

Break even analysis

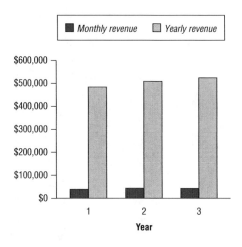

■ *Monthly revenue* □ *Yearly revenue*

7.9 Business Ratios

Business ratios—yearly

Year	1	2	3
Sales			
Sales growth	0.00%	7.00%	7.00%
Gross margin	70.00%	70.00%	70.00%
Financials			
Profit margin	11.43%	13.67%	14.80%
Assets to liabilities	1.27	1.37	1.48
Equity to liabilities	0.27	0.37	0.48
Assets to equity	4.75	3.73	3.07
Liquidity			
Acid test	0.45	0.47	0.48
Cash to assets	0.35	0.34	0.32

7.10 Three Year Profit and Loss Statement

Profit and loss statement (first year)

Months	1	2	3	4	5	6	7
Sales	$62,000	$62,500	$63,000	$63,500	$64,000	$64,500	$65,000
Cost of goods sold	$18,600	$18,750	$18,900	$19,050	$19,200	$19,350	$19,500
Gross margin	70.0%	70.0%	70.0%	70.0%	70.0%	70.0%	70.0%
Operating income	$43,400	$43,750	$44,100	$44,450	$44,800	$45,150	$45,500
Expenses							
Payroll	$17,333	$17,333	$17,333	$17,333	$17,333	$17,333	$17,333
General and administrative	$ 2,100	$ 2,100	$ 2,100	$ 2,100	$ 2,100	$ 2,100	$ 2,100
Marketing expenses	$ 1,943	$ 1,943	$ 1,943	$ 1,943	$ 1,943	$ 1,943	$ 1,943
Professional fees and licensure	$ 417	$ 417	$ 417	$ 417	$ 417	$ 417	$ 417
Insurance costs	$ 999	$ 999	$ 999	$ 999	$ 999	$ 999	$ 999
Travel and vehicle costs	$ 633	$ 633	$ 633	$ 633	$ 633	$ 633	$ 633
Rent and utilities	$ 2,021	$ 2,021	$ 2,021	$ 2,021	$ 2,021	$ 2,021	$ 2,021
Miscellaneous costs	$ 324	$ 324	$ 324	$ 324	$ 324	$ 324	$ 324
Payroll taxes	$ 2,600	$ 2,600	$ 2,600	$ 2,600	$ 2,600	$ 2,600	$ 2,600
Total operating costs	$28,369	$28,369	$28,369	$28,369	$28,369	$28,369	$28,369
EBITDA	$15,031	$15,381	$15,731	$16,081	$16,431	$16,781	$17,131
Federal income tax	$ 5,358	$ 5,401	$ 5,444	$ 5,487	$ 5,531	$ 5,574	$ 5,617
State income tax	$ 812	$ 818	$ 825	$ 831	$ 838	$ 845	$ 851
Interest expense	$ 1,875	$ 1,865	$ 1,856	$ 1,846	$ 1,836	$ 1,826	$ 1,816
Depreciation expense	$ 1,295	$ 1,295	$ 1,295	$ 1,295	$ 1,295	$ 1,295	$ 1,295
Net profit	$ 5,692	$ 6,002	$ 6,312	$ 6,622	$ 6,932	$ 7,242	$ 7,552

Profit and loss statement (first year cont.)

Month	8	9	10	11	12	1
Sales	$65,500	$66,000	$66,500	$67,000	$67,500	$777,000
Cost of goods sold	$19,650	$19,800	$19,950	$20,100	$20,250	$233,100
Gross margin	70.0%	70.0%	70.0%	70.0%	70.0%	70.0%
Operating income	$45,850	$46,200	$46,550	$46,900	$47,250	$543,900
Expenses						
Payroll	$17,333	$17,333	$17,333	$17,333	$17,333	$208,000
General and administrative	$ 2,100	$ 2,100	$ 2,100	$ 2,100	$ 2,100	$ 25,200
Marketing expenses	$ 1,943	$ 1,943	$ 1,943	$ 1,943	$ 1,943	$ 23,310
Professional fees and licensure	$ 417	$ 417	$ 417	$ 417	$ 417	$ 5,000
Insurance costs	$ 999	$ 999	$ 999	$ 999	$ 999	$ 11,987
Travel and vehicle costs	$ 633	$ 633	$ 633	$ 633	$ 633	$ 7,596
Rent and utilities	$ 2,021	$ 2,021	$ 2,021	$ 2,021	$ 2,021	$ 24,250
Miscellaneous costs	$ 324	$ 324	$ 324	$ 324	$ 324	$ 3,885
Payroll taxes	$ 2,600	$ 2,600	$ 2,600	$ 2,600	$ 2,600	$ 31,200
Total operating costs	$28,369	$28,369	$28,369	$28,369	$28,369	$340,428
EBITDA	$17,481	$17,831	$18,181	$18,531	$18,881	$203,472
Federal income tax	$ 5,660	$ 5,704	$ 5,747	$ 5,790	$ 5,833	$ 67,146
State income tax	$ 858	$ 864	$ 871	$ 877	$ 884	$ 10,174
Interest expense	$ 1,806	$ 1,795	$ 1,785	$ 1,775	$ 1,764	$ 21,844
Depreciation expense	$ 1,295	$ 1,295	$ 1,295	$ 1,295	$ 1,295	$ 15,536
Net profit	$ 7,863	$ 8,173	$ 8,484	$ 8,794	$ 9,105	$ 88,773

Profit and loss statement (second year)

Quarter	Q1	2 Q2	Q3	Q4	2
Sales	**$166,278**	**$207,848**	**$224,475**	**$232,789**	**$831,390**
Cost of goods sold	$ 49,883	$ 62,354	$ 67,343	$ 69,837	$249,417
Gross margin	70.0%	70.0%	70.0%	70.0%	70.0%
Operating income	**$116,395**	**$145,493**	**$157,133**	**$162,952**	**$581,973**
Expenses					
Payroll	$ 42,848	$ 53,560	$ 57,845	$ 59,987	$214,240
General and administrative	$ 5,242	$ 6,552	$ 7,076	$ 7,338	$ 26,208
Marketing expenses	$ 4,988	$ 6,235	$ 6,734	$ 6,984	$ 24,942
Professional fees and licensure	$ 1,030	$ 1,288	$ 1,391	$ 1,442	$ 5,150
Insurance costs	$ 2,517	$ 3,147	$ 3,398	$ 3,524	$ 12,586
Travel and vehicle costs	$ 1,671	$ 2,089	$ 2,256	$ 2,340	$ 8,356
Rent and utilities	$ 5,093	$ 6,366	$ 6,875	$ 7,130	$ 25,463
Miscellaneous costs	$ 831	$ 1,039	$ 1,122	$ 1,164	$ 4,157
Payroll taxes	$ 6,427	$ 8,034	$ 8,677	$ 8,998	$ 32,136
Total operating costs	**$ 70,647**	**$ 88,309**	**$ 95,374**	**$ 98,906**	**$353,237**
EBITDA	**$ 45,747**	**$ 57,184**	**$ 61,759**	**$ 64,046**	**$228,736**
Federal income tax	$ 13,755	$ 17,194	$ 18,569	$ 19,257	$ 68,774
State income tax	$ 2,084	$ 2,605	$ 2,814	$ 2,918	$ 10,420
Interest expense	$ 5,230	$ 5,133	$ 5,034	$ 4,932	$ 20,328
Depreciation expense	$ 3,884	$ 3,884	$ 3,884	$ 3,884	$ 15,536
Net profit	**$ 20,795**	**$ 28,369**	**$ 31,458**	**$ 33,055**	**$113,677**

Profit and loss statement (third year)

Quarter	Q1	3 Q2	Q3	Q4	3
Sales	**$177,917**	**$222,397**	**$240,189**	**$249,084**	**$889,587**
Cost of goods sold	$ 53,375	$ 66,719	$ 72,057	$ 74,725	$266,876
Gross margin	70.0%	70.0%	70.0%	70.0%	70.0%
Operating income	**$124,542**	**$155,678**	**$168,132**	**$174,359**	**$622,711**
Expenses					
Payroll	$ 44,133	$ 55,167	$ 59,580	$ 61,787	$220,667
General and administrative	$ 5,451	$ 6,814	$ 7,359	$ 7,632	$ 27,256
Marketing expenses	$ 5,338	$ 6,672	$ 7,206	$ 7,473	$ 26,688
Professional fees and licensure	$ 1,061	$ 1,326	$ 1,432	$ 1,485	$ 5,305
Insurance costs	$ 2,643	$ 3,304	$ 3,568	$ 3,700	$ 13,216
Travel and vehicle costs	$ 1,838	$ 2,298	$ 2,482	$ 2,574	$ 9,191
Rent and utilities	$ 5,347	$ 6,684	$ 7,219	$ 7,486	$ 26,736
Miscellaneous costs	$ 890	$ 1,112	$ 1,201	$ 1,245	$ 4,448
Payroll taxes	$ 6,620	$ 8,275	$ 8,937	$ 9,268	$ 33,100
Total operating costs	**$ 73,321**	**$ 91,652**	**$ 98,984**	**$102,650**	**$366,606**
EBITDA	**$ 51,221**	**$ 64,026**	**$ 69,148**	**$ 71,709**	**$256,105**
Federal income tax	$ 15,671	$ 19,588	$ 21,155	$ 21,939	$ 78,353
State income tax	$ 2,374	$ 2,968	$ 3,205	$ 3,324	$ 11,872
Interest expense	$ 4,829	$ 4,723	$ 4,615	$ 4,504	$ 18,671
Depreciation expense	$ 3,884	$ 3,884	$ 3,884	$ 3,884	$ 15,536
Net profit	**$ 24,463**	**$ 32,863**	**$ 36,289**	**$ 38,059**	**$131,674**

7.11 Three Year Cash Flow Analysis

Cash flow analysis (first year)

Month	1	2	3	4	5	6	7	8
Cash from operations	$ 6,986	$ 7,296	$ 7,606	$ 7,916	$ 8,227	$ 8,537	$ 8,847	$ 9,157
Cash from receivables	$ 0	$ 0	$ 0	$ 0	$ 0	$ 0	$ 0	$ 0
Operating cash inflow	**$ 6,986**	**$ 7,296**	**$ 7,606**	**$ 7,916**	**$ 8,227**	**$ 8,537**	**$ 8,847**	**$ 9,157**
Other cash inflows								
Equity investment	$ 50,000	$ 0	$ 0	$ 0	$ 0	$ 0	$ 0	$ 0
Increased borrowings	$250,000	$ 0	$ 0	$ 0	$ 0	$ 0	$ 0	$ 0
Sales of business assets	$ 0	$ 0	$ 0	$ 0	$ 0	$ 0	$ 0	$ 0
A/P increases	$ 3,159	$ 3,159	$ 3,159	$ 3,159	$ 3,159	$ 3,159	$ 3,159	$ 3,159
Total other cash inflows	**$303,159**	**$ 3,159**	**$ 3,159**	**$ 3,159**	**$ 3,159**	**$ 3,159**	**$ 3,159**	**$ 3,159**
Total cash inflow	**$310,145**	**$10,455**	**$ 10,765**	**$ 11,075**	**$ 11,385**	**$ 11,695**	**$ 12,006**	**$ 12,316**
Cash outflows								
Repayment of principal	$ 1,292	$ 1,302	$ 1,311	$ 1,321	$ 1,331	$ 1,341	$ 1,351	$ 1,361
A/P decreases	$ 2,075	$ 2,075	$ 2,075	$ 2,075	$ 2,075	$ 2,075	$ 2,075	$ 2,075
A/R increases	$ 0	$ 0	$ 0	$ 0	$ 0	$ 0	$ 0	$ 0
Asset purchases	$217,500	$ 0	$ 0	$ 0	$ 0	$ 0	$ 0	$ 0
Dividends	$ 0	$ 0	$ 0	$ 0	$ 0	$ 0	$ 0	$ 0
Total cash outflows	**$220,867**	**$ 3,376**	**$ 3,386**	**$ 3,396**	**$ 3,406**	**$ 3,416**	**$ 3,426**	**$ 3,436**
Net cash flow	**$ 89,278**	**$ 7,078**	**$ 7,379**	**$ 7,679**	**$ 7,979**	**$ 8,279**	**$ 8,580**	**$ 8,880**
Cash balance	**$ 89,278**	**$96,357**	**$103,735**	**$111,414**	**$119,394**	**$127,673**	**$136,253**	**$145,133**

Cash flow analysis (first year cont.)

Month	9	10	11	12	1
Cash from operations	$ 9,468	$ 9,778	$ 10,089	$ 10,400	$104,308
Cash from receivables	$ 0	$ 0	$ 0	$ 0	$ 0
Operating cash inflow	**$ 9,468**	**$ 9,778**	**$ 10,089**	**$ 10,400**	**$104,308**
Other cash inflows					
Equity investment	$ 0	$ 0	$ 0	$ 0	$ 50,000
Increased borrowings	$ 0	$ 0	$ 0	$ 0	$250,000
Sales of business assets	$ 0	$ 0	$ 0	$ 0	$ 0
A/P increases	$ 3,159	$ 3,159	$ 3,159	$ 3,159	$ 37,902
Total other cash inflows	**$ 3,159**	**$ 3,159**	**$ 3,159**	**$ 3,159**	**$337,902**
Total cash inflow	**$ 12,626**	**$ 12,937**	**$ 13,248**	**$ 13,558**	**$442,210**
Cash outflows					
Repayment of principal	$ 1,371	$ 1,382	$ 1,392	$ 1,403	$ 16,158
A/P decreases	$ 2,075	$ 2,075	$ 2,075	$ 2,075	$ 24,897
A/R increases	$ 0	$ 0	$ 0	$ 0	$ 0
Asset purchases	$ 0	$ 0	$ 0	$ 0	$217,500
Dividends	$ 0	$ 0	$ 0	$ 73,016	$ 73,016
Total cash outflows	**$ 3,446**	**$ 3,457**	**$ 3,467**	**$ 76,493**	**$331,571**
Net cash flow	**$ 9,180**	**$ 9,480**	**$ 9,781**	**−$ 62,935**	**$110,639**
Cash balance	**$154,313**	**$163,793**	**$173,574**	**$110,639**	**$110,639**

Cash flow analysis (second year)

Quarter	Q1	2 Q2	Q3	Q4	2
Cash from operations	$ 25,843	$ 32,303	$ 34,887	$ 36,180	$129,213
Cash from receivables	$ 0	$ 0	$ 0	$ 0	$ 0
Operating cash inflow	**$ 25,843**	**$ 32,303**	**$ 34,887**	**$ 36,180**	**$129,213**
Other cash inflows					
Equity investment	$ 0	$ 0	$ 0	$ 0	$ 0
Increased borrowings	$ 0	$ 0	$ 0	$ 0	$ 0
Sales of business assets	$ 0	$ 0	$ 0	$ 0	$ 0
A/P increases	$ 8,717	$ 10,897	$ 11,769	$ 12,204	$ 43,587
Total other cash inflows	**$ 8,717**	**$ 10,897**	**$ 11,769**	**$ 12,204**	**$ 43,587**
Total cash inflow	**$ 34,560**	**$ 43,200**	**$ 46,656**	**$ 48,384**	**$172,800**
Cash outflows					
Repayment of principal	$ 4,271	$ 4,368	$ 4,467	$ 4,568	$ 17,674
A/P decreases	$ 5,975	$ 7,469	$ 8,067	$ 8,365	$ 29,876
A/R increases	$ 0	$ 0	$ 0	$ 0	$ 0
Asset purchases	$ 6,461	$ 8,076	$ 8,722	$ 9,045	$ 32,303
Dividends	$ 18,090	$ 22,612	$ 24,421	$ 25,326	$ 90,449
Total cash outflows	**$ 34,797**	**$ 42,525**	**$ 45,677**	**$ 47,304**	**$170,303**
Net cash flow	**−$ 237**	**$ 675**	**$ 979**	**$ 1,080**	**$ 2,497**
Cash balance	**$110,402**	**$111,077**	**$112,057**	**$113,136**	**$113,136**

Cash flow analysis (third year)

Quarter	Q1	3 Q2	Q3	Q4	3
Cash from operations	$ 29,442	$ 36,802	$ 39,747	$ 41,219	$147,209
Cash from receivables	$ 0	$ 0	$ 0	$ 0	$ 0
Operating cash inflow	**$ 29,442**	**$ 36,802**	**$ 39,747**	**$ 41,219**	**$147,209**
Other cash inflows					
Equity investment	$ 0	$ 0	$ 0	$ 0	$ 0
Increased borrowings	$ 0	$ 0	$ 0	$ 0	$ 0
Sales of business assets	$ 0	$ 0	$ 0	$ 0	$ 0
A/P increases	$ 10,025	$ 12,531	$ 13,534	$ 14,035	$ 50,125
Total other cash inflows	**$ 10,025**	**$ 12,531**	**$ 13,534**	**$ 14,035**	**$ 50,125**
Total cash inflow	**$ 39,467**	**$ 49,334**	**$ 53,280**	**$ 55,254**	**$197,335**
Cash outflows					
Repayment of principal	$ 4,672	$ 4,778	$ 4,886	$ 4,997	$ 19,332
A/P decreases	$ 7,170	$ 8,963	$ 9,680	$ 10,038	$ 35,852
A/R increases	$ 0	$ 0	$ 0	$ 0	$ 0
Asset purchases	$ 7,360	$ 9,201	$ 9,937	$ 10,305	$ 36,802
Dividends	$ 20,609	$ 25,762	$ 27,823	$ 28,853	$103,047
Total cash outflows	**$ 39,812**	**$ 48,703**	**$ 52,325**	**$ 54,193**	**$195,033**
Net cash flow	**−$ 345**	**$ 631**	**$ 955**	**$ 1,061**	**$ 2,302**
Cash balance	**$112,791**	**$113,422**	**$114,377**	**$115,438**	**$115,438**

Pet Sitting Business

Pet Watchers Inc.

29 Pine St., # 4
Montgomery Ridge, MN 55489

Paul Greenland

Pet Watchers is a pet sitting business. Instead of pet owners bringing their animals to a kennel or boarding facility while they are away, we provide a variety of in-home services that allow their pets to stay in a safe, familiar environment.

EXECUTIVE SUMMARY

Business Overview

Just as there are many benefits associated with pet ownership, there also are many responsibilities. Irregular work schedules, business trips, and vacations can present challenges for pet owners who must balance such demands with the needs of their pets.

Pet Watchers is a pet sitting business. Instead of pet owners bringing their animals to a kennel or boarding facility while they are away, we provide a variety of in-home services that allow their pets to stay in a safe, familiar environment. Our services include everything from periodic daily visits to overnight stays. In addition to feeding and walking pets, we administer medications and take pets to grooming or veterinarian appointments. We also offer concurrent "home sitting" services for our clients, such as bringing in mail, turning on and off lights, and watering plants.

Pet Watchers is a new business established by Brian and Anita Phillips. After retiring from a 20-year law-enforcement career that included service as a K-9 officer, Brian began searching for a new opportunity that would allow him to continue interacting with the public. A part-time veterinary technician, Anita had been thinking about establishing her own business for several years. After many conversations and a great deal of research, the Phillips decided that pet sitting would not only satisfy their interests and needs, it also would leverage their existing skills.

MARKET ANALYSIS

According to the American Pet Products Association's *2009-2010 National Pet Owners Survey*, an estimated 45.6 million U.S. households owned dogs. In all, Americans owned 77.5 million dogs. Pet industry expenditures, which totaled $43.2 million in 2008, reached $45.5 million in 2009, and were expected to total $47.7 million in 2010.

According to data from Elliot Greenfield Research Inc., the community of Montgomery Ridge included approximately 3,649 households in 2009. Using formulas from the 2007 *U.S. Pet Ownership & Demographics Sourcebook*, the community includes an estimated 2,095 pet-owning households. More specifically, this total includes 1,357 dog-owning households; 1,182 cat-owning households; and 142 bird-owning households. Based upon population projections, these figures are expected to remain relatively flat through 2014, when the community will consist of 3,792 households (a 3.7% increase from 2009).

Montgomery Ridge is an excellent market for pet sitting services. In 2009 the average household income was $155,646. This is expected to increase 11.7 percent by 2014, reaching $173,931. In 2009 an estimated 19 percent of households had incomes between $100,000 and $149,999. The largest category consisted of households with incomes of more than $150,000 (37.1%).

In addition to targeting working professionals, Pet Watchers also will focus on promoting its services to several other key segments which, according to the industry association Pet Sitters International, represent the greatest demand for pet sitting services. These include:

- Couples without children

- Couples with children

- Single Females

The majority of residents in Montgomery Ridge are professional/white-collar workers (85.4%) who lead busy lives. Oftentimes, these individuals work long hours and have commitments that keep them away from home during the evening. They also travel frequently for business purposes.

INDUSTRY ANALYSIS

For 16 years, the pet sitting industry has been served by a member-based association called Pet Sitters International (PSI) that "promotes excellence in pet care through education." The organization benefits its members by offering an accreditation program, as well as a Pet Sitter Locator on its Web site that receives approximately 30,000 hits per month.

According to an industry survey conducted by PSI in 2008, pet sitting businesses make more than 17 million visits to clients each year. The majority of industry businesses are independently owned (98%).

The survey indicated that the most popular services requested by clients include:

1. Basic pet care

2. Dog walking

3. Care of special needs pets

4. Pet transportation service

5. Overnight pet sitting

6. House sitting with no pet

7. Errand services

8. Pooper scooper services

PSI further reports that, on average, industry players serve approximately 190 clients, and generate gross revenue of roughly $37,000.

Another leading industry association is Professional United Pet Sitters, which offers a lifetime membership, a message board, forms, a directory listing, and more.

PERSONNEL

The best pet sitters share several key characteristics. Specifically, these are:

- Patience
- Flexibility
- Caring
- Trustworthy
- Reliability

As individuals, the Phillips naturally have all of these traits, which have been honed over the years during their careers in law enforcement and the veterinary sciences.

Owners

Brian Phillips

After earning an undergraduate degree in criminal justice and graduating from the police academy, Brian Phillips spent the first eight years of his career working as a regular police officer in Brighton Park, Minnesota. However, his love for animals inspired him to apply for a position with the K9 unit, where he worked with a number of different dogs, including a 75-pound German Shepherd named Duke who was cross-trained for both patrol and narcotics searches. Ultimately, Phillips was promoted to sergeant and given responsibility for the K9 unit, which included five dogs. Following a 20-year law-enforcement career, Brian identified pet sitting as a business opportunity that will allow him to continue working with both dogs and the public.

Anita Phillips

Anita's love of animals dates back to her childhood. Most of the time, her family had at least two dogs, as well as a number of cats. After high school, Anita spent seven years working for a Minneapolis-area pet store. Eventually, she attended Paul Roberts Community College, which offered a two-year Associates degree in veterinary technology. After graduation, she passed a credentialing exam and found employment with Golden Crest Animal Hospital, where she has spent the last 18 years. In that role, her responsibilities have included assisting veterinarians with procedures and performing a wide range of tests to diagnose and treat medical conditions in small animals. Anita has been thinking about establishing her own business for several years, and is confident that pet sitting is the right opportunity.

Professional & Advisory Support

Pet Watchers has established a business banking account with Montgomery Ridge Community Bank, as well as a merchant account for accepting credit card payments. Legal services are provided by the firm of Smithfield & McCoy. Finally, Elliot James LLC will provide our business with tax advice.

GROWTH STRATEGY

We plan to grow Pet Watchers at a steady pace. Our objective is to identify reliable customers with whom we can build long-term relationships. Working from a small base of existing clients (we already pet sit for several people on an individual basis), we plan to grow as follows:

Year 1: 50 customers

Year 2: 125 customers

Year 3: 175 customers

Year 4: 225 customers

During year five, we will likely need to add an employee if we wish to continue growing our business. Another option at this point would be to franchise Pet Watchers, which is something that pet sitting businesses have done in other markets.

SERVICES

Pet Watchers provides a wide range of basic services, including:

- Companionship
- Special-Needs Pet Care
- Walking/Exercise
- Overnight Pet Sitting
- Medication Administration
- Basic Grooming
- Feeding/Watering
- Veterinary Visits
- Owner e-Mail Updates
- Kennel/Cage Cleaning
- Pet Waste Removal
- Plant Watering
- Newspaper/Mail
- Turning Lights On/Off

We care for many different kinds of small animals, including (but not limited to):

- Dogs
- Cats
- Fish
- Ferrets
- Rabbits
- Hamsters
- Guinea Pigs
- Gerbils
- Turtles
- Lizards
- Snakes
- Birds

MARKETING & SALES

Pet Watchers has developed a marketing plan that involves the following primary tactics:

1. Printed collateral describing our business.

2. A Yellow Page listing.

3. Relationship building with area veterinarians, groomers, trainers, and breeders in order to build a consistent referral base.

4. A Web site with complete details about our business and the services we offer.

5. Flyers distributed to local pet stores, veterinary offices, breeders, dog trainers, animal hospitals, and groomers to generate awareness of our services.

6. Direct mail campaigns to area pet owners. For this purpose, we will rent the names of subscribers to a popular pet magazine.

7. The submission of "success/human interest" stories to local media demonstrating how we have helped busy pet owners.

8. Birthday cards to the pets we care for on a regular basis, in order to build relationships with pet owners and encourage word-of-mouth referrals.

9. Because word-of-mouth referrals are the most significant source of new business, we will offer customers one free basic visit for each new customer we receive as a result of their referral.

OPERATIONS

Process

Pet Watchers will follow a formal process with all of its new customers. We will begin by offering a free initial consultation with the pet owner, at which time information will be gathered about the animal(s) background/history, including health problems, behavioral habits, medications, washing/grooming, favorite toys, nutrition, etc. In addition, we will obtain the name of the pet's veterinarian and discuss emergency care/first aid expectations. This information will be gathered on a simple intake form that we have developed.

In addition to gathering information, we will provide information about bonding and insurance, as well as a list of references. We will discuss our fees, and identify the specific services needed by the client. We will outline services in a written contract, to be signed by the pet owner and Brian or Anita Phillips. For new customers, we will require the payment of 50 percent of agreed-upon charges in advance, as well as a credit card number to which we can bill the remainder of charges upon successful completion of services.

Finally, Pet Watchers will make arrangements to obtain a key to the customer's home, as well as alarm codes and any necessary remote controls for entry gates or garage doors.

Facility & Location

Pet Watchers will operate as a home-based business. The Phillips have dedicated 100-square-feet of space for a home office, equipped with a personal computer, printer, telephone and voicemail system, and filing cabinet. No services will be provided directly in the Phillips' home.

Payment & Fees

Our business will charge $20 for a daily home visit and $50 for overnight stays. Transportation services (within a 15-mile radius of Montgomery Ridge) will be offered at a rate of $20 per trip.

LEGAL

Pet Watchers is bonded and insured (documentation is available upon request). In addition, our business is registered with the appropriate local and state government agencies.

RESOURCES

We have consulted outside resources while planning to establish our new business. In addition to conversations with pet sitters in other markets, we have consulted the following sources of information:

Moran, Patti. *Pet Sitting for Profit*, 3rd ed. John Wiley & Sons, 2006.

Williams Duea, Angela. *How to Open and Operate a Financially Successful Pet Sitting Business*. Atlantic Publishing, 2008.

FINANCIAL ANALYSIS

The accounting firm Elliot James LLC has developed a spreadsheet (available upon request) to illustrate projected cash flow for Pet Watchers during the first year of operation. The statement includes data on sales, operating expenses, taxes, etc.

Pet Watchers will incur the following start-up expenses during its first year, which the Phillips will cover from personal savings.

Start-up budget

Advertising and marketing	$ 5,000
Fuel	$ 2,750
Miscellaneous items	$ 500
Legal	$ 975
Accounting	$ 750
Office supplies	$ 325
Office equipment	$ 725
Laptop computer/peripherals (2)	$ 1,845
Liability insurance/surety bond	$ 548
Internet-enabled mobile phones (2)	$ 1,678
Membership dues and subscriptions	$ 350
Total	**$15,446**

REFERENCES

A list of references is available upon request.

Pet Waste Removal Business

The Scoop

2543 Peachtree Ave.
Primrose, IL 60054

Paul Greenland

The Scoop is a pet waste removal business serving the central Illinois community of Primrose.

EXECUTIVE SUMMARY

Business Overview

According to the American Pet Products Association's *2009-2010 National Pet Owners Survey*, an estimated 45.6 million U.S. households owned dogs during 2010. Each week, these dogs collectively produce a massive amount of waste. For busy families and elderly or disabled pet owners, "scooping poop" can be difficult and inconvenient.

Pet waste also is an environmental hazard. In addition to containing nitrogen and phosphorus, dog waste can spread bacteria infections such as Campylobacteriosis and Salmonellosis, as well as Toxocarisis (roundworms transmitted from animals to humans).

According to a bulletin from the U.S. Environmental Protection Agency, which designated pet waste as a form of pollution during the early 1990s: "Pets, particularly dogs, are significant contributors to source water contamination. Studies performed on watersheds in the Seattle, Washington, area found that nearly 20 percent of the bacteria found in water samples were matched with dogs as the host animals."

The Scoop is a pet waste removal business serving the central Illinois community of Primrose. As professional animal waste specialists, we take the hassle out of yard cleanup for pet owners, allowing them to spend their time doing more important things. At the same time, we minimize the environmental hazards connected with infrequent and/or improper pet waste removal.

The Scoop's origins are rooted in economic necessity. After an eight-year career working as a lawn care specialist for Handfield Lawn Services, which provided fertilizer, weed treatment, and pesticide applications, Jay Johnson lost his job when economic conditions forced his company to reduce staff. Unable to find a similar position at another company, Jay began considering ways to support his family. During his career as a lawn care specialist, unpleasant encounters with pet waste were all too common. Sensing an opportunity, Jay decided to combine his route management and lawn care skills and test the market for his own pet waste removal business.

MARKET ANALYSIS

According to the American Pet Products Association's *2009-2010 National Pet Owners Survey*, an estimated 45.6 million U.S. households owned dogs in 2010. In all, Americans owned 77.5 million dogs. Pet industry expenditures, which totaled $43.2 million in 2008, reached $45.5 million in 2009, and were expected to total $47.7 million in 2010.

According to data from Smith Research & Associates LLC, the community of Primrose, Illinois, consists of approximately 13,155 households. Using formulas from the 2007 *U.S. Pet Ownership & Demographics Sourcebook*, the community includes an estimated 4,894 dog-owning households (8,314 dogs). Based upon population projections, these figures are expected to remain relatively flat through 2014, when the community will consist of 13,167 households.

Because they have higher levels of discretionary income, as well as a greater prevalence of health issues that may make pet waste removal more challenging, individuals over the age of 55 are a prime market for our services. In 2009 the 55-plus segment comprised 30 percent of the Primrose population. Specifically, those aged 55 to 64 (3,439) accounted for 11.2 percent of the population, followed by those aged 65 to 74 (2,613; 8.5%), and those over the age of 75 (3,150; 10.3%).

In 2009 average household income in Primrose totaled $48,638. This figure was expected to increase 3.8 percent by 2014, reaching $50,479. In our market, the most significant household income growth is expected among those earning between $75,000 and $99,000 (4.8%); $100,000 and $149,000 (25.4%); and those earning more than $150,000 (32.5%).

We are fortunate in that competition is virtually nonexistent in the Primrose area. We will have two direct competitors. Abe Swanson is a local retiree who performs pet waste removal on a part-time basis. Green Fields Lawn Services Inc. is a local lawn maintenance company that began offering pet waste removal last season. However, this mainly is an add-on service for them, as their main focus is traditional fertilizer and weed treatment applications.

INDUSTRY ANALYSIS

During the early 2000s *USA Today* indicated that about 40 percent of the nation's pet owners did not pick up their dogs' waste. This reluctance, coupled with increased environmental sensitivity (and hefty fines in some communities) over rising bacteria levels in rivers and lakes, has set the stage for the pet waste removal industry's success. Our industry includes a large number of independent operations as well as industry leaders that have begun to offer franchising opportunities. One leader is DoodyCalls, which has been ranked as the leading pet waste removal franchise in the nation by *Entrepreneur Magazine*. Each year, DoodyCalls claims to remove more than 3 million pieces of dog waste. The company's operations span 21 states, and it serves approximately 8,000 dogs. In 2007 the company reported annual sales of $612,000.

GROWTH STRATEGY

While performing pet waste removal services independently, Jay Johnson discovered that he was able to clean five yards per hour, on average. During his first year of operations Jay plans to spend four hours per day (five days per week) performing pet waste removal. He will devote the remainder of each workday to planning, administrative tasks, and growing the business. By performing pet waste removal four hours per day, he will be able to provide service for 100 dogs during year one. During year two, Jay expects to provide service to 150 dogs, which he estimates will take six hours per day. Finally, during year three Jay will hire one full-time employee, allowing the business to serve 200 dogs and prepare for continued expansion in the coming years.

Households	2010	2011	2012
One dog	80	120	160
Two dogs	15	22	30
Three dogs	5	8	10
Total	**100**	**150**	**200**

SERVICE OPTIONS

Although the service we provide (scooping poop) is straightforward, we provide customers with several different options to meet their specific needs. Based on the owner's experience as an independent contractor, as well as discussions with pet waste removal business operators in other markets, most customers desire weekly service. However, we also will offer bi-weekly service for those with multiple dogs, as well as a semi-weekly option for those who only require the occasional cleanup. Substantial cleanup services (e.g., for first-time customers, as well as existing customers in the springtime) are available on a prescheduled basis.

OPERATIONS

Equipment

The main capital purchase for The Scoop will be a dedicated pickup truck for business use. Jay Johnson has made arrangements to purchase a reliable used truck with low miles from a private owner:

2003 Toyota Tundra SR5

- V8 engine
- 4 x 4
- 150,000 Mile Powertrain Warranty
- 68,200 miles
- Extended cab
- Sprayed in Bed Liner/Rubber Bed Mat

In addition, several additional rakes and dustpans will be purchased, along with several closed containers (for disposal) and a bulk supply of plastic disposal bags.

Location

The Scoop will operate from a home office. Jay Johnson has dedicated 150 square feet in his home for the business. He will use a personal computer and an off-the-shelf accounting program to store customer records, generate invoices, etc. He will use a dedicated cellular phone for telecommunications, given the mobile nature of his business.

Hours of Operation

Normal operating hours for The Scoop will be from 8 a.m. to 4:30 p.m., Monday to Friday.

Fees

For routine cleanup, The Scoop charges $15 per dog per visit (monthly minimum of two visits). We will require customers to commit to service in increments of three months.

Disposal

The Scoop will adhere to all local and state regulations regarding pet waste disposal. Specifically, we have made arrangements to lease a dumpster, where we can dispose of pet waste in secure plastic bags.

MANAGEMENT SUMMARY

The Scoop's origins are rooted in economic necessity. After an eight-year career working for as a lawn care specialist for Handfield Lawn Services, which provided fertilizer, weed treatment, and pesticide applications, Jay Johnson lost his job when economic conditions forced his company to reduce staff. Unable to find a similar position with Handfield's competitors, Jay began considering ways to support his family. During his career as a lawn care specialist, unpleasant encounters with pet waste were all too common.

Sensing an opportunity, Jay decided to combine his route management and lawn care skills and test the market. He purchased a small rake and a dustpan, printed off some basic flyers, and called upon a few of his former Handfield customers that were dog owners. To his surprise, Jay's new business idea was well received. After six months, he had developed a steady customer base, mainly through word-of-mouth referrals, and was earning a decent income. Moving forward, Jay has decided to formally establish The Scoop, which will commence operations in the summer of 2010.

MARKETING & SALES

We have developed a marketing plan for The Scoop that includes the following tactics:

- **Brand Identity**—A local graphic designer has developed an eye-catching logo for The Scoop, which we can use on all of our marketing materials.

- **Business Cards**—Although these go without saying for a new business, The Scoop has identified a supplier of magnetic business cards, which will allow our service to remain visible (on the fridge).

- **Word-of-Mouth Advertising**—In speaking with pet waste removal business operators in other markets, word-of-mouth referrals are very important. With this in mind, we will offer "refer a friend" discounts amounting to one free weekly visit (one dog) for each new customer referral.

- **Web Site**—We will develop a simple Web site describing our business, hours of operation, specials, and service options offered.

- **Yellow Page Advertising**—Arrangements have been made to list The Scope with Yellowbook under the category Pet Waste Removal Service.

- **Promotional Flyer**—We have developed a colorful flyer describing the services we provide. In addition to listing our rates, the flier contains customer testimonials and a coupon for one free weekly visit (one dog) for all new customers who sign a three-month contract.

- **Direct Marketing**—To raise awareness about our services in advance of the warm weather season, The Scoop has planned to do a direct mail campaign during the months of March and April to select neighborhoods in the Primrose community. A list broker has been identified that can provide us with mailing lists based on household income and pet ownership.

- **Vehicle Advertising**—Primrose Graphics, a local large-format printer, will produce vehicle graphics displaying our logo, phone number, and Web site on the company truck.

FINANCIAL ANALYSIS

Balance sheet

Sales	2010	2011	2012
Total sales	$52,500	$78,750	$105,000
Expenses			
Marketing and advertising	$ 3,000	$ 3,000	$ 3,000
General/administrative	$ 500	$ 500	$ 500
Accounting/legal	$ 800	$ 400	$ 400
Office supplies	$ 350	$ 350	$ 350
Equipment	$ 500	$ 500	$ 500
Auto loan	$ 3,276	$ 3,276	$ 3,276
Insurance	$ 1,500	$ 1,600	$ 1,700
Salary	$35,000	$40,000	$ 65,000
Payroll taxes	$ 3,600	$ 9,450	$ 12,600
Vendor permits and licenses	$ 250	$ 250	$ 250
Postage	$ 700	$ 350	$ 350
Gasoline	$ 1,500	$ 2,000	$ 3,000
Wireless telecommunications	$ 750	$ 800	$ 1,500
Total expenses	$51,726	$62,476	$ 92,426
Net income	$ 774	$16,274	$ 12,574

Retail Clothing

Clothes as Art Inc.

49567 Main St.
Los Angeles, CA 55550

Clothes as Art offers a creative alternative in the retail clothing industry: customers create and then produce their own designs on garments. Faced with strong competition, this plan outlines several marketing strategies and provides insight into factors like location and demography when planning a clothing venture.

This plan originally appeared in Business Plans Handbook, Volume 1; it has been updated for this volume.

EXECUTIVE SUMMARY

Clothes as Art Inc. will be a wearable art retail store. Clothes as Art Inc. enables people, male or female, young or old, to design their own clothing—whether they have any artistic abilities or not. It will be fashion art that's unique and original. Most of all, customers will be entertained while creating their own fashion art. Clothes as Art will begin conservatively by offering T-shirts and sweatshirts as in-store inventory from which the customer can choose. In addition to blanks for the customers to design, Clothes as Art Inc. will have a moderate inventory (30% of projected sales) of pre-painted shirts and sweatshirts. This will tap into the market of those who like the clothing but are more spontaneous buyers.

Any customer will be allowed to bring in pieces from their own wardrobe to paint. In addition, at the end of the day the spin drum is coated with a strip of the paint around the edge. This dries over night and becomes a durable, pliable material. This can be fashioned into belts, cut into earrings and other jewelry that will match all clothing produced by the artist. These will be offered as accessories at Clothes as Art.

Clothes as Art's products have two target markets. The first market consists of females, 21 to 35 years of age, with household income of $45,000 per year or higher. The second target market is 50 percent male, 50 percent female, 5 to 16 years of age, with household income of $45,000 per year or higher. The only location that would be conducive to the sale of these products is in a small location with very high walk-by traffic. Therefore, the location requirements are a high traffic, indoor mall.

Clothes as Art will have no true direct competition by another store in the area. Clothes as Art's edge will be its price. Of the existing indirect competition, there are few companies that will be able to compete with Clothes as Art's price. This will be a major advantage for the business during the difficult economic conditions of the early 2010s. Clothes as Art's financial statements have been compiled with the greatest degree of conservatism. Clothes as Art will require a loan of $179,077. The loan will comprise 31 percent up-front expenses and 69 percent working capital needs. Close analysis will show that Clothes as Art's gross profit margin is 77 percent before tax.

DESCRIPTION OF THE BUSINESS

Clothes as Art will be a wearable art and accessory retail store. I wish to incorporate the business and trademark its products, which will give rise to legal costs. Today's consumers want to do their own thing. Clothes as Art enables people, male or female, young or old, to design their own clothing—whether they have any artistic abilities or not. It's fun, it's exciting, and it will be inexpensive for them. It will be fashion art that is unique and original. The consumer will be able to design any number of pieces to go with any other articles of clothing they own. Most of all they will be entertained while creating their own fashion art. In addition, accessories will be fabricated from the byproduct of the artwork. Therefore, the accessories will complement any article sold in the store.

(Pictures are available for a more visual demonstration of the product.)

The service procedure of the store is quite simple. The customer enters the store and picks out an article of clothing they wish to paint on, or they may bring in a piece of their own wardrobe (I will use "shirt" to identify the clothing article). The customer then takes a number to await a free work table at which they will paint. The customer then chooses four colors that they will paint with. The paints are applied with squeeze bottles full of bright colors. While they are choosing their colors their shirt will be clipped and stretched on a cardboard board the same size as the shirt. This prepares the shirt to be a canvas for the artist. The attendant will then give the customer brief instructions on how and where to paint on the shirt. The customer then paints on the shirt in any way they believe will look good when it is spun.

When the customer is done he/she hands the shirt to the attendant who spins it. This is where the excitement begins. Spinning at about 450 RPM, the paint that was applied to the shirt quickly evolves into original art right before the eyes of the customer. (Pictures are available for a more visual demonstration of the product.) The centrifugal force caused by the spinning causes the paint to be drawn from the center of the shirt to the edges resulting in a star-burst (spin art) look to the design. The colors swirl together but don't blend into new colors. The original colors remain separate colors.

While this is happening crowds gather to watch the artist and they quickly form a line to do their own thing. The shirt is then sent through a large belt drier that adheres the paint permanently to the shirt. When the shirt is done drying, the customer's number is called at the cash register and another happy artist is born. The finished product is a self-made piece of artwork that can be machine washed and dried for years along with the customer's regular clothing. The entire services process takes an average of only 20 minutes, so the turnover is great. This includes an average time to paint (5 minutes), spin (30 seconds), and dry (15 minutes). There will be several tables at which to work. The drier can dry up to six shirts on a continuously moving conveyor belt.

Clothes as Art will begin conservatively by offering T-shirts and sweatshirts as in-store inventory. In addition to blanks for the customers to design, Clothes as Art will have moderate inventory (30% of projected sales) of pre-painted shirts and sweats. This will tap into the markets who like the clothing but are more spontaneous buyers. Any customer will be allowed to bring in pieces from their own wardrobe to paint. A caution will be given that the shop won't guarantee the results and no flammable materials will be allowed. When in-house inventory expansion is warranted, Clothes as Art will expand into jeans, jackets, women's casual suit coats, jean jackets, leather jackets, collared shirts, canvasses, placemats, jewelry, sweatpants, ties, belts, and shoes.

With respect to canvasses, Clothes as Art will have blank canvasses on which the customer can paint. Many people decorate their homes with certain color schemes. This will give the decorator the ability to create their own piece of artwork. At the end of the day the spin drum is coated with a strip of the paint around the edge. This dries overnight and becomes a durable, rubber-like material that can be fashioned into accessories such as belts, or cut into earrings and other jewelry-type articles that will match all clothing produced by the artist.

MARKET

Target Market

In accordance with the manufacturer and my own experience, Clothes as Art will be tapping primarily in to two separate markets.

Target market A

Sex	Female
Type	Working woman who is fashion conscious
Age	21–35
Education	Some college or degree holders
Household income	$45,000+

Target market B

Sex	50% male, 50% female
Age	5–16
Education	Grade school
Household income	$45,000+

As you will see in my biography (available upon request), I have previously worked for a retail store of this nature. It has been my experience that this product's market is both sexless and ageless (age 5 to 50). I have also spoken with another shop owner who agrees that the product has this type of wide appeal. For analysis I will deal with these two target markets.

My choice for location is the Shelby Corners Mall (no traffic studies are available for this mall). According to their "Primary Trade Market, Neighborhood/Lifestyle Composition," Target Market A fits into those categories called Blue Blood Estates, Money and Brains, Urban Gold Coast, and Young Influentials. This accounts for 81.8 percent of the 1.1 million people in this mall trade market. Target Market B fits into the category called Furs and Station Wagons. This accounts for 2 percent of the 1.1 million trade market figure. With respect to Target Market B showing such a low market share, please keep in mind that the mall offers no traffic studies. If you visit the mall you will see quite a few more children and teenagers than the mall market study shows. Therefore, the overall market with respect to children is very healthy.

Total Market

According to the North American Industry Classification System, Clothes as Art's Industry Group Number is 44819, Other Clothing Stores. After reaching an estimated $11.16 billion in 2006, sales increased to $12.05 billion in 2007 and $12.08 billion in 2008. During the early 2010s, the retail industry operated in a very difficult economic climate. More than ever before, value was of prime importance to customers.

As Janet Hoffman, global managing director of Accenture's Retail Practice, explained in the March 2010 issue of *Chain Store Age:* "Today's consumer is redefining the nature of value. Price is paramount, but consumers also demand the same or greater value for less money. Penny pinchers will not suddenly become big spenders given constraints on disposable cash, reduced asset values, clampdowns on corporate bonuses and, for many baby boomers, upcoming retirement. Retailers must identify and serve that price-value sweet spot to win loyalty and market share."

COMPETITION

Direct Competition

According to Spin and Dry Inc., the manufacturers of the spinning and drying equipment, there is no other equipment-based store of this kind in the metropolitan area. Therefore, Clothes as Art would have no direct competition in the Los Angeles area.

Clothes as Art's toughest competition is Art Wear, Custom Designs, and Clothes Etc. This is mainly due to the fact that their capital strength is greater than Clothes as Art's. In addition, their prices will be competitive, and their lines will be fuller.

Clothes as Art's main drawback will be a lack of capital necessary to compete with these stores. Clothes as Art can handle this drawback in one of two ways: either avoid them altogether or have a location that has a large enough market to handle all of the shops. The only way to avoid them is to choose another location; this would greatly affect our chances for success. Clothes as Art's location in the mall will have a large enough market for all of the shops.

Currently, the mall houses only two of our competitors. A recent expansion has added mainly high-end, high priced shops to the roster. Clothes as Art's main marketing device will be the low price of the goods; therefore, the new expansion has had little effect on the competition but it has increased the number of potential customers. Clothes as Art will bring a product to the market that each of these shops either do not carry or carry in small quantities. Most, with the exception of Clothes Etc., have prices that are quite a bit higher than Clothes as Art's.

We may not have the capital strength, but we also don't have the expenses that the other stores have to cover. We will be highly competitive with our prices.

Indirect Competition

The remaining T-shirt retailers are men's and women's sportswear stores and little shops that sell small proportions of T-shirts. Clothes as Art will be competing with them by giving the customer something that they don't offer. We will meet a market niche that is not being filled by the current stores. Other T-shirt retailers are generally custom silk screeners. Clothes as Art is not going to directly compete with them by doing silk screening, per se. We will be competing with them in that a proportion of Clothes as Art's sales will be to fraternities, sororities, church groups, etc., to supply items such as baseball jerseys and event T-shirts.

MARKETING STRATEGY

Based on experience in this market, with respect to T-shirts, price sells. This will be the same case with Clothes as Art's sweats. The cost of a finished T-shirt at our store will be $19 and a sweatshirt will be $25. This will be the store's major selling point. Even with this low price the goal of profit and positive cash flow can be achieved. This price may even be able to be raised given the superiority of the location and relative price flexibility of the mall's patrons.

In addition to my own advertising, the mall does quite a bit of advertising itself and will be augmenting other advertising.

The greater proportion of Clothes as Art's advertising will be in give-a-ways to local groups such as high schools, fraternities, and church groups. This will be the best way to build local support in both target markets, given that the product is relatively difficult to describe on the radio. In addition, this is a community-oriented advertising device that will help to build the store's credibility. In contacting local fund raising organizations, such as fraternities and church groups, they will be very apt to become return customers when their next fund raising drive comes around.

Another shop owner has commented that birthday parties are a very effective means of advertising. By bringing in a group of children (Target Market B) to paint, they will either return themselves or show our product to others. This is achieved by advertising in small local newspapers and church leaflets.

Another marketing avenue we will explore is contacting the local art clubs at high schools and colleges. The object of an art club promotion will be to teach people how to use the process efficiently. That would in turn help to make them repeat customers. Once they have mastered the techniques they would now be in a position to create wearable art gifts or garments for themselves. They also will bring in their friends, who they will attempt to teach. In addition, this would be a great method of getting artistically done pre-painted inventory for Clothes as Art. This would be done with the understanding that all designs must be pre-approved. This could also give rise to a special "gallery" section of the store for local artists' work, thus adding to the stature of Clothes as Art.

Clothes as Art will be advertising toward local schools. The store will bring in local art classes and charge a nominal fee if they bring their own shirts. The object will be to derive repeat customers out of the class and new customers out of the school. This is another avenue to exploit Target Market B.

Logo identification will be another advertising method. Garments can be manufactured for local bowling groups, fraternities, restaurants, and companies. The logo can be screen printed and brought in for establishment or hand painted with the Clothes as Art system. Clothes as Art will attempt to exploit the logos of local professional sports teams. The need for licensing agreements will be explored. It is my impression that as long as Clothes as Art is not doing the initial screen printing, Clothes as Art will not have to incur the large costs of acquiring a licensing agreement. Clothes as Art can create shirts for special events such as Valentine's Day, Mother's Day, and Father's Day.

LOCATION

Clothes as Art will require very little space. The space needed is only 850 square feet so the rent will be lower than a regular retail store. T-shirts and sweatshirts can be stored in stacked cubicles that take up very little space while storing large amounts of inventory. The pre-painted inventory will constitute 30 percent of sales and will therefore require a small amount of space. In using cubicles there will be very little space needed in a storeroom to store other inventory.

Through my experience with this product, Clothes as Art must be located in a very high walk-by traffic mall with high visibility, through a glass storefront. A large selling point of this product is entertainment. Therefore, in addition to the aforementioned marketing techniques, it is sold by one person watching another spin their shirt and then wanting to paint one themselves.

The mall affords the greatest visibility for Clothes as Art's product. As mentioned earlier, the mall has no traffic studies but it is known as the most successful mall in the metro area. It also affords the greatest means of reaching Clothes as Art's two target markets. A simple trip through the mall shows overwhelming evidence that Clothes as Art's two target markets will be very effectively reached.

The costs associated with the mall are quite steep. The track record of the mall owners (who also own several plazas) in the area of delivering a fruitful market to their renters has been shown conclusively by the longevity of and need for expansion of both the malls and plazas.

Clothes as Art's first choice would be to secure a pre-built space. This would lower the store's construction costs. The pre-constructed space would have to be in a good location. It is the experience of the mall's owners that the shops that fail were in the worst positions; therefore, the chance of Clothes as Art finding an adequate, pre-constructed space is very remote. To be as conservative as possible, financial statements are based on a few unfinished store sites in the expanded section of the mall. The average cost per square foot is $25.

Analysis of the completion indicates that the Shelby Corners Mall is the best location to access our target markets, while avoiding locations that house direct competition.

MANAGEMENT

Owner

Cathy Wood earned a Master of Business Administration from St. Louis University in May of 2001. She completed her Bachelor of Science in Business Administration/Finance at St. Louis University in December of 1999.

Throughout her life she has been very involved in entrepreneurship. She has owned her own house cleaning business since she was in grade eight. During the summer of 1997 she completed and entrepreneurial internship in North Carolina with a retail store specializing in Clothes as Art's product. There she learned many aspects of the business, from inventory control to cash management.

In addition, during the summer of 1998 she was an original partner in a car part retailing business registered in the State of California as Core Enterprises. She has done work for the Small Business Institute as a small business counselor for Bellni Baby and Children's Furniture in Glenwood, California. She was also commissioned by South County Landscaping and Construction Company in Sacramento, California, as a small business counselor. During her last year of undergraduate work she was the founding vice president of the Association of Collegiate Entrepreneurs (ACE). The association was initiated on campus to help students who aspire to become entrepreneurs get needed information and meet the necessary people. In this association she was responsible for the promotion and scheduling of speakers and events.

This plan received an Honorable Mention from the Kennesaw State business plan competition. This competition is international in nature and highly competitive.

Ms. Wood currently is employed as a business planner for Fox Associates. Fox Associates is an entertainment business in Los Angeles, which owns and operates the Bijou Theater (a local landmark).

Manager

Clothes as Art will not have a manager in the first year of operation. The owner will perform the duties of a manager. When the time comes for the company to hire a manager, he or she will have to have two outstanding abilities. They will have to perform all the normal managerial duties such as scheduling, employee guidance, and sales computing, and have adequate artistic abilities to lend in the sales process by giving advice to prospective customers.

Directors

The directors will include the owner Cathy Wood. Other directors will include people currently involved in local small business, the local artist community, and the local financial community.

PERSONNEL

General Hiring Philosophy: Each employee of Clothes as Art will have to possess enough artistic ability to aid and advise the customers. We already know that Clothes as Art requires almost no artistic abilities to produce a shirt. Therefore, with respect to customer aid, the employee's ability to give advice will need to be the strongest. They will have to be pleasant and sales-oriented. They will have to be able to emphasize the ease of the painting process and sell the product effectively. In addition to their customer-related duties, they will have to be able to design shirts for the pre-painted in-store inventory. With respect to pre-painted inventory, their artistic abilities will need to be strong. They must be able to excel in design beyond the average customer.

FINANCIAL ANALYSIS

Analyses, financial statements, and projections/information concerning competition and location have been prepared and are available upon request.

The requested loan will be collateralized with inventory, equipment, and leasehold improvement. Clothes as Art will always have 8 weeks worth of inventory in the shop at all times. T-shirts and sweatshirts are a staple item for screen printers and will therefore have a high resale value in the event of default. In addition, the dryer is commonly used by screen printers; therefore, it is not considered specialized equipment like the spinner and has a high resale price. I will attempt to persuade the mall to take a subordinated position on the leasehold improvements as another form of collateral. It is my intention to use all available net cash flow to pay down the outstanding long term liabilities of Clothes as Art. In addition, the unused portion of the loan will be held in short-term certificates of deposit at the loaning bank.

Financial statements for year 1, as well as supporting documents, have been prepared. Financial statements for years 2-5 consist of monthly income statements and year-end balance sheets.

I have assumed a 10 percent growth in sales for years 2 and 3. This is due to the time it takes for the product to take hold of its market. The sales then level off at an 8 percent growth rate for years 4 and 5. This is due to the fact that the store will become an established business in the mall. I have assummed a 5 percent increase in the cost of my inventory.

Specialty Bakery

Creative Cupcakes

99991 Gratiot Ave.
Eastpointe, MI 48021

Heidi Denler

Creative Cupcakes is a start-up retail establishment in Metropolitan Detroit. The bakery expects to fill a niche in the current trend for upscale, creative cupcakes, building a loyal customer base.

INTRODUCTION

Creative Cupcakes is a start-up retail establishment in Metropolitan Detroit. The bakery expects to fill a niche in the current trend for upscale, creative cupcakes, building a loyal customer base. The owner's bakery experience and home-based cake business will enhance short-term and long-term growth in an up and coming pastry industry segment. Competitive pricing will encourage customers to return for quality products and innovative ideas when the need arises for cupcakes, whether for a family dinner or an upscale party.

MANAGEMENT SUMMARY

The company will be established as an LLC (limited liability corporation) by the owners, Jake and Sally Pratt, who are brother and sister. Jake has 8 years experience in bakery retail sales at Antoine's Pastry Shop, and Sally has been running a home-based cake decorating business for the last five years. She recently began to focus on the cupcake niche of the market with an eye toward opening Creative Cupcakes and developing a loyal following of current customers.

The management team will assume a hands-on approach to baking, decorating, and dealing with customer service until the store is established and employees have proven their abilities to manage.

PRODUCTS AND SERVICES

Creative Cupcakes will offer cupcakes baked daily from scratch, replenishing bakery cases through-out the day to ensure the availability of freshly baked and decorated cupcakes. The aroma of baking cupcakes will encourage prospective customers to stop in as they walk past the shop.

MISSION STATEMENT

The mission of Creative Cupcakes is to provide high-quality, freshly-baked cupcakes for all occasions. Customer satisfaction, reasonable prices, high quality, unique products, and innovative flavors are paramount.

VISION STATEMENT

Growth in customer base will be accomplished via customer service, word-of-mouth and media advertising, and giving back to the community. Creative Cupcake will expand its initial site and identify up to three new locations in Southeastern Michigan within the first five years of operation.

VALUES STATEMENT

Jake and Sally Pratt are dedicated to quality products made from quality materials, offered in comfortable surroundings in a warm and friendly atmosphere to encourage repeat business.

BUSINESS PHILOSOPHY

Creative Cupcakes will offer every customer friendly service in a pleasant setting to encourage repeat business and customer goodwill with an eye to future growth.

GOALS AND OBJECTIVES

Sally and Jake Pratt will build on Sally's home-based cake and cupcake business through continued high-quality products to their customer base. Initially, promotion will include flyers and coupons distributed to current customers announcing their new location. Print ads will be purchased in local free and paid weekly and monthly publications.

Initially, Jake will manage the shop and customer service, leaving Sally in charge of the kitchen responsibilities. Co-op students from the local high school(s) will be hired to work part-time. Plans include hiring one professional baker to assist Sally full-time and up to two part-time bakers will be hired from the local culinary school.

ORGANIZATION STRUCTURE

Creative Cupcakes will be a limited liability corporation (LLC) with all assets and liabilities shared by the Pratt siblings. They will hire co-op student from the local high school(s) to staff the front counter, dealing with the general foot traffic. Students from the culinary institute will be hired as trainees with the possibility of becoming full-time cupcake bakers and decorators.

An employee policy handbook that outlines job descriptions, training, reviews, and staff meetings is under development. The Pratts will use staff meetings as a time to discuss what is working and what might need adjusting. They will encourage the staff to offer suggestions and voice concerns they might have. Employees must have an appreciation for the unique products offered by Creative Cupcakes.

ADVERTISING AND PROMOTION

Initially, advertising and promotion will be flyers placed on cars in local parking lots and hand-delivered door-to-door. A Web site is under development to build a strong customer base. Ads will be placed in local newspapers. Patrons will be asked to provide their e-mail addresses to receive advance notice for special events and coupons at Creative Cupcakes.

Press releases announcing the opening of the store and ensuing promotional events, such as high teas and tea tastings, will be sent to all local print, radio, and television. Personal phone and e-mail follow-up will be made to build a relationship with area media personalities, which are expected to result in free positive marketing and promotion.

CUSTOMER BASE

The Pratt siblings plans are predicated on the assumption that Sally's current customer base will follow her to the new location. The market position for Creative Cupcakes is expected to be strong due to Sally's current customers and a lack of competition in this bakery niche. Only two other cupcake stores are in the Metropolitan Detroit area.

Word of mouth referrals from friends will be supplemented by print advertising as well as flyers and coupons that will be distributed at local coffee shops. Creative Cupcakes plans to establish a large customer base among local residents to ensure consistent revenue as well as the stability of the enterprise. High visibility due to location along a busy main artery with ample parking and an inviting exterior and window displays will draw customers to the store. Once they are inside, they will discover family-friendly service and high-quality products that will keep them returning, whether for special occasions, a family dessert, or just a well-earned reward after a hard day at work. Current customers will be given coupons to be used on purchases at the new store, and all customers will be offered frequent buyer cards to encourage repeat business.

Teenagers looking for an afterschool treat or first date spot, young mothers looking for a quick dessert or treat for their pre-schooler, young adults who want a different dessert for a potluck, and business-people who want something besides bagels or muffins for an afternoon meeting comprise the target market for Creative Cupcakes.

PRODUCTS AND SERVICES

Creative Cupcakes will be open from 11AM to 9PM Tuesday through Saturday. The store will be closed for street traffic on Sundays and Mondays, although special orders will be delivered to customers who need orders on those days of the week. Customers will be able to pay by cash, VISA, MasterCard, or debit card.

Cupcake flavor choices will be monitored via interaction with customers as well as via charting sales. The menu will offer "standard" flavor cupcakes with a variety of fillings and frostings. Other flavors will rotate weekly and seasonally. A sample menu is attached as Appendix A.

While walk-in business will dominate sales, the Pratts will also offer special orders for any special occasion from an intimate dinner for two to a wedding. Creative Cupcake is ready to offer its versions of unique, flavorful, decorated cupcakes, the latest trend in desserts.

LOCATION

The proposed location for Creative Cupcakes is in Eastpointe, a middle-class suburb of Detroit. The area has abundant restaurants and bars, but only a few bakeries, none of which specialize in desserts, particularly cupcakes. The average age of Eastpointe residents is 36, and the average annual income is $46,261. Given the 2010 economic forecast, the area is well-suited to a new venture in an up and coming dessert area such as Creative Cupcakes.

The Pratts have identified a former coffee shop/restaurant near city hall on Gratiot as their prime location. The 1,700-square-foot building is available to rent for $699 per month. The kitchen equipment will require minimal upgrading and remodeling to accommodate the necessary ovens for baking the cupcakes, as well as countertops islands for decorating the cupcakes.

The store is on a major commuter route and is well-travelled by shoppers. Its location near city hall offers an opportunity to market cupcakes for individual workers as well as city-sponsored events.

STORE DESIGN AND EQUIPMENT

When customers walk into the store, they will see cases with trays of cupcakes, with flavors and frostings identified on cupcake-shaped markers. There will be a small eating area with two or three tables for those who choose to enjoy their cupcakes on the premises.

The kitchen area will comprise at least one-half of the store. It will have a walk-in refrigerator, a combination of commercial ovens and convection ovens to allow baking in large quantities. A small commercial stove will be necessary for the creation of decorations. At least four commercial Kitchen-Aid mixers will be used for making batter and frostings. The current kitchen has a three basin commercial grade sink and dishwasher. Metal shelving units will be used to store baking supplies (flour, sugar, flavorings, etc.), cupcake pans, cupcake liners, utensils, bowls, etc.

FINANCIAL

Start up costs will include standard security deposits and licensing by state and local health boards. Some interior work will need to be done to the building, especially in the kitchen as noted in the "Store Design and Equipment" section of this business plan. The unisex lavatory is serviceable and clean, but the Pratts would like to update the fixtures and will work with the landlord to do so.

The entire shop will require painting and placement of photos of specialty cupcakes to complete the ambience sought by the owners. One point of service cash register will be at the customer service area of the store. It will be linked to a laptop in the office area at the rear of the store to facilitate inventory control. Software for payroll, taxes, and other company business will be required. An all-in-one (AIO) printer/fax/copier will be purchased for day-to-day operations at the outset. Within six months, Creative Cupcakes plans to lease a copy machine so they can reduce their costs for printing flyers, coupons, brochures, etc., that Jake can design.

Other start up costs will include any fees for registration of the name and the business with all federal, state, and local government authorities. In addition, the owners will have typical overhead costs of rent payments, taxes, payroll, payroll taxes, key man insurance, property insurance, liability insurance, inventory, telephone and utilities, an alarm system, and advertising.

A small business administration (SBA) loan has been approved by the local Huntington Bank branch to cover start up costs and provide liquid cash for miscellaneous expenses.

Creative Cupcakes expects to show a profit immediately, due to Sally Pratt's current customer base following her from her cottage industry to the store-front bakery.

PROFESSIONAL AND ADVISORY SUPPORT

Jake and Sally Pratt will continue to use the legal services of the attorney Sally currently uses for her home-based cake and cupcake business. She is well-versed in small businesses and is a CPA as well as an attorney, so she will advise the siblings on financial as well as legal matters.

A local property-casualty insurance agency has been advising Creative Cupcakes' owners on securing insurance for the store and its inventory. As an LLC, the Pratts will assume responsibility for their own health insurance and will not offer it to any employees.

The Pratts have an established relationship with Huntington Bank, and have secured financing for their start-up costs, as well as a line of credit to cover unforeseen expenses.

Macomb County Business Assistance Center has been helpful with such details as planning, marketing, sales strategies, loan applications, and licensing, and the Pratts will continue to seek advice and mentoring from the Center.

BUSINESS AND GROWTH STRATEGY

A percentage of the profits will be saved for the purpose of expansion in additional locations. The Pratts' long-range plan is to open a second store within a year, and a third store several months later. These stores will be managed by staff at the original store who have proven their knowledge of and dedication to the business, as well as baking, decorating, and management skills.

Marketing will center on local advertising, flyers, print advertising, and securing interviews on local cable television shows to promote Creative Cupcakes.

The Pratts have begun to investigate working with local caterers to provide cupcakes for unusual dessert options for parties and other events.

COMPETITION

As of mid-2010, only two stand-alone cupcake bakeries are within a 50-mile radius of Creative Cupcake's planned Eastpointe location, although the large commercial franchise, Happy Belly, has kiosks in nearby shopping malls. There are only a handful of bakeries in the area, and they provide breads, pies, breakfast pastries, and cakes to their customers. Local grocery store cupcakes are not of the quality of Creative Cupcake. None of the area bakeries offer the variety of flavors, frostings, or decorations that give Creative Cupcake a competitive edge based on a unique product niche.

By providing high-quality cupcakes at a competitive price in a convenient location, Creative Cupcake is expected to serve its niche segment profitably.

WEB SITE

Creative Cupcakes is working with a Web site designer to create an online presence that will provide store hours, a store map, and contact information. One page will be dedicated to a complete menu of available cupcakes. Within six months, the Web site will include interactive forms to place orders to be ready for pickup.

The URL will be included on all printed materials, such as flyers, brochures, and business cards.

CONCLUSION

Creative Cupcakes expects to be profitable immediately, and expects to pay down its SBA loan from Huntington Bank within five years. A highly visible location on a busy thoroughfare in a middle class suburb, with a solid customer following and a unique, high-quality product, combined with friendly, knowledgeable staff will make this possible.

Several factors will combine to make Creative Cupcakes profitable immediately: location, store design, service, marketing, and staff. The location is highly visible on a busy thoroughfare in a middle class suburb. The store design and window displays will be visually attractive and welcoming to new customers as well as returning customers. Service will be prompt, with attention paid to customer input for flavor ideas. Effective marketing via attractive flyers, brochures, and a Web site presence will boost sales, along with a frequent buyer program to encourage repeat business. The staff will be knowledgeable about not only the product but also about customer service, and the promise of promotion within the company to manage new stores will encourage employee retention.

First impressions will be important to return business, as will relationships with the health department inspectors and licensing agencies. To that end, Creative Cupcakes will maintain a good working relationship with the Macomb County Business Center to remain up-to-date on state laws and regulations regarding the fledgling business.

APPENDIX A

Standard Cupcakes on the Daily Menu

- *Chocolate*—chocolate cupcake with vanilla buttercream frosting, with or without sprinkles
- *Classic Red Velvet*—red velvet cupcake with a traditional cream cheese frosting, drizzled with chocolate
- *Chocolate Lovers*—dark chocolate cupcake with dark chocolate frosting, topped with dark chocolate shavings
- *Vanilla*—vanilla bean cupcake with chocolate buttercream frosting, with or without sprinkles
- *Vanilla Vegan*—vegan vanilla bean cupcake with vegan "buttercream" frosting (chocolate or vanilla)
- *Chocolate Vegan*—vegan chocolate cupcake with vegan "buttercream" frosting (chocolate or vanilla)
- *Marble*—vanilla bean and chocolate swirled cupcake with either vanilla or chocolate buttercream frosting and rolled in sanding sugar of the customer's choosing
- *PB&J*—vanilla bean cupcake filled with strawberry jam and covered with peanut-butter buttercream frosting, drizzled with strawberry jam and topped with a fondant strawberry
- *Vanilla-filled*—vanilla bean cupcake filled with vanilla cream and frosted with milk chocolate buttercream
- *Chocolate-filled*—chocolate cupcake filled with milk chocolate cream and frosted with milk chocolate buttercream

Rotating Flavors (always available with 24-hour notice)

- *Vanilla Caramel*—vanilla bean cupcake, filled with caramel and frosted with caramel buttercream, drizzled with white chocolate

- *Chocolate Chip*— Chocolate or Pure Vanilla cake w/ chocolate or vanilla butter cream frosting, loaded w/ chocolate chips

- *German Chocolate*—chocolate cupcake covered with a caramel-pecan-coconut frosting and drizzled with chocolate

- *Banana Pecan*—moist banana cupcake with pecans covered with cream cheese frosting and topped with a whole pecan

- *Cinnamon Spice*—spice cupcake covered with cinnamon frosting with cinnamon-sugar sprinkles

- *Cappuccino*—milk chocolate cupcake covered with cappuccino buttercream frosting and mini-chocolate chips

- *Mochalata*—dark chocolate cupcake covered with espresso infused buttercream frosting and chocolate covered coffee beans

- *Vanillalata*—vanilla bean cake covered with cappuccino buttercream frosting and chocolate covered coffee beans

- *Carrot*—carrot-cake cupcake filled with shredded carrots, pineapple, and raisins covered with cream cheese frosting and a candy carrot (may be rolled in nuts)

- *Banana Split*—moist banana cupcake filled with strawberry jam covered with whipped vanilla buttercream frosting and drizzled with chocolate

- *Boston Cream*—vanilla bean cupcake filled with vanilla custard, topped with a rich chocolate ganache

- *It's the Razz!*—vanilla bean cupcake filled with raspberry jam covered with raspberry cream cheese frosting and drizzled with chocolate

- *Chocolate-covered Cherry*—vanilla bean cupcake filled with cherry preserves and frosting with milk chocolate buttercream frosting

- *Give Me "Samoa"*—vanilla bean cupcake frosting with vanilla buttercream frosting, rolled in lightly-toasted flaked coconut, drizzled with caramel and milk chocolate

Seasonal Cupcakes (available by special order with 24-hour notice)

- *Hawai'ian*—pineapple and macadamia nut cupcake covered with coconut cream frosting

- *Coconutty*—vanilla bean cupcake covered with vanilla (or chocolate!) buttercream frosting, topped with lightly-toasted flaked coconut

- *Citrus Delight*—lemon cupcake topped with lemon-infused whipped frosting and sprinkled with crushed lemon drop candies

- *Key Lime*—vanilla bean cupcake topped with key-lime whipped frosting and sprinkled with coconut, topped with a candy lime slice

- *Pumpkin*—pumpkin spice cupcake covered with cream cheese frosting, topped with cinnamon-sugar sprinkles

- *Caramel Apple*—vanilla bean cupcake filled with apple pie filling covered with vanilla buttercream drizzled with caramel

- *Sweet Potato Pie*—sweet-potato cupcake covered with cream cheese frosting topped with graham cracker crumbs and a slice of crystallized ginger

- *Hot Cocoa*—milk chocolate cupcake filled with marshmallow cream and covered with whipped vanilla frosting drizzled with chocolate
- *Holiday Mint*—dark chocolate cupcake covered with soft green, mint-infused vanilla buttercream frosting, drizzled with chocolate
- *Peppermint Delight*—vanilla bean cupcake covered with mint-infused chocolate buttercream frosting, topped with crushed peppermint candies
- *Gingerbread*—ginger infused cupcake covered with cream cheese frosting with cinnamon-sugar sprinkles
- *Eggnog*—eggnog-infused vanilla bean cupcake covered with nutmeg cream cheese frosting topped with cinnamon-sugar sprinkles

Available frostings include: Buttercream (vanilla, chocolate, caramel, cream cheese, German chocolate, lemon, raspberry, banana, peanut butter, strawberry); Whipped (vanilla, chocolate).

Available fillings include: Vanilla, chocolate, lemon, lime, banana, and fruit jams or preserves upon request.

All cupcakes can be decorated according to the wishes of the customers with sprinkles, sanding sugar, drizzled frosting, and fondant creations (flowers, butterflies, pumpkins, candy canes, snowmen, fruits, etc.)

Steak House

1 8 4 5   S t e a k h o u s e

777 Franklin St.
Buffalo, New York 14202

BizPlanDB.com

1845 Steakhouse is a New York-based corporation that will develop a restaurant that will serve steak, chops, and other American-based cuisine in the Buffalo, New York metropolitan area.

1.0 EXECUTIVE SUMMARY

The purpose of this business plan is to raise $175,000 for the development of a steak house while showcasing the expected financials and operations over the next three years. 1845 Steakhouse is a New York-based corporation that will develop a restaurant that will serve steak, chops, and other American-based cuisine. The Company was founded by Tyler Austin.

1.1 The Restaurant

1845 Steakhouse intends to serve a wide variety of entrées that will be of American origin. These entrees include steak, chops, seafood, and related dishes.

Additionally, the business will offer a wide variety of alcoholic beverages, which Management expects will generate a significant portion of the Company's revenues and profits.

1.2 Financing

Mr. Austin is seeking to raise $175,000 from as a bank loan. The interest rate and loan agreement are to be further discussed during negotiation. This business plan assumes that the business will receive a 10 year loan with a 9% fixed interest rate. The financing will be used for the following:

• Development of the location

• Financing for the first six months of operation

• Capital to purchase kitchen equipment

• Working capital

Mr. Austin will contribute $25,000 to the venture.

1.3 Mission Statement

Mr. Austin's mission is to provide customers with an outstanding line of American cuisine dishes with a focus on steak while concurrently remaining within the letter of the law regarding the sale of food and alcohol in the State of New York.

1.4 Management Team

The Company was founded by Tyler Austin. Mr. Austin has more than 10 years of experience in the food service industry. Through his expertise, he will be able to bring the operations of the business to profitability within its first year of operations.

1.5 Sales Forecasts

Mr. Austin expects a strong rate of growth at the start of operations. Below are the expected financials over the next three years.

Proforma profit and loss (yearly)

Year	1	2	3
Sales	$710,790	$781,869	$860,056
Operating costs	$343,912	$356,898	$370,495
EBITDA	$126,680	$160,753	$198,921
Taxes, interest, and depreciation	$ 74,144	$ 80,623	$ 94,407
Net profit	$ 52,536	$ 80,130	$104,514

Sales, operating costs, and profit forecast

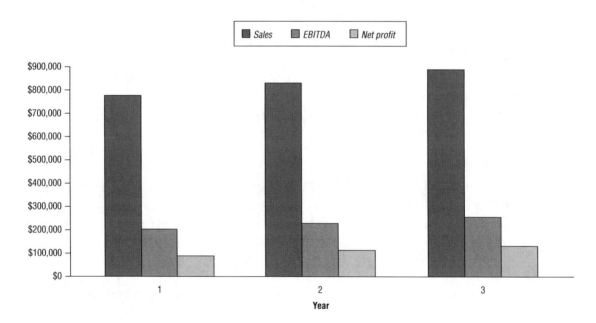

1.6 Expansion Plan

Mr. Austin expects that the business will aggressively expand during the first three years of operation. He intends to implement marketing campaigns that will effectively target individuals within the target market of Buffalo, New York and the surrounding communities. Mr. Austin may also seek to increase the number of locations he owns after the fifth year of operations.

2.0 COMPANY AND FINANCING SUMMARY

2.1 Registered Name and Corporate Structure

1845 Steakhouse is registered as a corporation in the State of New York.

2.2 Required Funds

At this time, the Mr. Austin requires $175,000 of debt funds. Below is a breakdown of how these funds will be used:

Projected startup costs

Initial lease payments and deposits	$ 25,000
Working capital	$ 40,000
FF&E	$ 20,000
Leasehold improvements	$ 35,000
Security deposits	$ 15,000
Insurance	$ 5,000
Kitchen equipment	$ 45,000
Marketing budget	$ 10,000
Miscellaneous and unforeseen costs	$ 5,000
Total startup costs	**$200,000**

Use of funds

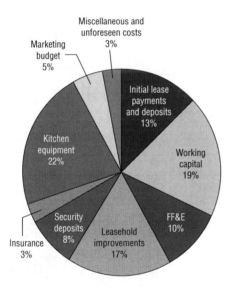

2.3 Investor Equity

Mr. Austin is not seeking an investment from a third party at this time.

2.4 Management Equity

Tyler Austin owns 100% of 1845 Steakhouse.

2.5 Exit Strategy

If the business is very successful, Mr. Austin may seek to sell the business to a third party for a significant earnings multiple. Most likely, the Company will hire a qualified business broker to sell the business. Based on historical numbers, the business could fetch a sales premium of up to 5 to 7 times earnings.

3.0 RESTAURANT PRODUCTS

Below is a description of the products offered by 1845 Steakhouse.

3.1 Steak and American Cuisine

As stated in the executive summary, the primary focus of 1845 Steakhouse will be the sale of aged steaks and American cuisine products throughout the restaurant's location. The Company will offer an expansive menu of steaks, chops, seafood, and related cuisine, which will include vegetarian items such as grilled stir-fry and other cooked entrees. The Company will also provide a number of appetizers. The preliminary pricing schedule for the business can be found in the fifth section of the business plan.

3.2 Beverages

The Company will serve a wide variety of liquors and alcoholic beverages that are available on the menu. The specialty drinks offered by the restaurant include a number of cocktails. These drinks are primary rum, vodka, and liqueur drinks that combine a number of sweet and flavored mixes. Depending on the size and alcohols used for the beverages, prices of these cocktails range from $5 to $8 per serving.

The business will also serve bottled waters, sodas, and other non-alcoholic beverages.

4.0 STRATEGIC AND MARKET ANALYSIS

4.1 Economic Outlook

This section of the analysis will detail the economic climate, the restaurant industry, the customer profile, and the competition that the business will face as it progresses through its business operations.

Currently, the economic market condition in the United States is in recession. This slowdown in the economy has also greatly impacted real estate sales, which has halted to historical lows. Many economists expect that this recession will continue until mid-2010, at which point the economy will begin a prolonged recovery period.

4.2 Industry Analysis

There over 600,000 restaurants and eateries in the United States. Gross annual receipts total more than $172 billion dollars per year. It is one of the country's largest grossing industries. The industry also employs over ten million people, and generates an average annual payroll of more than $34 billion dollars per year.

As the country has become significantly wealthier of the last ten years, more and more Americans are eating out. Time has also become a concern for the average American family. Studies have shown that more than 40% of American families eat out at least one night per week. Americans, on the whole, have also become much busier. More and more families now have two incomes, and as such, the tradition of staying at home and cooking meals is vanishing. 1845 Steakhouse will seek to capitalize on this trend by providing American cuisine entrees to its customers.

Among these establishments, Management anticipates that 30,000 restaurants offer steak as their food genre.

4.3 Customer Profile

The 1845 Steakhouse's average customer will be a middle to upper middle class man or woman living in the Company's targeted market. Common traits among clients will include:

- Annual household income exceeding $40,000

- Lives or works no more than 20 miles from 1845 Steakhouse

- Will spend $25 to $35 per visit (per person)

There are approximately 1 million people living within Erie County. Among these people, median family income is $48,522. Given the very high population density of the area, 1845 Steakhouse should be able to remain profitable in most economic climates.

4.4 Competition

New York is renowned for having a number of steak houses that have been in operation for several decades. As such, it is imperative that the business create an atmosphere that clearly differentiates itself from famous competitors. Management intends to accomplish this task by combining the sale of classic steak entrees with a modern setting.

5.0 MARKETING PLAN

Mr. Austin intends to maintain an extensive marketing campaign that will ensure maximum visibility for the business in its location. Below is an overview of the marketing strategies and objectives that Mr. Austin will use once he launches 1845 Steakhouse.

5.1 Marketing Objectives

- Implement a local campaign with the Company's targeted market via the use of flyers, local newspaper advertisements, and word of mouth advertising.

- Hire a public relations firm to provide reviews and articles about the Company's grand opening.

5.2 Marketing Strategies

Mr. Austin intends on using a number of marketing strategies that will allow 1845 Steakhouse to easily target men and women within targeted market. These strategies include traditional print advertisements and discounts offered as a part of a grand opening campaign. Below is a description of how the business intends to market its services to the general public.

The Company also intends on hiring a local public relations firm that will promote reviews and articles about the restaurant, its steak and American cuisine, and relevant hours of operation and pricing. Mr. Austin will invite local food critics to 1845 Steakhouse in order to generate positive publicity about the restaurant.

The Company will maintain a sizable amount of print and traditional advertising methods within local the local market to promote the American cuisine products that the Company is selling. At the onset of operations, the Company will distribute an expansive number of coupons for lower priced fare within local circulars.

5.3 Pricing

Management anticipates that the business will generate approximately $35 per person for an entrée. If alcohol is served, Management expects that the total per person revenues generated for a meal will range from $45 to $55.

6.0 ORGANIZATIONAL PLAN AND PERSONNEL SUMMARY

6.1 Corporate Organization

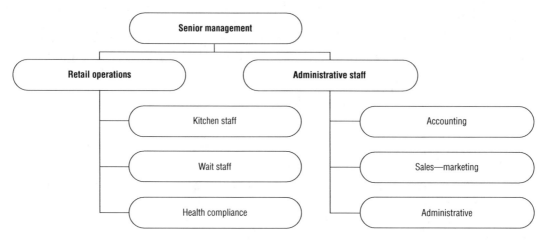

6.2 Organizational Budget

Personnel plan—yearly

Year	1	2	3
Owner	$ 40,000	$ 41,200	$ 42,436
Chefs	$105,000	$108,150	$111,395
Wait staff	$ 40,000	$ 41,200	$ 42,436
Busing staff	$ 25,000	$ 25,750	$ 26,523
Administrative	$ 20,000	$ 20,600	$ 21,218
Total	**$230,000**	**$236,900**	**$244,007**

Numbers of personnel

Owner	1	1	1
Chefs	3	3	3
Wait staff	4	4	4
Busing staff	2	2	2
Administrative	1	1	1
Totals	**11**	**11**	**11**

Personnel expense breakdown

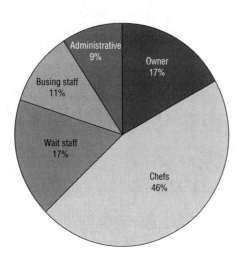

7.0 FINANCIAL PLAN

7.1 Underlying Assumptions

The Company has based its proforma financial statements on the following:

- 1845 Steakhouse will have an annual revenue growth rate of 10% per year.

- The Owner will acquire $175,000 of debt funds to develop the business.

- The loan will have a 10 year term with a 9% interest rate.

7.2 Sensitivity Analysis

In the event of an economic downturn, the business may have a decline in its revenues. However, 1845 Steakhouse will generate substantial gross margins from its food and beverage sales, and despite a decrease in top line income, the business will be able to remain profitable and cash flow positive.

7.3 Source of Funds

Financing

Equity contributions	
Management investment	$ 25,000.00
Total equity financing	**$ 25,000.00**
Banks and lenders	
Banks and lenders	$175,000.00
Total debt financing	**$175,000.00**
Total financing	**$200,000.00**

7.4 General Assumptions

General assumptions

Year	1	2	3
Short term interest rate	9.5%	9.5%	9.5%
Long term interest rate	10.0%	10.0%	10.0%
Federal tax rate	33.0%	33.0%	33.0%
State tax rate	5.0%	5.0%	5.0%
Personnel taxes	15.0%	15.0%	15.0%

7.5 Profit and Loss Statements

Proforma profit and loss (yearly)

Year	1	2	3
Sales	**$710,790**	**$781,869**	**$860,056**
Cost of goods sold	$240,198	$264,218	$290,640
Gross margin	66.21%	66.21%	66.21%
Operating income	**$470,592**	**$517,651**	**$569,416**
Expenses			
Payroll	$230,000	$236,900	$244,007
General and administrative	$ 9,000	$ 9,360	$ 9,734
Marketing expenses	$ 15,637	$ 17,201	$ 18,921
Professional fees and licensure	$ 5,000	$ 5,150	$ 5,305
Insurance costs	$ 15,000	$ 15,750	$ 16,538
Travel and vehicle costs	$ 7,500	$ 8,250	$ 9,075
Rent and utilities	$ 25,000	$ 26,250	$ 27,563
Miscellaneous costs	$ 2,275	$ 2,502	$ 2,752
Payroll taxes	$ 34,500	$ 35,535	$ 36,601
Total operating costs	**$343,912**	**$356,898**	**$370,495**
EBITDA	**$126,680**	**$160,753**	**$198,921**
Federal income tax	$ 41,804	$ 48,353	$ 61,331
State income tax	$ 6,334	$ 7,326	$ 9,293
Interest expense	$ 15,291	$ 14,230	$ 13,069
Depreciation expenses	$ 10,714	$ 10,714	$ 10,714
Net profit	**$ 52,536**	**$ 80,130**	**$104,514**
Profit margin	**7.39%**	**10.25%**	**12.15%**

Sales, operating costs, and profit forecast

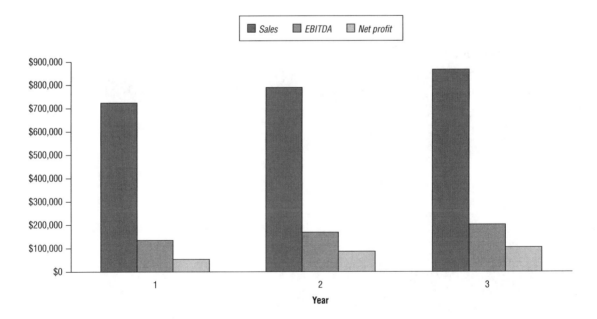

7.6 Cash Flow Analysis

Proforma cash flow analysis—yearly

Year	1	2	3
Cash from operations	$ 63,251	$90,844	$115,228
Cash from receivables	$ 0	$ 0	$ 0
Operating cash inflow	**$ 63,251**	**$90,844**	**$115,228**
Other cash inflows			
Equity investment	$ 25,000	$ 0	$ 0
Increased borrowings	$175,000	$ 0	$ 0
Sales of business assets	$ 0	$ 0	$ 0
A/P increases	$ 1,700	$ 1,955	$ 2,248
Total other cash inflows	**$201,700**	**$ 1,955**	**$ 2,248**
Total cash inflow	**$264,951**	**$92,799**	**$117,476**
Cash outflows			
Repayment of principal	$ 11,311	$12,372	$ 13,533
A/P decreases	$ 1,600	$ 1,920	$ 2,304
A/R increases	$ 0	$ 0	$ 0
Asset purchases	$150,000	$ 9,084	$ 11,523
Dividends	$ 44,275	$63,591	$ 80,660
Total cash outflows	**$207,186**	**$86,967**	**$108,019**
Net cash flow	**$ 57,764**	**$ 5,832**	**$ 9,457**
Cash balance	**$ 57,764**	**$63,596**	**$ 73,053**

Proforma cash flow (yearly)

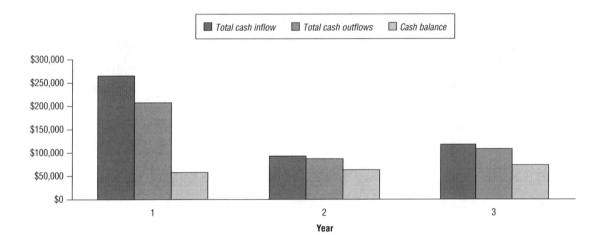

7.7 Balance Sheet

Proforma balance sheet—yearly

Year	1	2	3
Assets			
Cash	$ 57,764	$ 63,596	$ 73,053
Amortized expansion costs	$ 85,000	$ 85,908	$ 87,061
Kitchen equipment	$ 45,000	$ 51,813	$ 60,455
FF&E	$ 20,000	$ 21,363	$ 23,091
Accumulated depreciation	($ 10,714)	($ 21,429)	($ 32,143)
Total assets	**$197,050**	**$201,252**	**$211,518**
Liabilities and equity			
Accounts payable	$ 100	$ 135	$ 79
Long term liabilities	$163,689	$151,317	$138,945
Other liabilities	$ 0	$ 0	$ 0
Total liabilities	**$163,789**	**$151,452**	**$139,024**
Net worth	**$ 33,261**	**$ 49,800**	**$ 72,493**
Total liabilities and equity	**$197,050**	**$201,252**	**$211,518**

Proforma balance sheet

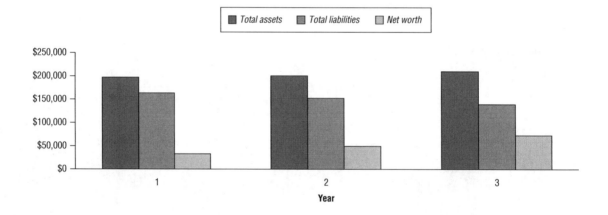

7.8 Breakeven Analysis

Monthly break even analysis

Year	1	2	3
Monthly revenue	$ 43,288	$ 44,922	$ 46,634
Yearly revenue	$519,450	$539,065	$559,602

Break even analysis

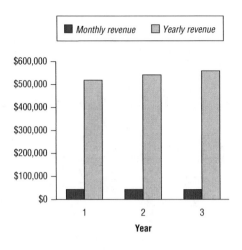

7.9 Business Ratios

Business ratios—yearly

Year	1	2	3
Sales			
Sales growth	00.00%	10.00%	10.00%
Gross margin	66.20%	66.20%	66.20%
Financials			
Profit margin	7.39%	10.25%	12.15%
Assets to liabilities	1.20	1.33	1.52
Equity to liabilities	0.20	0.33	0.52
Assets to equity	5.92	4.04	2.92
Liquidity			
Acid test	0.35	0.42	0.53
Cash to assets	0.29	0.32	0.35

7.10 Three Year Profit and Loss Statement

Profit and loss statement (first year)

Months	1	2	3	4	5	6	7
Sales	**$53,650**	**$54,665**	**$55,680**	**$56,695**	**$57,710**	**$58,725**	**$59,740**
Cost of goods sold	$18,130	$18,473	$18,816	$19,159	$19,502	$19,845	$20,188
Gross margin	66.2%	66.2%	66.2%	66.2%	66.2%	66.2%	66.2%
Operating income	**$35,520**	**$36,192**	**$36,864**	**$37,536**	**$38,208**	**$38,880**	**$39,552**
Expenses							
Payroll	$19,167	$19,167	$19,167	$19,167	$19,167	$19,167	$19,167
General and administrative	$ 750	$ 750	$ 750	$ 750	$ 750	$ 750	$ 750
Marketing expenses	$ 1,303	$ 1,303	$ 1,303	$ 1,303	$ 1,303	$ 1,303	$ 1,303
Professional fees and licensure	$ 417	$ 417	$ 417	$ 417	$ 417	$ 417	$ 417
Insurance costs	$ 1,250	$ 1,250	$ 1,250	$ 1,250	$ 1,250	$ 1,250	$ 1,250
Travel and vehicle costs	$ 625	$ 625	$ 625	$ 625	$ 625	$ 625	$ 625
Rent and utilities	$ 2,083	$ 2,083	$ 2,083	$ 2,083	$ 2,083	$ 2,083	$ 2,083
Miscellaneous costs	$ 190	$ 190	$ 190	$ 190	$ 190	$ 190	$ 190
Payroll taxes	$ 2,875	$ 2,875	$ 2,875	$ 2,875	$ 2,875	$ 2,875	$ 2,875
Total operating costs	**$28,659**	**$28,659**	**$28,659**	**$28,659**	**$28,659**	**$28,659**	**$28,659**
EBITDA	**$ 6,861**	**$ 7,533**	**$ 8,205**	**$ 8,877**	**$ 9,549**	**$10,221**	**$10,893**
Federal income tax	$ 3,155	$ 3,215	$ 3,275	$ 3,334	$ 3,394	$ 3,454	$ 3,514
State income tax	$ 478	$ 487	$ 496	$ 505	$ 514	$ 523	$ 532
Interest expense	$ 1,313	$ 1,306	$ 1,299	$ 1,292	$ 1,285	$ 1,278	$ 1,271
Depreciation expense	$ 893	$ 893	$ 893	$ 893	$ 893	$ 893	$ 893
Net profit	**$ 1,022**	**$ 1,632**	**$ 2,242**	**$ 2,852**	**$ 3,462**	**$ 4,073**	**$ 4,683**

Profit and loss statement (first year cont.)

Month	8	9	10	11	12	1
Sales	**$60,755**	**$61,770**	**$62,785**	**$63,800**	**$64,815**	**$710,790**
Cost of goods sold	$20,531	$20,874	$21,217	$21,560	$21,903	$240,198
Gross margin	66.2%	66.2%	66.2%	66.2%	66.2%	66.2%
Operating income	**$40,224**	**$40,896**	**$41,568**	**$42,240**	**$42,912**	**$470,592**
Expenses						
Payroll	$19,167	$19,167	$19,167	$19,167	$19,167	$230,000
General and administrative	$ 750	$ 750	$ 750	$ 750	$ 750	$ 9,000
Marketing expenses	$ 1,303	$ 1,303	$ 1,303	$ 1,303	$ 1,303	$ 15,637
Professional fees and licensure	$ 417	$ 417	$ 417	$ 417	$ 417	$ 5,000
Insurance costs	$ 1,250	$ 1,250	$ 1,250	$ 1,250	$ 1,250	$ 15,000
Travel and vehicle costs	$ 625	$ 625	$ 625	$ 625	$ 625	$ 7,500
Rent and utilities	$ 2,083	$ 2,083	$ 2,083	$ 2,083	$ 2,083	$ 25,000
Miscellaneous costs	$ 190	$ 190	$ 190	$ 190	$ 190	$ 2,275
Payroll taxes	$ 2,875	$ 2,875	$ 2,875	$ 2,875	$ 2,875	$ 34,500
Total operating costs	**$28,659**	**$28,659**	**$28,659**	**$28,659**	**$28,659**	**$343,912**
EBITDA	**$11,565**	**$12,237**	**$12,909**	**$13,581**	**$14,253**	**$126,680**
Federal income tax	$ 3,573	$ 3,633	$ 3,693	$ 3,752	$ 3,812	$ 41,804
State income tax	$ 541	$ 550	$ 559	$ 569	$ 578	$ 6,334
Interest expense	$ 1,264	$ 1,257	$ 1,250	$ 1,242	$ 1,235	$ 15,291
Depreciation expense	$ 893	$ 893	$ 893	$ 893	$ 893	$ 10,714
Net profit	**$ 5,293**	**$ 5,904**	**$ 6,514**	**$ 7,125**	**$ 7,735**	**$ 52,536**

Profit and loss statement (second year)

Quarter	Q1	2 Q2	Q3	Q4	2
Sales	$156,374	$195,467	$211,105	$218,923	$781,869
Cost of goods sold	$ 52,844	$ 66,054	$ 71,339	$ 73,981	$264,218
Gross margin	66.2%	66.2%	66.2%	66.2%	66.2%
Operating income	$103,530	$129,413	$139,766	$144,942	$517,651
Expenses					
Payroll	$ 47,380	$ 59,225	$ 63,963	$ 66,332	$236,900
General and administrative	$ 1,872	$ 2,340	$ 2,527	$ 2,621	$ 9,360
Marketing expenses	$ 3,440	$ 4,300	$ 4,644	$ 4,816	$ 17,201
Professional fees and licensure	$ 1,030	$ 1,288	$ 1,391	$ 1,442	$ 5,150
Insurance costs	$ 3,150	$ 3,938	$ 4,253	$ 4,410	$ 15,750
Travel and vehicle costs	$ 1,650	$ 2,063	$ 2,228	$ 2,310	$ 8,250
Rent and utilities	$ 5,250	$ 6,563	$ 7,088	$ 7,350	$ 26,250
Miscellaneous costs	$ 500	$ 625	$ 676	$ 701	$ 2,502
Payroll taxes	$ 7,107	$ 8,884	$ 9,594	$ 9,950	$ 35,535
Total operating costs	$ 71,380	$ 89,225	$ 96,362	$ 99,931	$356,898
EBITDA	$ 32,151	$ 40,188	$ 43,403	$ 45,011	$160,753
Federal income tax	$ 9,671	$ 12,088	$ 13,055	$ 13,539	$ 48,353
State income tax	$ 1,465	$ 1,832	$ 1,978	$ 2,051	$ 7,326
Interest expense	$ 3,661	$ 3,593	$ 3,524	$ 3,453	$ 14,230
Depreciation expense	$ 2,679	$ 2,679	$ 2,679	$ 2,679	$ 10,714
Net profit	$ 14,676	$ 19,997	$ 22,168	$ 23,290	$ 80,130

Profit and loss statement (third year)

Quarter	Q1	3 Q2	Q3	Q4	3
Sales	$172,011	$215,014	$232,215	$240,816	$860,056
Cost of goods sold	$ 58,128	$ 72,660	$ 78,473	$ 81,379	$290,640
Gross margin	66.2%	66.2%	66.2%	66.2%	66.2%
Operating income	$113,883	$142,354	$153,742	$159,437	$569,416
Expenses					
Payroll	$ 48,801	$ 61,002	$ 65,882	$ 68,322	$244,007
General and administrative	$ 1,947	$ 2,434	$ 2,628	$ 2,726	$ 9,734
Marketing expenses	$ 3,784	$ 4,730	$ 5,109	$ 5,298	$ 18,921
Professional fees and licensure	$ 1,061	$ 1,326	$ 1,432	$ 1,485	$ 5,305
Insurance costs	$ 3,308	$ 4,134	$ 4,465	$ 4,631	$ 16,538
Travel and vehicle costs	$ 1,815	$ 2,269	$ 2,450	$ 2,541	$ 9,075
Rent and utilities	$ 5,513	$ 6,891	$ 7,442	$ 7,718	$ 27,563
Miscellaneous costs	$ 550	$ 688	$ 743	$ 771	$ 2,752
Payroll taxes	$ 7,320	$ 9,150	$ 9,882	$ 10,248	$ 36,601
Total operating costs	$ 74,099	$ 92,624	$100,034	$103,739	$370,495
EBITDA	$ 39,784	$ 49,730	$ 53,709	$ 55,698	$198,921
Federal income tax	$ 12,266	$ 15,333	$ 16,559	$ 17,173	$ 61,331
State income tax	$ 1,859	$ 2,323	$ 2,509	$ 2,602	$ 9,293
Interest expense	$ 3,380	$ 3,306	$ 3,230	$ 3,153	$ 13,069
Depreciation expense	$ 2,679	$ 2,679	$ 2,679	$ 2,679	$ 10,714
Net profit	$ 19,601	$ 26,090	$ 28,731	$ 30,092	$104,514

7.11 Three Year Cash Flow Analysis

Cash flow analysis (first year)

Month	1	2	3	4	5	6	7	8
Cash from operations	$ 1,915	$ 2,525	$ 3,135	$ 3,745	$ 4,355	$ 4,965	$ 5,576	$ 6,186
Cash from receivables	$ 0	$ 0	$ 0	$ 0	$ 0	$ 0	$ 0	$ 0
Operating cash inflow	**$ 1,915**	**$ 2,525**	**$ 3,135**	**$ 3,745**	**$ 4,355**	**$ 4,965**	**$ 5,576**	**$ 6,186**
Other cash inflows								
Equity investment	$ 25,000	$ 0	$ 0	$ 0	$ 0	$ 0	$ 0	$ 0
Increased borrowings	$175,000	$ 0	$ 0	$ 0	$ 0	$ 0	$ 0	$ 0
Sales of business assets	$ 0	$ 0	$ 0	$ 0	$ 0	$ 0	$ 0	$ 0
A/P increases	$ 142	$ 142	$ 142	$ 142	$ 142	$ 142	$ 142	$ 142
Total other cash inflows	**$200,142**	**$ 142**	**$ 142**	**$ 142**	**$ 142**	**$ 142**	**$ 142**	**$ 142**
Total cash inflow	**$202,056**	**$ 2,666**	**$ 3,277**	**$ 3,887**	**$ 4,497**	**$ 5,107**	**$ 5,717**	**$ 6,328**
Cash outflows								
Repayment of principal	$ 904	$ 911	$ 918	$ 925	$ 932	$ 939	$ 946	$ 953
A/P decreases	$ 133	$ 133	$ 133	$ 133	$ 133	$ 133	$ 133	$ 133
A/R increases	$ 0	$ 0	$ 0	$ 0	$ 0	$ 0	$ 0	$ 0
Asset purchases	$150,000	$ 0	$ 0	$ 0	$ 0	$ 0	$ 0	$ 0
Dividends	$ 0	$ 0	$ 0	$ 0	$ 0	$ 0	$ 0	$ 0
Total cash outflows	**$151,038**	**$ 1,044**	**$ 1,051**	**$ 1,058**	**$ 1,065**	**$ 1,072**	**$ 1,079**	**$ 1,086**
Net cash flow	**$ 51,019**	**$ 1,622**	**$ 2,225**	**$ 2,828**	**$ 3,432**	**$ 4,035**	**$ 4,638**	**$ 5,242**
Cash balance	**$ 51,019**	**$52,641**	**$54,866**	**$57,694**	**$61,126**	**$65,161**	**$69,799**	**$75,041**

Cash flow analysis (first year cont.)

Month	9	10	11	12	1
Cash from operations	$ 6,796	$ 7,407	$ 8,017	$ 8,628	$ 63,251
Cash from receivables	$ 0	$ 0	$ 0	$ 0	$ 0
Operating cash inflow	**$ 6,796**	**$ 7,407**	**$ 8,017**	**$ 8,628**	**$ 63,251**
Other cash inflows					
Equity investment	$ 0	$ 0	$ 0	$ 0	$ 25,000
Increased borrowings	$ 0	$ 0	$ 0	$ 0	$175,000
Sales of business assets	$ 0	$ 0	$ 0	$ 0	$ 0
A/P increases	$ 142	$ 142	$ 142	$ 142	$ 1,700
Total other cash inflows	**$ 142**	**$ 142**	**$ 142**	**$ 142**	**$201,700**
Total cash inflow	**$ 6,938**	**$ 7,549**	**$ 8,159**	**$ 8,770**	**$264,951**
Cash Outflows					
Repayment of principal	$ 961	$ 967	$ 974	$ 982	$ 11,311
A/P decreases	$ 133	$ 133	$ 133	$ 133	$ 1,600
A/R increases	$ 0	$ 0	$ 0	$ 0	$ 0
Asset purchases	$ 0	$ 0	$ 0	$ 0	$150,000
Dividends	$ 0	$ 0	$ 0	$44,275	$ 44,275
Total cash outflows	**$ 1,094**	**$ 1,101**	**$ 1,108**	**$45,390**	**$207,186**
Net cash flow	**$ 5,844**	**$ 6,448**	**$ 7,051**	**−$36,620**	**$ 57,764**
Cash balance	**$80,885**	**$87,333**	**$94,384**	**$57,764**	**$ 57,764**

Cash flow analysis (second year)

		2			
Quarter	Q1	Q2	Q3	Q4	2
Cash from operations	$18,169	$22,711	$24,528	$25,436	$90,844
Cash from receivables	$ 0	$ 0	$ 0	$ 0	$ 0
Operating cash inflow	**$18,169**	**$22,711**	**$24,528**	**$25,436**	**$90,844**
Other cash inflows					
Equity investment	$ 0	$ 0	$ 0	$ 0	$ 0
Increased borrowings	$ 0	$ 0	$ 0	$ 0	$ 0
Sales of business assets	$ 0	$ 0	$ 0	$ 0	$ 0
A/P increases	$ 391	$ 489	$ 528	$ 547	$ 1,955
Total other cash inflows	**$ 391**	**$ 489**	**$ 528**	**$ 547**	**$ 1,955**
Total cash inflow	**$18,560**	**$23,200**	**$25,056**	**$25,984**	**$92,799**
Cash outflows					
Repayment of principal	$ 2,990	$ 3,058	$ 3,127	$ 3,198	$12,372
A/P decreases	$ 384	$ 480	$ 518	$ 538	$ 1,920
A/R increases	$ 0	$ 0	$ 0	$ 0	$ 0
Asset purchases	$ 1,817	$ 2,271	$ 2,453	$ 2,544	$ 9,084
Dividends	$12,718	$15,898	$17,170	$17,805	$63,591
Total cash outflows	**$17,909**	**$21,706**	**$23,268**	**$24,084**	**$86,967**
Net cash flow	**$ 651**	**$ 1,493**	**$ 1,788**	**$ 1,899**	**$ 5,832**
Cash balance	**$58,415**	**$59,909**	**$61,697**	**$63,596**	**$63,596**

Cash flow analysis (third year)

		3			
Quarter	Q1	Q2	Q3	Q4	3
Cash from operations	$23,046	$28,807	$31,112	$32,264	$115,228
Cash from receivables	$ 0	$ 0	$ 0	$ 0	$ 0
Operating cash inflow	**$23,046**	**$28,807**	**$31,112**	**$32,264**	**$115,228**
Other cash inflows					
Equity investment	$ 0	$ 0	$ 0	$ 0	$ 0
Increased borrowings	$ 0	$ 0	$ 0	$ 0	$ 0
Sales of business assets	$ 0	$ 0	$ 0	$ 0	$ 0
A/P increases	$ 450	$ 562	$ 607	$ 630	$ 2,248
Total other cash inflows	**$ 450**	**$ 562**	**$ 607**	**$ 630**	**$ 2,248**
Total cash inflow	**$23,495**	**$29,369**	**$31,719**	**$32,893**	**$117,476**
Cash outflows					
Repayment of principal	$ 3,270	$ 3,344	$ 3,420	$ 3,498	$ 13,533
A/P decreases	$ 461	$ 576	$ 622	$ 645	$ 2,304
A/R increases	$ 0	$ 0	$ 0	$ 0	$ 0
Asset purchases	$ 2,305	$ 2,881	$ 3,111	$ 3,226	$ 11,523
Dividends	$16,132	$20,165	$21,778	$22,585	$ 80,660
Total cash outflows	**$22,168**	**$26,966**	**$28,932**	**$29,954**	**$108,019**
Net cash flow	**$ 1,328**	**$ 2,403**	**$ 2,787**	**$ 2,939**	**$ 9,457**
Cash balance	**$64,924**	**$67,327**	**$70,114**	**$73,053**	**$ 73,053**

Teacher Continuing Education

The Institute for the Advancement of Teacher Education (IATE)

3456 Main St.
St. Louis, MO 63101

Sam Maguire, Mike Holthaus, Hannah Dust, and Christina Garcia

The Institute for the Advancement of Teacher Education, or IATE, is a school for teachers from preschool to high school. It will operate from governmental grants, public school board funding, and private donations. The main goal of the school is to provide continuing education and resources to educators that would enable them to reach students in the best way possible to achieve both personal and academic success. The school will stress teaching from an ethical point of view.

BUSINESS DESCRIPTION

Our business originated from an idea that surfaced after reflecting on several personal experiences. The first experience occurred at a local elementary school, where a teacher was overheard while disciplining his class in an incredibly inappropriate manner.

Another experience occurred while reading *Freakonomics* by Steven Levitt and Stephen Dubner. One of the chapters in the book focuses on education systems and standardized tests. Rather than focusing on the students, the book focuses on the teachers. The book explains a study where teachers were actually found cheating in various ways to improve their image as a teacher. It is known to inhabitants of St. Louis,

Missouri that when a school's overall performance dips below the acceptable standard, it is closed down. Our idea would help solve those problems as well. The final experience occurred in our first meeting in class. Professor Tang stated that Professor Goede's presence in class has greatly increased the productivity and experience for students. From this I realized that my idea could truly work.

From these experiences, our team developed an idea of a school for teachers from preschool to high school. This school would operate from governmental grants, public school board funding, and private donations. The main goal of the school would be to provide continuing education and resources to educators that would enable them to reach students in the best way possible to achieve both personal and academic success. The school would stress teaching from an ethical point of view, which would hopefully minimize "teacher cheating" as well as teach effective and proper forms of student discipline and encouragement. Also, the school would provide as a retreat for teachers, which could reduce teacher stress, as well as encourage networking, idea exchange, teaching methods, and general advisement from someone outside of the school's administration. Another idea that the school could participate in is providing small research grants to teachers to seek out new information; much like a college or university.

The school will create a requirement as well as a desire for teacher education. Through contractual obligations between the teachers and the school board, as well as offering performance-based incentives to teachers, the school will be a center for educational reform, which will lead to academic success in the St. Louis Public School System.

THE SERVICE

Our service is for the teachers in the St. Louis Public School System. Our intended impact is to create new and innovative forms of education, so as to improve the educational facilities of the St. Louis Public Schools. By providing teacher education, we will be able to increase the ability of our current teachers, as well as attract new people into the educational system, with hopes to decrease the cost of educating the average student. Teachers would be required to take 12 credit hours of class per year in classes that range from 2 credit hours to 4 credit hours. Each credit hour a class is worth would result in five hours of time in classroom, which results in 60 total hours per year for teachers to spend in our facility. Classes would be offered year round, allowing for summer, night, and weekend classes.

UNIQUE BENEFITS

The bonus system would act as a motivating force for teachers so that they improve their teaching styles, with a reward that would hopefully keep teachers in the system. Having a base of experienced teachers is critical to school reform. It aids the process of networking, which provides more opportunities for resources and idea exchange. Expanding the number of teachers with years of studying and research would increase the number of classes taught by highly qualified teachers. In St. Louis only 84% of teachers are highly qualified, which is 9.3% lower than the average in Missouri.

Award based incentives

G.P.A.	4.0	3.7	3.3	3.0	2.7	2.3	2.0
Award	$3,000	$2,500	$2,000	$1,500	$1,000	$750	$500

Every grade will consist of in class evaluations performed by IATE staff, where they will physically attend classes taught by IATE students within the school system. This, partnered with overall student performance evaluations such as Iowa Basics test scores will determine the award level.

UNIQUE LIMITATIONS

The main limitation with the IATE program is that it is the only program of its kind. Therefore we must prove that a program like IATE can truly be beneficial to a school system. Additionally, the teaching profession has been labeled a second rate job. This means that less qualified people are becoming teachers, and those that are teachers are not choosing to stay with the profession due to opportunities available outside of the education system. Teachers are tired of defending their career choice. In an article in *The Washington Post* Sarah Fine explains, "Schools need teachers like me. I just can't stay (Fine, 2009)." Fine explains that, especially in the era of Teach for America, many college graduates burn out after only a few years in the education system.

STAGE OF DEVELOPMENT

Currently, we are working on a feasible study in order to determine whether the Institute for the Advancement of Teacher Education (IATE) will be beneficial to society. It is our plan to conduct a case study using a reserved room at a university or public library and having certified educators volunteer their time to teach sample courses including ethics, teaching methods, and organizational leadership. It is our hope that we can conduct the case study using minimal funding by utilizing the above-mentioned bootstrapping methods.

LEGAL RESTRICTIONS

A number of legal restrictions and rights exist that we must abide by throughout our endeavors in establishing the Institute for the Advancement of Teacher Education.

- We must make certain that school boards are including mandatory attendance at our school when creating teacher contracts. The teachers must be aware of this requirement, so as not to have any legal disagreements.

- Because the school operates from governmental grants and public school funding, we must target the public school system and the teachers involved. At this point in our projects development, we are only targeting public school teachers. This avoids any conflict that private and parochial schools may add.

- While designing our plan, we must consider the aspect of teacher certification. It is crucial that we make certain the teachers are fully qualified to not only teach the students in the first place, but also to attend IATE. The teachers must earn a bachelor's degree in education from an accredited college. After earning this degree, graduates must apply to the state for a teaching certificate, and it is this certificate that qualifies them to teach in public schools. We will establish this requirement, as it will be the identical one for attending the IATE.

- We must be confident that the public schools and our program are abiding by the No Child Left Behind Act (NCLB). This Act was approved in 2002 and contains a number of requirements for public schools and education systems regarding student responsibilities, teacher qualifications, funding, accountability, special needs education, and other initiatives. Just as public schools must abide by this Act in order to receive federal government funding, so will the IATE and the members involved.

- It is necessary that the IATE abide by state legislation. Just as it is required that all schools provide a safe teaching environment for teachers and students (sanitary codes, fire drills, violence, transportation availability, etc.), the IATE will be compelled to abide by these regulations as well.

INSURANCE REQUIREMENTS

After speaking with an expert in the Chicago Public School System Tressie Dust, we found out that there are only certain liabilities that we must be aware of. There is no type of insurance available for purchase that would benefit us outside of property and on-site general liability. A legal expert would be hired to assist us in any sort of position where liability must be determined. As far as insurance for our employees, we assume that we would qualify to fall under the St. Louis School District insurance policy, reducing our costs.

TRENDS RELATED TO SERVICE

There are not many "current trends" in our industry, simply because our product is a new and innovative one. However, there are a number of trends relating to the current public school system that our program must abide by. According to the Missouri State Teachers Association (MSTA), both teachers with less than four years of experience and college graduates must maintain a four-year license in order to qualify for their career certificate. They are obligated to perform a number of requirements, some including completing a criminal background check, participating in a district mentoring program for a minimum of two years, and completing thirty contact hours of professional development; which may include hours in an appropriate college class. We have decided that attending the IATE would be a way for teachers to maintain this teaching certificate. As teachers are required to complete thirty contact hours of professional development, they could attend our school in order to attain the hours necessary. Furthermore, "student teaching" is a current trend that has been around for years, and is ultimately a college-supervised instructional experience for students who are not yet certified to teach. It gives aspiring teachers help and guidance in order for them to attain hands-on experience. Upon reflecting on our idea, we realized that it might be difficult to teach the teachers "how to teach" without having students involved. Therefore, we will incorporate the idea of "student teaching" into the IATE. One aspect of our business would be that the school provides coaching options, whereby people from the IATE are sent out to the elementary/high school to "coach" the teachers and help them develop professionally. Finally, in the IATE we will stick with the current trend of simply teaching professional development through curriculum (just like the classic learning system) and standard studies.

THE INDUSTRY AND MARKET

CURRENT INDUSTRY

There is not necessarily a current industry for a program like the Institute for the Advancement of Teacher Education. However, there are other programs that are working for improvement in the quality of teachers.

Current cost per student

St. Louis	$15,635.00
Missouri	$10,190.00
U.S.A.	$ 9,385.00

Teach for America
- The mission of Teach for America is to eliminate educational inequity by enlisting our nation's most promising future leaders in the effort.

President Obama's Success Through Education Program

- Teaching begins with recruitment efforts that restore prestige and financial incentives to education careers.

- Included are adequate entry-level salaries and service scholarships that cover high-quality teacher education programs.

- See "Current Industry" for further detail.

The Teacher Education Institute

- The goal is to improve student achievement through professional development.

- TEI offers mostly online courses, and does not allow for collaboration among teachers. Another program in the current industry is the Lawrence Hall of Science.

Lawrence Hall of Science.

- A dynamic center for teacher education, research, and curriculum development in kindergarten through twelfth grade.

- Simply focuses on science and math education.

Title II.

- A government grant program through the U.S. Department of Education, where the goal is to increase academic achievement by improving the teacher and principal quality.

- Title II works to hold the schools accountable for the improvements in student success.

These programs in the current industry are not competitors, but instead they are means to help start the IATE. For instance, the creators of Teach for America would be a great resource because they possess an understanding of why school reform is necessary in the United States. They could potentially be used as teachers at the IATE. Since Title II is a grant program working to increase the number of qualified teachers, it is possible that they would be willing to provide money for the IATE. Given Obama's "Success Through Education Plan," the IATE would be likely to receive government support. Overall, the Institute for the Advancement of Teacher Education has serious potential in the market. Given the current school systems in St. Louis City and the recognition of the need for change by the government, IATE is sure to be a successful program. There is a need for better teachers in today's society and the IATE is sure to provide that change.

CURRENT INDUSTRY IN ST. LOUIS

Currently, there is a great need for reform. Graduation rates, communication arts status, and mathematics status have not been met in the adequate yearly progress report. The only aspect of the progress report that had been met in 2009 was the attendance rate. Additionally, the certification status of teachers in St. Louis City is below the Missouri average. There are even portions of teachers that have expired certificates or no teaching certificate at all. Given a few of the tragic statistics of St. Louis City schools, it is apparent that there is a great need for better teachers.

Graduation rate

	2005	2006	2007	2008	2009
Missouri	86.0	85.8	86.3	85.8	85.0
St. Louis	60.2	55.7	55.8	52.9	45.7

Accreditation

MSIP Accreditation as of July 2009

St. Louis City School District is: Unaccredited

	Number of Missouri Districts		
Accredited	**Provisionally**	**Interim**	**Unaccredited**
512	8	1	2
(97.9%)	(1.5%)	(0.2%)	(0.4%)

Attendance

	2005	2006	2007	2008	2009
Missouri	94.6	94.8	94.7	94.8	95.1
St. Louis	89.0	88.7	88.7	88.6	90.3

Dropout rate

Missouri	**2005**	**2006**	**2007**	**2008**	**2009**
Total	**3.5**	**3.9**	**3.7**	**4.0**	**4.3**
Asian	1.5	1.9	2.4	2.1	2.2
Black	5.8	7.0	6.5	8.0	9.5
Hispanic	4.8	5.5	6.8	5.8	5.0
Indian	4.9	5.9	4.5	3.5	4.9
White	3.1	3.1	3.0	3.0	3.1
St. Louis					
Total	**13.0**	**18.7**	**12.1**	**23.9**	**27.5**
Asian	7.2	15.1	9.2	16.3	16.9
Black	13.3	17.9	12.6	24.1	28.4
Hispanic	11.6	25.6	8.2	33.4	19.0
Indian	7.4	13.8	7.1	7.4	0.0
White	12.5	23.5	9.7	21.8	24.5

MARKET POTENTIAL

It is our belief that there is great potential for the Institute for the Advancement of Teacher Education. Not only does the above data provide proof that there much needed reform for school in the city of St. Louis, but the entire country is currently working to reform the education system.

President Obama is currently working on The American Recovery and Reinvestment Act, which has a large focus on education. The White House website, explains what is included in the Act. This includes:

- $77 billion for reforms to strengthen elementary and secondary education, including $48.6 billion to stabilize state education budgets. The hope is that this will provide encouragement for states to reform.

- One hope is that American public schools will make improvements in teacher effectiveness and ensure that all schools have highly qualified teachers.

- This will also help schools to gather information to improve student learning and teacher performance.

The Act also provides around $5 billion in competitive funds to spur innovation and chart ambitious reform to close the achievement gap. Within the American Recovery and Reinvestment Act, President Obama and the U.S. Secretary of Education, Arne Duncan, created a "Race to The Top" competition, where states come up with reform plans for their education systems. The top states will compete for $4.35 billion in grants to support education reform and innovation in classrooms.

We believe that the IATE is an innovative idea that could receive funding through this act, or possibly be included in Missouri's Race to the Top Application. Missouri was not chosen in the first round. However, it is working on making changes to enter into the next round. Missouri's Race to the Top plan focuses on five reform initiatives. Specifically:

- Developing a model curriculum based on Common Core Standards.

- Developing a comprehensive education data system.

- Improving the preparation of teachers and school leaders.

- Measuring teacher/leader effects.

- Improving the efficiency and effectiveness of the Department of Education.

President Obama's Success Through Education Plan does focus on the necessity of reform for teachers. The White House website explains, "Teachers are the single most important resource to a child's education. President Obama will ensure that teachers are supported as professionals in the classroom, while also holding them more accountable. He will invest in innovative strategies to help teachers to improve student outcomes, and use rewards and incentives to keep talented teachers in the schools that need them the most. President Obama will invest in a national effort to prepare and reward outstanding teachers, while recruiting the best and brightest to the field of teaching. Additionally, he will challenge state school districts to remove ineffective teachers from the classroom."

Overall, there is great market potential because the Institute for the Advancement of Teacher Education is inventive, and has the potential to bring the state of Missouri money if there is proof of reform. This is a program that would do well because the City of St. Louis is practically demanding reform in the education areas.

COMPETITION

Potential competition for the IATE would include other means for teachers to be provided continued education and resources. These entail teacher workshops, seminars, tutorials, and discussion groups. As Missouri teachers are able to complete their thirty contact hours of professional development through spending time in an appropriate college class, these college classes would be our competition as well. Another form of competition would be beginning teacher assistance (BTA) programs. Even though hours spent in these programs do not count toward teachers' professional development hours, they would still be competition, as teachers may prefer to attend these programs instead of the IATE.

Other forms of competition include the Teacher Education Institute, which designs and delivers meticulous and intricate graduate-level professional development courses for K-12 classroom teachers and other opportunities for teachers to attain their professional development hours.

CUSTOMERS

When creating an educational resource such as ours, there are many people affected by our service. This makes it hard for us to identify our customer. However, we will be targeting teachers as our demographic, seeing as they will be the primary people involved in our institution. In order to enter the market, we will need to target our idea to politicians, primarily at a local and state level, seeing as in 2009 the St. Louis Public School system received 85.5% (St. Louis Public Schools, 2009) of its funding from those two levels of government. Due to the fact that boards run all public school systems, we must target the St. Louis Public School system board. These people set the policy that all schools within its district must follow; including teacher contracts, certification standards, and system wide goals. They also direct the budget as seen appropriate, once the politicians agree on a fiscal number.

After entering the market, our target demographic will be able to switch to our main goal, being faculty and teachers in the St. Louis public school system, which teaches grades K-12. The reason that we are focusing our attention to this particular demographic is because we noticed a trend in the St. Louis public school system of poor teacher/student performance. It would be near impossible to address the problem on a student basis, but to reach the students through the teachers at a ratio of 18 to 1 is a completely plausible idea.

Although not a target demographic for our organization, the individual taxpayer will be affected by our organization. We are hoping that the formation of our organization will result in lower costs per student in the education system that is in place in St. Louis. This will cause the taxpayers' dollars to be spent in an efficient manner, allowing for community improvements, or even lower tax rates down the road.

MARKET PENETRATION

In order to penetrate the market for our business we need to make organization known to the public; particularly the school districts. As of recent, we are trying to get in contact with the St. Louis City School Board to collaborate and brainstorm ideas on how to make our organization and vision known to the public. Solely based on a few statistics we are confident that our organization will gain community support.

FUTURE ACTION PLAN

We are planning our business endeavor by starting in small quantities, possibly with a focus school. Once we show improvement in student education through our method of teacher education, our project would gain support from within the school board as well as from local and possibly national politicians. Through bootstrapping, we plan on starting our first year by offering a limited number of classes in public libraries, school space, and other forms of donated space. These classes would focus on the core of our organizations mission.

BEGINNING CAPITAL

When beginning in an environment that is funded by tax dollars, it is pertinent that our organization runs by our bootstraps. For this reason, we plan on limiting the amount of new capital needed. We will do so by using the following capital that already exists. Note that this capital will be needed when we create the actual school, and not the test case.

- School building already owned by school district (Auditorium, gymnasium, and room for offices required.)

- Tables, desks, chairs, chalkboards and other room equipment already owned by school district.

- New computers and technology, similar to that available in the classrooms at local schools.

- Generic office supplies and furniture would be needed as well.

Seeing as though our facility will develop from an off-site based case study in a public location, more demands for start-up capital are sure to surface. Facilities for our business will need to be refurbished properly, so as to accommodate faculty, and hopefully provide a positive atmosphere for all of our patrons.

Sources of capital would be through financing from the school board, donations by leading members of the community, politicians, and educational charity organizations.

SOURCES OF CAPITAL

In our first year of operation (case study year), we would not need a large bankroll, due to our low expenses and donated time. For the sake of this feasibility report, we will recognize our first year of operation as our first year of actually having a facility that operates at full capacity.

Current Revenue for St. Louis School District

	Federal	State	Local
Percent	14.50	58.20	27.30
Cash	$2,473,622,877.66	$1,160,307,638.49	$616,280,613.85

As stated above, 85.5% of the financial resources available to the public school system are channeled through the state and local governments. The other 14.5% is given from federal sources. We believe that our organization will qualify for federal grants, which will serve as part of our financial base. Hopefully, due to the affect that our organization will have on a large population, we will qualify for a large grant. However, we feel as though local politicians and school board members in the St. Louis area will help direct funds towards our institution, due to the fact that the St. Louis school system is in such disrepair. Currently, there are already goals formed to improve the teacher's affect on students. The goal is to "ensure that every student is taught by a highly qualified teacher who holds certification in the area of his/her assignments and whose professional practices consistently demonstrate a high level of skill and proficiency".

The goal of our organization, as previously stated, is to reduce the average expenditure per student by at least 33%. This would lower St. Louis's expense per student to reach that of Missouri.

Delete	Current A.D.A.	# of students	Total cost
Current	15,635.55	26,108	$ 408,212,939.40
I.A.T.E.	10,475.45	26,108	$ 273,493,048.60
Total amount available after I.A.T.E. establishment			**$134,719,890.80**

Based on our research, there is tremendous inefficiency prevalent in the St. Louis Public School District. By having the Institute for the Advancement of Teacher Education, the St. Louis School district can hope to save close to $134,719,890.80 per year in the future. Although this cut in average cost per student would not be seen immediately, it would cut costs long-term and eventually pay for itself. For this reason we see no major problems in our future while asking the St. Louis Public School District for almost $10,000,000.00 in our first year and $4,000,000.00 per year after that. Through federal grants and financing, we would hope to attain near $5,000,000.00 initially, and near $1,500,000.00 per year after that.

INFORMATION NEEDED

Further information is needed to determine the best way to reach teachers effectively as well as their students. Support is needed from local universities, specifically in the liberal arts and psychological departments. We also must find the best manner to interact with the SLPS board, as well as key officials in the Missouri and U.S. Department of Education.

WRITING THE BUSINESS PLAN

Currently we are in the feasibility stage of this project. We have decided that our plan is feasible, so we can now begin writing our business plan.

SUPPORT NEEDED

It is obvious that our institution will not be able to begin or last without the support of our community. It is imperative that we quickly establish connections with local leaders in the academic and business world. Mixing the faculty of the public schools with professors who teach psychology, economics, entrepreneurship, philosophy, ethics, and other such fields will create new and exciting methods of teaching, while providing out of the norm resources for K-12 teachers. It is important to reach out to entrepreneurs as well, seeing as though they are continuously thinking of ways to improve the status quo. Without the participation of the school board, there would be almost no incentive to attend the school, unless if enough money could be raised as a private organization. Therefore, their support is completely needed. With that being said, the community and taxpayer support would be necessary as well. Without their help, IATE would be unable to convince local politicians to support our school with federal, state, and local tax dollars.

Tutoring Service

Stuart Tutoring

22111 Ardmore
Saint Clair Shores, MI 48081

Heidi Denler

Stuart Tutoring will offer tutoring services primarily for high school students, but also for select middle school students, in a wide range of academic subject. Kathy Stuart is the sole proprietor, but over the next two years, she plans to add staff and incorporate as an LLC.

COMPANY SUMMARY

Stuart Tutoring will offer tutoring services primarily for high school students, but also for select middle school students, in a wide range of academic subject. Kathy Stuart is the sole proprietor, but over the next two years, she plans to add staff and incorporate as an LLC. Stuart began tutoring when she was an education major at Wayne State University in Detroit, Michigan. As class sizes in the district where she teaches began to increase and teaching jobs became difficult to find, she decided to increase her income by tutoring students after school and on weekends. She expects to expand her services by offering tutoring over the summer months to keep students' minds engaged in the learning process.

MANAGEMENT SUMMARY

Kathy Stuart is certified to teach kindergarten through eighth grade in an inclusive classroom (all subjects are taught) and recently completed her M.Ed. She also received certification to teach English and social studies at the high school level. She has 12 years of experience teaching upper elementary school, four years teaching high school, and two years teaching community college classes. Stuart has been tutoring on an informal basis since she was in high school and volunteered her time as a member of National Honor Society to tutor fellow students in all subjects. She has also volunteered as a literacy instructor at a local church, teaching adults to read, and at the Tutoring Tree, working with elementary students. Stuart has created a home-based business, but wants to expand her services to include all subjects. To that end, she plans to add teaching colleagues in math and science to be able to offer full-service tutoring to students.

MISSION STATEMENT

Stuart Tutoring will help all students succeed academically by making connections between the subject(s) being studied and each student's interests and academic goals.

VISION STATEMENT

Kathy Stuart will work with teaching colleagues, as well school counselors and advisers to identify students who would benefit from being tutored by an experienced teacher.

VALUES STATEMENT

Kathy Stuart recognizes that academic success is critical for personal advancements in the early 21st century. She also recognizes that every student is capable of learning, and that one teacher's approach does not work for every student in a particular classroom. There are multiple routes to academic success, and Stuart Tutoring will find the best route for each individual.

BUSINESS PHILOSOPHY

Each student will learn how to approach and learn concepts that are challenging to them in a typical classroom setting. Kathy Stuart will use her connections with local educators and counselors to identify students in need of an individual approach to learning. Listening to each student to diagnose the breakdown in learning and developing a plan for academic success is the basic philosophy of Stuart Tutoring.

ORGANIZATION STRUCTURE

Stuart Tutoring will be run as a sole proprietorship for the first two to three years of operation. It is the formal organization of a small but effective tutoring service owner Kathy Stuart has been operating for five years. Stuart's plan is to add staff, hiring two or three colleagues with specialties in math and science who would eventually become partners in a limited liability company (LLC).

All tutors will be teachers certified in individual core subjects of English/language arts, social studies, math, and science. They will be "highly qualified" teachers who have proven their experience in their fields (certified as "highly qualified" under the No Child Left Behind Act), as well as having proven their ability to connect with students and help them learn. Every teacher who is hired as a tutor for Stuart Tutoring will have demonstrated their education philosophy to include a belief that every student can learn.

ADVERTISING AND PROMOTION

Initially, Stuart Tutoring will only advertise its tutoring services via paid ads in the high school newspaper. These ads will incur minimal costs and reach the target audience. The majority of tutoring clientele will be reached by way of recommendations of fellow teachers and counselors. Recommendations from colleagues and counselors will be the primary form of promotion, so Stuart will provide them with brochures and business cards to give to students that have been identifies as needing extra help in core subjects.

Testimonials from former students will be available for students, parents, counselors, and teachers to review. Past successes are a key form of promotion for tutoring. A reduced rate will be offered for the first session to encourage students to try tutoring and make sure that Stuart Tutoring's services will meet their expectations.

As the business grows and expands to offer services to students in neighboring school districts, Stuart plans to advertise in those school newspapers. After opening at least one storefront location, ads will be placed in local, weekly newspapers.

CUSTOMER BASE

The target market for Stuart Tutoring will be high school students who are having difficulty keeping pace with class progress. In addition, Stuart Tutoring will provide a place for students who want to make the most of their learning experience and gain an edge for college admissions. Stuart will offer preparation sessions for all manner of standardized testing geared to every level of learner, as well as sessions in basic study skills and organization. She recognizes the importance of ongoing networking with teachers and counselors not only at the local high school, but also a the middle schools, where 8 th grade students in need of extra help and encouragement as they prepare to enter high school can also be identified as potential tutoring clients.

Kathy Stuart recognizes the importance of working with parents of students to encourage not only studying, but also good study habits that will serve every student for years to come. She has maintained an open door policy for parents over the years she has tutored and will continue that policy as she formalizes her tutoring services.

PRODUCTS AND SERVICES

Stuart Tutoring will offer long-term tutoring primarily for high school students in the core subject areas of:

- English/language arts, including literature, creative writing, non-fiction writing, and journalism

- Social studies, including history, geography, and economics

- Math, including algebra, geometry, pre-calculus, calculus, trigonometry, and statistics

- Science, including biology, chemistry, and physics

In addition, short-term sessions will be offered on a rotating basis throughout the year for:

- Test preparation, including how to answer multiple choice, short answer, and essay questions, as well as how to get through the maze of standardized testing for state tests and college admissions testing

- Effective study habits

- Organization for academic success

Homework help will always be part of the program, but ensuring complete understanding of basic concepts required to complete that homework will be a primary goal of Stuart Tutoring.

In the late winter and early spring, group sessions will be offered to review for advanced placement (AP) testing that takes place in spring for college credits to be earned for classes taken in high school.

Hours of operation will be from 4:30 PM to 9:30 PM Monday through Thursday and 9 AM to 4 PM Saturday.

Prices will be competitive for individual tutoring at $25 an hour, as well as for short-term sessions at between $50 and $150 per two-to-three meeting session.

PERSONNEL REQUIREMENTS

As founder, Kathy Stuart will be the primary tutor for immediate clients of Stuart Tutoring. She will hire additional teachers as the client list grows and as students, parents, and counselors indicate a need for additional subjects to be included, such as foreign languages and technology.

LOCATION

Stuart Tutoring will begin operations the way Kathy Stuart has been tutoring for years—in her home or at the students' homes. She will rent space at a neighborhood facility or church for group sessions. Within six months, she plans to find a storefront near the school that she can rent or purchase as a permanent facility so students can come to Stuart Tutoring and work with qualified educators in more than one subject.

STORE DESIGN AND EQUIPMENT

Making the change from operating a home-based business to having a stand-alone storefront facility, Stuart will organize the floor plan to include:

- An office for herself to keep accounting and legal records with a desk and chair, bookshelves, and filing cabinet

- An office to be shared by other tutors that will have two or three desks with chairs, a filing cabinet, a work table and chairs, copy machine, printer for tutors to use with their laptops to allow printing of individualized teaching aids for each student

- A large conference room with a table and chairs for 12 students that will also have a white board and computer link

- Double study carrels for one-on-one tutoring in specific subjects for private lessons

- Bookshelves for textbooks purchased from the local school district and study aids

- A small break room with a refrigerator, microwave, sink and counter space where tutors can eat a quick snack and relax between tutoring sessions

- A unisex bathroom

FINANCIAL

Start-up costs for the first six months will be minimal because Stuart is formalizing her current tutoring operations. Moving into the storefront, she will incur costs of furnishing the space with desks and chairs, a conference table and chairs, work table and chairs, filing cabinets, white board, Wi-Fi Internet access, printers, a copy machine, textbooks, refrigerator, and microwave. In addition, Stuart will incur costs for the following items:

- Office supplies (paper, staplers, paper clips, pencils, pens, pocket folders)

- School supplies (notebook paper, pencils, pens)

- Kitchen supplies (paper toweling, hand soap, dish soap, paper plates, plasticware, paper cups)

- Bathroom supplies (toilet paper, soap, paper toweling, cleaning supplies).

Stuart will also purchase computer software as needed to assist students, property and casualty insurance, and an alarm system. Other costs will include security deposits, fees for registering the name of the service with state and local authorities and necessary licensing, and typical overhead costs for rent, utilities, taxes, and legal and accounting fees.

PROFESSIONAL AND ADVISORY SUPPORT

Stuart Tutoring will work with the state board of education to ensure compliance with all laws that relate to tutoring. While legal counsel is not expected to be an ongoing expense, Stuart will hire an attorney to handle the initial start-up requirements and all lease arrangements. She will hire a CPA to handle taxes, payroll, and other business financial matters.

Stuart is working with the local Fifth Third Bank branch for a line of credit to cover major start-up costs for opening her storefront facility. Other costs will be covered by her savings accounts. She expects to show a strong profit margin immediately.

BUSINESS AND GROWTH STRATEGY

Stuart plans to build her tutoring business slowly in order to conserve financial reserves and not overextend her line of credit. The community at large is heavily invested in the education of their children, and she expects to be able to develop her clientele steadily, adding teachers as tutors as the company grows.

As business increases, Stuart plans to retire from teaching in schools and run Stuart Tutoring full-time. She will add online tutoring, using web cam technology, and homework help. She will also add sessions to address the increasing need for elementary students who are struggling to overcome reading challenges, such as dyslexia, which can impede learning.

To that end, she will hire a information technology assistant part-time to maintain the company Web site and reading specialists.

COMPETITION

Many high school and college students tutor fellow classmates and those younger than they are, but they do not have the educational background and experience that Stuart has. There is a local outlet of the nationally-syndicated Sylvan Learning Center and a local storefront tutoring service, run by a former administrator of a nearby school district. Several college students offer tutoring on a limited basis, much the way Stuart started tutoring.

However, Stuart's experience as a highly qualified teacher and as a tutor since her high school days, combined with her connections to the local school district give her a competitive edge for attracting students and helping them become successful academically.

WEB SITE

Kathy Stuart is working with the computer and technology teachers at the local high school, who have identified students who will earn extra credit by creating an informational Web site about Stuart Tutoring. Contact information, hours, and testimonials will be available, along with credentials of the tutoring staff. As business increases, Stuart will add online, face-to-face tutoring and homework help.

CONCLUSION

High school students who are need help conquering the challenges of one or more classes or who simply want to enrich classroom learning to be more competitive for college admissions and testing will be treated equally. All staff will recognize that every student can learn, and that sometimes a different approach is required to allow understanding of a subject or process. Study skills and organization are equally important to academic success and, having been recognized as such, will be addressed as needed for each student. The bottom line is that every student at Stuart Tutoring will empowered for future learning and success.

Minimal monthly overhead costs beyond rent, utilities, and a small payroll ensure that Stuart Tutoring will be profitable immediately. Kathy Stuart's financial goal is to have all start-up costs incurred to outfit the storefront paid within two years.

Stuart Tutoring promises to be a win-win situation for Stuart and for the students she helps.

Used Furniture Business

Furniture xCHANGE

2135 17th Ave.
Dekalb, IL 61005

Paul Greenland

Furniture xCHANGE provides college students, apartment dwellers, non-profit organizations, and businesses with functional used furniture at the very best prices.

EXECUTIVE SUMMARY

Business Overview

During the early 2010s, difficult economic conditions were affecting everyone. Cash-strapped consumers faced layoffs, reduced hours, and unemployment. Many businesses were streamlining their operations or closing their doors. Nonprofit organizations were forced to contend with increased demand for their services, coupled with fewer resources. Amidst these conditions, saving money was more important than ever before.

Headquartered in Dekalb, Illinois, Furniture xCHANGE provides college students, apartment dwellers, non-profit organizations, and businesses with functional used furniture at the very best prices. Our business model is simple: we acquire "gently used" furniture (from garage sales, flea markets, estate sales, auctions, distressed businesses, and similar sources), make minimal repairs and touch-ups required to maximize resale value, and sell it for profit.

Based on feedback from industry players in other markets, turning over inventory quickly (e.g., every 90 days) is essential for success in the used furniture business. One business owner reported that storage of one executive desk costs $50 per month in floor space, for example. For this reason, our business will concentrate on moving furniture in and out of our warehouse as quickly as possible.

Furniture xCHANGE is owned by husband-and-wife team Mark and Carly Costello. A carpenter who has worked mainly in the commercial sector, Mark has been out of work for extended periods of time during the recent economic downturn. Mechanically inclined, he is skilled at repairing things and training others to do so (he has excellent supervisory and teaching skills). Carly works as a part-time bookkeeper for a local manufacturing company, and has time to handle the administrative tasks associated with the new business.

MARKET ANALYSIS

Furniture xCHANGE is based in Dekalb, Illinois, which is located in close geographic proximity to both Rockford, Illinois, and the greater Chicago area. Our new business will serve two specific markets:

1. College students and apartment dwellers in need of decent, basic furniture for their dwellings.

2. Small and mid-sized businesses (especially new startups) and/or non-profit organizations in need of affordable office furniture.

College Students and Apartment Dwellers

There are a large number of colleges and universities in our market area, including:

Community Colleges
- Richard J. Daley College
- College of DuPage
- Elgin Community College
- Harper College
- Joliet Junior College
- Kennedy–King College
- College of Lake County
- MacCormac College
- Malcolm X College
- McHenry County College
- Moraine Valley Community College
- Morton College
- Oakton Community College
- Olive–Harvey College
- Prairie State College
- South Suburban College
- Triton College
- Harry S Truman College
- Harold Washington College
- Waubonsee Community College
- Wilbur Wright College

Four-year Colleges
- Calumet College of St. Joseph
- Carthage College
- Columbia College Chicago
- Elmhurst College
- Harrington College of Design
- Hebrew Theological College
- Illinois Institute of Art—Chicago
- Kendall College
- Lake Forest College

- Lexington College
- Moody Bible Institute
- North Central College
- St. Augustine College
- Saint Joseph's College
- School of the Art Institute of Chicago
- Shimer College
- Telshe Yeshiva
- Trinity Christian College
- VanderCook College of Music
- Westwood College
- Wheaton College

Universities
- Aurora University
- Benedictine University
- Chicago State University
- Concordia University Chicago
- DePaul University
- Dominican University
- East–West University
- Governors State University
- Illinois Institute of Technology
- Indiana University Northwest
- Judson University
- Lewis University
- Loyola University Chicago
- Midwestern University
- National–Louis University
- North Park University
- Northeastern Illinois University
- Northern Illinois University
- Northwestern University
- Purdue University Calumet
- Purdue University North Central
- Robert Morris University
- Roosevelt University

- Rush University

- University of St. Francis

- University of Saint Mary of the Lake

- Saint Xavier University

- Trinity International University

- University of Chicago

- University of Illinois at Chicago

- University of Wisconsin—Parkside

- Valparaiso University

In 2009 there were 47,053 housing units within a 15-mile radius of our business, 482,888 units within a 30-mile radius, and 3.83 million units within a 60-mile radius (which includes the city of Chicago). Within these radii, renter-occupied housing totaled 33.7 percent, 18.8 percent, and 25.6 percent, respectively.

Small and Mid-sized Businesses

According to data from Cityscape Research Associates LLC, there are more than 350,000 businesses in our market, employing more than 4.9 million people. By size, the majority of the businesses within our market are small or mid-sized:

- 1-4 Employees (58.2%)

- 5-9 Employees (19.0%)

- 10-19 Employees (10.8%)

- 20-49 Employees (7.0%)

- 50-99 Employees (2.8%)

- 100-249 Employees (1.6%)

- 250-499 Employees (0.4%)

- 500-999 Employees (0.1%)

- 1,000+ Employees (0.1%)

Competition

Furniture xCHANGE will face competition from new furniture stores, used furniture stores, charitable organizations such as Goodwill and Salvation Army, flea markets, and individual sellers. Our total market area (including the city of Chicago) includes 1,959 furniture stores (2.9% of all establishments). However, this figure includes establishments selling new furniture.

Our key market differential will be our "truckload sale" model of bringing affordable furniture to strategic locations near college campuses at key times (e.g., namely at the beginning of the school year). For business furniture, we will develop a reputation for being "first in line" when organizations liquidate furniture. This will allow us to offer a consistent supply, and the greatest selection, of used office furniture to our customers.

INDUSTRY ANALYSIS

The production and sale of furniture is a $12 billion industry, according to a recent analysis performed by George Sparkman & Associates. Furniture xCHANGE is part of the used merchandise stores industry, which includes 20,000 stores and generates annual revenues of approximately $8 billion.

The used furniture segment of the used merchandise stores industry accounts for approximately 10 percent of annual sales.

PERSONNEL

Furniture xCHANGE will begin operations with the following employed staff:

- Mark Costello (full-time, owner)
- Carly Costello (part-time, administrative)
- Roger Hendrix (full-time, repair/refinishing)
- Henry Parks (full-time, acquisitions/deliveries)
- Len Cambry (part-time, acquisitions/deliveries)

We will hire student workers on a contract/as-needed basis to help with college-related tent sales/ acquisition events, allowing us to quickly scale our labor up or down as needed.

Professional & Advisory Support

Furniture xCHANGE will rely upon Illinois Financial Services LLC for tax assistance. Legal counsel will be received from Maryann Skinner, an independent attorney. Finally, our business has established both checking and merchant accounts with Dekalb Community Bank.

BUSINESS STRATEGY

An important component of our business strategy will involve the placement of large tents in strategic locations near college campuses and apartment complexes at key times (especially in August, when students are moving into new housing for a new school year). We will promote our availability via flyers sent to college admission offices (with hopes that they include the information in student correspondence regarding housing arrangements), and to the owners of private apartment complexes.

Following the same approach used by college bookstores, we will offer to repurchase furniture (at a significant discount) from students in the spring, as they exit housing. Essentially, we will do them a favor by taking structurally sound furniture off of their hands. We will follow a similar approach with the general public, offering a free haul-away service (usually in one or two business days) for individuals who, instead of attempting to sell their old furniture, simply want it off of their hands. After acquiring this furniture for free, or at a minimal cost, we will then make any necessary repairs, and prepare the furniture for resale.

In regard to office furniture, our strategy will place a heavy emphasis upon being "first in line" when organizations decided to liquidate furniture (for bankruptcy or other reasons). This will involve monitoring bankruptcy notices in newspapers throughout our market area, and periodic promotional mailings to law firms that handle bankruptcy cases, among other approaches.

SERVICES

Our business will provide the following types of furniture for the college/apartment markets:

- Bed Frames
- Bookshelves

- Side Tables

- Dining Tables

- Chest of Drawers

- Chairs

- Sofas

We will provide some or all of the following types of office furniture:

- Bookcases

- Carts

- Chairs (Swivel, Desk, Ergonomic, Folding)

- Chair Mats

- Coat Racks

- Computer Armoires & Cabinets

- Computer Carts & Stands

- Computer Desks

- Conference Tables

- Desks

- Display Cases

- Drafting Furniture

- Filing Cabinets

- Lecterns

- Literature Racks

- Mailroom Furniture

- Office Panels

- Reception Desks

- Reception Seating

- Roll Top Desks

- Waste Receptacles

MARKETING & SALES

Furniture xCHANGE has developed a marketing plan that involves the following tactics:

- Word-of-mouth marketing within the college campus and business communities.

- Printed fliers promoting our truckload sale and acquisition events, which will be distributed via college housing offices, and through the help of temporary student employees on a flat-fee basis.

- Direct mailings to newly established businesses (which have applied for permits from area county clerk offices).

- A Yellow Page advertisement.

- Print and online classified ads promoting our free furniture pick-up and haul-away service.

- Membership in the local chamber of commerce.

- A Web site with complete details about our business, including the services we offer and the types of furniture we have for sale.

- Vehicle graphics promoting our brand and Web site.

OPERATIONS

Facility & Location

Furniture xCHANGE has made arrangements to lease a 12,000-square-foot section of a 48,000-square-foot warehouse in Dekalb. The facility, formerly home to an agricultural supply company that declared bankruptcy, has been vacant for some time, and has been a burden for the owner to insure. For this reason, we were able to negotiate a very competitive three-year lease. The warehouse owner has agreed to lease the space to us at a steep discount for the first year ($17,500). We will have an option to renew our lease after one year for $34,200 annually ($2.85 per square foot). Benefiting us is the fact that the entire facility is vacant, providing opportunity for us to expand our operations. In addition, the facility is equipped with storage racks that are suitable for our purposes.

Significant thought has been devoted to the layout of our operations. Used furniture will be received through a garage door at the front of the facility, were space has been dedicated for furniture intake and assessment. An adjacent space will be used for furniture repair. This area is further subdivided for the repair of wood furniture, metal furniture, and reupholstering. Finally, the remainder of the space will be used for furniture storage. At the rear of the facility, there is a dedicated area for loading furniture onto trucks, as well as a second garage door for moving refurbished furniture out of the facility.

A detailed floor plan of our warehouse is available upon request.

Vehicles

Our business has negotiated for the purchase of a used, 17-foot diesel box truck (135,016 miles) from a local U-Haul dealer at a cost of $3,996. Complete maintenance records are available for the vehicle, and it has been well maintained. Based on the growth of our business, a second 14-foot or 17-foot diesel box truck will be purchased during our second year of operations. For large truckload sales, when we need to transport large volumes of furniture, we will rent a 26-foot U-Haul from the same dealer.

Miscellaneous

Furniture xCHANGE will rent large tents from a local rental firm when hosting truckload sales at various locations throughout our market area. Tent sizes and rates will vary, depending on location.

FINANCIAL ANALYSIS

Financial Projections

Based on conversations with several used office furniture dealers in other markets, and experience hosting several independent truckload sales prior to establishing this business, we estimate Furniture xCHANGE's gross sales will total $185,000 during the first year. Assuming our business model is successful, we anticipate annual growth of at least 15 percent during our second and third years. Detailed projections are available on request.

Startup Expenses

Furniture xCHANGE will incur start-up costs of $16,500, in order to procure the following:

Vehicles

- Used 17-foot truck

Safety Supplies

- Rubber Gloves
- Earplugs
- Safety Goggles
- Safety Glasses
- Shop Aprons

Hardware & Fasteners (assorted pieces)

Hand Tools

- Hammers
- Tape Measures
- Clamps (Bar, Band, C)
- Screwdrivers
- Rafter Squares
- Angle Irons
- Scratch Awls
- Nail Sets
- Pliers
- Pry Bars

Power Tools

- Power Drills
- Air Compressors
- Finishing Nailers
- Belt Sanders
- Finishing Sanders
- Biscuit Joiner
- Router/Router Table
- Tablesaw
- Drill Press
- Bandsaw
- Circular Saw

Refinishing/Touch-up Supplies

- Drop Cloths
- Rags/Shop Towels
- Touch Up Markers

- Touch Up Pen
- Touch Up Brushes
- Dry Powder
- Soft Wax Filler
- Retouch Crayons
- Paste Wax
- Cotton Rags
- Cheese Cloth Wipes
- Wood Polishes
- Burnishing Cream
- Metal Polish
- Shellac
- Oil Finishes
- Varnishes
- Wood Glue
- Steel Wool Pads & Rolls
- Sandpaper
- Hand Brush
- Wood Putty
- Wood Dye
- Silicone Molding Putty
- Frame Filler
- Turpentine
- Furniture Wax
- Lubricating Wax
- Metal Polish
- Metal Polishing Mitts
- Iron Paste
- Rust Remover
- Universal Tints
- Metal Acid Dye

To cover these expenses, and provide funds for continuing operations, the owners will provide $25,000 from their personal savings and retirement. In addition, they are seeking a business loan in the amount of $50,000.

Virtual Assistance

AdminiStar Services

14201 Gnarled Tree Lane
Smithfield Ridge, TX 75217

Paul Greenland

AdminiStar Services provides administrative assistance to businesses and individual professionals on an independent contract basis. Services are provided on retainer, as well as on a pay-as-you-go and per-project basis. Our business serves clients in our local market of Dallas, Texas, and also in other states.

EXECUTIVE SUMMARY

Business Overview

Difficult economic conditions have resulted in layoffs and downsizing at businesses and organizations of all sizes and types. This has been especially true at smaller and mid–sized businesses. Although workforce reductions can produce cost savings, the resulting understaffing means that everyone's plate gets a little fuller. When workloads are excessively high, organizations can experience a number of problems, including mistakes, absenteeism, poor morale, and missed deadlines. When quality suffers, so do an organization's performance and reputation.

AdminiStar Services provides administrative and secretarial assistance to businesses and individual professionals on an independent contract basis. Services are provided on retainer, as well as on a pay-as-you-go or per-project basis. Simply put, we handle executive and administrative tasks for companies (especially small and mid-sized operations) as needed, allowing them to dedicate more of their resources toward what they do best. In addition, we allow companies to reduce or minimize their investment in office equipment and space.

AdminiStar Services is a sole proprietorship owned by Janet Stewart. After a 20-year career in the corporate world, where her experience included working as a senior administrative assistant for a large consumer products company, Janet decided to take her advanced skills and abilities to the marketplace and work for herself, enjoying greater flexibility, and providing her with better life balance.

MARKET ANALYSIS

Our virtual assistance business will serve clients in any state; we will not limit operations to our local market. We will concentrate on marketing our services to small businesses (especially those with less than 10 employees) that may not employ full-time administrative support personnel. According to an article in the September 23, 2010, issue of *The Huffington Post*, the United States is home to approximately 27 million small businesses.

According to ALISR Research, within our local market alone (Dallas, Texas), there were 62,600 businesses with fewer than nine employees in 2009. Specifically, there were 49,447 establishments with 1 to 4 employees, accounting for 64.8 percent of all establishments. In addition, establishments with 5 to 9 employees numbered 13,157 (17.2% of all establishments).

INDUSTRY

In 2008 the Virtual Assistance Chamber of Commerce provided valuable insight into the industry when it published a survey based on responses from approximately 600 individuals. According to the survey, more than 90 percent of respondents indicated that their virtual assistance business had an administrative focus.

The virtual assistance industry is dominated by women, according to the chamber's survey. In terms of age, the largest percentage of respondents (36.68%) were between the ages of 40 and 49, followed by those aged 30 to 39 (28.23%), and those in the 50 to 59 age group (22.43%). In terms of education, the survey found that many virtual assistants (34.4% of respondents) have at least some college education. Some 22.4 percent of respondents reported having a four-year college degree, while 16.8 percent had a two-year degree.

Most virtual assistants (96.25% of respondents) work from a home office, according to the chamber survey. In terms of structure, the majority of businesses are sole proprietorships (72.92%), while 18.23 percent are limited liability companies, 2.95 percent are S-corporations, and 2.41 percent are traditional corporations. When asked how many clients they have, 14.64 percent of respondents reported having four clients, followed by two clients (14.36%), three clients (13.81%), five clients (9.94%), one client (9.12%), more than 11 (5.25%), and six clients (4.70%). Finally, the most common base hourly rate range for virtual assistants was $30-$39 (31.53%), followed by $40-$49 (20.74%), $50-$59 (16.48%), and $20-$29 (13.35%).

According to data from the U.S. Bureau of Labor Statistics' *Occupational Outlook Handbook, 2010-11 Edition*, 4.35 million secretaries and administrative assistants were employed in 2008. This number was projected to increase 11 percent by 2018, when projected employment would total 4.82 million workers. According to the bureau, secretaries earned median annual wages of $29,050 in mid-2008. Those in the lowest 10 percent earned $18,440, while those in the highest 10 percent enjoyed annual salaries exceeding $43,240.

Some within the virtual assistance industry specialize in a particular type of administrative assistant work (e.g., legal, medical, executive, etc.). A wide range of associations exist for particular administrative specialties, and most offer different types of certifications or designations (e.g., Certified Professional Secretary, Certified Administrative Professional, Accredited Legal Secretary, Certified Legal Secretary Specialist, etc.). Just as different industry sub-specialties are served by specific professional organizations, the virtual assistance industry is served by industry associations. These include the Virtual Assistance Chamber of Commerce and the International Virtual Assistants Association.

PERSONNEL

Janet Stewart is the sole employee of AdminiStar Services. After a 20-year career in the corporate world (résumé available upon request), where her experience included working as a senior administrative assistant for a large consumer products company, Janet decided to take her advanced skills and abilities to the marketplace and work for herself, enjoying greater flexibility, and providing her with better life balance.

Although Janet has no intention of hiring additional staff (at least initially), she has developed a solid network of reliable resources that can be of use to her clients. These include graphic designers, mail houses, freelance writers and editors, Web designers/programmers, video editors, advertising agencies, and printers/copy shops. When needed, AdminiStar Services will either connect the appropriate vendors with her clients or subcontract services that it cannot provide directly.

AdminiStar Services has established a business banking account with Hollingsworth Credit Union, as well as a merchant account for accepting credit card payments. If needed, legal counsel will be provided by the firm of Mayer & Holland. Finally, accounting and tax services will be provided by Greater Dallas Financial Associates Inc.

GROWTH STRATEGY

AdminiStar Services is fortunate to begin operations with one client, CGM Amber-Helton Inc., a start-up manufacturer of high-performance sporting goods for women. CGM Amber-Helton has agreed to a one-year contract with AdminiStar Services for 12 hours of weekly billable services (the equivalent of 1.5 workdays). Based on Janet Stewart's familiarity with CGM Amber-Helton's business plan and discussions with the owner, it is highly likely that additional service hours will be required after the first year.

Moving forward, AdminiStar Services plans to grow at a steady, measured pace. Janet will attempt to secure clients who are willing to agree to retainer arrangements. This will allow her to better protect her billings and schedule. However, she may need to take on a larger pool of clients whose needs are variable (e.g., pay-as-you-go) or variable/project-based.

Following are three-year billable hour projections for AdminiStar Services:

2010	2011	2012
1,225	1,715	2,205

These projections are based on 25 hours of weekly billable hours during the first year, 35 hours of billable time during the second year, and 45 hours during the third year. Factoring in holidays and vacation time, billings are based on 49 work weeks per year. Unless a decision is made to add additional staff, the business will be at maximum capacity during its third year, considering that Janet will need to devote between five and 10 hours per week to non-billable work (e.g., invoicing, marketing, and administrative tasks).

SERVICES

Our services, which focus more on high-level administrative support and less on basic clerical tasks, include:

- Scheduling appointments and meetings
- Setting up Web meetings/conferences
- Coordinating document duplication and delivery
- Database management
- Presentation development
- Business-related correspondence (e.g., letters, memos, etc.)
- Proofreading/editing

- Simple financial statements

- Writing reports

- Producing news releases

- Making travel arrangements

- Invoice management

- Web site content management

- Social media assistance (e.g., updating blogs based on pre-defined guidelines, monitoring Facebook postings, etc.)

- Ordering supplies

- Research (e.g., sales leads, vendors, etc.)

- Special projects

Examples of the businesses that we will concentrate on providing services to include:

- Retail startups

- Consumer product startups

- Entrepreneurs

- Health & medical clinics

- Law firms

- Professional service firms

- Museums

MARKETING & SALES

Even though AdminiStar Services is a new enterprise, Janet Stewart is in a strong position to build her business. Over the years, she has developed a reputation for excellence and efficiency while interacting with her employers' suppliers, vendors, customers, and board members. Stewart plans to capitalize on the relationship she has developed in order to secure new clients.

In speaking with virtual assistants in other markets, she has discovered that word-of-mouth marketing is the most successful tactic for generating new business. With this in mind, word-of-mouth marketing will play a central role in her marketing efforts. Stewart will personally call upon contacts in an effort to (1) determine if her services are of interest to them and (2) ask them to spread the word about her new enterprise.

Online directories also are a key referral source for virtual assistants. AdminiStar Services will secure listings in the top industry directories (detailed list available upon request) in order to stay visible among prospective customers. Whenever possible, directory listings will include a link to a Web site with complete details about AdminiStar Services. In addition to providing information about our services, the site will include a fact-gathering/intake form for potential new clients.

In speaking with other industry players, Janet Stewart has learned that a very small percentage make cold calls to prospective clients. Because her background includes some telesales experience, and because she is very persuasive, Stewart will rely heavily upon cold calls to top prospects. Initially focusing on the Dallas, Texas, area she will make 15 cold calls per business day during the first six months of operation. If necessary, she will adjust her volume of sales calls accordingly (based upon the growth strategy outlined in this business plan) and begin concentrating on other national markets.

Finally, AdminiStar Services will develop a simple tri-fold brochure and business cards that can be sent to prospective customers via mail, or left behind following personal meetings.

OPERATIONS

Facility & Location

Janet Stewart will operate AdminiStar Services as a home-based business. She has devoted space within her home for business purposes. In addition, Stewart has installed an Internet-based telephone line that allows her to call anywhere in North America or Europe for one low monthly fee. In addition to voice mail, the service offers features such as call forwarding (so that calls can be routed to her cell phone in the event that she is not in the office) and the ability to set up multi-party conference calls. Fortunately, Stewart already has a computer, multi-functional peripheral device (e.g., copy, fax, scanner), and filing cabinets in her home, so additional equipment will not need to be purchased.

Payment & Fees

Although AdminiStar Services' fees are somewhat negotiable, we typically will charge $45 per hour for our services. Rates may be slightly higher for special, complex projects. Although we will give preference to retainer arrangements (for which we will provide services at a slight discount in exchange for a regular number of pre-paid, billable hours), we also will accept work on a pay-as-you-go or per-project basis.

Insurance

Although many virtual assistants do not carry any type of business insurance, AdminiStar Services will secure a business liability policy, as well as specific coverage related to errors and omissions. In addition, Janet Stewart will add a home office rider to her homeowner's insurance policy.

FINANCIAL ANALYSIS

Following are three-year financial projections for AdminiStar Services, based on Janet Stewart's knowledge of the virtual assistance market. This plan will be revised in year four (2013).

	2010	2011	2012
Revenue	$55,125	$77,175	$99,225
Expenses			
Advertising and marketing	$ 750	$ 600	$ 600
Miscellaneous items	$ 250	$ 300	$ 350
Legal	$ 1,250	$ 250	$ 250
Accounting	$ 500	$ 500	$ 500
Office supplies	$ 500	$ 500	$ 500
Computers/peripherals	$ 250	$ 250	$ 1,000
Business insurance	$ 500	$ 500	$ 500
Salary	$40,000	$65,000	$75,000
Postage	$ 450	$ 550	$ 650
Business travel	$ 500	$ 600	$ 700
Telecommunications	$ 500	$ 500	$ 500
Broadband internet	$ 600	$ 650	$ 700
Total expenses	**$46,050**	**$70,200**	**$81,250**
Net income	**$ 9,075**	**$ 6,975**	**$17,975**

Wedding Planning Service

Together Forever Wedding Planners

515 West Cherry St.
Jefferson City, MO 65109

Kari Lucke

Together Forever is a wedding planning service that is designed to provide couples with all the services they need for an extraordinary wedding and reception while keeping within the proposed budget. Because planning a wedding can be a very stressful and complicated process, Together Forever exists to help couples navigate all the challenges to creating a beautiful wedding that meets all of their expectations.

1.0. INTRODUCTION

1.1. Executive Summary

Together Forever is a wedding planning service that is designed to provide couples with all the services they need for an extraordinary wedding and reception while keeping within the proposed budget. Because planning a wedding can be a very stressful and complicated process, Together Forever exists to help couples navigate all the challenges to creating a beautiful wedding that meets all of their expectations.

1.2. Business Philosophy

Owner Elaine Nixon is a member of the Association for Wedding Professionals International (AFWPI) and the Association of Certified Professional Wedding Consultants (ACPWC), and thus Together Forever follows each of these organizations' Code of Ethics:

- Exhibit professional and ethical behavior

- Communicate completely with customers regarding prices, what the service/product includes and what is in the contract

- If a dispute arises, settle it professionally and promptly

- Return phone calls to current as well as potential customers

- Treat other wedding professionals with respect

- Assist in the advancement of the wedding industry by helping to educate the public and potential wedding professionals

- Observe all laws and obtain any license(s) required by law for any businesses as well as your type of business

- Honor all agreements made with customers, suppliers, and services provided

- Maintain the highest standards of professionalism at all times

- Practice good business ethics at all times
- Practice professional integrity
- Be accountable, objective, and tactful
- Promote and maintain good business skills
- Represent each client fairly and honestly
- Provide quality service in a timely and cost-effective manner
- Establish reasonable and proper fees for services
- Use honest and factual advertising
- Maintain a positive and professional attitude in all business relationships
- Operate a business that is a credit to the ACPWC

1.3. Goals and Objectives

- Establish a reputation as a premier wedding planning service in the mid-Missouri area
- Plan 30 weddings a year by the third year of business

1.4. Company History

Elaine Nixon and Julie Patrick founded Today's Wedding LLC in Bloomington, Minnesota, in 2000 as equal partners. They worked as full-service wedding planners in the area for eight years; the partnership ended when Elaine moved to Jefferson City in 2008. During the time Elaine and Julie conducted business under the Today's Wedding name, they planned an average of 30 weddings a year. These events consisted of everything from small ceremonies with two attendants to very large and elaborate weddings with 12- to 15-member wedding parties. Elaine and Julie also planned and coordinated destination weddings in several locations, including Jamaica, the Bahamas, Mexico, and Italy. Although Elaine will operate under a different business name in the mid-Missouri area, she carries with her both her certification as a professional wedding planner and her years of experience in the business.

2.0. INDUSTRY AND MARKET

2.1. Industry Analysis

According to AFWPI, there were 2.2 million weddings held in the United States in 2008. The most popular months for weddings are June through September, with the fewest weddings performed in January and February. Other statistics show that about one-third of U.S. couples hire a wedding consultant.

According to the Personal Money Store (http://www.personalmoneystore.com), in 2010 the wedding industry was worth $120 billion and the average wedding cost $27,000. In addition, Michael Eckenrod of the Personal Money Store stated, "Although wedding planners used to be solely for the affluent, lately they are much more mainstream, playing parts in even the smallest wedding affairs." A publication titled "The Wedding Report" by Shane McMurray attributed the growth in the wedding planning industry to people "waiting longer to marry and [being]... too busy pursuing careers to plan their big day."

2.2 Market Analysis

Jefferson City is the capital of Missouri and has a population of about 40,000. Eighty percent of the city's population is white, 15 percent black, 2 percent Asian, 2 percent Hispanic, and 11 percent other. Columbia, Missouri, which is 30 miles north of Jefferson City, is also a primary market. Columbia's population is 94,000 and consists of a large concentration of young adults; 35 percent are ages 20 to 34.

Columbia's race distribution is 81 percent white, 11 percent black, 4 percent Asian, 2 percent Hispanic, and 2 percent other.

It is important to note that although the primary market for Together Forever consists of young adults, their parents (especially the bride's mother) are also potential clients, because traditionally the bride's parents foot the bill for the wedding and are very involved in its planning.

2.3. Competition

The main competitor in the Jefferson City area for Together Forever is Weddings by Joan. This is the only full-service wedding planner in the city; other establishments offer specific services such booking the location, arranging for flowers, and so on, whereas others focus on the reception (entertainment, catering, the cake), but none offer the range of services covered by Together Forever. In addition, the operator of Weddings by Joan is a recent college graduate, is not yet certified, and does not have as much experience in the business as Elaine, which gives Together Forever a competitive advantage.

There are several event planners in Columbia, but only four focus on weddings in particular, and, of those, only two offer a full range of services: Your Day Events and The Princess Bride LLC. Both of these offer services and prices comparable to Together Forever. However, Together Forever has an edge on both of these businesses. First, Your Day Events does not have a website, which puts it at a distinct disadvantage as compared to Together Forever. Second, The Princess Bride is locally known for its unusual themed weddings and seems to have created a niche for itself in this area. Therefore, couples that are looking for a traditional wedding may not think of that service as their best option.

3.0. PERSONNEL

3.1. Management

Elaine Nixon is the sole owner and proprietor of Together Forever. Elaine graduated with a bachelor's degree in interior design from the University of Minnesota in 1997, worked as an assistant to a designer for three years in the Minneapolis area, then started a wedding planning business with partner Julie Patrick in 2000. Elaine has all of the professional requirements needed to run a successful wedding planning business in the mid-Missouri area, including eight years experience as a wedding planner, certification by the Association of Certified Professional Wedding Consultants, and the educational background and skills needed to put together a wedding that is aesthetically attractive. In addition, Elaine has the personal characteristics required for success in this business: a professional demeanor, a diplomatic style, and a calm and tolerant personality. Because brides, grooms, family members, and others involved in the wedding can get extremely anxious, frenzied, and even panicked as the wedding day approaches, it is essential that the consultant in charge remain level-headed, patient, and organized. Elaine has worked with a wide variety of personalities and has successfully negotiated several tense situations to conclusions that satisfied everyone involved. Such a skill is indispensable in the wedding planning business.

3.2. Staffing

Initially, Elaine will be the sole employee of Together Forever. She will perform all necessary functions for operation of the business, including record-keeping and billing. However, as the business grows, Elaine may hire additional help on a part-time basis. This could consist of an administrative assistant and/or a person to help coordinate and set up on wedding days. Another option would be to provide an unpaid or low-pay internship or apprenticeship for a college student who is interested in becoming a wedding planner.

3.3. Professional and Advisory Support

Elaine is a member of two trade organizations, both of which provide extensive professional support and resources.

The Association for Wedding Professionals International (AFWPI) provides a free listing and web site link for each member business in its online directory; a subscription to the trade journal for wedding professionals, *Vows Magazine*; a monthly mailing list of brides who have requested information on wedding planners; discounts on booth rental at bridal shows nationwide as well as on services such as car rental and hotel accommodations; a quarterly newsletter; the right to use the AFWPI logo in promotional materials; and a variety of conferences and training programs. The membership fee is $240 annually.

The Association of Certified Professional Wedding Consultants (ACPWC) offers training for certification, a listing in the membership directory, monthly updates on the industry, use of the ACPWC logo, and many networking opportunities. As an ACPWC-certified wedding consultant, Elaine positions herself at the top of the industry in terms of credentials.

Other support will be provided by George Smith, attorney; Dennis Naught, insurance agent; Tina Caldwell, personal banker; and Sheila Johnston, accountant.

4.0. STRATEGIES

4.1. Business Strategy

After identifying a potential client, Elaine meets with the couple for a one-hour complimentary consultation in which she gives a brief summary of her services and prices and tells the couple what they can expect if they hire Together Forever to plan their wedding. She also gives the couple a brochure that provides details about the service. At the same time, the couple can explain to Elaine what they have in mind for the wedding, where they are in the process of planning for it, and what budgetary restrictions they may have. If both parties are comfortable that they are a good fit, Elaine schedules the initial appointment as well as some subsequent appointments, if possible. Sometimes, the couple wants time to think over whether they will use Together Forever, in which case Elaine gives them her card and encourages them to look at her web site and call her with any questions. Elaine follows up with a phone call or email to the couple if she has not heard from them within a week to ten days, but she does not employ any pressure tactics in order to convince the couple to choose Together Forever. Usually, if Elaine can provide the services the couple needs and they get a good first impression, they will choose to hire her.

4.2 Growth Strategy

One area of growth for Together Forever will be in the destination wedding sector. Destination weddings, which often take place in exotic locations, are becoming more popular in the United States. In fact, according to *Brides* magazine, the number of destination weddings increased by 400 percent between 1996 and 2006. Planning these weddings involves a distinct set of challenges, such as helping the couple choose a location that is right for them, securing airline tickets and hotel reservations for the wedding party and guests, managing details such as flowers, tuxedo rental, and reception details from a distance, and so on, but there is also huge potential for growth. One option is to develop packages that are specific to a certain location—Together Forever can then maintain ongoing contacts with vendors in that location, and all the couple has to do is choose one of the locations. This option can also mean less time and work for Elaine, as she would already have a familiarity with the location, which vendors to use, what facilities are available, and so on.

5.0. PRODUCTS AND SERVICES

5.1. Description

Together Forever offers two basic packages: a full-service package and a consultation package.

The full-service package includes an unlimited number of consultations and the following assistance and services, all of which can be adjusted based on the individual couple's needs:

Decision-Making Assistance: This includes help with decisions on:

- Overall theme and tone of the wedding and reception

- Rehearsal dinner menu, location, format

- Location for the wedding and reception

- Selection of dresses, tuxes, and other apparel for the wedding party

- Favors, wedding-party gifts, flowers, candles, other decorations

- Selection of vendors (photographer, musicians, flower shop, caterer, etc.)

- Invitations and guest list

Preparation Services: Together Forever will perform all of the following tasks prior to the wedding day:

- Reserve location for rehearsal dinner, wedding, and reception

- Create, print, and mail (if requested) Save-the-Date cards

- Order and mail wedding invitations; track RSVPs (if requested)

- Work with vendors to design and set up ceremony site

- Design and set up the reception area, includes details like ordering napkins, renting tableware, and setting up/decorating tables

- Coordinate bridal gown and bridesmaid dress fittings

- Coordinate all appointments with pastor, vendors, others

- Set up and track agreements with vendors

- Schedule appointments for personal services for bride, bridesmaids, mothers, etc. (e.g., hair, nails)

- Help with obtaining marriage license, change of name form (if requested)

- Negotiate and reserve hotel room blocks for wedding party and guests

- Create and deliver to hotel gift bags for out-of-town guests, if requested

Day-of-Wedding Services: Together Forever will perform all of the following services on the day of the wedding:

- Verify and coordinate the on-time delivery and services of florist, musicians, caterers, photographer, limo/car service

- Ensure ceremony site and rehearsal site are set up and ready

- Provide snacks and drinks for the wedding party prior to the wedding

- Assist bride and female members of wedding party with dresses, last-minute needs

The consultation package, on the other hand, is for couples who want to make most of the decisions and arrangements on their own and includes the services decided on by Elaine and the couple at the initial consultation.

5.2. Pricing

The full-service package is priced at a base rate of $2,500, whereas the consultation package is charged at an hourly rate of $75. For the full-service package, a deposit of $500, which is applied to the total cost, is due at the time of the first scheduled consultation. If the couple cancels within seven days, half of the deposit is returned. Cancellations after seven days receive no refund. There is no deposit fee for the consultation package.

6.0. MARKETING AND SALES

6.1. Advertising and Promotion

Advertising for Together Forever will consist of the following: business cards, a trifold brochure, a 2-inch by 3-inch display ad in the local telephone company's Yellow Pages, a 2-inch by 3-inch display ad in the local monthly lifestyles magazine *Inside Columbia*, and a professionally designed and easy-to-navigate web site. For the web site, "professionally designed" is key, as many wedding planners (and countless other services) have web sites that look unprofessional and provide questionable first impressions.

Word of mouth is considered another form of advertising. As people use Together Forever and are satisfied, they will recommend the company to friends and family. Word of mouth is considered one of the most effective means of advertising for this type of company.

Finally, Elaine will participate in two local bridal shows a year. The booth rental for each averages $300 for a two-day event.

6.2. Cost

Total cost of start-up advertising is estimated at $800: $300 for the Yellow Pages ad, $200 for the *Inside Columbia* ad, $200 for brochures, and $100 for business cards. Booth rental for bridal shows will run $600 a year.

7.0. OPERATIONS

7.1. Customers

Customers are engaged couples, primarily brides-to-be, in the mid-Missouri area, including the cities of Jefferson City and Columbia. Because the average age of brides is now 26 and the average age of grooms is 28, this is the age group that will be targeted by Together Forever. Customers also include brides' parents, as they are often the ones who pay for the wedding.

7.2. Equipment

The only equipment necessary to begin the business consists of a computer and related software and hardware, as well as basic office supplies. Elaine will also invest in furniture for the office, as described in Section 7.4.

7.3. Hours

Appointments are scheduled on an individual basis. There are no "walk-in" hours for a consultation business such as wedding planning, but the designated business phone line will be answered 24 hours a day by Elaine herself or an answering machine.

7.4. Facility and Location

Elaine will work from her home at 515 West Cherry Street in Jefferson City, Missouri. The house is a brick two-story that has been completely remodeled and updated. The front lawn is professionally landscaped with flowers, shrubs, trees, and other features that add to the house's "curb appeal" and make clients feel welcome and confident in the occupant's good taste and level of professionalism. Elaine will meet with clients at her home at times, and she has designed an office specifically for that purpose. The office is outfitted with an executive meeting table, leather chairs, and an audio-visual system including a flat-screen TV, DVD player, CD player, and quality sound system. This office also contains Elaine's work desk and computer, magazines and books, DVDs, CDs, and other resources, and any other equipment or supplies that may be needed when Elaine meets with clients. Because first impressions are important in this business, the office, as well as the entire house, is tastefully and professionally decorated and includes such special touches as fresh flowers and fine art. The office is located directly off the entryway of the home.

7.5. Legal Environment

Due to the nature of the consultation business, couples will sign a contract with Elaine at the first official appointment. The contract will list services, prices, legal rights and responsibilities of both parties, and do on. Elaine will have the contract reviewed by an attorney before finalizing the document.

8.0. FINANCIAL ANALYSIS

Wedding planning is a low start-up cost business. However, in order to provide a professional image, Elaine will invest in some extra items such as furniture for her office. Money for start-up costs will come from a personal savings account.

Start-Up Costs

Office furniture	$ 2,000
Computer and related equip.	$ 1,500
Office supplies	$ 200
Advertising	$ 800
ACPWC membership	$ 240
Insurance	$ 200
Total	**$ 4,940**

Income will depend on number of weddings per year as well as the level of services performed. According to Elaine's experience with Today's Wedding as well as research on specific demographics and characteristics of the mid-Missouri area, the average profit for planning a wedding is $2,000. This allows for all operating expenses including salary for part-time assistants and out-of-pocket incidental costs. Based on this conservative estimate, the first three years' profit may be projected as follows.

	No. of weddings	Profit
Year 1	15	$30,000
Year 2	20	$40,000
Year 3	30	$60,000

Business Plan Template

USING THIS TEMPLATE

A business plan carefully spells out a company's projected course of action over a period of time, usually the first two to three years after the start-up. In addition, banks, lenders, and other investors examine the information and financial documentation before deciding whether or not to finance a new business venture. Therefore, a business plan is an essential tool in obtaining financing and should describe the business itself in detail as well as all important factors influencing the company, including the market, industry, competition, operations and management policies, problem solving strategies, financial resources and needs, and other vital information. The plan enables the business owner to anticipate costs, plan for difficulties, and take advantage of opportunities, as well as design and implement strategies that keep the company running as smoothly as possible.

This template has been provided as a model to help you construct your own business plan. Please keep in mind that there is no single acceptable format for a business plan, and that this template is in no way comprehensive, but serves as an example.

The business plans provided in this section are fictional and have been used by small business agencies as models for clients to use in compiling their own business plans.

GENERIC BUSINESS PLAN

Main headings included below are topics that should be covered in a comprehensive business plan. They include:

Business Summary

Purpose
Provides a brief overview of your business, succinctly highlighting the main ideas of your plan.

Includes

- Name and Type of Business
- Description of Product/Service
- Business History and Development
- Location
- Market

- Competition
- Management
- Financial Information
- Business Strengths and Weaknesses
- Business Growth

Table of Contents

Purpose
Organized in an Outline Format, the Table of Contents illustrates the selection and arrangement of information contained in your plan.

Includes

- Topic Headings and Subheadings
- Page Number References

Business History and Industry Outlook

Purpose

Examines the conception and subsequent development of your business within an industry specific context.

Includes

- Start-up Information
- Owner/Key Personnel Experience
- Location
- Development Problems and Solutions
- Investment/Funding Information

- Future Plans and Goals
- Market Trends and Statistics
- Major Competitors
- Product/Service Advantages
- National, Regional, and Local Economic Impact

Product/Service

Purpose

Introduces, defines, and details the product and/or service that inspired the information of your business.

Includes

- Unique Features
- Niche Served
- Market Comparison
- Stage of Product/Service Development

- Production
- Facilities, Equipment, and Labor
- Financial Requirements
- Product/Service Life Cycle
- Future Growth

Market Examination

Purpose

Assessment of product/service applications in relation to consumer buying cycles.

Includes

- Target Market
- Consumer Buying Habits
- Product/Service Applications
- Consumer Reactions
- Market Factors and Trends

- Penetration of the Market
- Market Share
- Research and Studies
- Cost
- Sales Volume and Goals

Competition

Purpose

Analysis of Competitors in the Marketplace.

Includes

- Competitor Information
- Product/Service Comparison
- Market Niche

- Product/Service Strengths and Weaknesses
- Future Product/Service Development

Marketing

Purpose

Identifies promotion and sales strategies for your product/service.

Includes

- Product/Service Sales Appeal
- Special and Unique Features
- Identification of Customers
- Sales and Marketing Staff
- Sales Cycles
- Type of Advertising/ Promotion
- Pricing
- Competition
- Customer Services

Operations

Purpose

Traces product/service development from production/inception to the market environment.

Includes

- Cost Effective Production Methods
- Facility
- Location
- Equipment
- Labor
- Future Expansion

Administration and Management

Purpose

Offers a statement of your management philosophy with an in-depth focus on processes and procedures.

Includes

- Management Philosophy
- Structure of Organization
- Reporting System
- Methods of Communication
- Employee Skills and Training
- Employee Needs and Compensation
- Work Environment
- Management Policies and Procedures
- Roles and Responsibilities

Key Personnel

Purpose

Describes the unique backgrounds of principle employees involved in business.

Includes

- Owner(s)/Employee Education and Experience
- Positions and Roles
- Benefits and Salary
- Duties and Responsibilities
- Objectives and Goals

Potential Problems and Solutions

Purpose

Discussion of problem solving strategies that change issues into opportunities.

Includes

- Risks
- Litigation
- Future Competition
- Economic Impact
- Problem Solving Skills

Financial Information

Purpose

Secures needed funding and assistance through worksheets and projections detailing financial plans, methods of repayment, and future growth opportunities.

Includes

- Financial Statements
- Bank Loans
- Methods of Repayment
- Tax Returns

- Start-up Costs
- Projected Income (3 years)
- Projected Cash Flow (3 Years)
- Projected Balance Statements (3 years)

Appendices

Purpose

Supporting documents used to enhance your business proposal.

Includes

- Photographs of product, equipment, facilities, etc.
- Copyright/Trademark Documents
- Legal Agreements
- Marketing Materials
- Research and or Studies

- Operation Schedules
- Organizational Charts
- Job Descriptions
- Resumes
- Additional Financial Documentation

Fictional Food Distributor

Commercial Foods, Inc.

3003 Avondale Ave.
Knoxville, TN 37920

This plan demonstrates how a partnership can have a positive impact on a new business. It demonstrates how two individuals can carve a niche in the specialty foods market by offering gourmet foods to upscale restaurants and fine hotels. This plan is fictional and has not been used to gain funding from a bank or other lending institution.

STATEMENT OF PURPOSE

Commercial Foods, Inc. seeks a loan of $75,000 to establish a new business. This sum, together with $5,000 equity investment by the principals, will be used as follows:

- Merchandise inventory $25,000

- Office fixture/equipment $12,000

- Warehouse equipment $14,000

- One delivery truck $10,000

- Working capital $39,000

- Total $100,000

DESCRIPTION OF THE BUSINESS

Commercial Foods, Inc. will be a distributor of specialty food service products to hotels and upscale restaurants in the geographical area of a 50 mile radius of Knoxville. Richard Roberts will direct the sales effort and John Williams will manage the warehouse operation and the office. One delivery truck will be used initially with a second truck added in the third year. We expect to begin operation of the business within 30 days after securing the requested financing.

MANAGEMENT

A. Richard Roberts is a native of Memphis, Tennessee. He is a graduate of Memphis State University with a Bachelor's degree from the School of Business. After graduation, he worked for a major manufacturer of specialty food service products as a detail sales person for five years, and, for the past three years, he has served as a product sales manager for this firm.

B. John Williams is a native of Nashville, Tennessee. He holds a B.S. Degree in Food Technology from the University of Tennessee. His career includes five years as a product development chemist in gourmet food products and five years as operations manager for a food service distributor.

Both men are healthy and energetic. Their backgrounds complement each other, which will ensure the success of Commercial Foods, Inc. They will set policies together and personnel decisions will be made jointly. Initial salaries for the owners will be $1,000 per month for the first few years. The spouses of both principals are successful in the business world and earn enough to support the families.

They have engaged the services of Foster Jones, CPA, and William Hale, Attorney, to assist them in an advisory capacity.

PERSONNEL

The firm will employ one delivery truck driver at a wage of $8.00 per hour. One office worker will be employed at $7.50 per hour. One part-time employee will be used in the office at $5.00 per hour. The driver will load and unload his own trucks. Mr. Williams will assist in the warehouse operation as needed to assist one stock person at $7.00 per hour. An additional delivery truck and driver will be added the third year.

LOCATION

The firm will lease a 20,000 square foot building at 3003 Avondale Ave., in Knoxville, which contains warehouse and office areas equipped with two-door truck docks. The annual rental is $9,000. The building was previously used as a food service warehouse and very little modification to the building will be required.

PRODUCTS AND SERVICES

The firm will offer specialty food service products such as soup bases, dessert mixes, sauce bases, pastry mixes, spices, and flavors, normally used by upscale restaurants and nice hotels. We are going after a niche in the market with high quality gourmet products. There is much less competition in this market than in standard run of the mill food service products. Through their work experiences, the principals have contacts with supply sources and with local chefs.

THE MARKET

We know from our market survey that there are over 200 hotels and upscale restaurants in the area we plan to serve. Customers will be attracted by a direct sales approach. We will offer samples of our products and product application data on use of our products in the finished prepared foods. We will cultivate the chefs in these establishments. The technical background of John Williams will be especially useful here.

COMPETITION

We find that we will be only distributor in the area offering a full line of gourmet food service products. Other foodservice distributors offer only a few such items in conjunction with their standard product line. Our survey shows that many of the chefs are ordering products from Atlanta and Memphis because of a lack of adequate local supply.

SUMMARY

Commercial Foods, Inc. will be established as a foodservice distributor of specialty food in Knoxville. The principals, with excellent experience in the industry, are seeking a $75,000 loan to establish the business. The principals are investing $25,000 as equity capital.

The business will be set up as an S Corporation with each principal owning 50% of the common stock in the corporation.

Fictional Hardware Store

Oshkosh Hardware, Inc.

123 Main St.
Oshkosh, WI 54901

The following plan outlines how a small hardware store can survive competition from large discount chains by offering products and providing expert advice in the use of any product it sells. This plan is fictional and has not been used to gain funding from a bank or other lending institution.

EXECUTIVE SUMMARY

Oshkosh Hardware, Inc. is a new corporation that is going to establish a retail hardware store in a strip mall in Oshkosh, Wisconsin. The store will sell hardware of all kinds, quality tools, paint, and housewares. The business will make revenue and a profit by servicing its customers not only with needed hardware but also with expert advice in the use of any product it sells.

Oshkosh Hardware, Inc. will be operated by its sole shareholder, James Smith. The company will have a total of four employees. It will sell its products in the local market. Customers will buy our products because we will provide free advice on the use of all of our products and will also furnish a full refund warranty.

Oshkosh Hardware, Inc. will sell its products in the Oshkosh store staffed by three sales representatives. No additional employees will be needed to achieve its short and long range goals. The primary short range goal is to open the store by October 1, 1994. In order to achieve this goal a lease must be signed by July 1, 1994 and the complete inventory ordered by August 1, 1994.

Mr. James Smith will invest $30,000 in the business. In addition, the company will have to borrow $150,000 during the first year to cover the investment in inventory, accounts receivable, and furniture and equipment. The company will be profitable after six months of operation and should be able to start repayment of the loan in the second year.

THE BUSINESS

The business will sell hardware of all kinds, quality tools, paint, and housewares. We will purchase our products from three large wholesale buying groups.

In general our customers are homeowners who do their own repair and maintenance, hobbyists, and housewives. Our business is unique in that we will have a complete line of all hardware items and will be able to get special orders by overnight delivery. The business makes revenue and profits by servicing our customers not only with needed hardware but also with expert advice in the use of any product we sell. Our major costs for bringing our products to market are cost of merchandise of 36%, salaries of $45,000, and occupancy costs of $60,000.

197

Oshkosh Hardware, Inc.'s retail outlet will be located at 1524 Frontage Road, which is in a newly developed retail center of Oshkosh. Our location helps facilitate accessibility from all parts of town and reduces our delivery costs. The store will occupy 7500 square feet of space. The major equipment involved in our business is counters and shelving, a computer, a paint mixing machine, and a truck.

THE MARKET

Oshkosh Hardware, Inc. will operate in the local market. There are 15,000 potential customers in this market area. We have three competitors who control approximately 98% of the market at present. We feel we can capture 25% of the market within the next four years. Our major reason for believing this is that our staff is technically competent to advise our customers in the correct use of all products we sell.

After a careful market analysis, we have determined that approximately 60% of our customers are men and 40% are women. The percentage of customers that fall into the following age categories are:

Under 16: 0%
17-21: 5%
22-30: 30%
31-40: 30%
41-50: 20%
51-60: 10%
61-70: 5%
Over 70: 0%

The reasons our customers prefer our products is our complete knowledge of their use and our full refund warranty.

We get our information about what products our customers want by talking to existing customers. There seems to be an increasing demand for our product. The demand for our product is increasing in size based on the change in population characteristics.

SALES

At Oshkosh Hardware, Inc. we will employ three sales people and will not need any additional personnel to achieve our sales goals. These salespeople will need several years experience in home repair and power tool usage. We expect to attract 30% of our customers from newspaper ads, 5% of our customers from local directories, 5% of our customers from the yellow pages, 10% of our customers from family and friends, and 50% of our customers from current customers. The most cost effect source will be current customers. In general our industry is growing.

MANAGEMENT

We would evaluate the quality of our management staff as being excellent. Our manager is experienced and very motivated to achieve the various sales and quality assurance objectives we have set. We will use a management information system that produces key inventory, quality assurance, and sales data on a weekly basis. All data is compared to previously established goals for that week, and deviations are the primary focus of the management staff.

GOALS IMPLEMENTATION

The short term goals of our business are:

1. Open the store by October 1, 1994
2. Reach our breakeven point in two months
3. Have sales of $100,000 in the first six months

In order to achieve our first short term goal we must:

1. Sign the lease by July 1, 1994
2. Order a complete inventory by August 1, 1994

In order to achieve our second short term goal we must:

1. Advertise extensively in Sept. and Oct.
2. Keep expenses to a minimum

In order to achieve our third short term goal we must:

1. Promote power tool sales for the Christmas season
2. Keep good customer traffic in Jan. and Feb.

The long term goals for our business are:

1. Obtain sales volume of $600,000 in three years
2. Become the largest hardware dealer in the city
3. Open a second store in Fond du Lac

The most important thing we must do in order to achieve the long term goals for our business is to develop a highly profitable business with excellent cash flow.

FINANCE

Oshkosh Hardware, Inc. Faces some potential threats or risks to our business. They are discount house competition. We believe we can avoid or compensate for this by providing quality products complimented by quality advice on the use of every product we sell. The financial projections we have prepared are located at the end of this document.

JOB DESCRIPTION-GENERAL MANAGER

The General Manager of the business of the corporation will be the president of the corporation. He will be responsible for the complete operation of the retail hardware store which is owned by the corporation. A detailed description of his duties and responsibilities is as follows.

Sales

Train and supervise the three sales people. Develop programs to motivate and compensate these employees. Coordinate advertising and sales promotion effects to achieve sales totals as outlined in budget. Oversee purchasing function and inventory control procedures to insure adequate merchandise at all times at a reasonable cost.

Finance

Prepare monthly and annual budgets. Secure adequate line of credit from local banks. Supervise office personnel to insure timely preparation of records, statements, all government reports, control of receivables and payables, and monthly financial statements.

Administration

Perform duties as required in the areas of personnel, building leasing and maintenance, licenses and permits, and public relations.

Organizations, Agencies, & Consultants

A listing of Associations and Consultants of interest to entrepreneurs, followed by the ten Small Business Administration Regional Offices, Small Business Development Centers, Service Corps of Retired Executives offices, and Venture Capital and Finance Companies.

Organizations, Agencies, & Consultants

Associations

This section contains a listing of associations and other agencies of interest to the small business owner. Entries are listed alphabetically by organization name.

American Business Women's Association
9100 Ward Pkwy.
PO Box 8728
Kansas City, MO 64114-0728
(800)228-0007
E-mail: abwa@abwa.org
Website: http://www.abwa.org
Jeanne Banks, National President

American Franchisee Association
53 W Jackson Blvd., Ste. 1157
Chicago, IL 60604
(312)431-0545
E-mail: info@franchisee.org
Website: http://www.franchisee.org
Susan P. Kezios, President

American Independent Business Alliance
222 S Black Ave.
Bozeman, MT 59715
(406)582-1255
E-mail: info@amiba.net
Website: http://www.amiba.net
Jennifer Rockne, Director

American Small Businesses Association
206 E College St., Ste. 201
Grapevine, TX 76051
800-942-2722
E-mail: info@asbaonline.org
Website: http://www.asbaonline.org/

American Women's Economic Development Corporation
216 East 45th St., 10th Floor
New York, NY 10017
(917)368-6100

Fax: (212)986-7114
E-mail: info@awed.org
Website: http://www.awed.org
Roseanne Antonucci, Exec. Dir.

Association for Enterprise Opportunity
1601 N Kent St., Ste. 1101
Arlington, VA 22209
(703)841-7760
Fax: (703)841-7748
E-mail: aeo@assoceo.org
Website: http://www.micro
enterpriseworks.org
Bill Edwards, Exec.Dir.

Association of Small Business Development Centers
c/o Don Wilson
8990 Burke Lake Rd.
Burke, VA 22015
(703)764-9850
Fax: (703)764-1234
E-mail: info@asbdc-us.org
Website: http://www.asbdc-us.org
Don Wilson, Pres./CEO

BEST Employers Association
2505 McCabe Way
Irvine, CA 92614
(949)253-4080
800-433-0088
Fax: (714)553-0883
E-mail: info@bestlife.com
Website: http://www.bestlife.com
Donald R. Lawrenz, CEO

Center for Family Business
PO Box 24219
Cleveland, OH 44124
(440)460-5409
E-mail: grummi@aol.com
Dr. Leon A. Danco, Chm.

Coalition for Government Procurement
1990 M St. NW, Ste. 400
Washington, DC 20036
(202)331-0975
E-mail: info@thecgp.org
Website: http://www.coalgovpro.org
Paul Caggiano, Pres.

Employers of America
PO Box 1874
Mason City, IA 50402-1874
(641)424-3187
800-728-3187
Fax: (641)424-1673
E-mail: employer@employerhelp.org
Website: http://www.employerhelp.org
Jim Collison, Pres.

Family Firm Institute
200 Lincoln St., Ste. 201
Boston, MA 02111
(617)482-3045
Fax: (617)482-3049
E-mail: ffi@ffi.org
Website: http://www.ffi.org
Judy L. Green, Ph.D., Exec.Dir.

Independent Visually Impaired Enterprisers
500 S 3rd St., Apt. H
Burbank, CA 91502
(818)238-9321
E-mail: abazyn@bazyn
communications.com
http://www.acb.org/affiliates
Adris Bazyn, Pres.

International Association for Business Organizations
3 Woodthorn Ct., Ste. 12
Owings Mills, MD 21117
(410)581-1373
E-mail: nahbb@msn.com
Rudolph Lewis, Exec. Officer

International Council for Small Business
The George Washington University
School of Business and Public
Management
2115 G St. NW, Ste. 403
Washington, DC 20052
(202)994-0704
Fax: (202)994-4930
E-mail: icsb@gwu.edu
Website: http://www.icsb.org
Susan G. Duffy. Admin.

International Small Business Consortium
3309 Windjammer St.
Norman, OK 73072
E-mail: sb@isbc.com
Website: http://www.isbc.com

Kauffman Center for Entrepreneurial Leadership
4801 Rockhill Rd.
Kansas City, MO 64110-2046
(816)932-1000
E-mail: info@kauffman.org
Website: http://www.entreworld.org

National Alliance for Fair Competition
3 Bethesda Metro Center, Ste. 1100
Bethesda, MD 20814
(410)235-7116
Fax: (410)235-7116
E-mail: ampesq@aol.com
Tony Ponticelli, Exec.Dir.

National Association for the Self-Employed
PO Box 612067
DFW Airport
Dallas, TX 75261-2067
(800)232-6273
E-mail: mpetron@nase.org
Website: http://www.nase.org
Robert Hughes, Pres.

National Association of Business Leaders
4132 Shoreline Dr., Ste. J & H
Earth City, MO 63045
Fax: (314)298-9110
E-mail: nabl@nabl.com
Website: http://www.nabl.com/
Gene Blumenthal, Contact

National Association of Private Enterprise
PO Box 15550
Long Beach, CA 90815
888-224-0953

Fax: (714)844-4942
Website: http://www.napeonline.net
Laura Squiers, Exec.Dir.

National Association of Small Business Investment Companies
666 11th St. NW, Ste. 750
Washington, DC 20001
(202)628-5055
Fax: (202)628-5080
E-mail: nasbic@nasbic.org
Website: http://www.nasbic.org
Lee W. Mercer, Pres.

National Business Association
PO Box 700728
5151 Beltline Rd., Ste. 1150
Dallas, TX 75370
(972)458-0900
800-456-0440
Fax: (972)960-9149
E-mail: info@nationalbusiness.org
Website: http://www.national
business.org
Raj Nisankarao, Pres.

National Business Owners Association
PO Box 111
Stuart, VA 24171
(276)251-7500
(866)251-7505
Fax: (276)251-2217
E-mail: membershipservices@nboa.org
Website: http://www.rvmdb.com.nboa
Paul LaBarr, Pres.

National Center for Fair Competition
PO Box 220
Annandale, VA 22003
(703)280-4622
Fax: (703)280-0942
E-mail: kentonp1@aol.com
Kenton Pattie, Pres.

National Family Business Council
1640 W. Kennedy Rd.
Lake Forest, IL 60045
(847)295-1040
Fax: (847)295-1898
E-mail: lmsnfbc@email.msn.com
Jogn E. Messervey, Pres.

National Federation of Independent Business
53 Century Blvd., Ste. 250
Nashville, TN 37214
(615)872-5800
800-NFIBNOW
Fax: (615)872-5353
Website: http://www.nfib.org
Jack Faris, Pres. and CEO

National Small Business Association
1156 15th St. NW, Ste. 1100
Washington, DC 20005
(202)293-8830
800-345-6728
Fax: (202)872-8543
E-mail: press@nsba.biz
Website: http://www.nsba.biz
Rob Yunich, Dir. of Communications

PUSH Commercial Division
930 E 50th St.
Chicago, IL 60615-2702
(773)373-3366
Fax: (773)373-3571
E-mail: info@rainbowpush.org
Website: http://www.rainbowpush.org
Rev. Willie T. Barrow, Co-Chm.

Research Institute for Small and Emerging Business
722 12th St. NW
Washington, DC 20005
(202)628-8382
Fax: (202)628-8392
E-mail: info@riseb.org
Website: http://www.riseb.org
Allan Neece, Jr., Chm.

Sales Professionals USA
PO Box 149
Arvada, CO 80001
(303)534-4937
888-736-7767
E-mail: salespro@salesprofessionals-usa.com
Website: http://www.salesprofessionals-usa.com
Sharon Herbert, Natl. Pres.

Score Association - Service Corps of Retired Executives
409 3rd St. SW, 6th Fl.
Washington, DC 20024
(202)205-6762
800-634-0245
Fax: (202)205-7636
E-mail: media@score.org
Website: http://www.score.org
W. Kenneth Yancey, Jr., CEO

Small Business and Entrepreneurship Council
1920 L St. NW, Ste. 200
Washington, DC 20036
(202)785-0238
Fax: (202)822-8118
E-mail: membership@sbec.org
Website: http://www.sbecouncil.org
Karen Kerrigan, Pres./CEO

Small Business in Telecommunications
1331 H St. NW, Ste. 500
Washington, DC 20005
(202)347-4511
Fax: (202)347-8607
E-mail: sbt@sbthome.org
Website: http://www.sbthome.org
Lonnie Danchik, Chm.

Small Business Legislative Council
1010 Massachusetts Ave. NW, Ste. 540
Washington, DC 20005
(202)639-8500
Fax: (202)296-5333
E-mail: email@sblc.org
Website: http://www.sblc.org
John Satagaj, Pres.

Small Business Service Bureau
554 Main St.
PO Box 15014
Worcester, MA 01615-0014
(508)756-3513
800-343-0939
Fax: (508)770-0528
E-mail: membership@sbsb.com
Website: http://www.sbsb.com
Francis R. Carroll, Pres.

**Small Publishers Association
of North America**
1618 W COlorado Ave.
Colorado Springs, CO 80904
(719)475-1726
Fax: (719)471-2182
E-mail: span@spannet.org
Website: http://www.spannet.org
Scott Flora, Exec. Dir.

SOHO America
PO Box 941
Hurst, TX 76053-0941
800-495-SOHO
E-mail: soho@1sas.com
Website: http://www.soho.org

**Structured Employment Economic
Development Corporation**
915 Broadway, 17th Fl.
New York, NY 10010
(212)473-0255
Fax: (212)473-0357
E-mail: info@seedco.org
Website: http://www.seedco.org
William Grinker, CEO

Support Services Alliance
107 Prospect St.
Schoharie, NY 12157
800-836-4772

E-mail: info@ssamembers.com
Website: http://www.ssainfo.com
Steve COle, Pres.

**United States Association for Small
Business and Entrepreneurship**
975 University Ave., No. 3260
Madison, WI 53706
(608)262-9982
Fax: (608)263-0818
E-mail: jgillman@wisc.edu
Website: http://www.ususbe.org
Joan Gillman, Exec. Dir.

Consultants

This section contains a listing of consultants specializing in small business development. It is arranged alphabetically by country, then by state or province, then by city, then by firm name.

Canada

Alberta

Common Sense Solutions
3405 16A Ave.
Edmonton, AB, Canada
(403)465-7330
Fax: (403)465-7380
E-mail: gcoulson@comsense
solutions.com
Website: http://www.comsense
solutions.com

Varsity Consulting Group
School of Business
University of Alberta
Edmonton, AB, Canada T6G 2R6
(780)492-2994
Fax: (780)492-5400
Website: http://www.bus.ualberta.ca/vcg

Viro Hospital Consulting
42 Commonwealth Bldg., 9912 - 106
St. NW
Edmonton, AB, Canada T5K 1C5
(403)425-3871
Fax: (403)425-3871
E-mail: rpb@freenet.edmonton.ab.ca

British Columbia

SRI Strategic Resources Inc.
4330 Kingsway, Ste. 1600
Burnaby, BC, Canada V5H 4G7
(604)435-0627
Fax: (604)435-2782

E-mail: inquiry@sri.bc.ca
Website: http://www.sri.com

Andrew R. De Boda Consulting
1523 Milford Ave.
Coquitlam, BC, Canada V3J 2V9
(604)936-4527
Fax: (604)936-4527
E-mail: deboda@intergate.bc.ca
Website: http://www.ourworld.
compuserve.com/homepages/deboda

The Sage Group Ltd.
980 - 355 Burrard St.
744 W Haistings, Ste. 410
Vancouver, BC, Canada V6C 1A5
(604)669-9269
Fax: (604)669-6622

Tikkanen-Bradley
1345 Nelson St., Ste. 202
Vancouver, BC, Canada V6E 1J8
(604)669-0583
E-mail: webmaster@tikkanen
bradley.com
Website: http://www.tikkanenbradley.com

Ontario

The Cynton Co.
17 Massey St.
Brampton, ON, Canada L6S 2V6
(905)792-7769
Fax: (905)792-8116
E-mail: cynton@home.com
Website: http://www.cynton.com

Begley & Associates
RR 6
Cambridge, ON, Canada N1R 5S7
(519)740-3629
Fax: (519)740-3629
E-mail: begley@in.on.ca
Website: http://www.in.on.ca/~begley/
index.htm

CRO Engineering Ltd.
1895 William Hodgins Ln.
Carp, ON, Canada K0A 1L0
(613)839-1108
Fax: (613)839-1406
E-mail: J.Grefford@ieee.ca
Website: http://www.geocities.com/
WallStreet/District/7401/

Task Enterprises
Box 69, RR 2 Hamilton
Flamborough, ON, Canada L8N 2Z7
(905)659-0153
Fax: (905)659-0861

HST Group Ltd.
430 Gilmour St.
Ottawa, ON, Canada K2P 0R8
(613)236-7303
Fax: (613)236-9893

Harrison Associates
BCE Pl.
181 Bay St., Ste. 3740
PO Box 798
Toronto, ON, Canada M5J 2T3
(416)364-5441
Fax: (416)364-2875

TCI Convergence Ltd. Management Consultants
99 Crown's Ln.
Toronto, ON, Canada M5R 3P4
(416)515-4146
Fax: (416)515-2097
E-mail: tci@inforamp.net
Website: http://tciconverge.com/index.1.html

Ken Wyman & Associates Inc.
64B Shuter St., Ste. 200
Toronto, ON, Canada M5B 1B1
(416)362-2926
Fax: (416)362-3039
E-mail: kenwyman@compuserve.com

JPL Business Consultants
82705 Metter Rd.
Wellandport, ON, Canada L0R 2J0
(905)386-7450
Fax: (905)386-7450
E-mail: plamarch@freenet.npiec.on.ca

Quebec

The Zimmar Consulting Partnership Inc.
Westmount
PO Box 98
Montreal, QC, Canada H3Z 2T1
(514)484-1459
Fax: (514)484-3063

Saskatchewan

Trimension Group
No. 104-110 Research Dr.
Innovation Place, SK, Canada S7N 3R3
(306)668-2560
Fax: (306)975-1156
E-mail: trimension@trimension.ca
Website: http://www.trimension.ca

Corporate Management Consultants
40 Government Road - PO Box 185
Prud Homme, SK, Canada, SOK 3K0
(306)654-4569
Fax: (650)618-2742

E-mail: cmccorporatemanagement@shaw.ca
Website: http://www.Corporate managementconsultants.com
Gerald Rekve

United States

Alabama

Business Planning Inc.
300 Office Park Dr.
Birmingham, AL 35223-2474
(205)870-7090
Fax: (205)870-7103

Tradebank of Eastern Alabama
546 Broad St., Ste. 3
Gadsden, AL 35901
(205)547-8700
Fax: (205)547-8718
E-mail: mansion@webex.com
Website: http://www.webex.com/~tea

Alaska

AK Business Development Center
3335 Arctic Blvd., Ste. 203
Anchorage, AK 99503
(907)562-0335
Free: 800-478-3474
Fax: (907)562-6988
E-mail: abdc@gci.net
Website: http://www.abdc.org

Business Matters
PO Box 287
Fairbanks, AK 99707
(907)452-5650

Arizona

Carefree Direct Marketing Corp.
8001 E Serene St.
PO Box 3737
Carefree, AZ 85377-3737
(480)488-4227
Fax: (480)488-2841

Trans Energy Corp.
1739 W 7th Ave.
Mesa, AZ 85202
(480)827-7915
Fax: (480)967-6601
E-mail: aha@clean-air.org
Website: http://www.clean-air.org

CMAS
5125 N 16th St.
Phoenix, AZ 85016

(602)395-1001
Fax: (602)604-8180

Comgate Telemanagement Ltd.
706 E Bell Rd., Ste. 105
Phoenix, AZ 85022
(602)485-5708
Fax: (602)485-5709
E-mail: comgate@netzone.com
Website: http://www.comgate.com

Moneysoft Inc.
1 E Camelback Rd. #550
Phoenix, AZ 85012
Free: 800-966-7797
E-mail: mbray@moneysoft.com

Harvey C. Skoog
PO Box 26439
Prescott Valley, AZ 86312
(520)772-1714
Fax: (520)772-2814

LMC Services
8711 E Pinnacle Peak Rd., No. 340
Scottsdale, AZ 85255-3555
(602)585-7177
Fax: (602)585-5880
E-mail: louws@earthlink.com

Sauerbrun Technology Group Ltd.
7979 E Princess Dr., Ste. 5
Scottsdale, AZ 85255-5878
(602)502-4950
Fax: (602)502-4292
E-mail: info@sauerbrun.com
Website: http://www.sauerbrun.com

Gary L. McLeod
PO Box 230
Sonoita, AZ 85637
Fax: (602)455-5661

Van Cleve Associates
6932 E 2nd St.
Tucson, AZ 85710
(520)296-2587
Fax: (520)296-3358

California

Acumen Group Inc.
(650)949-9349
Fax: (650)949-4845
E-mail: acumen-g@ix.netcom.com
Website: http://pw2.netcom.com/~janed/acumen.html

On-line Career and Management Consulting
420 Central Ave., No. 314
Alameda, CA 94501

(510)864-0336
Fax: (510)864-0336
E-mail: career@dnai.com
Website: http://www.dnai.com/~career

Career Paths-Thomas E. Church & Associates Inc.
PO Box 2439
Aptos, CA 95001
(408)662-7950
Fax: (408)662-7955
E-mail: church@ix.netcom.com
Website: http://www.careerpaths-tom.com

Keck & Co. Business Consultants
410 Walsh Rd.
Atherton, CA 94027
(650)854-9588
Fax: (650)854-7240
E-mail: info@keckco.com
Website: http://www.keckco.com

Ben W. Laverty III, PhD, REA, CEI
4909 Stockdale Hwy., Ste. 132
Bakersfield, CA 93309
(661)283-8300
Free: 800-833-0373
Fax: (661)283-8313
E-mail: cstc@cstcsafety.com
Website: http://www.cstcsafety.com/cstc

Lindquist Consultants-Venture Planning
225 Arlington Ave.
Berkeley, CA 94707
(510)524-6685
Fax: (510)527-6604

Larson Associates
PO Box 9005
Brea, CA 92822
(714)529-4121
Fax: (714)572-3606
E-mail: ray@consultlarson.com
Website: http://www.consultlarson.com

Kremer Management Consulting
PO Box 500
Carmel, CA 93921
(408)626-8311
Fax: (408)624-2663
E-mail: ddkremer@aol.com

W and J PARTNERSHIP
PO Box 2499
18876 Edwin Markham Dr.
Castro Valley, CA 94546
(510)583-7751
Fax: (510)583-7645
E-mail: wamorgan@wjpartnership.com
Website: http://www.wjpartnership.com

JB Associates
21118 Gardena Dr.
Cupertino, CA 95014
(408)257-0214
Fax: (408)257-0216
E-mail: semarang@sirius.com

House Agricultural Consultants
PO Box 1615
Davis, CA 95617-1615
(916)753-3361
Fax: (916)753-0464
E-mail: infoag@houseag.com
Website: http://www.houseag.com/

3C Systems Co.
16161 Ventura Blvd., Ste. 815
Encino, CA 91436
(818)907-1302
Fax: (818)907-1357
E-mail: mark@3CSysCo.com
Website: http://www.3CSysCo.com

Technical Management Consultants
3624 Westfall Dr.
Encino, CA 91436-4154
(818)784-0626
Fax: (818)501-5575
E-mail: tmcrs@aol.com

RAINWATER-GISH & Associates, Business Finance & Development
317 3rd St., Ste. 3
Eureka, CA 95501
(707)443-0030
Fax: (707)443-5683

Global Tradelinks
451 Pebble Beach Pl.
Fullerton, CA 92835
(714)441-2280
Fax: (714)441-2281
E-mail: info@globaltradelinks.com
Website: http://www.globaltradelinks.com

Strategic Business Group
800 Cienaga Dr.
Fullerton, CA 92835-1248
(714)449-1040
Fax: (714)525-1631

Burnes Consulting
20537 Wolf Creek Rd.
Grass Valley, CA 95949
(530)346-8188
Free: 800-949-9021
Fax: (530)346-7704
E-mail: kent@burnesconsulting.com
Website: http://www.burnesconsulting.com

Pioneer Business Consultants
9042 Garfield Ave., Ste. 312
Huntington Beach, CA 92646
(714)964-7600

Beblie, Brandt & Jacobs Inc.
16 Technology, Ste. 164
Irvine, CA 92618
(714)450-8790
Fax: (714)450-8799
E-mail: darcy@bbjinc.com
Website: http://198.147.90.26

Fluor Daniel Inc.
3353 Michelson Dr.
Irvine, CA 92612-0650
(949)975-2000
Fax: (949)975-5271
E-mail: sales.consulting@fluordaniel.com
Website: http://www.fluordaniel
consulting.com

MCS Associates
18300 Von Karman, Ste. 710
Irvine, CA 92612
(949)263-8700
Fax: (949)263-0770
E-mail: info@mcsassociates.com
Website: http://www.mcsassociates.com

Inspired Arts Inc.
4225 Executive Sq., Ste. 1160
La Jolla, CA 92037
(619)623-3525
Free: 800-851-4394
Fax: (619)623-3534
E-mail: info@inspiredarts.com
Website: http://www.inspiredarts.com

The Laresis Companies
PO Box 3284
La Jolla, CA 92038
(619)452-2720
Fax: (619)452-8744

RCL & Co.
PO Box 1143
737 Pearl St., Ste. 201
La Jolla, CA 92038
(619)454-8883
Fax: (619)454-8880

Comprehensive Business Services
3201 Lucas Cir.
Lafayette, CA 94549
(925)283-8272
Fax: (925)283-8272

The Ribble Group
27601 Forbes Rd., Ste. 52
Laguna Niguel, CA 92677

(714)582-1085
Fax: (714)582-6420
E-mail: ribble@deltanet.com

Norris Bernstein, CMC
9309 Marina Pacifica Dr. N
Long Beach, CA 90803
(562)493-5458
Fax: (562)493-5459
E-mail: norris@ctecomputer.com
Website: http://foodconsultants.com/
bernstein/

Horizon Consulting Services
1315 Garthwick Dr.
Los Altos, CA 94024
(415)967-0906
Fax: (415)967-0906

Brincko Associates Inc.
1801 Avenue of the Stars, Ste. 1054
Los Angeles, CA 90067
(310)553-4523
Fax: (310)553-6782

Rubenstein/Justman Management Consultants
2049 Century Park E, 24th Fl.
Los Angeles, CA 90067
(310)282-0800
Fax: (310)282-0400
E-mail: info@rjmc.net
Website: http://www.rjmc.net

F.J. Schroeder & Associates
1926 Westholme Ave.
Los Angeles, CA 90025
(310)470-2655
Fax: (310)470-6378
E-mail: fjsacons@aol.com
Website: http://www.mcninet.com/
GlobalLook/Fjschroe.html

Western Management Associates
5959 W Century Blvd., Ste. 565
Los Angeles, CA 90045-6506
(310)645-1091
Free: (888)788-6534
Fax: (310)645-1092
E-mail: gene@cfoforrent.com
Website: http://www.cfoforrent.com

Darrell Sell and Associates
Los Gatos, CA 95030
(408)354-7794
E-mail: darrell@netcom.com

Leslie J. Zambo
3355 Michael Dr.
Marina, CA 93933
(408)384-7086

Fax: (408)647-4199
E-mail: 104776.1552@compuserve.com

Marketing Services Management
PO Box 1377
Martinez, CA 94553
(510)370-8527
Fax: (510)370-8527
E-mail: markserve@biotechnet.com

William M. Shine Consulting Service
PO Box 127
Moraga, CA 94556-0127
(510)376-6516

Palo Alto Management Group Inc.
2672 Bayshore Pky., Ste. 701
Mountain View, CA 94043
(415)968-4374
Fax: (415)968-4245
E-mail: mburwen@pamg.com

BizplanSource
1048 Irvine Ave., Ste. 621
Newport Beach, CA 92660
Free: 888-253-0974
Fax: 800-859-8254
E-mail: info@bizplansource.com
Website: http://www.bizplansource.com
Adam Greengrass, President

The Market Connection
4020 Birch St., Ste. 203
Newport Beach, CA 92660
(714)731-6273
Fax: (714)833-0253

Muller Associates
PO Box 7264
Newport Beach, CA 92658
(714)646-1169
Fax: (714)646-1169

International Health Resources
PO Box 329
North San Juan, CA 95960-0329
(530)292-1266
Fax: (530)292-1243
Website: http://www.futureof
healthcare.com

NEXUS - Consultants to Management
PO Box 1531
Novato, CA 94948
(415)897-4400
Fax: (415)898-2252
E-mail: jimnexus@aol.com

Aerospcace.Org
PO Box 28831
Oakland, CA 94604-8831

(510)530-9169
Fax: (510)530-3411
Website: http://www.aerospace.org

Intelequest Corp.
722 Gailen Ave.
Palo Alto, CA 94303
(415)968-3443
Fax: (415)493-6954
E-mail: frits@iqix.com

McLaughlin & Associates
66 San Marino Cir.
Rancho Mirage, CA 92270
(760)321-2932
Fax: (760)328-2474
E-mail: jackmcla@msn.com

Carrera Consulting Group, a division of Maximus
2110 21st St., Ste. 400
Sacramento, CA 95818
(916)456-3300
Fax: (916)456-3306
E-mail: central@carreraconsulting.com
Website: http://www.carreraconsulting.com

Bay Area Tax Consultants and Bayhill Financial Consultants
1150 Bayhill Dr., Ste. 1150
San Bruno, CA 94066-3004
(415)952-8786
Fax: (415)588-4524
E-mail: baytax@compuserve.com
Website: http://www.baytax.com/

AdCon Services, LLC
8871 Hillery Dr.
Dan Diego, CA 92126
(858)433-1411
E-mail: adam@adconservices.com
Website: http://www.adconservices.com
Adam Greengrass

California Business Incubation Network
101 W Broadway, No. 480
San Diego, CA 92101
(619)237-0559
Fax: (619)237-0521

G.R. Gordetsky Consultants Inc.
11414 Windy Summit Pl.
San Diego, CA 92127
(619)487-4939
Fax: (619)487-5587
E-mail: gordet@pacbell.net

Freeman, Sullivan & Co.
131 Steuart St., Ste. 500
San Francisco, CA 94105
(415)777-0707

Free: 800-777-0737
Fax: (415)777-2420
Website: http://www.fsc-research.com

Ideas Unlimited
2151 California St., Ste. 7
San Francisco, CA 94115
(415)931-0641
Fax: (415)931-0880

Russell Miller Inc.
300 Montgomery St., Ste. 900
San Francisco, CA 94104
(415)956-7474
Fax: (415)398-0620
E-mail: rmi@pacbell.net
Website: http://www.rmisf.com

PKF Consulting
425 California St., Ste. 1650
San Francisco, CA 94104
(415)421-5378
Fax: (415)956-7708
E-mail: callahan@pkfc.com
Website: http://www.pkfonline.com

Welling & Woodard Inc.
1067 Broadway
San Francisco, CA 94133
(415)776-4500
Fax: (415)776-5067

Highland Associates
16174 Highland Dr.
San Jose, CA 95127
(408)272-7008
Fax: (408)272-4040

ORDIS Inc.
6815 Trinidad Dr.
San Jose, CA 95120-2056
(408)268-3321
Free: 800-446-7347
Fax: (408)268-3582
E-mail: ordis@ordis.com
Website: http://www.ordis.com

Stanford Resources Inc.
20 Great Oaks Blvd., Ste. 200
San Jose, CA 95119
(408)360-8400
Fax: (408)360-8410
E-mail: sales@stanfordsources.com
Website: http://www.stanfordresources.com

Technology Properties Ltd. Inc.
PO Box 20250
San Jose, CA 95160
(408)243-9898
Fax: (408)296-6637
E-mail: sanjose@tplnet.com

Helfert Associates
1777 Borel Pl., Ste. 508
San Mateo, CA 94402-3514
(650)377-0540
Fax: (650)377-0472

Mykytyn Consulting Group Inc.
185 N Redwood Dr., Ste. 200
San Rafael, CA 94903
(415)491-1770
Fax: (415)491-1251
E-mail: info@mcgi.com
Website: http://www.mcgi.com

Omega Management Systems Inc.
3 Mount Darwin Ct.
San Rafael, CA 94903-1109
(415)499-1300
Fax: (415)492-9490
E-mail: omegamgt@ix.netcom.com

The Information Group Inc.
4675 Stevens Creek Blvd., Ste. 100
Santa Clara, CA 95051
(408)985-7877
Fax: (408)985-2945
E-mail: dvincent@tig-usa.com
Website: http://www.tig-usa.com

Cast Management Consultants
1620 26th St., Ste. 2040N
Santa Monica, CA 90404
(310)828-7511
Fax: (310)453-6831

Cuma Consulting Management
Box 724
Santa Rosa, CA 95402
(707)785-2477
Fax: (707)785-2478

The E-Myth Academy
131B Stony Cir., Ste. 2000
Santa Rosa, CA 95401
(707)569-5600
Free: 800-221-0266
Fax: (707)569-5700
E-mail: info@e-myth.com
Website: http://www.e-myth.com

Reilly, Connors & Ray
1743 Canyon Rd.
Spring Valley, CA 91977
(619)698-4808
Fax: (619)460-3892
E-mail: davidray@adnc.com

Management Consultants
Sunnyvale, CA 94087-4700
(408)773-0321

RJR Associates
1639 Lewiston Dr.
Sunnyvale, CA 94087
(408)737-7720
E-mail: bobroy@rjrassoc.com
Website: http://www.rjrassoc.com

Schwafel Associates
333 Cobalt Way, Ste. 21
Sunnyvale, CA 94085
(408)720-0649
Fax: (408)720-1796
E-mail: schwafel@ricochet.net
Website: http://www.patca.org

Staubs Business Services
23320 S Vermont Ave.
Torrance, CA 90502-2940
(310)830-9128
Fax: (310)830-9128
E-mail: Harry_L_Staubs@Lamg.com

Out of Your Mind...and Into the Marketplace
13381 White Sands Dr.
Tustin, CA 92780-4565
(714)544-0248
Free: 800-419-1513
Fax: (714)730-1414
E-mail: lpinson@aol.com
Website: http://www.business-plan.com

Independent Research Services
PO Box 2426
Van Nuys, CA 91404-2426
(818)993-3622

Ingman Company Inc.
7949 Woodley Ave., Ste. 120
Van Nuys, CA 91406-1232
(818)375-5027
Fax: (818)894-5001

Innovative Technology Associates
3639 E Harbor Blvd., Ste. 203E
Ventura, CA 93001
(805)650-9353

Grid Technology Associates
20404 Tufts Cir.
Walnut, CA 91789
(909)444-0922
Fax: (909)444-0922
E-mail: grid_technology@msn.com

Ridge Consultants Inc.
100 Pringle Ave., Ste. 580
Walnut Creek, CA 94596
(925)274-1990
Fax: (510)274-1956
E-mail: info@ridgecon.com
Website: http://www.ridgecon.com

Bell Springs Publishing
PO Box 1240
Willits, CA 95490
(707)459-6372
E-mail: bellsprings@sabernet
Website: http://www.bellsprings.com

Hutchinson Consulting and Appraisal
23245 Sylvan St., Ste. 103
Woodland Hills, CA 91367
(818)888-8175
Free: 800-977-7548
Fax: (818)888-8220
E-mail: r.f.hutchinson-cpa@worldnet.
att.net

Colorado

Sam Boyer & Associates
4255 S Buckley Rd., No. 136
Aurora, CO 80013
Free: 800-785-0485
Fax: (303)766-8740
E-mail: samboyer@samboyer.com
Website: http://www.samboyer.com/

Ameriwest Business Consultants Inc.
PO Box 26266
Colorado Springs, CO 80936
(719)380-7096
Fax: (719)380-7096
E-mail: email@abchelp.com
Website: http://www.abchelp.com

GVNW Consulting Inc.
2270 La Montana Way
Colorado Springs, CO 80936
(719)594-5800
Fax: (719)594-5803
Website: http://www.gvnw.com

M-Squared Inc.
755 San Gabriel Pl.
Colorado Springs, CO 80906
(719)576-2554
Fax: (719)576-2554

Thornton Financial FNIC
1024 Centre Ave., Bldg. E
Fort Collins, CO 80526-1849
(970)221-2089
Fax: (970)484-5206

TenEyck Associates
1760 Cherryville Rd.
Greenwood Village, CO 80121-1503
(303)758-6129
Fax: (303)761-8286

Associated Enterprises Ltd.
13050 W Ceder Dr., Unit 11
Lakewood, CO 80228

(303)988-6695
Fax: (303)988-6739
E-mail: ael1@classic.msn.com

The Vincent Company Inc.
200 Union Blvd., Ste. 210
Lakewood, CO 80228
(303)989-7271
Free: 800-274-0733
Fax: (303)989-7570
E-mail: vincent@vincentco.com
Website: http://www.vincentco.com

Johnson & West Management Consultants Inc.
7612 S Logan Dr.
Littleton, CO 80122
(303)730-2810
Fax: (303)730-3219

Western Capital Holdings Inc.
10050 E Applwood Dr.
Parker, CO 80138
(303)841-1022
Fax: (303)770-1945

Connecticut

Stratman Group Inc.
40 Tower Ln.
Avon, CT 06001-4222
(860)677-2898
Free: 800-551-0499
Fax: (860)677-8210

Cowherd Consulting Group Inc.
106 Stephen Mather Rd.
Darien, CT 06820
(203)655-2150
Fax: (203)655-6427

Greenwich Associates
8 Greenwich Office Park
Greenwich, CT 06831-5149
(203)629-1200
Fax: (203)629-1229
E-mail: lisa@greenwich.com
Website: http://www.greenwich.com

Follow-up News
185 Pine St., Ste. 818
Manchester, CT 06040
(860)647-7542
Free: 800-708-0696
Fax: (860)646-6544
E-mail: Followupnews@aol.com

Lovins & Associates Consulting
309 Edwards St.
New Haven, CT 06511
(203)787-3367

Fax: (203)624-7599
E-mail: Alovinsphd@aol.com
Website: http://www.lovinsgroup.com

JC Ventures Inc.
4 Arnold St.
Old Greenwich, CT 06870-1203
(203)698-1990
Free: 800-698-1997
Fax: (203)698-2638

Charles L. Hornung Associates
52 Ned's Mountain Rd.
Ridgefield, CT 06877
(203)431-0297

Manus
100 Prospect St., S Tower
Stamford, CT 06901
(203)326-3880
Free: 800-445-0942
Fax: (203)326-3890
E-mail: manus1@aol.com
Website: http://www.RightManus.com

RealBusinessPlans.com
156 Westport Rd.
Wilton, CT 06897
(914)837-2886
E-mail: ct@realbusinessplans.com
Website: http://www.RealBusinessPlans.com
Tony Tecce

Delaware

Focus Marketing
61-7 Habor Dr.
Claymont, DE 19703
(302)793-3064

Daedalus Ventures Ltd.
PO Box 1474
Hockessin, DE 19707
(302)239-6758
Fax: (302)239-9991
E-mail: daedalus@mail.del.net

The Formula Group
PO Box 866
Hockessin, DE 19707
(302)456-0952
Fax: (302)456-1354
E-mail: formula@netaxs.com

Selden Enterprises Inc.
2502 Silverside Rd., Ste. 1
Wilmington, DE 19810-3740
(302)529-7113
Fax: (302)529-7442
E-mail: selden2@bellatlantic.net
Website: http://www.seldenenterprises.com

District of Columbia

Bruce W. McGee and Associates
7826 Eastern Ave. NW, Ste. 30
Washington, DC 20012
(202)726-7272
Fax: (202)726-2946

McManis Associates Inc.
1900 K St. NW, Ste. 700
Washington, DC 20006
(202)466-7680
Fax: (202)872-1898
Website: http://www.mcmanis-mmi.com

Smith, Dawson & Andrews Inc.
1000 Connecticut Ave., Ste. 302
Washington, DC 20036
(202)835-0740
Fax: (202)775-8526
E-mail: webmaster@sda-inc.com
Website: http://www.sda-inc.com

Florida

BackBone, Inc.
20404 Hacienda Court
Boca Raton, FL 33498
(561)470-0965
Fax: 516-908-4038
E-mail: BPlans@backboneinc.com
Website: http://www.backboneinc.com
Charles Epstein, President

Whalen & Associates Inc.
4255 Northwest 26 Ct.
Boca Raton, FL 33434
(561)241-5950
Fax: (561)241-7414
E-mail: drwhalen@ix.netcom.com

E.N. Rysso & Associates
180 Bermuda Petrel Ct.
Daytona Beach, FL 32119
(386)760-3028
E-mail: erysso@aol.com

Virtual Technocrats LLC
560 Lavers Circle, #146
Delray Beach, FL 33444
(561)265-3509
E-mail: josh@virtualtechnocrats.com;
info@virtualtechnocrats.com
Website: http://www.virtualtechno
crats.com
Josh Eikov, Managing Director

Eric Sands Consulting Services
6193 Rock Island Rd., Ste. 412
Fort Lauderdale, FL 33319
(954)721-4767

Fax: (954)720-2815
E-mail: easands@aol.com
Website: http://www.ericsandsconsultig.com

Professional Planning Associates, Inc.
1975 E. Sunrise Blvd. Suite 607
Fort Lauderdale, FL 33304
(954)764-5204
Fax: 954-463-4172
E-mail: Mgoldstein@proplana.com
Website: http://proplana.com
Michael Goldstein, President

Host Media Corp.
3948 S 3rd St., Ste. 191
Jacksonville Beach, FL 32250
(904)285-3239
Fax: (904)285-5618
E-mail: msconsulting@compuserve.com
Website: http://www.media
servicesgroup.com

William V. Hall
1925 Brickell, Ste. D-701
Miami, FL 33129
(305)856-9622
Fax: (305)856-4113
E-mail: williamvhall@compuserve.com

F.A. McGee Inc.
800 Claughton Island Dr., Ste. 401
Miami, FL 33131
(305)377-9123

Taxplan Inc.
Mirasol International Ctr.
2699 Collins Ave.
Miami Beach, FL 33140
(305)538-3303

T.C. Brown & Associates
8415 Excalibur Cir., Apt. B1
Naples, FL 34108
(941)594-1949
Fax: (941)594-0611
E-mail: tcater@naples.net.com

RLA International Consulting
713 Lagoon Dr.
North Palm Beach, FL 33408
(407)626-4258
Fax: (407)626-5772

Comprehensive Franchising Inc.
2465 Ridgecrest Ave.
Orange Park, FL 32065
(904)272-6567
Free: 800-321-6567
Fax: (904)272-6750
E-mail: theimp@cris.com
Website: http://www.franchise411.com

Hunter G. Jackson Jr. - Consulting Environmental Physicist
PO Box 618272
Orlando, FL 32861-8272
(407)295-4188
E-mail: hunterjackson@juno.com

F. Newton Parks
210 El Brillo Way
Palm Beach, FL 33480
(561)833-1727
Fax: (561)833-4541

Avery Business Development Services
2506 St. Michel Ct.
Ponte Vedra Beach, FL 32082
(904)285-6033
Fax: (904)285-6033

Strategic Business Planning Co.
PO Box 821006
South Florida, FL 33082-1006
(954)704-9100
Fax: (954)438-7333
E-mail: info@bizplan.com
Website: http://www.bizplan.com

Dufresne Consulting Group Inc.
10014 N Dale Mabry, Ste. 101
Tampa, FL 33618-4426
(813)264-4775
Fax: (813)264-9300
Website: http://www.dcgconsult.com

Agrippa Enterprises Inc.
PO Box 175
Venice, FL 34284-0175
(941)355-7876
E-mail: webservices@agrippa.com
Website: http://www.agrippa.com

Center for Simplified Strategic Planning Inc.
PO Box 3324
Vero Beach, FL 32964-3324
(561)231-3636
Fax: (561)231-1099
Website: http://www.cssp.com

Georgia

Marketing Spectrum Inc.
115 Perimeter Pl., Ste. 440
Atlanta, GA 30346
(770)395-7244
Fax: (770)393-4071

Business Ventures Corp.
1650 Oakbrook Dr., Ste. 405
Norcross, GA 30093
(770)729-8000
Fax: (770)729-8028

Informed Decisions Inc.
100 Falling Cheek
Sautee Nacoochee, GA 30571
(706)878-1905
Fax: (706)878-1802
E-mail: skylake@compuserve.com

Tom C. Davis & Associates, P.C.
3189 Perimeter Rd.
Valdosta, GA 31602
(912)247-9801
Fax: (912)244-7704
E-mail: mail@tcdcpa.com
Website: http://www.tcdcpa.com/

Illinois

TWD and Associates
431 S Patton
Arlington Heights, IL 60005
(847)398-6410
Fax: (847)255-5095
E-mail: tdoo@aol.com

Management Planning Associates Inc.
2275 Half Day Rd., Ste. 350
Bannockburn, IL 60015-1277
(847)945-2421
Fax: (847)945-2425

Phil Faris Associates
86 Old Mill Ct.
Barrington, IL 60010
(847)382-4888
Fax: (847)382-4890
E-mail: pfaris@meginsnet.net

Seven Continents Technology
787 Stonebridge
Buffalo Grove, IL 60089
(708)577-9653
Fax: (708)870-1220

Grubb & Blue Inc.
2404 Windsor Pl.
Champaign, IL 61820
(217)366-0052
Fax: (217)356-0117

ACE Accounting Service Inc.
3128 N Bernard St.
Chicago, IL 60618
(773)463-7854
Fax: (773)463-7854

AON Consulting Worldwide
200 E Randolph St., 10th Fl.
Chicago, IL 60601
(312)381-4800
Free: 800-438-6487
Fax: (312)381-0240
Website: http://www.aon.com

FMS Consultants
5801 N Sheridan Rd., Ste. 3D
Chicago, IL 60660
(773)561-7362
Fax: (773)561-6274

Grant Thornton
800 1 Prudential Plz.
130 E Randolph St.
Chicago, IL 60601
(312)856-0001
Fax: (312)861-1340
E-mail: gtinfo@gt.com
Website: http://www.grantthornton.com

Kingsbury International Ltd.
5341 N Glenwood Ave.
Chicago, IL 60640
(773)271-3030
Fax: (773)728-7080
E-mail: jetlag@mcs.com
Website: http://www.kingbiz.com

MacDougall & Blake Inc.
1414 N Wells St., Ste. 311
Chicago, IL 60610-1306
(312)587-3330
Fax: (312)587-3699
E-mail: jblake@compuserve.com

James C. Osburn Ltd.
6445 N. Western Ave., Ste. 304
Chicago, IL 60645
(773)262-4428
Fax: (773)262-6755
E-mail: osburnltd@aol.com

Tarifero & Tazewell Inc.
211 S Clark
Chicago, IL 60690
(312)665-9714
Fax: (312)665-9716

Human Energy Design Systems
620 Roosevelt Dr.
Edwardsville, IL 62025
(618)692-0258
Fax: (618)692-0819

China Business Consultants Group
931 Dakota Cir.
Naperville, IL 60563
(630)778-7992
Fax: (630)778-7915
E-mail: cbcq@aol.com

Center for Workforce Effectiveness
500 Skokie Blvd., Ste. 222
Northbrook, IL 60062
(847)559-8777
Fax: (847)559-8778

E-mail: office@cwelink.com
Website: http://www.cwelink.com

Smith Associates
1320 White Mountain Dr.
Northbrook, IL 60062
(847)480-7200
Fax: (847)480-9828

Francorp Inc.
20200 Governors Dr.
Olympia Fields, IL 60461
(708)481-2900
Free: 800-372-6244
Fax: (708)481-5885
E-mail: francorp@aol.com
Website: http://www.francorpinc.com

Camber Business Strategy Consultants
1010 S Plum Tree Ct
Palatine, IL 60078-0986
(847)202-0101
Fax: (847)705-7510
E-mail: camber@ameritech.net

Partec Enterprise Group
5202 Keith Dr.
Richton Park, IL 60471
(708)503-4047
Fax: (708)503-9468

Rockford Consulting Group Ltd.
Century Plz., Ste. 206
7210 E State St.
Rockford, IL 61108
(815)229-2900
Free: 800-667-7495
Fax: (815)229-2612
E-mail: rligus@RockfordConsulting.com
Website: http://www.Rockford
Consulting.com

RSM McGladrey Inc.
1699 E Woodfield Rd., Ste. 300
Schaumburg, IL 60173-4969
(847)413-6900
Fax: (847)517-7067
Website: http://www.rsmmcgladrey.com

A.D. Star Consulting
320 Euclid
Winnetka, IL 60093
(847)446-7827
Fax: (847)446-7827
E-mail: startwo@worldnet.att.net

Indiana

Modular Consultants Inc.
3109 Crabtree Ln.
Elkhart, IN 46514

(219)264-5761
Fax: (219)264-5761
E-mail: sasabo5313@aol.com

Midwest Marketing Research
PO Box 1077
Goshen, IN 46527
(219)533-0548
Fax: (219)533-0540
E-mail: 103365.654@compuserve

Ketchum Consulting Group
8021 Knue Rd., Ste. 112
Indianapolis, IN 46250
(317)845-5411
Fax: (317)842-9941

**MDI Management
Consulting**
1519 Park Dr.
Munster, IN 46321
(219)838-7909
Fax: (219)838-7909

Iowa

McCord Consulting Group Inc.
4533 Pine View Dr. NE
PO Box 11024
Cedar Rapids, IA 52410
(319)378-0077
Fax: (319)378-1577
E-mail: smmccord@hom.com
Website: http://www.mccordgroup.com

Management Solutions L.C.
3815 Lincoln Pl. Dr.
Des Moines, IA 50312
(515)277-6408
Fax: (515)277-3506
E-mail: wasunimers@uswest.net

Grandview Marketing
15 Red Bridge Dr.
Sioux City, IA 51104
(712)239-3122
Fax: (712)258-7578
E-mail: eandrews@pionet.net

Kansas

Assessments in Action
513A N Mur-Len
Olathe, KS 66062
(913)764-6270
Free: (888)548-1504
Fax: (913)764-6495
E-mail: lowdene@qni.com
Website: http://www.assessments-
in-action.com

Maine

Edgemont Enterprises
PO Box 8354
Portland, ME 04104
(207)871-8964
Fax: (207)871-8964

Pan Atlantic Consultants
5 Milk St.
Portland, ME 04101
(207)871-8622
Fax: (207)772-4842
E-mail: pmurphy@maine.rr.com
Website: http://www.panatlantic.net

Maryland

Clemons & Associates Inc.
5024-R Campbell Blvd.
Baltimore, MD 21236
(410)931-8100
Fax: (410)931-8111
E-mail: info@clemonsmgmt.com
Website: http://www.clemonsmgmt.com

Imperial Group Ltd.
305 Washington Ave., Ste. 204
Baltimore, MD 21204-6009
(410)337-8500
Fax: (410)337-7641

Leadership Institute
3831 Yolando Rd.
Baltimore, MD 21218
(410)366-9111
Fax: (410)243-8478
E-mail: behconsult@aol.com

Burdeshaw Associates Ltd.
4701 Sangamore Rd.
Bethesda, MD 20816-2508
(301)229-5800
Fax: (301)229-5045
E-mail: jstacy@burdeshaw.com
Website: http://www.burdeshaw.com

Michael E. Cohen
5225 Pooks Hill Rd., Ste. 1119 S
Bethesda, MD 20814
(301)530-5738
Fax: (301)530-2988
E-mail: mecohen@crosslink.net

World Development Group Inc.
5272 River Rd., Ste. 650
Bethesda, MD 20816-1405
(301)652-1818
Fax: (301)652-1250
E-mail: wdg@has.com
Website: http://www.worlddg.com

Swartz Consulting
PO Box 4301
Crofton, MD 21114-4301
(301)262-6728

Software Solutions International Inc.
9633 Duffer Way
Gaithersburg, MD 20886
(301)330-4136
Fax: (301)330-4136

Strategies Inc.
8 Park Center Ct., Ste. 200
Owings Mills, MD 21117
(410)363-6669
Fax: (410)363-1231
E-mail: strategies@strat1.com
Website: http://www.strat1.com

Hammer Marketing Resources
179 Inverness Rd.
Severna Park, MD 21146
(410)544-9191
Fax: (305)675-3277
E-mail: info@gohammer.com
Website: http://www.gohammer.com

Andrew Sussman & Associates
13731 Kretsinger
Smithsburg, MD 21783
(301)824-2943
Fax: (301)824-2943

Massachusetts

Geibel Marketing and Public Relations
PO Box 611
Belmont, MA 02478-0005
(617)484-8285
Fax: (617)489-3567
E-mail: jgeibel@geibelpr.com
Website: http://www.geibelpr.com

Bain & Co.
2 Copley Pl.
Boston, MA 02116
(617)572-2000
Fax: (617)572-2427
E-mail: corporate.inquiries@bain.com
Website: http://www.bain.com

Mehr & Co.
62 Kinnaird St.
Cambridge, MA 02139
(617)876-3311
Fax: (617)876-3023
E-mail: mehrco@aol.com

Monitor Company Inc.
2 Canal Park
Cambridge, MA 02141

(617)252-2000
Fax: (617)252-2100
Website: http://www.monitor.com

Information & Research Associates
PO Box 3121
Framingham, MA 01701
(508)788-0784

Walden Consultants Ltd.
252 Pond St.
Hopkinton, MA 01748
(508)435-4882
Fax: (508)435-3971
Website: http://www.waldencon
sultants.com

Jeffrey D. Marshall
102 Mitchell Rd.
Ipswich, MA 01938-1219
(508)356-1113
Fax: (508)356-2989

Consulting Resources Corp.
6 Northbrook Park
Lexington, MA 02420
(781)863-1222
Fax: (781)863-1441
E-mail: res@consultingresources.net
Website: http://www.consulting
resources.net

Planning Technologies Group L.L.C.
92 Hayden Ave.
Lexington, MA 02421
(781)778-4678
Fax: (781)861-1099
E-mail: ptg@plantech.com
Website: http://www.plantech.com

Kalba International Inc.
23 Sandy Pond Rd.
Lincoln, MA 01773
(781)259-9589
Fax: (781)259-1460
E-mail: info@kalbainternational.com
Website: http://www.kalbainter
national.com

VMB Associates Inc.
115 Ashland St.
Melrose, MA 02176
(781)665-0623
Fax: (425)732-7142
E-mail: vmbinc@aol.com

The Company Doctor
14 Pudding Stone Ln.
Mendon, MA 01756
(508)478-1747
Fax: (508)478-0520

Data and Strategies Group Inc.
190 N Main St.
Natick, MA 01760
(508)653-9990
Fax: (508)653-7799
E-mail: dsginc@dsggroup.com
Website: http://www.dsggroup.com

The Enterprise Group
73 Parker Rd.
Needham, MA 02494
(617)444-6631
Fax: (617)433-9991
E-mail: lsacco@world.std.com
Website: http://www.enterprise-group.com

PSMJ Resources Inc.
10 Midland Ave.
Newton, MA 02458
(617)965-0055
Free: 800-537-7765
Fax: (617)965-5152
E-mail: psmj@tiac.net
Website: http://www.psmj.com

Scheur Management Group Inc.
255 Washington St., Ste. 100
Newton, MA 02458-1611
(617)969-7500
Fax: (617)969-7508
E-mail: smgnow@scheur.com
Website: http://www.scheur.com

I.E.E.E., Boston Section
240 Bear Hill Rd., 202B
Waltham, MA 02451-1017
(781)890-5294
Fax: (781)890-5290

Business Planning and Consulting Services
20 Beechwood Ter.
Wellesley, MA 02482
(617)237-9151
Fax: (617)237-9151

Michigan

Walter Frederick Consulting
1719 South Blvd.
Ann Arbor, MI 48104
(313)662-4336
Fax: (313)769-7505

Fox Enterprises
6220 W Freeland Rd.
Freeland, MI 48623
(517)695-9170
Fax: (517)695-9174
E-mail: foxjw@concentric.net
Website: http://www.cris.com/~foxjw

G.G.W. and Associates
1213 Hampton
Jackson, MI 49203
(517)782-2255
Fax: (517)782-2255

Altamar Group Ltd.
6810 S Cedar, Ste. 2-B
Lansing, MI 48911
(517)694-0910
Free: 800-443-2627
Fax: (517)694-1377

Sheffieck Consultants Inc.
23610 Greening Dr.
Novi, MI 48375-3130
(248)347-3545
Fax: (248)347-3530
E-mail: cfsheff@concentric.net

Rehmann, Robson PC
5800 Gratiot
Saginaw, MI 48605
(517)799-9580
Fax: (517)799-0227
Website: http://www.rrpc.com

Francis & Co.
17200 W 10 Mile Rd., Ste. 207
Southfield, MI 48075
(248)559-7600
Fax: (248)559-5249

Private Ventures Inc.
16000 W 9 Mile Rd., Ste. 504
Southfield, MI 48075
(248)569-1977
Free: 800-448-7614
Fax: (248)569-1838
E-mail: pventuresi@aol.com

JGK Associates
14464 Kerner Dr.
Sterling Heights, MI 48313
(810)247-9055
Fax: (248)822-4977
E-mail: kozlowski@home.com

Minnesota

Health Fitness Corp.
3500 W 80th St., Ste. 130
Bloomington, MN 55431
(612)831-6830
Fax: (612)831-7264

Consatech Inc.
PO Box 1047
Burnsville, MN 55337
(612)953-1088
Fax: (612)435-2966

Robert F. Knotek
14960 Ironwood Ct.
Eden Prairie, MN 55346
(612)949-2875

DRI Consulting
7715 Stonewood Ct.
Edina, MN 55439
(612)941-9656
Fax: (612)941-2693
E-mail: dric@dric.com
Website: http://www.dric.com

Markin Consulting
12072 87th Pl. N
Maple Grove, MN 55369
(612)493-3568
Fax: (612)493-5744
E-mail: markin@markinconsulting.com
Website: http://www.markin
consulting.com

Minnesota Cooperation Office for Small Business & Job Creation Inc.
5001 W 80th St., Ste. 825
Minneapolis, MN 55437
(612)830-1230
Fax: (612)830-1232
E-mail: mncoop@msn.com
Website: http://www.mnco.org

Enterprise Consulting Inc.
PO Box 1111
Minnetonka, MN 55345
(612)949-5909
Fax: (612)906-3965

Amdahl International
724 1st Ave. SW
Rochester, MN 55902
(507)252-0402
Fax: (507)252-0402
E-mail: amdahl@best-service.com
Website: http://www.wp.com/amdahl_int

Power Systems Research
1365 Corporate Center Curve, 2nd Fl.
St. Paul, MN 55121
(612)905-8400
Free: (888)625-8612
Fax: (612)454-0760
E-mail: Barb@Powersys.com
Website: http://www.powersys.com

Missouri

Business Planning and Development Corp.
4030 Charlotte St.
Kansas City, MO 64110
(816)753-0495

E-mail: humph@bpdev.demon.co.uk
Website: http://www.bpdev.demon.co.uk

CFO Service
10336 Donoho
St. Louis, MO 63131
(314)750-2940
E-mail: jskae@cfoservice.com
Website: http://www.cfoservice.com

Nebraska

International Management Consulting Group Inc.
1309 Harlan Dr., Ste. 205
Bellevue, NE 68005
(402)291-4545
Free: 800-665-IMCG
Fax: (402)291-4343
E-mail: imcg@neonramp.com
Website: http://www.mgtcon
sulting.com

Heartland Management Consulting Group
1904 Barrington Pky.
Papillion, NE 68046
(402)339-2387
Fax: (402)339-1319

Nevada

The DuBois Group
865 Tahoe Blvd., Ste. 108
Incline Village, NV 89451
(775)832-0550
Free: 800-375-2935
Fax: (775)832-0556
E-mail: DuBoisGrp@aol.com

New Hampshire

Wolff Consultants
10 Buck Rd.
Hanover, NH 03755
(603)643-6015

BPT Consulting Associates Ltd.
12 Parmenter Rd., Ste. B-6
Londonderry, NH 03053
(603)437-8484
Free: (888)278-0030
Fax: (603)434-5388
E-mail: bptcons@tiac.net
Website: http://www.bptconsulting.com

New Jersey

Bedminster Group Inc.
1170 Rte. 22 E
Bridgewater, NJ 08807

(908)500-4155
Fax: (908)766-0780
E-mail: info@bedminstergroup.com
Website: http://www.bedminster
group.com
Fax: (202)806-1777
Terry Strong, Acting Regional Dir.

Delta Planning Inc.
PO Box 425
Denville, NJ 07834
(913)625-1742
Free: 800-672-0762
Fax: (973)625-3531
E-mail: DeltaP@worldnet.att.net
Website: http://deltaplanning.com

Kumar Associates Inc.
1004 Cumbermeade Rd.
Fort Lee, NJ 07024
(201)224-9480
Fax: (201)585-2343
E-mail: mail@kumarassociates.com
Website: http://kumarassociates.com

John Hall & Company Inc.
PO Box 187
Glen Ridge, NJ 07028
(973)680-4449
Fax: (973)680-4581
E-mail: jhcompany@aol.com

Market Focus
PO Box 402
Maplewood, NJ 07040
(973)378-2470
Fax: (973)378-2470
E-mail: mcss66@marketfocus.com

Vanguard Communications Corp.
100 American Rd.
Morris Plains, NJ 07950
(973)605-8000
Fax: (973)605-8329
Website: http://www.vanguard.net/

ConMar International Ltd.
1901 US Hwy. 130
North Brunswick, NJ 08902
(732)940-8347
Fax: (732)274-1199

KLW New Products
156 Cedar Dr.
Old Tappan, NJ 07675
(201)358-1300
Fax: (201)664-2594
E-mail: lrlarsen@usa.net
Website: http://www.klwnew
products.com

Organizations, Agencies, & Consultants

PA Consulting Group
315A Enterprise Dr.
Plainsboro, NJ 08536
(609)936-8300
Fax: (609)936-8811
E-mail: info@paconsulting.com
Website: http://www.pa-consulting.com

Aurora Marketing Management Inc.
66 Witherspoon St., Ste. 600
Princeton, NJ 08542
(908)904-1125
Fax: (908)359-1108
E-mail: aurora2@voicenet.com
Website: http://www.auroramarketing.net

Smart Business Supersite
88 Orchard Rd., CN-5219
Princeton, NJ 08543
(908)321-1924
Fax: (908)321-5156
E-mail: irv@smartbiz.com
Website: http://www.smartbiz.com

Tracelin Associates
1171 Main St., Ste. 6K
Rahway, NJ 07065
(732)381-3288

Schkeeper Inc.
130-6 Bodman Pl.
Red Bank, NJ 07701
(732)219-1965
Fax: (732)530-3703

Henry Branch Associates
2502 Harmon Cove Twr.
Secaucus, NJ 07094
(201)866-2008
Fax: (201)601-0101
E-mail: hbranch161@home.com

Robert Gibbons & Company Inc.
46 Knoll Rd.
Tenafly, NJ 07670-1050
(201)871-3933
Fax: (201)871-2173
E-mail: crisisbob@aol.com

PMC Management Consultants Inc.
6 Thistle Ln.
Three Bridges, NJ 08887-0332
(908)788-1014
Free: 800-PMC-0250
Fax: (908)806-7287
E-mail: int@pmc-management.com
Website: http://www.pmc-management.com

R.W. Bankart & Associates
20 Valley Ave., Ste. D-2

Westwood, NJ 07675-3607
(201)664-7672

New Mexico

Vondle & Associates Inc.
4926 Calle de Tierra, NE
Albuquerque, NM 87111
(505)292-8961
Fax: (505)296-2790
E-mail: vondle@aol.com

InfoNewMexico
2207 Black Hills Rd., NE
Rio Rancho, NM 87124
(505)891-2462
Fax: (505)896-8971

New York

Powers Research and Training Institute
PO Box 78
Bayville, NY 11709
(516)628-2250
Fax: (516)628-2252
E-mail: powercocch@compuserve.com
Website: http://www.nancypowers.com

Consortium House
296 Wittenberg Rd.
Bearsville, NY 12409
(845)679-8867
Fax: (845)679-9248
E-mail: eugenegs@aol.com
Website: http://www.chpub.com

Progressive Finance Corp.
3549 Tiemann Ave.
Bronx, NY 10469
(718)405-9029
Free: 800-225-8381
Fax: (718)405-1170

Wave Hill Associates Inc.
2621 Palisade Ave., Ste. 15-C
Bronx, NY 10463
(718)549-7368
Fax: (718)601-9670
E-mail: pepper@compuserve.com

Management Insight
96 Arlington Rd.
Buffalo, NY 14221
(716)631-3319
Fax: (716)631-0203
E-mail: michalski@foodservice insight.com
Website: http://www.foodservice insight.com

Samani International Enterprises, Marions Panyaught Consultancy
2028 Parsons
Flushing, NY 11357-3436
(917)287-8087
Fax: 800-873-8939
E-mail: vjp2@biostrategist.com
Website: http://www.biostrategist.com

Marketing Resources Group
71-58 Austin St.
Forest Hills, NY 11375
(718)261-8882

Mangabay Business Plans & Development Subsidiary of Innis Asset Allocation
125-10 Queens Blvd., Ste. 2202
Kew Gardens, NY 11415
(905)527-1947
Fax: 509-472-1935
E-mail: mangabay@mangabay.com
Website: http://www.mangabay.com
Lee Toh, Managing Partner

ComputerEase Co.
1301 Monmouth Ave.
Lakewood, NY 08701
(212)406-9464
Fax: (914)277-5317
E-mail: crawfordc@juno.com

Boice Dunham Group
30 W 13th St.
New York, NY 10011
(212)924-2200
Fax: (212)924-1108

Elizabeth Capen
27 E 95th St.
New York, NY 10128
(212)427-7654
Fax: (212)876-3190

Haver Analytics
60 E 42nd St., Ste. 2424
New York, NY 10017
(212)986-9300
Fax: (212)986-5857
E-mail: data@haver.com
Website: http://www.haver.com

The Jordan, Edmiston Group Inc.
150 E 52nd Ave., 18th Fl.
New York, NY 10022
(212)754-0710
Fax: (212)754-0337

KPMG International
345 Park Ave.
New York, NY 10154-0102
(212)758-9700

Fax: (212)758-9819
Website: http://www.kpmg.com

Mahoney Cohen Consulting Corp.
111 W 40th St., 12th Fl.
New York, NY 10018
(212)490-8000
Fax: (212)790-5913

Management Practice Inc.
342 Madison Ave.
New York, NY 10173-1230
(212)867-7948
Fax: (212)972-5188
Website: http://www.mpiweb.com

Moseley Associates Inc.
342 Madison Ave., Ste. 1414
New York, NY 10016
(212)213-6673
Fax: (212)687-1520

Practice Development Counsel
60 Sutton Pl. S
New York, NY 10022
(212)593-1549
Fax: (212)980-7940
E-mail: pwhaserot@pdcounsel.com
Website: http://www.pdcounsel.com

Unique Value International Inc.
575 Madison Ave., 10th Fl.
New York, NY 10022-1304
(212)605-0590
Fax: (212)605-0589

The Van Tulleken Co.
126 E 56th St.
New York, NY 10022
(212)355-1390
Fax: (212)755-3061
E-mail: newyork@vantulleken.com

Vencon Management Inc.
301 W 53rd St.
New York, NY 10019
(212)581-8787
Fax: (212)397-4126
Website: http://www.venconinc.com

Werner International Inc.
55 E 52nd, 29th Fl.
New York, NY 10055
(212)909-1260
Fax: (212)909-1273
E-mail: richard.downing@rgh.com
Website: http://www.wernertex.com

Zimmerman Business Consulting Inc.
44 E 92nd St., Ste. 5-B
New York, NY 10128

(212)860-3107
Fax: (212)860-7730
E-mail: ljzzbci@aol.com
Website: http://www.zbcinc.com

Overton Financial
7 Allen Rd.
Peekskill, NY 10566
(914)737-4649
Fax: (914)737-4696

Stromberg Consulting
2500 Westchester Ave.
Purchase, NY 10577
(914)251-1515
Fax: (914)251-1562
E-mail: strategy@stromberg_consul
ting.com
Website: http://www.stromberg_
consulting.com

Innovation Management Consulting Inc.
209 Dewitt Rd.
Syracuse, NY 13214-2006
(315)425-5144
Fax: (315)445-8989
E-mail: missonneb@axess.net

M. Clifford Agress
891 Fulton St.
Valley Stream, NY 11580
(516)825-8955
Fax: (516)825-8955

Destiny Kinal Marketing Consultancy
105 Chemung St.
Waverly, NY 14892
(607)565-8317
Fax: (607)565-4083

Valutis Consulting Inc.
5350 Main St., Ste. 7
Williamsville, NY 14221-5338
(716)634-2553
Fax: (716)634-2554
E-mail: valutis@localnet.com
Website: http://www.valutisconsulting.com

North Carolina

Best Practices L.L.C.
6320 Quadrangle Dr., Ste. 200
Chapel Hill, NC 27514
(919)403-0251
Fax: (919)403-0144
E-mail: best@best:in/class
Website: http://www.best-in-class.com

Norelli & Co.
Bank of America Corporate Ctr.
100 N Tyron St., Ste. 5160

Charlotte, NC 28202-4000
(704)376-5484
Fax: (704)376-5485
E-mail: consult@norelli.com
Website: http://www.norelli.com

North Dakota

Center for Innovation
4300 Dartmouth Dr.
PO Box 8372
Grand Forks, ND 58202
(701)777-3132
Fax: (701)777-2339
E-mail: bruce@innovators.net
Website: http://www.innovators.net

Ohio

Transportation Technology Services
208 Harmon Rd.
Aurora, OH 44202
(330)562-3596

Empro Systems Inc.
4777 Red Bank Expy., Ste. 1
Cincinnati, OH 45227-1542
(513)271-2042
Fax: (513)271-2042

Alliance Management International Ltd.
1440 Windrow Ln.
Cleveland, OH 44147-3200
(440)838-1922
Fax: (440)838-0979
E-mail: bgruss@amiltd.com
Website: http://www.amiltd.com

Bozell Kamstra Public Relations
1301 E 9th St., Ste. 3400
Cleveland, OH 44114
(216)623-1511
Fax: (216)623-1501
E-mail: jfeniger@cleveland.bozellk
amstra.com
Website: http://www.bozellk
amstra.com

Cory Dillon Associates
111 Schreyer Pl. E
Columbus, OH 43214
(614)262-8211
Fax: (614)262-3806

Holcomb Gallagher Adams
300 Marconi, Ste. 303
Columbus, OH 43215
(614)221-3343
Fax: (614)221-3367
E-mail: riadams@acme.freenet.oh.us

Young & Associates
PO Box 711
Kent, OH 44240
(330)678-0524
Free: 800-525-9775
Fax: (330)678-6219
E-mail: online@younginc.com
Website: http://www.younginc.com

Robert A. Westman & Associates
8981 Inversary Dr. SE
Warren, OH 44484-2551
(330)856-4149
Fax: (330)856-2564

Oklahoma

Innovative Partners L.L.C.
4900 Richmond Sq., Ste. 100
Oklahoma City, OK 73118
(405)840-0033
Fax: (405)843-8359
E-mail: ipartners@juno.com

Oregon

**INTERCON - The International
Converting Institute**
5200 Badger Rd.
Crooked River Ranch, OR 97760
(541)548-1447
Fax: (541)548-1618
E-mail: johnbowler@
crookedriverranch.com

Talbott ARM
HC 60, Box 5620
Lakeview, OR 97630
(541)635-8587
Fax: (503)947-3482

Management Technology Associates Ltd.
2768 SW Sherwood Dr, Ste. 105
Portland, OR 97201-2251
(503)224-5220
Fax: (503)224-5334
E-mail: lcuster@mta-ltd.com
Website: http://www.mgmt-tech.com

Pennsylvania

Healthscope Inc.
400 Lancaster Ave.
Devon, PA 19333
(610)687-6199
Fax: (610)687-6376
E-mail: health@voicenet.com
Website: http://www.healthscope.net/

Elayne Howard & Associates Inc.
3501 Masons Mill Rd., Ste. 501

Huntingdon Valley, PA 19006-3509
(215)657-9550

GRA Inc.
115 West Ave., Ste. 201
Jenkintown, PA 19046
(215)884-7500
Fax: (215)884-1385
E-mail: gramail@gra-inc.com
Website: http://www.gra-inc.com

**Mifflin County Industrial Development
Corp.**
Mifflin County Industrial Plz.
6395 SR 103 N
Bldg. 50
Lewistown, PA 17044
(717)242-0393
Fax: (717)242-1842
E-mail: mcide@acsworld.net

Autech Products
1289 Revere Rd.
Morrisville, PA 19067
(215)493-3759
Fax: (215)493-9791
E-mail: autech4@yahoo.com

Advantage Associates
434 Avon Dr.
Pittsburgh, PA 15228
(412)343-1558
Fax: (412)362-1684
E-mail: ecocba1@aol.com

Regis J. Sheehan & Associates
Pittsburgh, PA 15220
(412)279-1207

James W. Davidson Company Inc.
23 Forest View Rd.
Wallingford, PA 19086
(610)566-1462

Puerto Rico

Diego Chevere & Co.
Metro Parque 7, Ste. 204
Metro Office
Caparra Heights, PR 00920
(787)774-9595
Fax: (787)774-9566
E-mail: dcco@coqui.net

Manuel L. Porrata and Associates
898 Munoz Rivera Ave., Ste. 201
San Juan, PR 00927
(787)765-2140
Fax: (787)754-3285
E-mail: m_porrata@manuelporrata.com
Website: http://manualporrata.com

South Carolina

Aquafood Business Associates
PO Box 13267
Charleston, SC 29422
(843)795-9506
Fax: (843)795-9477
E-mail: rraba@aol.com

Profit Associates Inc.
PO Box 38026
Charleston, SC 29414
(803)763-5718
Fax: (803)763-5719
E-mail: bobrog@awod.com
Website: http://www.awod.com/gallery/
business/proasc

Strategic Innovations International
12 Executive Ct.
Lake Wylie, SC 29710
(803)831-1225
Fax: (803)831-1177
E-mail: stratinnov@aol.com
Website: http://www.
strategicinnovations.com

Minus Stage
Box 4436
Rock Hill, SC 29731
(803)328-0705
Fax: (803)329-9948

Tennessee

Daniel Petchers & Associates
8820 Fernwood CV
Germantown, TN 38138
(901)755-9896

Business Choices
1114 Forest Harbor, Ste. 300
Hendersonville, TN 37075-9646
(615)822-8692
Free: 800-737-8382
Fax: (615)822-8692
E-mail: bz-ch@juno.com

**RCFA Healthcare Management
Services L.L.C.**
9648 Kingston Pke., Ste. 8
Knoxville, TN 37922
(865)531-0176
Free: 800-635-4040
Fax: (865)531-0722
E-mail: info@rcfa.com
Website: http://www.rcfa.com

Growth Consultants of America
3917 Trimble Rd.
Nashville, TN 37215

(615)383-0550
Fax: (615)269-8940
E-mail: 70244.451@compuserve.com

Texas

**Integrated Cost Management
Systems Inc.**
2261 Brookhollow Plz. Dr., Ste. 104
Arlington, TX 76006
(817)633-2873
Fax: (817)633-3781
E-mail: abm@icms.net
Website: http://www.icms.net

Lori Williams
1000 Leslie Ct.
Arlington, TX 76012
(817)459-3934
Fax: (817)459-3934

Business Resource Software Inc.
2013 Wells Branch Pky., Ste. 305
Austin, TX 78728
Free: 800-423-1228
Fax: (512)251-4401
E-mail: info@brs-inc.com
Website: http://www.brs-inc.com

Erisa Adminstrative Services Inc.
12325 Hymeadow Dr., Bldg. 4
Austin, TX 78750-1847
(512)250-9020
Fax: (512)250-9487
Website: http://www.cserisa.com

R. Miller Hicks & Co.
1011 W 11th St.
Austin, TX 78703
(512)477-7000
Fax: (512)477-9697
E-mail: millerhicks@rmhicks.com
Website: http://www.rmhicks.com

Pragmatic Tactics Inc.
3303 Westchester Ave.
College Station, TX 77845
(409)696-5294
Free: 800-570-5294
Fax: (409)696-4994
E-mail: ptactics@aol.com
Website: http://www.ptatics.com

Perot Systems
12404 Park Central Dr.
Dallas, TX 75251
(972)340-5000
Free: 800-688-4333
Fax: (972)455-4100
E-mail: corp.comm@ps.net
Website: http://www.perotsystems.com

ReGENERATION Partners
3838 Oak Lawn Ave.
Dallas, TX 75219
(214)559-3999
Free: 800-406-1112
E-mail: info@regeneration-partner.com
Website: http://www.regeneration-
partners.com

**High Technology Associates - Division
of Global Technologies Inc.**
1775 St. James Pl., Ste. 105
Houston, TX 77056
(713)963-9300
Fax: (713)963-8341
E-mail: hta@infohwy.com

MasterCOM
103 Thunder Rd.
Kerrville, TX 78028
(830)895-7990
Fax: (830)443-3428
E-mail: jmstubblefield@master
training.com
Website: http://www.mastertraining.com

PROTEC
4607 Linden Pl.
Pearland, TX 77584
(281)997-9872
Fax: (281)997-9895
E-mail: p.oman@ix.netcom.com

Alpha Quadrant Inc.
10618 Auldine
San Antonio, TX 78230
(210)344-3330
Fax: (210)344-8151
E-mail: mbussone@sbcglobal.net
Website:http://www.a-quadrant.com
Michele Bussone

Bastian Public Relations
614 San Dizier
San Antonio, TX 78232
(210)404-1839
E-mail: lisa@bastianpr.com
Website: http://www.bastianpr.com
Lisa Bastian CBC

**Business Strategy Development
Consultants**
PO Box 690365
San Antonio, TX 78269
(210)696-8000
Free: 800-927-BSDC
Fax: (210)696-8000

Tom Welch, CPC
6900 San Pedro Ave., Ste. 147
San Antonio, TX 78216-6207

(210)737-7022
Fax: (210)737-7022
E-mail: bplan@iamerica.net
Website: http://www.moneywords.com

Utah

Business Management Resource
PO Box 521125
Salt Lake City, UT 84152-1125
(801)272-4668
Fax: (801)277-3290
E-mail: pingfong@worldnet.att.net

Virginia

Tindell Associates
209 Oxford Ave.
Alexandria, VA 22301
(703)683-0109
Fax: 703-783-0219
E-mail: scott@tindell.net
Website: http://www.tindell.net
Scott Lockett, President

Elliott B. Jaffa
2530-B S Walter Reed Dr.
Arlington, VA 22206
(703)931-0040
E-mail: thetrainingdoctor@excite.com
Website: http://www.tregistry.com/
jaffa.htm

Koach Enterprises - USA
5529 N 18th St.
Arlington, VA 22205
(703)241-8361
Fax: (703)241-8623

Federal Market Development
5650 Chapel Run Ct.
Centreville, VA 20120-3601
(703)502-8930
Free: 800-821-5003
Fax: (703)502-8929

Huff, Stuart & Carlton
2107 Graves Mills Rd., Ste. C
Forest, VA 24551
(804)316-9356
Free: (888)316-9356
Fax: (804)316-9357
Website: http://www.wealthmgt.net

AMX International Inc.
1420 Spring Hill Rd. , Ste. 600
McLean, VA 22102-3006
(703)690-4100
Fax: (703)643-1279
E-mail: amxmail@amxi.com
Website: http://www.amxi.com

Charles Scott Pugh (Investor)
4101 Pittaway Dr.
Richmond, VA 23235-1022
(804)560-0979
Fax: (804)560-4670

John C. Randall and Associates Inc.
PO Box 15127
Richmond, VA 23227
(804)746-4450
Fax: (804)730-8933
E-mail: randalljcx@aol.com
Website: http://www.johncrandall.com

McLeod & Co.
410 1st St.
Roanoke, VA 24011
(540)342-6911
Fax: (540)344-6367
Website: http://www.mcleodco.com/

Salzinger & Company Inc.
8000 Towers Crescent Dr., Ste. 1350
Vienna, VA 22182
(703)442-5200
Fax: (703)442-5205
E-mail: info@salzinger.com
Website: http://www.salzinger.com

The Small Business Counselor
12423 Hedges Run Dr., Ste. 153
Woodbridge, VA 22192
(703)490-6755
Fax: (703)490-1356

Washington

Burlington Consultants
10900 NE 8th St., Ste. 900
Bellevue, WA 98004
(425)688-3060
Fax: (425)454-4383
E-mail: partners@burlington
consultants.com
Website: http://www.burlington
consultants.com

Perry L. Smith Consulting
800 Bellevue Way NE, Ste. 400
Bellevue, WA 98004-4208
(425)462-2072
Fax: (425)462-5638

St. Charles Consulting Group
1420 NW Gilman Blvd.
Issaquah, WA 98027
(425)557-8708
Fax: (425)557-8731
E-mail: info@stcharlesconsulting.com
Website: http://www.stcharlescon
sulting.com

Independent Automotive Training Services
PO Box 334
Kirkland, WA 98083
(425)822-5715
E-mail: ltunney@autosvccon.com
Website: http://www.autosvccon.com

Kahle Associate Inc.
6203 204th Dr. NE
Redmond, WA 98053
(425)836-8763
Fax: (425)868-3770
E-mail: randykahle@kahleassociates.com
Website: http://www.kahleassociates.com

Dan Collin
3419 Wallingord Ave N, No. 2
Seattle, WA 98103
(206)634-9469
E-mail: dc@dancollin.com
Website: http://members.home.net/
dcollin/

ECG Management Consultants Inc.
1111 3rd Ave., Ste. 2700
Seattle, WA 98101-3201
(206)689-2200
Fax: (206)689-2209
E-mail: ecg@ecgmc.com
Website: http://www.ecgmc.com

Northwest Trade Adjustment Assistance Center
900 4th Ave., Ste. 2430
Seattle, WA 98164-1001
(206)622-2730
Free: 800-667-8087
Fax: (206)622-1105
E-mail: matchingfunds@nwtaac.org
Website: http://www.taacenters.org

Business Planning Consultants
S 3510 Ridgeview Dr.
Spokane, WA 99206
(509)928-0332
Fax: (509)921-0842
E-mail: bpci@nextdim.com

West Virginia

**Stanley & Associates Inc./
BusinessandMarketingPlans.com**
1687 Robert C. Byrd Dr.
Beckley, WV 25801
(304)252-0324
Free: 888-752-6720
Fax: (304)252-0470
E-mail: cclay@charterinternet.com

Website: http://www.Businessand
MarketingPlans.com
Christopher Clay

Wisconsin

White & Associates Inc.
5349 Somerset Ln. S
Greenfield, WI 53221
(414)281-7373
Fax: (414)281-7006
E-mail: wnaconsult@aol.com

Small business administration regional offices

This section contains a listing of Small Business Administration offices arranged numerically by region. Service areas are provided. Contact the appropriate office for a referral to the nearest field office, or visit the Small Business Administration online at www.sba.gov.

Region 1

U.S. Small Business Administration
Region I Office
10 Causeway St., Ste. 812
Boston, MA 02222-1093
Phone: (617)565-8415
Fax: (617)565-8420
Serves Connecticut, Maine, Massachusetts, New Hampshire, Rhode Island, and Vermont.

Region 2

U.S. Small Business Administration
Region II Office
26 Federal Plaza, Ste. 3108
New York, NY 10278
Phone: (212)264-1450
Fax: (212)264-0038
Serves New Jersey, New York, Puerto Rico, and the Virgin Islands.

Region 3

U.S. Small Business Administration
Region III Office
Robert N C Nix Sr. Federal Building
900 Market St., 5th Fl.
Philadelphia, PA 19107
(215)580-2807
Serves Delaware, the District of Columbia, Maryland, Pennsylvania, Virginia, and West Virginia.

Region 4

U.S. Small Business Administration
Region IV Office
233 Peachtree St. NE
Harris Tower 1800
Atlanta, GA 30303
Phone: (404)331-4999
Fax: (404)331-2354
Serves Alabama, Florida, Georgia, Kentucky, Mississippi, North Carolina, South Carolina, and Tennessee.

Region 5

U.S. Small Business Administration
Region V Office
500 W. Madison St.
Citicorp Center, Ste. 1240
Chicago, IL 60661-2511
Phone: (312)353-0357
Fax: (312)353-3426
Serves Illinois, Indiana, Michigan, Minnesota, Ohio, and Wisconsin.

Region 6

U.S. Small Business Administration
Region VI Office
4300 Amon Carter Blvd., Ste. 108
Fort Worth, TX 76155
Phone: (817)684-5581
Fax: (817)684-5588
Serves Arkansas, Louisiana, New Mexico, Oklahoma, and Texas.

Region 7

U.S. Small Business Administration
Region VII Office
323 W. 8th St., Ste. 307
Kansas City, MO 64105-1500
Phone: (816)374-6380
Fax: (816)374-6339
Serves Iowa, Kansas, Missouri, and Nebraska.

Region 8

U.S. Small Business Administration
Region VIII Office
721 19th St., Ste. 400
Denver, CO 80202
Phone: (303)844-0500
Fax: (303)844-0506
Serves Colorado, Montana, North Dakota, South Dakota, Utah, and Wyoming.

Region 9

U.S. Small Business Administration
Region IX Office
330 N Brand Blvd., Ste. 1270
Glendale, CA 91203-2304
Phone: (818)552-3434
Fax: (818)552-3440
Serves American Samoa, Arizona, California, Guam, Hawaii, Nevada, and the Trust Territory of the Pacific Islands.

Region 10

U.S. Small Business Administration
Region X Office
2401 Fourth Ave., Ste. 400
Seattle, WA 98121
Phone: (206)553-5676
Fax: (206)553-4155
Serves Alaska, Idaho, Oregon, and Washington.

Small business development centers

This section contains a listing of all Small Business Development Centers, organized alphabetically by state/U.S. territory, then by city, then by agency name.

Alabama

Alabama SBDC
UNIVERSITY OF ALABAMA
2800 Milan Court Suite 124
Birmingham, AL 35211-6908
Phone: 205-943-6750
Fax: 205-943-6752
E-Mail: wcampbell@provost.uab.edu
Website: http://www.asbdc.org
Mr. William Campbell Jr, State Director

Alaska

Alaska SBDC
UNIVERSITY OF ALASKA - ANCHORAGE
430 West Seventh Avenue, Suite 110
Anchorage, AK 99501
Phone: 907-274 -7232
Fax: 907-274-9524
E-Mail: anerw@uaa.alaska.edu
Website: http://www.aksbdc.org
Ms. Jean R. Wall, State Director

American Samoa

American Samoa SBDC
AMERICAN SAMOA COMMUNITY COLLEGE
P.O. Box 2609
Pago Pago, American Samoa 96799
Phone: 011-684-699-4830
Fax: 011-684-699-6132
E-Mail: htalex@att.net
Mr. Herbert Thweatt, Director

Arizona

Arizona SBDC
MARICOPA COUNTY COMMUNITY COLLEGE
2411 West 14th Street, Suite 132
Tempe, AZ 85281
Phone: 480-731-8720
Fax: 480-731-8729
E-Mail: mike.york@domail.maricopa.edu
Website: http://www.dist.maricopa.edu.sbdc
Mr. Michael York, State Director

Arkansas

Arkansas SBDC
UNIVERSITY OF ARKANSAS
2801 South University Avenue
Little Rock, AR 72204
Phone: 501-324-9043
Fax: 501-324-9049
E-Mail: jmroderick@ualr.edu
Website: http://asbdc.ualr.edu
Ms. Janet M. Roderick, State Director

California

California - San Francisco SBDC
Northern California SBDC Lead Center
HUMBOLDT STATE UNIVERSITY
Office of Economic Development
1 Harpst Street 2006A, Siemens Hall
Arcata, CA, 95521
Phone: 707-826-3922
Fax: 707-826-3206
E-Mail: gainer@humboldt.edu
Ms. Margaret A. Gainer, Regional Director

California - Sacramento SBDC
CALIFORNIA STATE UNIVERSITY - CHICO
Chico, CA 95929-0765
Phone: 530-898-4598
Fax: 530-898-4734

E-Mail: dripke@csuchico.edu
Website: http://gsbdc.csuchico.edu
Mr. Dan Ripke, Interim Regional Director

California - San Diego SBDC
SOUTHWESTERN COMMUNITY
COLLEGE DISTRICT
900 Otey Lakes Road
Chula Vista, CA 91910
Phone: 619-482-6388
Fax: 619-482-6402
E-Mail: dtrujillo@swc.cc.ca.us
Website: http://www.sbditc.org
Ms. Debbie P. Trujillo, Regional Director

California - Fresno SBDC
UC Merced Lead Center
UNIVERSITY OF CALIFORNIA -
MERCED
550 East Shaw, Suite 105A
Fresno, CA 93710
Phone: 559-241-6590
Fax: 559-241-7422
E-Mail: crosander@ucmerced.edu
Website: http://sbdc.ucmerced.edu
Mr. Chris Rosander, State Director

California - Santa Ana SBDC
Tri-County Lead SBDC
CALIFORNIA STATE UNIVERSITY -
FULLERTON
800 North State College Boulevard, LH640
Fullerton, CA 92834
Phone: 714-278-2719
Fax: 714-278-7858
E-Mail: vpham@fullerton.edu
Website: http://www.leadsbdc.org
Ms. Vi Pham, Lead Center Director

California - Los Angeles Region SBDC
LONG BEACH COMMUNITY
COLLEGE DISTRICT
3950 Paramount Boulevard, Ste 101
Lakewood, CA 90712
Phone: 562-938-5004
Fax: 562-938-5030
E-Mail: ssloan@lbcc.edu
Ms. Sheneui Sloan, Interim Lead Center
Director

Colorado

Colorado SBDC
OFFICE OF ECONOMIC
DEVELOPMENT
1625 Broadway, Suite 170
Denver, CO 80202
Phone: 303-892-3864
Fax: 303-892-3848
E-Mail: Kelly.Manning@state.co.us

Website: http://www.state.co.us/oed/sbdc
Ms. Kelly Manning, State Director

Connecticut

Connecticut SBDC
UNIVERSITY OF CONNECTICUT
1376 Storrs Road, Unit 4094
Storrs, CT 06269-1094
Phone: 860-870-6370
Fax: 860-870-6374
E-Mail: richard.cheney@uconn.edu
Website: http://www.sbdc.uconn.edu
Mr. Richard Cheney, Interim State Director

Delaware

Delaware SBDC
DELAWARE TECHNOLOGY PARK
1 Innovation Way, Suite 301
Newark, DE 19711
Phone: 302-831-2747
Fax: 302-831-1423
E-Mail: Clinton.tymes@mvs.udel.edu
Website: http://www.delawaresbdc.org
Mr. Clinton Tymes, State Director

District of Columbia

District of Columbia SBDC
HOWARD UNIVERSITY
2600 6th Street, NW Room 128
Washington, DC 20059
Phone: 202-806-1550
Fax: 202-806-1777
E-Mail: hturner@howard.edu
Website: http://www.dcsbdc.com/
Mr. Henry Turner, Executive Director

Florida

Florida SBDC
UNIVERSITY OF WEST FLORIDA
401 East Chase Street, Suite 100
Pensacola, FL 32502
Phone: 850-473-7800
Fax: 850-473-7813
E-Mail: jcartwri@uwf.edu
Website: http://www.floridasbdc.com
Mr. Jerry Cartwright, State Director

Georgia

Georgia SBDC
UNIVERSITY OF GEORGIA
1180 East Broad Street
Athens, GA 30602
Phone: 706-542-6762
Fax: 706-542-6776
E-mail: aadams@sbdc.uga.edu

Website: http://www.sbdc.uga.edu
Mr. Allan Adams, Interim State Director

Guam

Guam Small Business Development
Center
UNIVERSITY OF GUAM
Pacific Islands SBDC
P.O. Box 5014 - U.O.G. Station
Mangilao, GU 96923
Phone: 671-735-2590
Fax: 671-734-2002
E-mail: casey@pacificsbdc.com
Website: http://www.uog.edu/sbdc
Mr. Casey Jeszenka, Director

Hawaii

Hawaii SBDC
UNIVERSITY OF HAWAII - HILO
308 Kamehameha Avenue, Suite 201
Hilo, HI 96720
Phone: 808-974-7515
Fax: 808-974-7683
E-Mail: darrylm@interpac.net
Website: http://www.hawaii-sbdc.org
Mr. Darryl Mleynek, State Director

Idaho

Idaho SBDC
BOISE STATE UNIVERSITY
1910 University Drive
Boise, ID 83725
Phone: 208-426-3799
Fax: 208-426-3877
E-mail: jhogge@boisestate.edu
Website: http://www.idahosbdc.org
Mr. Jim Hogge, State Director

Illinois

Illinois SBDC
DEPARTMENT OF COMMERCE
AND ECONOMIC OPPORTUNITY
620 E. Adams, S-4
Springfield, IL 62701
Phone: 217-524-5700
Fax: 217-524-0171
E-mail: mpatrilli@ildceo.net
Website: http://www.ilsbdc.biz
Mr. Mark Petrilli, State Director

Indiana

Indiana SBDC
INDIANA ECONOMIC
DEVELOPMENT CORPORATION
One North Capitol, Suite 900
Indianapolis, IN 46204

Phone: 317-234-8872
Fax: 317-232-8874
E-mail: dtrocha@isbdc.org
Website: http://www.isbdc.org
Ms. Debbie Bishop Trocha, State Director

Iowa

Iowa SBDC
IOWA STATE UNIVERSITY
340 Gerdin Business Bldg.
Ames, IA 50011-1350
Phone: 515-294-2037
Fax: 515-294-6522
E-mail: jonryan@iastate.edu
Website: http://www.iabusnet.org
Mr. Jon Ryan, State Director

Kansas

Kansas SBDC
FORT HAYS STATE UNIVERSITY
214 SW Sixth Street, Suite 301
Topeka, KS 66603
Phone: 785-296-6514
Fax: 785-291-3261
E-mail: ksbdc.wkearns@fhsu.edu
Website: http://www.fhsu.edu/ksbdc
Mr. Wally Kearns, State Director

Kentucky

Kentucky SBDC
UNIVERSITY OF KENTUCKY
225 Gatton College of Business
Economics Building
Lexington, KY 40506-0034
Phone: 859-257-7668
Fax: 859-323-1907
E-mail: lrnaug0@pop.uky.edu
Website: http://www.ksbdc.org
Ms. Becky Naugle, State Director

Louisiana

Louisiana SBDC
UNIVERSITY OF LOUISIANA - MONROE
College of Business Administration
700 University Avenue
Monroe, LA 71209
Phone: 318-342-5506
Fax: 318-342-5510
E-mail: wilkerson@ulm.edu
Website: http://www.lsbdc.org
Ms. Mary Lynn Wilkerson, State Director

Maine

Maine SBDC
UNIVERSITY OF SOUTHERN MAINE
96 Falmouth Street P.O. Box 9300
Portland, ME 04103
Phone: 207-780-4420
Fax: 207-780-4810
E-mail: jrmassaua@maine.edu
Website: http://www.mainesbdc.org
Mr. John Massaua, State Director

Maryland

Maryland SBDC
UNIVERSITY OF MARYLAND
7100 Baltimore Avenue, Suite 401
College Park, MD 20742
Phone: 301-403-8300
Fax: 301-403-8303
E-mail: rsprow@mdsbdc.umd.edu
Website: http://www.mdsbdc.umd.edu
Ms. Renee Sprow, State Director

Massachusetts

Massachusetts SBDC
UNIVERSITY OF MASSACHUSETTS
School of Management, Room 205
Amherst, MA 01003-4935
Phone: 413-545-6301
Fax: 413-545-1273
E-mail: gep@msbdc.umass.edu
Website: http://msbdc.som.umass.edu
Ms. Georgianna Parkin, State Director

Michigan

Michigan SBTDC
GRAND VALLEY STATE UNIVERSITY
510 West Fulton Avenue
Grand Rapids, MI 49504
Phone: 616-331-7485
Fax: 616-331-7389
E-mail: lopuckic@gvsu.edu
Website: http://www.misbtdc.org
Ms. Carol Lopucki, State Director

Minnesota

Minnesota SBDC
MINNESOTA SMALL BUSINESS DEVELOPMENT CENTER
1st National Bank Building
332 Minnesota Street, Suite E200
St. Paul, MN 55101-1351
Phone: 651-297-5773
Fax: 651-296-5287

E-mail: michael.myhre@state.mn.us
Website: http://www.mnsbdc.com
Mr. Michael Myhre, State Director

Mississippi

Mississippi SBDC
UNIVERSITY OF MISSISSIPPI
B-19 Jeanette Phillips Drive
P.O. Box 1848
University, MS 38677
Phone: 662-915-5001
Fax: 662-915-5650
E-mail: wgurley@olemiss.edu
Website: http://www.olemiss.edu/depts/mssbdc
Mr. Doug Gurley, Jr., State Director

Missouri

Missouri SBDC
UNIVERSITY OF MISSOURI
1205 University Avenue, Suite 300
Columbia, MO 65211
Phone: 573-882-1348
Fax: 573-884-4297
E-mail: summersm@missouri.edu
Website: http://www.mo-sbdc.org/index.shtml
Mr. Max Summers, State Director

Montana

Montana SBDC
DEPARTMENT OF COMMERCE
301 South Park Avenue, Room 114 /
P.O. Box 200505
Helena, MT 59620
Phone: 406-841-2746
Fax: 406-444-1872
E-mail: adesch@state.mt.us
Website: http://commerce.state.mt.us/brd/BRD_SBDC.html
Ms. Ann Desch, State Director

Nebraska

Nebraska SBDC
UNIVERSITY OF NEBRASKA - OMAHA
60th & Dodge Street, CBA Room 407
Omaha, NE 68182
Phone: 402-554-2521
Fax: 402-554-3473
E-mail: rbernier@unomaha.edu
Website: http://nbdc.unomaha.edu
Mr. Robert Bernier, State Director

Nevada

Nevada SBDC
UNIVERSITY OF NEVADA - RENO
Reno College of Business
Administration, Room 411
Reno, NV 89557-0100
Phone: 775-784-1717
Fax: 775-784-4337
E-mail: males@unr.edu
Website: http://www.nsbdc.org
Mr. Sam Males, State Director

New Hampshire

New Hampshire SBDC
UNIVERSITY OF NEW HAMPSHIRE
108 McConnell Hall
Durham, NH 03824-3593
Phone: 603-862-4879
Fax: 603-862-4876
E-mail: Mary.Collins@unh.edu
Website: http://www.nhsbdc.org
Ms. Mary Collins, State Director

New Jersey

New Jersey SBDC
RUTGERS UNIVERSITY
49 Bleeker Street
Newark, NJ 07102-1993
Phone: 973-353-5950
Fax: 973-353-1110
E-mail: bhopper@njsbdc.com
Website: http://www.njsbdc.com/home
Ms. Brenda Hopper, State Director

New Mexico

New Mexico SBDC
SANTA FE COMMUNITY COLLEGE
6401 Richards Avenue
Santa Fe, NM 87505
Phone: 505-428-1362
Fax: 505-471-9469
E-mail: rmiller@santa-fe.cc.nm.us
Website: http://www.nmsbdc.org
Mr. Roy Miller, State Director

New York

New York SBDC
STATE UNIVERSITY OF NEW YORK
SUNY Plaza, S-523
Albany, NY 12246
Phone: 518-443-5398
Fax: 518-443-5275
E-mail: j.king@nyssbdc.org
Website: http://www.nyssbdc.org
Mr. Jim King, State Director

North Carolina

North Carolina SBDTC
UNIVERSITY OF NORTH CAROLINA
5 West Hargett Street, Suite 600
Raleigh, NC 27601
Phone: 919-715-7272
Fax: 919-715-7777
E-mail: sdaugherty@sbtdc.org
Website: http://www.sbtdc.org
Mr. Scott Daugherty, State Director

North Dakota

North Dakota SBDC
UNIVERSITY OF NORTH DAKOTA
1600 E. Century Avenue, Suite 2
Bismarck, ND 58503
Phone: 701-328-5375
Fax: 701-328-5320
E-mail: christine.martin@und.nodak.edu
Website: http://www.ndsbdc.org
Ms. Christine Martin-Goldman, State
Director

Ohio

Ohio SBDC
**OHIO DEPARTMENT
OF DEVELOPMENT**
77 South High Street
Columbus, OH 43216
Phone: 614-466-5102
Fax: 614-466-0829
E-mail: mabraham@odod.state.oh.us
Website: http://www.ohiosbdc.org
Ms. Michele Abraham, State Director

Oklahoma

Oklahoma SBDC
**SOUTHEAST OKLAHOMA STATE
UNIVERSITY**
517 University, Box 2584, Station A
Durant, OK 74701
Phone: 580-745-7577
Fax: 580-745-7471
E-mail: gpennington@sosu.edu
Website: http://www.osbdc.org
Mr. Grady Pennington, State Director

Oregon

Oregon SBDC
LANE COMMUNITY COLLEGE
99 West Tenth Avenue, Suite 390
Eugene, OR 97401-3021
Phone: 541-463-5250
Fax: 541-345-6006
E-mail: carterb@lanecc.edu

Website: http://www.bizcenter.org
Mr. William Carter, State Director

Pennsylvania

Pennsylvania SBDC
UNIVERSITY OF PENNSYLVANIA
The Wharton School
3733 Spruce Street
Philadelphia, PA 19104-6374
Phone: 215-898-1219
Fax: 215-573-2135
E-mail: ghiggins@wharton.upenn.edu
Website: http://pasbdc.org
Mr. Gregory Higgins, State Director

Puerto Rico

Puerto Rico SBDC
**INTER-AMERICAN UNIVERSITY
OF PUERTO RICO**
416 Ponce de Leon Avenue, Union Plaza,
Seventh Floor
Hato Rey, PR 00918
Phone: 787-763-6811
Fax: 787-763-4629
E-mail: cmarti@prsbdc.org
Website: http://www.prsbdc.org
Ms. Carmen Marti, Executive Director

Rhode Island

Rhode Island SBDC
BRYANT UNIVERSITY
1150 Douglas Pike
Smithfield, RI 02917
Phone: 401-232-6923
Fax: 401-232-6933
E-mail: adawson@bryant.edu
Website: http://www.risbdc.org
Ms. Diane Fournaris, Interim State Director

South Carolina

South Carolina SBDC
UNIVERSITY OF SOUTH CAROLINA
College of Business Administration
1710 College Street
Columbia, SC 29208
Phone: 803-777-4907
Fax: 803-777-4403
E-mail: lenti@moore.sc.edu
Website: http://scsbdc.moore.sc.edu
Mr. John Lenti, State Director

South Dakota

South Dakota SBDC
UNIVERSITY OF SOUTH DAKOTA
414 East Clark Street, Patterson Hall
Vermillion, SD 57069

Phone: 605-677-6256
Fax: 605-677-5427
E-mail: jshemmin@usd.edu
Website: http://www.sdsbdc.org
Mr. John S. Hemmingstad, State Director

Tennessee

Tennessee SBDC
TENNESSEE BOARD OF REGENTS
1415 Murfressboro Road, Suite 540
Nashville, TN 37217-2833
Phone: 615-898-2745
Fax: 615-893-7089
E-mail: pgeho@mail.tsbdc.org
Website: http://www.tsbdc.org
Mr. Patrick Geho, State Director

Texas

Texas-North SBDC
DALLAS COUNTY COMMUNITY COLLEGE
1402 Corinth Street
Dallas, TX 75215
Phone: 214-860-5835
Fax: 214-860-5813
E-mail: emk9402@dcccd.edu
Website: http://www.ntsbdc.org
Ms. Liz Klimback, Region Director

Texas-Houston SBDC
UNIVERSITY OF HOUSTON
2302 Fannin, Suite 200
Houston, TX 77002
Phone: 713-752-8425
Fax: 713-756-1500
E-mail: fyoung@uh.edu
Website: http://sbdcnetwork.uh.edu
Mr. Mike Young, Executive Director

Texas-NW SBDC
TEXAS TECH UNIVERSITY
2579 South Loop 289, Suite 114
Lubbock, TX 79423
Phone: 806-745-3973
Fax: 806-745-6207
E-mail: c.bean@nwtsbdc.org
Website: http://www.nwtsbdc.org
Mr. Craig Bean, Executive Director

Texas-South-West Texas Border Region SBDC
UNIVERSITY OF TEXAS - SAN ANTONIO
501 West Durango Boulevard
San Antonio, TX 78207-4415
Phone: 210-458-2742
Fax: 210-458-2464

E-mail: albert.salgado@utsa.edu
Website: http://www.iedtexas.org
Mr. Alberto Salgado, Region Director

Utah

Utah SBDC
SALT LAKE COMMUNITY COLLEGE
9750 South 300 West
Sandy, UT 84070
Phone: 801-957-3493
Fax: 801-957-3488
E-mail: Greg.Panichello@slcc.edu
Website:http://www.slcc.edu/sbdc
Mr. Greg Panichello, State Director

Vermont

Vermont SBDC
VERMONT TECHNICAL COLLEGE
PO Box 188, 1 Main Street
Randolph Center, VT 05061-0188
Phone: 802-728-9101
Fax: 802-728-3026
E-mail: lquillen@vtc.edu
Website: http://www.vtsbdc.org
Ms. Lenae Quillen-Blume, State Director

Virgin Islands

Virgin Islands SBDC
UNIVERSITY OF THE VIRGIN ISLANDS
8000 Nisky Center, Suite 720
St. Thomas, VI 00802-5804
Phone: 340-776-3206
Fax: 340-775-3756
E-mail: wbush@webmail.uvi.edu
Website: http://rps.uvi.edu/SBDC
Mr. Warren Bush, State Director

Virginia

Virginia SBDC
GEORGE MASON UNIVERSITY
4031 University Drive, Suite 200
Fairfax, VA 22030-3409
Phone: 703-277-7727
Fax: 703-352-8515
E-mail: jkeenan@gmu.edu
Website: http://www.virginiasbdc.org
Ms. Jody Keenan, Director

Washington

Washington SBDC
WASHINGTON STATE UNIVERSITY
534 E. Trent Avenue
P.O. Box 1495
Spokane, WA 99210-1495

Phone: 509-358-7765
Fax: 509-358-7764
E-mail: barogers@wsu.edu
Website: http://www.wsbdc.org
Mr. Brett Rogers, State Director

West Virginia

West Virginia SBDC
WEST VIRGINIA DEVELOPMENT OFFICE
Capital Complex, Building 6, Room 652
Charleston, WV 25301
Phone: 304-558-2960
Fax: 304-558-0127
E-mail: csalyer@wvsbdc.org
Website: http://www.wvsbdc.org
Mr. Conley Salyor, State Director

Wisconsin

Wisconsin SBDC
UNIVERSITY OF WISCONSIN
432 North Lake Street, Room 423
Madison, WI 53706
Phone: 608-263-7794
Fax: 608-263-7830
E-mail: erica.kauten@uwex.edu
Website: http://www.wisconsinsbdc.org
Ms. Erica Kauten, State Director

Wyoming

Wyoming SBDC
UNIVERSITY OF WYOMING
P.O. Box 3922
Laramie, WY 82071-3922
Phone: 307-766-3505
Fax: 307-766-3406
E-mail: DDW@uwyo.edu
Website: http://www.uwyo.edu/sbdc
Ms. Debbie Popp, Acting State Director

Service corps of retired executives (score) offices
This section contains a listing of all SCORE offices organized alphabetically by state/U.S. territory, then by city, then by agency name.

Alabama

SCORE Office (Northeast Alabama)
1330 Quintard Ave.
Anniston, AL 36202
(256)237-3536

Organizations, Agencies, & Consultants

SCORE Office (North Alabama)
901 South 15th St, Rm. 201
Birmingham, AL 35294-2060
(205)934-6868
Fax: (205)934-0538

SCORE Office (Baldwin County)
29750 Larry Dee Cawyer Dr.
Daphne, AL 36526
(334)928-5838

SCORE Office (Shoals)
612 S. COurt
Florence, AL 35630
(256)764-4661
Fax: (256)766-9017
E-mail: shoals@shoalschamber.com

SCORE Office (Mobile)
600 S Court St.
Mobile, AL 36104
(334)240-6868
Fax: (334)240-6869

SCORE Office (Alabama Capitol City)
600 S. Court St.
Montgomery, AL 36104
(334)240-6868
Fax: (334)240-6869

SCORE Office (East Alabama)
601 Ave. A
Opelika, AL 36801
(334)745-4861
E-mail: score636@hotmail.com
Website: http://www.angelfire.com/sc/
score636/

SCORE Office (Tuscaloosa)
2200 University Blvd.
Tuscaloosa, AL 35402
(205)758-7588

Alaska

SCORE Office (Anchorage)
510 L St., Ste. 310
Anchorage, AK 99501
(907)271-4022
Fax: (907)271-4545

Arizona

SCORE Office (Lake Havasu)
10 S. Acoma Blvd.
Lake Havasu City, AZ 86403
(520)453-5951
E-mail: SCORE@ctaz.com
Website: http://www.scorearizona.org/
lake_havasu/

SCORE Office (East Valley)
Federal Bldg., Rm. 104
26 N. MacDonald St.
Mesa, AZ 85201
(602)379-3100
Fax: (602)379-3143
E-mail: 402@aol.com
Website: http://www.scorearizona.
org/mesa/

SCORE Office (Phoenix)
2828 N. Central Ave., Ste. 800
Central & One Thomas
Phoenix, AZ 85004
(602)640-2329
Fax: (602)640-2360
E-mail: e-mail@SCORE-phoenix.org
Website: http://www.score-phoenix.org/

SCORE Office (Prescott Arizona)
1228 Willow Creek Rd., Ste. 2
Prescott, AZ 86301
(520)778-7438
Fax: (520)778-0812
E-mail: score@northlink.com
Website: http://www.scorearizona.org/
prescott/

SCORE Office (Tucson)
110 E. Pennington St.
Tucson, AZ 85702
(520)670-5008
Fax: (520)670-5011
E-mail: score@azstarnet.com
Website: http://www.scorearizona.org/
tucson/

SCORE Office (Yuma)
281 W. 24th St., Ste. 116
Yuma, AZ 85364
(520)314-0480
E-mail: score@C2i2.com
Website: http://www.scorearizona.org/
yuma

Arkansas

SCORE Office (South Central)
201 N. Jackson Ave.
El Dorado, AR 71730-5803
(870)863-6113
Fax: (870)863-6115

SCORE Office (Ozark)
Fayetteville, AR 72701
(501)442-7619

SCORE Office (Northwest Arkansas)
Glenn Haven Dr., No. 4
Ft. Smith, AR 72901
(501)783-3556

SCORE Office (Garland County)
Grand & Ouachita
PO Box 6012
Hot Springs Village, AR 71902
(501)321-1700

SCORE Office (Little Rock)
2120 Riverfront Dr., Rm. 100
Little Rock, AR 72202-1747
(501)324-5893
Fax: (501)324-5199

SCORE Office (Southeast Arkansas)
121 W. 6th
Pine Bluff, AR 71601
(870)535-7189
Fax: (870)535-1643

California

SCORE Office (Golden Empire)
1706 Chester Ave., No. 200
Bakersfield, CA 93301
(805)322-5881
Fax: (805)322-5663

SCORE Office (Greater Chico Area)
1324 Mangrove St., Ste. 114
Chico, CA 95926
(916)342-8932
Fax: (916)342-8932

SCORE Office (Concord)
2151-A Salvio St., Ste. B
Concord, CA 94520
(510)685-1181
Fax: (510)685-5623

SCORE Office (Covina)
935 W. Badillo St.
Covina, CA 91723
(818)967-4191
Fax: (818)966-9660

SCORE Office (Rancho Cucamonga)
8280 Utica, Ste. 160
Cucamonga, CA 91730
(909)987-1012
Fax: (909)987-5917

SCORE Office (Culver City)
PO Box 707
Culver City, CA 90232-0707
(310)287-3850
Fax: (310)287-1350

SCORE Office (Danville)
380 Diablo Rd., Ste. 103
Danville, CA 94526
(510)837-4400

SCORE Office (Downey)
11131 Brookshire Ave.
Downey, CA 90241
(310)923-2191
Fax: (310)864-0461

SCORE Office (El Cajon)
109 Rea Ave.
El Cajon, CA 92020
(619)444-1327
Fax: (619)440-6164

SCORE Office (El Centro)
1100 Main St.
El Centro, CA 92243
(619)352-3681
Fax: (619)352-3246

SCORE Office (Escondido)
720 N. Broadway
Escondido, CA 92025
(619)745-2125
Fax: (619)745-1183

SCORE Office (Fairfield)
1111 Webster St.
Fairfield, CA 94533
(707)425-4625
Fax: (707)425-0826

SCORE Office (Fontana)
17009 Valley Blvd., Ste. B
Fontana, CA 92335
(909)822-4433
Fax: (909)822-6238

SCORE Office (Foster City)
1125 E. Hillsdale Blvd.
Foster City, CA 94404
(415)573-7600
Fax: (415)573-5201

SCORE Office (Fremont)
2201 Walnut Ave., Ste. 110
Fremont, CA 94538
(510)795-2244
Fax: (510)795-2240

SCORE Office (Central California)
2719 N. Air Fresno Dr., Ste. 200
Fresno, CA 93727-1547
(559)487-5605
Fax: (559)487-5636

SCORE Office (Gardena)
1204 W. Gardena Blvd.
Gardena, CA 90247
(310)532-9905
Fax: (310)515-4893

SCORE Office (Lompoc)
330 N. Brand Blvd., Ste. 190
Glendale, CA 91203-2304

(818)552-3206
Fax: (818)552-3323

SCORE Office (Los Angeles)
330 N. Brand Blvd., Ste. 190
Glendale, CA 91203-2304
(818)552-3206
Fax: (818)552-3323

SCORE Office (Glendora)
131 E. Foothill Blvd.
Glendora, CA 91740
(818)963-4128
Fax: (818)914-4822

SCORE Office (Grover Beach)
177 S. 8th St.
Grover Beach, CA 93433
(805)489-9091
Fax: (805)489-9091

SCORE Office (Hawthorne)
12477 Hawthorne Blvd.
Hawthorne, CA 90250
(310)676-1163
Fax: (310)676-7661

SCORE Office (Hayward)
22300 Foothill Blvd., Ste. 303
Hayward, CA 94541
(510)537-2424

SCORE Office (Hemet)
1700 E. Florida Ave.
Hemet, CA 92544-4679
(909)652-4390
Fax: (909)929-8543

SCORE Office (Hesperia)
16367 Main St.
PO Box 403656
Hesperia, CA 92340
(619)244-2135

SCORE Office (Holloster)
321 San Felipe Rd., No. 11
Hollister, CA 95023

SCORE Office (Hollywood)
7018 Hollywood Blvd.
Hollywood, CA 90028
(213)469-8311
Fax: (213)469-2805

SCORE Office (Indio)
82503 Hwy. 111
PO Drawer TTT
Indio, CA 92202
(619)347-0676

SCORE Office (Inglewood)
330 Queen St.

Inglewood, CA 90301
(818)552-3206

SCORE Office (La Puente)
218 N. Grendanda St. D.
La Puente, CA 91744
(818)330-3216
Fax: (818)330-9524

SCORE Office (La Verne)
2078 Bonita Ave.
La Verne, CA 91750
(909)593-5265
Fax: (714)929-8475

SCORE Office (Lake Elsinore)
132 W. Graham Ave.
Lake Elsinore, CA 92530
(909)674-2577

SCORE Office (Lakeport)
PO Box 295
Lakeport, CA 95453
(707)263-5092

SCORE Office (Lakewood)
5445 E. Del Amo Blvd., Ste. 2
Lakewood, CA 90714
(213)920-7737

SCORE Office (Long Beach)
1 World Trade Center
Long Beach, CA 90831

SCORE Office (Los Alamitos)
901 W. Civic Center Dr., Ste. 160
Los Alamitos, CA 90720

SCORE Office (Los Altos)
321 University Ave.
Los Altos, CA 94022
(415)948-1455

SCORE Office (Manhattan Beach)
PO Box 3007
Manhattan Beach, CA 90266
(310)545-5313
Fax: (310)545-7203

SCORE Office (Merced)
1632 N. St.
Merced, CA 95340
(209)725-3800
Fax: (209)383-4959

SCORE Office (Milpitas)
75 S. Milpitas Blvd., Ste. 205
Milpitas, CA 95035
(408)262-2613
Fax: (408)262-2823

SCORE Office (Yosemite)
1012 11th St., Ste. 300
Modesto, CA 95354
(209)521-9333

SCORE Office (Montclair)
5220 Benito Ave.
Montclair, CA 91763

SCORE Office (Monterey Bay)
380 Alvarado St.
PO Box 1770
Monterey, CA 93940-1770
(408)649-1770

SCORE Office (Moreno Valley)
25480 Alessandro
Moreno Valley, CA 92553

SCORE Office (Morgan Hill)
25 W. 1st St.
PO Box 786
Morgan Hill, CA 95038
(408)779-9444
Fax: (408)778-1786

SCORE Office (Morro Bay)
880 Main St.
Morro Bay, CA 93442
(805)772-4467

SCORE Office (Mountain View)
580 Castro St.
Mountain View, CA 94041
(415)968-8378
Fax: (415)968-5668

SCORE Office (Napa)
1556 1st St.
Napa, CA 94559
(707)226-7455
Fax: (707)226-1171

SCORE Office (North Hollywood)
5019 Lankershim Blvd.
North Hollywood, CA 91601
(818)552-3206

SCORE Office (Northridge)
8801 Reseda Blvd.
Northridge, CA 91324
(818)349-5676

SCORE Office (Novato)
807 De Long Ave.
Novato, CA 94945
(415)897-1164
Fax: (415)898-9097

SCORE Office (East Bay)
519 17th St.
Oakland, CA 94612

(510)273-6611
Fax: (510)273-6015
E-mail: webmaster@eastbayscore.org
Website: http://www.eastbayscore.org

SCORE Office (Oceanside)
928 N. Coast Hwy.
Oceanside, CA 92054
(619)722-1534

SCORE Office (Ontario)
121 West B. St.
Ontario, CA 91762
Fax: (714)984-6439

SCORE Office (Oxnard)
PO Box 867
Oxnard, CA 93032
(805)385-8860
Fax: (805)487-1763

SCORE Office (Pacifica)
450 Dundee Way, Ste. 2
Pacifica, CA 94044
(415)355-4122

SCORE Office (Palm Desert)
72990 Hwy. 111
Palm Desert, CA 92260
(619)346-6111
Fax: (619)346-3463

SCORE Office (Palm Springs)
650 E. Tahquitz Canyon Way Ste. D
Palm Springs, CA 92262-6706
(760)320-6682
Fax: (760)323-9426

SCORE Office (Lakeside)
2150 Low Tree
Palmdale, CA 93551
(805)948-4518
Fax: (805)949-1212

SCORE Office (Palo Alto)
325 Forest Ave.
Palo Alto, CA 94301
(415)324-3121
Fax: (415)324-1215

SCORE Office (Pasadena)
117 E. Colorado Blvd., Ste. 100
Pasadena, CA 91105
(818)795-3355
Fax: (818)795-5663

SCORE Office (Paso Robles)
1225 Park St.
Paso Robles, CA 93446-2234
(805)238-0506
Fax: (805)238-0527

SCORE Office (Petaluma)
799 Baywood Dr., Ste. 3
Petaluma, CA 94954
(707)762-2785
Fax: (707)762-4721

SCORE Office (Pico Rivera)
9122 E. Washington Blvd.
Pico Rivera, CA 90660

SCORE Office (Pittsburg)
2700 E. Leland Rd.
Pittsburg, CA 94565
(510)439-2181
Fax: (510)427-1599

SCORE Office (Pleasanton)
777 Peters Ave.
Pleasanton, CA 94566
(510)846-9697

SCORE Office (Monterey Park)
485 N. Garey
Pomona, CA 91769

SCORE Office (Pomona)
485 N. Garey Ave.
Pomona, CA 91766
(909)622-1256

SCORE Office (Antelope Valley)
4511 West Ave. M-4
Quartz Hill, CA 93536
(805)272-0087
E-mail: avscore@ptw.com
Website: http://www.score.av.org/

SCORE Office (Shasta)
737 Auditorium Dr.
Redding, CA 96099
(916)225-2770

SCORE Office (Redwood City)
1675 Broadway
Redwood City, CA 94063
(415)364-1722
Fax: (415)364-1729

SCORE Office (Richmond)
3925 MacDonald Ave.
Richmond, CA 94805

SCORE Office (Ridgecrest)
PO Box 771
Ridgecrest, CA 93555
(619)375-8331
Fax: (619)375-0365

SCORE Office (Riverside)
3685 Main St., Ste. 350
Riverside, CA 92501
(909)683-7100

SCORE Office (Sacramento)
9845 Horn Rd., 260-B
Sacramento, CA 95827
(916)361-2322
Fax: (916)361-2164
E-mail: sacchapter@directcon.net

SCORE Office (Salinas)
PO Box 1170
Salinas, CA 93902
(408)424-7611
Fax: (408)424-8639

SCORE Office (Inland Empire)
777 E. Rialto Ave.
Purchasing
San Bernardino, CA 92415-0760
(909)386-8278

SCORE Office (San Carlos)
San Carlos Chamber of Commerce
PO Box 1086
San Carlos, CA 94070
(415)593-1068
Fax: (415)593-9108

SCORE Office (Encinitas)
550 W. C St., Ste. 550
San Diego, CA 92101-3540
(619)557-7272
Fax: (619)557-5894

SCORE Office (San Diego)
550 West C. St., Ste. 550
San Diego, CA 92101-3540
(619)557-7272
Fax: (619)557-5894
Website: http://www.score-sandiego.org

SCORE Office (Menlo Park)
1100 Merrill St.
San Francisco, CA 94105
(415)325-2818
Fax: (415)325-0920

SCORE Office (San Francisco)
455 Market St., 6th Fl.
San Francisco, CA 94105
(415)744-6827
Fax: (415)744-6750
E-mail: sfscore@sfscore.
Website: http://www.sfscore.com

SCORE Office (San Gabriel)
401 W. Las Tunas Dr.
San Gabriel, CA 91776
(818)576-2525
Fax: (818)289-2901

SCORE Office (San Jose)
Deanza College
208 S. 1st. St., Ste. 137
San Jose, CA 95113
(408)288-8479
Fax: (408)535-5541

SCORE Office (Silicon Valley)
84 W. Santa Clara St., Ste. 100
San Jose, CA 95113
(408)288-8479
Fax: (408)535-5541
E-mail: info@svscore.org
Website: http://www.svscore.org

SCORE Office (San Luis Obispo)
3566 S. Hiquera, No. 104
San Luis Obispo, CA 93401
(805)547-0779

SCORE Office (San Mateo)
1021 S. El Camino, 2nd Fl.
San Mateo, CA 94402
(415)341-5679

SCORE Office (San Pedro)
390 W. 7th St.
San Pedro, CA 90731
(310)832-7272

SCORE Office (Orange County)
200 W. Santa Anna Blvd., Ste. 700
Santa Ana, CA 92701
(714)550-7369
Fax: (714)550-0191
Website: http://www.score114.org

SCORE Office (Santa Barbara)
3227 State St.
Santa Barbara, CA 93130
(805)563-0084

SCORE Office (Central Coast)
509 W. Morrison Ave.
Santa Maria, CA 93454
(805)347-7755

SCORE Office (Santa Maria)
614 S. Broadway
Santa Maria, CA 93454-5111
(805)925-2403
Fax: (805)928-7559

SCORE Office (Santa Monica)
501 Colorado, Ste. 150
Santa Monica, CA 90401
(310)393-9825
Fax: (310)394-1868

SCORE Office (Santa Rosa)
777 Sonoma Ave., Rm. 115E
Santa Rosa, CA 95404

(707)571-8342
Fax: (707)541-0331
Website: http://www.pressdemo.com/community/score/score.html

SCORE Office (Scotts Valley)
4 Camp Evers Ln.
Scotts Valley, CA 95066
(408)438-1010
Fax: (408)438-6544

SCORE Office (Simi Valley)
40 W. Cochran St., Ste. 100
Simi Valley, CA 93065
(805)526-3900
Fax: (805)526-6234

SCORE Office (Sonoma)
453 1st St. E
Sonoma, CA 95476
(707)996-1033

SCORE Office (Los Banos)
222 S. Shepard St.
Sonora, CA 95370
(209)532-4212

SCORE Office (Tuolumne County)
39 North Washington St.
Sonora, CA 95370
(209)588-0128
E-mail: score@mlode.com

SCORE Office (South San Francisco)
445 Market St., Ste. 6th Fl.
South San Francisco, CA 94105
(415)744-6827
Fax: (415)744-6812

SCORE Office (Stockton)
401 N. San Joaquin St., Rm. 215
Stockton, CA 95202
(209)946-6293

SCORE Office (Taft)
314 4th St.
Taft, CA 93268
(805)765-2165
Fax: (805)765-6639

SCORE Office (Conejo Valley)
625 W. Hillcrest Dr.
Thousand Oaks, CA 91360
(805)499-1993
Fax: (805)498-7264

SCORE Office (Torrance)
3400 Torrance Blvd., Ste. 100
Torrance, CA 90503
(310)540-5858
Fax: (310)540-7662

SCORE Office (Truckee)
PO Box 2757
Truckee, CA 96160
(916)587-2757
Fax: (916)587-2439

SCORE Office (Visalia)
113 S. M St,
Tulare, CA 93274
(209)627-0766
Fax: (209)627-8149

SCORE Office (Upland)
433 N. 2nd Ave.
Upland, CA 91786
(909)931-4108

SCORE Office (Vallejo)
2 Florida St.
Vallejo, CA 94590
(707)644-5551
Fax: (707)644-5590

SCORE Office (Van Nuys)
14540 Victory Blvd.
Van Nuys, CA 91411
(818)989-0300
Fax: (818)989-3836

SCORE Office (Ventura)
5700 Ralston St., Ste. 310
Ventura, CA 93001
(805)658-2688
Fax: (805)658-2252
E-mail: scoreven@jps.net
Website: http://www.jps.net/scoreven

SCORE Office (Vista)
201 E. Washington St.
Vista, CA 92084
(619)726-1122
Fax: (619)226-8654

SCORE Office (Watsonville)
PO Box 1748
Watsonville, CA 95077
(408)724-3849
Fax: (408)728-5300

SCORE Office (West Covina)
811 S. Sunset Ave.
West Covina, CA 91790
(818)338-8496
Fax: (818)960-0511

SCORE Office (Westlake)
30893 Thousand Oaks Blvd.
Westlake Village, CA 91362
(805)496-5630
Fax: (818)991-1754

Colorado

SCORE Office (Colorado Springs)
2 N. Cascade Ave., Ste. 110
Colorado Springs, CO 80903
(719)636-3074
Website: http://www.cscc.org/score02/
index.html

SCORE Office (Denver)
US Custom's House, 4th Fl.
721 19th St.
Denver, CO 80201-0660
(303)844-3985
Fax: (303)844-6490
E-mail: score62@csn.net
Website: http://www.sni.net/score62

SCORE Office (Tri-River)
1102 Grand Ave.
Glenwood Springs, CO 81601
(970)945-6589

SCORE Office (Grand Junction)
2591 B & 3/4 Rd.
Grand Junction, CO 81503
(970)243-5242

SCORE Office (Gunnison)
608 N. 11th
Gunnison, CO 81230
(303)641-4422

SCORE Office (Montrose)
1214 Peppertree Dr.
Montrose, CO 81401
(970)249-6080

SCORE Office (Pagosa Springs)
PO Box 4381
Pagosa Springs, CO 81157
(970)731-4890

SCORE Office (Rifle)
0854 W. Battlement Pky., Apt. C106
Parachute, CO 81635
(970)285-9390

SCORE Office (Pueblo)
302 N. Santa Fe
Pueblo, CO 81003
(719)542-1704
Fax: (719)542-1624
E-mail: mackey@iex.net
Website: http://www.pueblo.org/score

SCORE Office (Ridgway)
143 Poplar Pl.
Ridgway, CO 81432

SCORE Office (Silverton)
PO Box 480

Silverton, CO 81433
(303)387-5430

SCORE Office (Minturn)
PO Box 2066
Vail, CO 81658
(970)476-1224

Connecticut

SCORE Office (Greater Bridgeport)
230 Park Ave.
Bridgeport, CT 06601-0999
(203)576-4369
Fax: (203)576-4388

SCORE Office (Bristol)
10 Main St. 1st. Fl.
Bristol, CT 06010
(203)584-4718
Fax: (203)584-4722

SCORE office (Greater Danbury)
246 Federal Rd.
Unit LL2, Ste. 7
Brookfield, CT 06804
(203)775-1151

SCORE Office (Greater Danbury)
246 Federal Rd., Unit LL2, Ste. 7
Brookfield, CT 06804
(203)775-1151

SCORE Office (Eastern Connecticut)
Administration Bldg., Rm. 313
PO 625
61 Main St. (Chapter 579)
Groton, CT 06475
(203)388-9508

SCORE Office (Greater Hartford County)
330 Main St.
Hartford, CT 06106
(860)548-1749
Fax: (860)240-4659
Website: http://www.score56.org

SCORE Office (Manchester)
20 Hartford Rd.
Manchester, CT 06040
(203)646-2223
Fax: (203)646-5871

SCORE Office (New Britain)
185 Main St., Ste. 431
New Britain, CT 06051
(203)827-4492
Fax: (203)827-4480

SCORE Office (New Haven)
25 Science Pk., Bldg. 25, Rm. 366

New Haven, CT 06511
(203)865-7645

SCORE Office (Fairfield County)
24 Beldon Ave., 5th Fl.
Norwalk, CT 06850
(203)847-7348
Fax: (203)849-9308

SCORE Office (Old Saybrook)
146 Main St.
Old Saybrook, CT 06475
(860)388-9508

SCORE Office (Simsbury)
Box 244
Simsbury, CT 06070
(203)651-7307
Fax: (203)651-1933

SCORE Office (Torrington)
23 North Rd.
Torrington, CT 06791
(203)482-6586

Delaware

SCORE Office (Dover)
Treadway Towers
PO Box 576
Dover, DE 19903
(302)678-0892
Fax: (302)678-0189

SCORE Office (Lewes)
PO Box 1
Lewes, DE 19958
(302)645-8073
Fax: (302)645-8412

SCORE Office (Milford)
204 NE Front St.
Milford, DE 19963
(302)422-3301

SCORE Office (Wilmington)
824 Market St., Ste. 610
Wilmington, DE 19801
(302)573-6652
Fax: (302)573-6092
Website: http://www.scoredelaware.com

District of Columbia

SCORE Office (George Mason University)
409 3rd St. SW, 4th Fl.
Washington, DC 20024
800-634-0245

SCORE Office (Washington DC)
1110 Vermont Ave. NW, 9th Fl.

Washington, DC 20043
(202)606-4000
Fax: (202)606-4225
E-mail: dcscore@hotmail.com
Website: http://www.scoredc.org/

Florida

SCORE Office (Desota County Chamber of Commerce)
16 South Velucia Ave.
Arcadia, FL 34266
(941)494-4033

SCORE Office (Suncoast/Pinellas)
Airport Business Ctr.
4707 - 140th Ave. N, No. 311
Clearwater, FL 33755
(813)532-6800
Fax: (813)532-6800

SCORE Office (DeLand)
336 N. Woodland Blvd.
DeLand, FL 32720
(904)734-4331
Fax: (904)734-4333

SCORE Office (South Palm Beach)
1050 S. Federal Hwy., Ste. 132
Delray Beach, FL 33483
(561)278-7752
Fax: (561)278-0288

SCORE Office (Ft. Lauderdale)
Federal Bldg., Ste. 123
299 E. Broward Blvd.
Ft. Lauderdale, FL 33301
(954)356-7263
Fax: (954)356-7145

SCORE Office (Southwest Florida)
The Renaissance
8695 College Pky., Ste. 345 & 346
Ft. Myers, FL 33919
(941)489-2935
Fax: (941)489-1170

SCORE Office (Treasure Coast)
Professional Center, Ste. 2
3220 S. US, No. 1
Ft. Pierce, FL 34982
(561)489-0548

SCORE Office (Gainesville)
101 SE 2nd Pl., Ste. 104
Gainesville, FL 32601
(904)375-8278

SCORE Office (Hialeah Dade Chamber)
59 W. 5th St.
Hialeah, FL 33010

(305)887-1515
Fax: (305)887-2453

SCORE Office (Daytona Beach)
921 Nova Rd., Ste. A
Holly Hills, FL 32117
(904)255-6889
Fax: (904)255-0229
E-mail: score87@dbeach.com

SCORE Office (South Broward)
3475 Sheridan St., Ste. 203
Hollywood, FL 33021
(305)966-8415

SCORE Office (Citrus County)
5 Poplar Ct.
Homosassa, FL 34446
(352)382-1037

SCORE Office (Jacksonville)
7825 Baymeadows Way, Ste. 100-B
Jacksonville, FL 32256
(904)443-1911
Fax: (904)443-1980
E-mail: scorejax@juno.com
Website: http://www.scorejax.org/

SCORE Office (Jacksonville Satellite)
3 Independent Dr.
Jacksonville, FL 32256
(904)366-6600
Fax: (904)632-0617

SCORE Office (Central Florida)
5410 S. Florida Ave., No. 3
Lakeland, FL 33801
(941)687-5783
Fax: (941)687-6225

SCORE Office (Lakeland)
100 Lake Morton Dr.
Lakeland, FL 33801
(941)686-2168

SCORE Office (St. Petersburg)
800 W. Bay Dr., Ste. 505
Largo, FL 33712
(813)585-4571

SCORE Office (Leesburg)
9501 US Hwy. 441
Leesburg, FL 34788-8751
(352)365-3556
Fax: (352)365-3501

SCORE Office (Cocoa)
1600 Farno Rd., Unit 205
Melbourne, FL 32935
(407)254-2288

SCORE Office (Melbourne)
Melbourne Professional Complex
1600 Sarno, Ste. 205
Melbourne, FL 32935
(407)254-2288
Fax: (407)245-2288

SCORE Office (Merritt Island)
1600 Sarno Rd., Ste. 205
Melbourne, FL 32935
(407)254-2288
Fax: (407)254-2288

SCORE Office (Space Coast)
Melbourn Professional Complex
1600 Sarno, Ste. 205
Melbourne, FL 32935
(407)254-2288
Fax: (407)254-2288

SCORE Office (Dade)
49 NW 5th St.
Miami, FL 33128
(305)371-6889
Fax: (305)374-1882
E-mail: score@netrox.net
Website: http://www.netrox.net/~score/

SCORE Office (Naples of Collier)
International College
2654 Tamiami Trl. E
Naples, FL 34112
(941)417-1280
Fax: (941)417-1281
E-mail: score@naples.net
Website: http://www.naples.net/clubs/
score/index.htm

SCORE Office (Pasco County)
6014 US Hwy. 19, Ste. 302
New Port Richey, FL 34652
(813)842-4638

SCORE Office (Southeast Volusia)
115 Canal St.
New Smyrna Beach, FL 32168
(904)428-2449
Fax: (904)423-3512

SCORE Office (Ocala)
110 E. Silver Springs Blvd.
Ocala, FL 34470
(352)629-5959

Clay County SCORE Office
Clay County Chamber of Commerce
1734 Kingsdey Ave.
PO Box 1441
Orange Park, FL 32073
(904)264-2651
Fax: (904)269-0363

SCORE Office (Orlando)
80 N. Hughey Ave.
Rm. 445 Federal Bldg.
Orlando, FL 32801
(407)648-6476
Fax: (407)648-6425

SCORE Office (Emerald Coast)
19 W. Garden St., No. 325
Pensacola, FL 32501
(904)444-2060
Fax: (904)444-2070

SCORE Office (Charlotte County)
201 W. Marion Ave., Ste. 211
Punta Gorda, FL 33950
(941)575-1818
E-mail: score@gls3c.com
Website: http://www.charlotte-
florida.com/business/scorepg01.htm

SCORE Office (St. Augustine)
1 Riberia St.
St. Augustine, FL 32084
(904)829-5681
Fax: (904)829-6477

SCORE Office (Bradenton)
2801 Fruitville, Ste. 280
Sarasota, FL 34237
(813)955-1029

SCORE Office (Manasota)
2801 Fruitville Rd., Ste. 280
Sarasota, FL 34237
(941)955-1029
Fax: (941)955-5581
E-mail: score116@gte.net
Website: http://www.score-suncoast.org/

SCORE Office (Tallahassee)
200 W. Park Ave.
Tallahassee, FL 32302
(850)487-2665

SCORE Office (Hillsborough)
4732 Dale Mabry Hwy. N, Ste. 400
Tampa, FL 33614-6509
(813)870-0125

SCORE Office (Lake Sumter)
122 E. Main St.
Tavares, FL 32778-3810
(352)365-3556

SCORE Office (Titusville)
2000 S. Washington Ave.
Titusville, FL 32780
(407)267-3036
Fax: (407)264-0127

SCORE Office (Venice)
257 N. Tamiami Trl.
Venice, FL 34285
(941)488-2236
Fax: (941)484-5903

SCORE Office (Palm Beach)
500 Australian Ave. S, Ste. 100
West Palm Beach, FL 33401
(561)833-1672
Fax: (561)833-1712

SCORE Office (Wildwood)
103 N. Webster St.
Wildwood, FL 34785

Georgia

SCORE Office (Atlanta)
Harris Tower, Suite 1900
233 Peachtree Rd., NE
Atlanta, GA 30309
(404)347-2442
Fax: (404)347-1227

SCORE Office (Augusta)
3126 Oxford Rd.
Augusta, GA 30909
(706)869-9100

SCORE Office (Columbus)
School Bldg.
PO Box 40
Columbus, GA 31901
(706)327-3654

SCORE Office (Dalton-Whitfield)
305 S. Thorton Ave.
Dalton, GA 30720
(706)279-3383

SCORE Office (Gainesville)
PO Box 374
Gainesville, GA 30503
(770)532-6206
Fax: (770)535-8419

SCORE Office (Macon)
711 Grand Bldg.
Macon, GA 31201
(912)751-6160

SCORE Office (Brunswick)
4 Glen Ave.
St. Simons Island, GA 31520
(912)265-0620
Fax: (912)265-0629

SCORE Office (Savannah)
111 E. Liberty St., Ste. 103
Savannah, GA 31401
(912)652-4335

Fax: (912)652-4184
E-mail: info@scoresav.org
Website: http://www.coastalempire.com/
score/index.htm

Guam

SCORE Office (Guam)
Pacific News Bldg., Rm. 103
238 Archbishop Flores St.
Agana, GU 96910-5100
(671)472-7308

Hawaii

SCORE Office (Hawaii, Inc.)
1111 Bishop St., Ste. 204
PO Box 50207
Honolulu, HI 96813
(808)522-8132
Fax: (808)522-8135
E-mail: hnlscore@juno.com

SCORE Office (Kahului)
250 Alamaha, Unit N16A
Kahului, HI 96732
(808)871-7711

SCORE Office (Maui, Inc.)
590 E. Lipoa Pkwy., Ste. 227
Kihei, HI 96753
(808)875-2380

Idaho

SCORE Office (Treasure Valley)
1020 Main St., No. 290
Boise, ID 83702
(208)334-1696
Fax: (208)334-9353

SCORE Office (Eastern Idaho)
2300 N. Yellowstone, Ste. 119
Idaho Falls, ID 83401
(208)523-1022
Fax: (208)528-7127

Illinois

SCORE Office (Fox Valley)
40 W. Downer Pl.
PO Box 277
Aurora, IL 60506
(630)897-9214
Fax: (630)897-7002

SCORE Office (Greater Belvidere)
419 S. State St.
Belvidere, IL 61008
(815)544-4357
Fax: (815)547-7654

SCORE Office (Bensenville)
1050 Busse Hwy. Suite 100
Bensenville, IL 60106
(708)350-2944
Fax: (708)350-2979

SCORE Office (Central Illinois)
402 N. Hershey Rd.
Bloomington, IL 61704
(309)644-0549
Fax: (309)663-8270
E-mail: webmaster@central-illinois-score.org
Website: http://www.central-illinois-score.org/

SCORE Office (Southern Illinois)
150 E. Pleasant Hill Rd.
Box 1
Carbondale, IL 62901
(618)453-6654
Fax: (618)453-5040

SCORE Office (Chicago)
Northwest Atrium Ctr.
500 W. Madison St., No. 1250
Chicago, IL 60661
(312)353-7724
Fax: (312)886-5688
Website: http://www.mcs.net/~bic/

SCORE Office (Chicago–Oliver Harvey College)
Pullman Bldg.
1000 E. 11th St., 7th Fl.
Chicago, IL 60628
Fax: (312)468-8086

SCORE Office (Danville)
28 W. N. Street
Danville, IL 61832
(217)442-7232
Fax: (217)442-6228

SCORE Office (Decatur)
Milliken University
1184 W. Main St.
Decatur, IL 62522
(217)424-6297
Fax: (217)424-3993
E-mail: charding@mail.millikin.edu
Website: http://www.millikin.edu/
academics/Tabor/score.html

SCORE Office (Downers Grove)
925 Curtis
Downers Grove, IL 60515
(708)968-4050
Fax: (708)968-8368

SCORE Office (Elgin)
24 E. Chicago, 3rd Fl.
PO Box 648
Elgin, IL 60120
(847)741-5660
Fax: (847)741-5677

SCORE Office (Freeport Area)
26 S. Galena Ave.
Freeport, IL 61032
(815)233-1350
Fax: (815)235-4038

SCORE Office (Galesburg)
292 E. Simmons St.
PO Box 749
Galesburg, IL 61401
(309)343-1194
Fax: (309)343-1195

SCORE Office (Glen Ellyn)
500 Pennsylvania
Glen Ellyn, IL 60137
(708)469-0907
Fax: (708)469-0426

SCORE Office (Greater Alton)
Alden Hall
5800 Godfrey Rd.
Godfrey, IL 62035-2466
(618)467-2280
Fax: (618)466-8289
Website: http://www.altonweb.com/
score/

SCORE Office (Grayslake)
19351 W. Washington St.
Grayslake, IL 60030
(708)223-3633
Fax: (708)223-9371

SCORE Office (Harrisburg)
303 S. Commercial
Harrisburg, IL 62946-1528
(618)252-8528
Fax: (618)252-0210

SCORE Office (Joliet)
100 N. Chicago
Joliet, IL 60432
(815)727-5371
Fax: (815)727-5374

SCORE Office (Kankakee)
101 S. Schuyler Ave.
Kankakee, IL 60901
(815)933-0376
Fax: (815)933-0380

SCORE Office (Macomb)
216 Seal Hall, Rm. 214

Macomb, IL 61455
(309)298-1128
Fax: (309)298-2520

SCORE Office (Matteson)
210 Lincoln Mall
Matteson, IL 60443
(708)709-3750
Fax: (708)503-9322

SCORE Office (Mattoon)
1701 Wabash Ave.
Mattoon, IL 61938
(217)235-5661
Fax: (217)234-6544

SCORE Office (Quad Cities)
622 19th St.
Moline, IL 61265
(309)797-0082
Fax: (309)757-5435
E-mail: score@qconline.com
Website: http://www.qconline.com/
business/score/

SCORE Office (Naperville)
131 W. Jefferson Ave.
Naperville, IL 60540
(708)355-4141
Fax: (708)355-8355

SCORE Office (Northbrook)
2002 Walters Ave.
Northbrook, IL 60062
(847)498-5555
Fax: (847)498-5510

SCORE Office (Palos Hills)
10900 S. 88th Ave.
Palos Hills, IL 60465
(847)974-5468
Fax: (847)974-0078

SCORE Office (Peoria)
124 SW Adams, Ste. 300
Peoria, IL 61602
(309)676-0755
Fax: (309)676-7534

SCORE Office (Prospect Heights)
1375 Wolf Rd.
Prospect Heights, IL 60070
(847)537-8660
Fax: (847)537-7138

SCORE Office (Quincy Tri-State)
300 Civic Center Plz., Ste. 245
Quincy, IL 62301
(217)222-8093
Fax: (217)222-3033

SCORE Office (River Grove)
2000 5th Ave.
River Grove, IL 60171
(708)456-0300
Fax: (708)583-3121

SCORE Office (Northern Illinois)
515 N. Court St.
Rockford, IL 61103
(815)962-0122
Fax: (815)962-0122

SCORE Office (St. Charles)
103 N. 1st Ave.
St. Charles, IL 60174-1982
(847)584-8384
Fax: (847)584-6065

SCORE Office (Springfield)
511 W. Capitol Ave., Ste. 302
Springfield, IL 62704
(217)492-4416
Fax: (217)492-4867

SCORE Office (Sycamore)
112 Somunak St.
Sycamore, IL 60178
(815)895-3456
Fax: (815)895-0125

SCORE Office (University)
Hwy. 50 & Stuenkel Rd. Ste. C3305
University Park, IL 60466
(708)534-5000
Fax: (708)534-8457

Indiana

SCORE Office (Anderson)
205 W. 11th St.
Anderson, IN 46015
(317)642-0264

SCORE Office (Bloomington)
Star Center
216 W. Allen
Bloomington, IN 47403
(812)335-7334
E-mail: wtfische@indiana.edu
Website: http://www.brainfreezemedia.
com/score527/

SCORE Office (South East Indiana)
500 Franklin St.
Box 29
Columbus, IN 47201
(812)379-4457

SCORE Office (Corydon)
310 N. Elm St.
Corydon, IN 47112

(812)738-2137
Fax: (812)738-6438

SCORE Office (Crown Point)
Old Courthouse Sq. Ste. 206
PO Box 43
Crown Point, IN 46307
(219)663-1800

SCORE Office (Elkhart)
418 S. Main St.
Elkhart, IN 46515
(219)293-1531
Fax: (219)294-1859

SCORE Office (Evansville)
1100 W. Lloyd Expy., Ste. 105
Evansville, IN 47708
(812)426-6144

SCORE Office (Fort Wayne)
1300 S. Harrison St.
Ft. Wayne, IN 46802
(219)422-2601
Fax: (219)422-2601

SCORE Office (Gary)
973 W. 6th Ave., Rm. 326
Gary, IN 46402
(219)882-3918

SCORE Office (Hammond)
7034 Indianapolis Blvd.
Hammond, IN 46324
(219)931-1000
Fax: (219)845-9548

SCORE Office (Indianapolis)
429 N. Pennsylvania St., Ste. 100
Indianapolis, IN 46204-1873
(317)226-7264
Fax: (317)226-7259
E-mail: inscore@indy.net
Website: http://www.score-
indianapolis.org/

SCORE Office (Jasper)
PO Box 307
Jasper, IN 47547-0307
(812)482-6866

SCORE Office (Kokomo/Howard Counties)
106 N. Washington St.
Kokomo, IN 46901
(765)457-5301
Fax: (765)452-4564

SCORE Office (Logansport)
300 E. Broadway, Ste. 103
Logansport, IN 46947
(219)753-6388

SCORE Office (Madison)
301 E. Main St.
Madison, IN 47250
(812)265-3135
Fax: (812)265-2923

SCORE Office (Marengo)
Rt. 1 Box 224D
Marengo, IN 47140
Fax: (812)365-2793

SCORE Office (Marion/Grant Counties)
215 S. Adams
Marion, IN 46952
(765)664-5107

SCORE Office (Merrillville)
255 W. 80th Pl.
Merrillville, IN 46410
(219)769-8180
Fax: (219)736-6223

SCORE Office (Michigan City)
200 E. Michigan Blvd.
Michigan City, IN 46360
(219)874-6221
Fax: (219)873-1204

SCORE Office (South Central Indiana)
4100 Charleston Rd.
New Albany, IN 47150-9538
(812)945-0066

SCORE Office (Rensselaer)
104 W. Washington
Rensselaer, IN 47978

SCORE Office (Salem)
210 N. Main St.
Salem, IN 47167
(812)883-4303
Fax: (812)883-1467

SCORE Office (South Bend)
300 N. Michigan St.
South Bend, IN 46601
(219)282-4350
E-mail: chair@southbend-score.org
Website: http://www.southbend-score.org/

SCORE Office (Valparaiso)
150 Lincolnway
Valparaiso, IN 46383
(219)462-1105
Fax: (219)469-5710

SCORE Office (Vincennes)
27 N. 3rd
PO Box 553
Vincennes, IN 47591
(812)882-6440
Fax: (812)882-6441

SCORE Office (Wabash)
PO Box 371
Wabash, IN 46992
(219)563-1168
Fax: (219)563-6920

Iowa

SCORE Office (Burlington)
Federal Bldg.
300 N. Main St.
Burlington, IA 52601
(319)752-2967

SCORE Office (Cedar Rapids)
2750 1st Ave. NE, Ste 350
Cedar Rapids, IA 52401-1806
(319)362-6405
Fax: (319)362-7861
E:mail: score@scorecr.org
Website: http://www.scorecr.org

SCORE Office (Illowa)
333 4th Ave. S
Clinton, IA 52732
(319)242-5702

SCORE Office (Council Bluffs)
7 N. 6th St.
Council Bluffs, IA 51502
(712)325-1000

SCORE Office (Northeast Iowa)
3404 285th St.
Cresco, IA 52136
(319)547-3377

SCORE Office (Des Moines)
Federal Bldg., Rm. 749
210 Walnut St.
Des Moines, IA 50309-2186
(515)284-4760

SCORE Office (Ft. Dodge)
Federal Bldg., Rm. 436
205 S. 8th St.
Ft. Dodge, IA 50501
(515)955-2622

SCORE Office (Independence)
110 1st. St. east
Independence, IA 50644
(319)334-7178
Fax: (319)334-7179

SCORE Office (Iowa City)
210 Federal Bldg.
PO Box 1853
Iowa City, IA 52240-1853
(319)338-1662

SCORE Office (Keokuk)
401 Main St.
Pierce Bldg., No. 1
Keokuk, IA 52632
(319)524-5055

SCORE Office (Central Iowa)
Fisher Community College
709 S. Center
Marshalltown, IA 50158
(515)753-6645

SCORE Office (River City)
15 West State St.
Mason City, IA 50401
(515)423-5724

SCORE Office (South Central)
SBDC, Indian Hills Community College
525 Grandview Ave.
Ottumwa, IA 52501
(515)683-5127
Fax: (515)683-5263

SCORE Office (Dubuque)
10250 Sundown Rd.
Peosta, IA 52068
(319)556-5110

SCORE Office (Southwest Iowa)
614 W. Sheridan
Shenandoah, IA 51601
(712)246-3260

SCORE Office (Sioux City)
Federal Bldg.
320 6th St.
Sioux City, IA 51101
(712)277-2324
Fax: (712)277-2325

SCORE Office (Iowa Lakes)
122 W. 5th St.
Spencer, IA 51301
(712)262-3059

SCORE Office (Vista)
119 W. 6th St.
Storm Lake, IA 50588
(712)732-3780

SCORE Office (Waterloo)
215 E. 4th
Waterloo, IA 50703
(319)233-8431

Kansas

SCORE Office (Southwest Kansas)
501 W. Spruce
Dodge City, KS 67801
(316)227-3119

SCORE Office (Emporia)
811 Homewood
Emporia, KS 66801
(316)342-1600

SCORE Office (Golden Belt)
1307 Williams
Great Bend, KS 67530
(316)792-2401

SCORE Office (Hays)
PO Box 400
Hays, KS 67601
(913)625-6595

SCORE Office (Hutchinson)
1 E. 9th St.
Hutchinson, KS 67501
(316)665-8468
Fax: (316)665-7619

SCORE Office (Southeast Kansas)
404 Westminster Pl.
PO Box 886
Independence, KS 67301
(316)331-4741

SCORE Office (McPherson)
306 N. Main
PO Box 616
McPherson, KS 67460
(316)241-3303

SCORE Office (Salina)
120 Ash St.
Salina, KS 67401
(785)243-4290
Fax: (785)243-1833

SCORE Office (Topeka)
1700 College
Topeka, KS 66621
(785)231-1010

SCORE Office (Wichita)
100 E. English, Ste. 510
Wichita, KS 67202
(316)269-6273
Fax: (316)269-6499

SCORE Office (Ark Valley)
205 E. 9th St.
Winfield, KS 67156
(316)221-1617

Kentucky

SCORE Office (Ashland)
PO Box 830
Ashland, KY 41105
(606)329-8011
Fax: (606)325-4607

SCORE Office (Bowling Green)
812 State St.
PO Box 51
Bowling Green, KY 42101
(502)781-3200
Fax: (502)843-0458

SCORE Office (Tri-Lakes)
508 Barbee Way
Danville, KY 40422-1548
(606)231-9902

SCORE Office (Glasgow)
301 W. Main St.
Glasgow, KY 42141
(502)651-3161
Fax: (502)651-3122

SCORE Office (Hazard)
B & I Technical Center
100 Airport Gardens Rd.
Hazard, KY 41701
(606)439-5856
Fax: (606)439-1808

SCORE Office (Lexington)
410 W. Vine St., Ste. 290, Civic C
Lexington, KY 40507
(606)231-9902
Fax: (606)253-3190
E-mail: scorelex@uky.campus.mci.net

SCORE Office (Louisville)
188 Federal Office Bldg.
600 Dr. Martin L. King Jr. Pl.
Louisville, KY 40202
(502)582-5976

SCORE Office (Madisonville)
257 N. Main
Madisonville, KY 42431
(502)825-1399
Fax: (502)825-1396

SCORE Office (Paducah)
Federal Office Bldg.
501 Broadway, Rm. B-36
Paducah, KY 42001
(502)442-5685

Louisiana

SCORE Office (Central Louisiana)
802 3rd St.
Alexandria, LA 71309
(318)442-6671

SCORE Office (Baton Rouge)
564 Laurel St.
PO Box 3217
Baton Rouge, LA 70801

(504)381-7130
Fax: (504)336-4306

SCORE Office (North Shore)
2 W. Thomas
Hammond, LA 70401
(504)345-4457
Fax: (504)345-4749

SCORE Office (Lafayette)
804 St. Mary Blvd.
Lafayette, LA 70505-1307
(318)233-2705
Fax: (318)234-8671
E-mail: score302@aol.com

SCORE Office (Lake Charles)
120 W. Pujo St.
Lake Charles, LA 70601
(318)433-3632

SCORE Office (New Orleans)
365 Canal St., Ste. 3100
New Orleans, LA 70130
(504)589-2356
Fax: (504)589-2339

SCORE Office (Shreveport)
400 Edwards St.
Shreveport, LA 71101
(318)677-2536
Fax: (318)677-2541

Maine

SCORE Office (Augusta)
40 Western Ave.
Augusta, ME 04330
(207)622-8509

SCORE Office (Bangor)
Peabody Hall, Rm. 229
One College Cir.
Bangor, ME 04401
(207)941-9707

SCORE Office (Central & Northern Arroostock)
111 High St.
Caribou, ME 04736
(207)492-8010
Fax: (207)492-8010

SCORE Office (Penquis)
South St.
Dover Foxcroft, ME 04426
(207)564-7021

SCORE Office (Maine Coastal)
Mill Mall
Box 1105
Ellsworth, ME 04605-1105

(207)667-5800
E-mail: score@arcadia.net

SCORE Office (Lewiston-Auburn)
BIC of Maine-Bates Mill Complex
35 Canal St.
Lewiston, ME 04240-7764
(207)782-3708
Fax: (207)783-7745

SCORE Office (Portland)
66 Pearl St., Rm. 210
Portland, ME 04101
(207)772-1147
Fax: (207)772-5581
E-mail: Score53@score.maine.org
Website: http://www.score.maine.org/
chapter53/

SCORE Office (Western Mountains)
255 River St.
PO Box 252
Rumford, ME 04257-0252
(207)369-9976

SCORE Office (Oxford Hills)
166 Main St.
South Paris, ME 04281
(207)743-0499

Maryland

SCORE Office (Southern Maryland)
2525 Riva Rd., Ste. 110
Annapolis, MD 21401
(410)266-9553
Fax: (410)573-0981
E-mail: score390@aol.com
Website: http://members.aol.com/
score390/index.htm

SCORE Office (Baltimore)
The City Crescent Bldg., 6th Fl.
10 S. Howard St.
Baltimore, MD 21201
(410)962-2233
Fax: (410)962-1805

SCORE Office (Bel Air)
108 S. Bond St.
Bel Air, MD 21014
(410)838-2020
Fax: (410)893-4715

SCORE Office (Bethesda)
7910 Woodmont Ave., Ste. 1204
Bethesda, MD 20814
(301)652-4900
Fax: (301)657-1973

SCORE Office (Bowie)
6670 Race Track Rd.
Bowie, MD 20715
(301)262-0920
Fax: (301)262-0921

SCORE Office (Dorchester County)
203 Sunburst Hwy.
Cambridge, MD 21613
(410)228-3575

SCORE Office (Upper Shore)
210 Marlboro Ave.
Easton, MD 21601
(410)822-4606
Fax: (410)822-7922

SCORE Office (Frederick County)
43A S. Market St.
Frederick, MD 21701
(301)662-8723
Fax: (301)846-4427

SCORE Office (Gaithersburg)
9 Park Ave.
Gaithersburg, MD 20877
(301)840-1400
Fax: (301)963-3918

SCORE Office (Glen Burnie)
103 Crain Hwy. SE
Glen Burnie, MD 21061
(410)766-8282
Fax: (410)766-9722

SCORE Office (Hagerstown)
111 W. Washington St.
Hagerstown, MD 21740
(301)739-2015
Fax: (301)739-1278

SCORE Office (Laurel)
7901 Sandy Spring Rd. Ste. 501
Laurel, MD 20707
(301)725-4000
Fax: (301)725-0776

SCORE Office (Salisbury)
300 E. Main St.
Salisbury, MD 21801
(410)749-0185
Fax: (410)860-9925

Massachusetts

SCORE Office (NE Massachusetts)
100 Cummings Ctr., Ste. 101 K
Beverly, MA 01923
(978)922-9441
Website: http://www1.shore.net/~score/

SCORE Office (Boston)
10 Causeway St., Rm. 265
Boston, MA 02222-1093
(617)565-5591
Fax: (617)565-5598
E-mail: boston-score-20@worldnet.att.net
Website: http://www.scoreboston.org/

SCORE office (Bristol/Plymouth County)
53 N. 6th St., Federal Bldg.
Bristol, MA 02740
(508)994-5093

SCORE Office (SE Massachusetts)
60 School St.
Brockton, MA 02401
(508)587-2673
Fax: (508)587-1340
Website: http://www.metrosouth
chamber.com/score.html

SCORE Office (North Adams)
820 N. State Rd.
Cheshire, MA 01225
(413)743-5100

SCORE Office (Clinton Satellite)
1 Green St.
Clinton, MA 01510
Fax: (508)368-7689

SCORE Office (Greenfield)
PO Box 898
Greenfield, MA 01302
(413)773-5463
Fax: (413)773-7008

SCORE Office (Haverhill)
87 Winter St.
Haverhill, MA 01830
(508)373-5663
Fax: (508)373-8060

SCORE Office (Hudson Satellite)
PO Box 578
Hudson, MA 01749
(508)568-0360
Fax: (508)568-0360

SCORE Office (Cape Cod)
Independence Pk., Ste. 5B
270 Communications Way
Hyannis, MA 02601
(508)775-4884
Fax: (508)790-2540

SCORE Office (Lawrence)
264 Essex St.
Lawrence, MA 01840
(508)686-0900
Fax: (508)794-9953

SCORE Office (Leominster Satellite)
110 Erdman Way
Leominster, MA 01453
(508)840-4300
Fax: (508)840-4896

SCORE Office (Bristol/Plymouth Counties)
53 N. 6th St., Federal Bldg.
New Bedford, MA 02740
(508)994-5093

SCORE Office (Newburyport)
29 State St.
Newburyport, MA 01950
(617)462-6680

SCORE Office (Pittsfield)
66 West St.
Pittsfield, MA 01201
(413)499-2485

SCORE Office (Haverhill-Salem)
32 Derby Sq.
Salem, MA 01970
(508)745-0330
Fax: (508)745-3855

SCORE Office (Springfield)
1350 Main St.
Federal Bldg.
Springfield, MA 01103
(413)785-0314

SCORE Office (Carver)
12 Taunton Green, Ste. 201
Taunton, MA 02780
(508)824-4068
Fax: (508)824-4069

SCORE Office (Worcester)
33 Waldo St.
Worcester, MA 01608
(508)753-2929
Fax: (508)754-8560

Michigan

SCORE Office (Allegan)
PO Box 338
Allegan, MI 49010
(616)673-2479

SCORE Office (Ann Arbor)
425 S. Main St., Ste. 103
Ann Arbor, MI 48104
(313)665-4433

SCORE Office (Battle Creek)
34 W. Jackson Ste. 4A
Battle Creek, MI 49017-3505

(616)962-4076
Fax: (616)962-6309

SCORE Office (Cadillac)
222 Lake St.
Cadillac, MI 49601
(616)775-9776
Fax: (616)768-4255

SCORE Office (Detroit)
477 Michigan Ave., Rm. 515
Detroit, MI 48226
(313)226-7947
Fax: (313)226-3448

SCORE Office (Flint)
708 Root Rd., Rm. 308
Flint, MI 48503
(810)233-6846

SCORE Office (Grand Rapids)
111 Pearl St. NW
Grand Rapids, MI 49503-2831
(616)771-0305
Fax: (616)771-0328
E-mail: scoreone@iserv.net
Website: http://www.iserv.net/
~scoreone/

SCORE Office (Holland)
480 State St.
Holland, MI 49423
(616)396-9472

SCORE Office (Jackson)
209 East Washington
PO Box 80
Jackson, MI 49204
(517)782-8221
Fax: (517)782-0061

SCORE Office (Kalamazoo)
345 W. Michigan Ave.
Kalamazoo, MI 49007
(616)381-5382
Fax: (616)384-0096
E-mail: score@nucleus.net

SCORE Office (Lansing)
117 E. Allegan
PO Box 14030
Lansing, MI 48901
(517)487-6340
Fax: (517)484-6910

SCORE Office (Livonia)
15401 Farmington Rd.
Livonia, MI 48154
(313)427-2122
Fax: (313)427-6055

SCORE Office (Madison Heights)
26345 John R
Madison Heights, MI 48071
(810)542-5010
Fax: (810)542-6821

SCORE Office (Monroe)
111 E. 1st
Monroe, MI 48161
(313)242-3366
Fax: (313)242-7253

SCORE Office (Mt. Clemens)
58 S/B Gratiot
Mt. Clemens, MI 48043
(810)463-1528
Fax: (810)463-6541

SCORE Office (Muskegon)
PO Box 1087
230 Terrace Plz.
Muskegon, MI 49443
(616)722-3751
Fax: (616)728-7251

SCORE Office (Petoskey)
401 E. Mitchell St.
Petoskey, MI 49770
(616)347-4150

SCORE Office (Pontiac)
Executive Office Bldg.
1200 N. Telegraph Rd.
Pontiac, MI 48341
(810)975-9555

SCORE Office (Pontiac)
PO Box 430025
Pontiac, MI 48343
(810)335-9600

SCORE Office (Port Huron)
920 Pinegrove Ave.
Port Huron, MI 48060
(810)985-7101

SCORE Office (Rochester)
71 Walnut Ste. 110
Rochester, MI 48307
(810)651-6700
Fax: (810)651-5270

SCORE Office (Saginaw)
901 S. Washington Ave.
Saginaw, MI 48601
(517)752-7161
Fax: (517)752-9055

SCORE Office (Upper Peninsula)
2581 I-75 Business Spur
Sault Ste. Marie, MI 49783
(906)632-3301

SCORE Office (Southfield)
21000 W. 10 Mile Rd.
Southfield, MI 48075
(810)204-3050
Fax: (810)204-3099

SCORE Office (Traverse City)
202 E. Grandview Pkwy.
PO Box 387
Traverse City, MI 49685
(616)947-5075
Fax: (616)946-2565

SCORE Office (Warren)
30500 Van Dyke, Ste. 118
Warren, MI 48093
(810)751-3939

Minnesota

SCORE Office (Aitkin)
Aitkin, MN 56431
(218)741-3906

SCORE Office (Albert Lea)
202 N. Broadway Ave.
Albert Lea, MN 56007
(507)373-7487

SCORE Office (Austin)
PO Box 864
Austin, MN 55912
(507)437-4561
Fax: (507)437-4869

SCORE Office (South Metro)
Ames Business Ctr.
2500 W. County Rd., No. 42
Burnsville, MN 55337
(612)898-5645
Fax: (612)435-6972
E-mail: southmetro@scoreminn.org
Website: http://www.scoreminn.org/
southmetro/

SCORE Office (Duluth)
1717 Minnesota Ave.
Duluth, MN 55802
(218)727-8286
Fax: (218)727-3113
E-mail: duluth@scoreminn.org
Website: http://www.scoreminn.org

SCORE Office (Fairmont)
PO Box 826
Fairmont, MN 56031
(507)235-5547
Fax: (507)235-8411

SCORE Office (Southwest Minnesota)
112 Riverfront St.

Box 999
Mankato, MN 56001
(507)345-4519
Fax: (507)345-4451
Website: http://www.scoreminn.org/

SCORE Office (Minneapolis)
North Plaza Bldg., Ste. 51
5217 Wayzata Blvd.
Minneapolis, MN 55416
(612)591-0539
Fax: (612)544-0436
Website: http://www.scoreminn.org/

SCORE Office (Owatonna)
PO Box 331
Owatonna, MN 55060
(507)451-7970
Fax: (507)451-7972

SCORE Office (Red Wing)
2000 W. Main St., Ste. 324
Red Wing, MN 55066
(612)388-4079

SCORE Office (Southeastern Minnesota)
220 S. Broadway, Ste. 100
Rochester, MN 55901
(507)288-1122
Fax: (507)282-8960
Website: http://www.scoreminn.org/

SCORE Office (Brainerd)
St. Cloud, MN 56301

SCORE Office (Central Area)
1527 Northway Dr.
St. Cloud, MN 56301
(320)240-1332
Fax: (320)255-9050
Website: http://www.scoreminn.org/

SCORE Office (St. Paul)
350 St. Peter St., No. 295
Lowry Professional Bldg.
St. Paul, MN 55102
(651)223-5010
Fax: (651)223-5048
Website: http://www.scoreminn.org/

SCORE Office (Winona)
Box 870
Winona, MN 55987
(507)452-2272
Fax: (507)454-8814

SCORE Office (Worthington)
1121 3rd Ave.
Worthington, MN 56187
(507)372-2919
Fax: (507)372-2827

Mississippi

SCORE Office (Delta)
915 Washington Ave.
PO Box 933
Greenville, MS 38701
(601)378-3141

SCORE Office (Gulfcoast)
1 Government Plaza
2909 13th St., Ste. 203
Gulfport, MS 39501
(228)863-0054

SCORE Office (Jackson)
1st Jackson Center, Ste. 400
101 W. Capitol St.
Jackson, MS 39201
(601)965-5533

SCORE Office (Meridian)
5220 16th Ave.
Meridian, MS 39305
(601)482-4412

Missouri

SCORE Office (Lake of the Ozark)
University Extension
113 Kansas St.
PO Box 1405
Camdenton, MO 65020
(573)346-2644
Fax: (573)346-2694
E-mail: score@cdoc.net
Website: http://sites.cdoc.net/score/

Chamber of Commerce (Cape Girardeau)
PO Box 98
Cape Girardeau, MO 63702-0098
(314)335-3312

SCORE Office (Mid-Missouri)
1705 Halstead Ct.
Columbia, MO 65203
(573)874-1132

SCORE Office (Ozark-Gateway)
1486 Glassy Rd.
Cuba, MO 65453-1640
(573)885-4954

SCORE Office (Kansas City)
323 W. 8th St., Ste. 104
Kansas City, MO 64105
(816)374-6675
Fax: (816)374-6692
E-mail: SCOREBIC@AOL.COM
Website: http://www.crn.org/score/

SCORE Office (Sedalia)
Lucas Place
323 W. 8th St., Ste.104
Kansas City, MO 64105
(816)374-6675

SCORE office (Tri-Lakes)
PO Box 1148
Kimberling, MO 65686
(417)739-3041

SCORE Office (Tri-Lakes)
HCRI Box 85
Lampe, MO 65681
(417)858-6798

SCORE Office (Mexico)
111 N. Washington St.
Mexico, MO 65265
(314)581-2765

SCORE Office (Southeast Missouri)
Rte. 1, Box 280
Neelyville, MO 63954
(573)989-3577

SCORE office (Poplar Bluff Area)
806 Emma St.
Poplar Bluff, MO 63901
(573)686-8892

SCORE Office (St. Joseph)
3003 Frederick Ave.
St. Joseph, MO 64506
(816)232-4461

SCORE Office (St. Louis)
815 Olive St., Rm. 242
St. Louis, MO 63101-1569
(314)539-6970
Fax: (314)539-3785
E-mail: info@stlscore.org
Website: http://www.stlscore.org/

SCORE Office (Lewis & Clark)
425 Spencer Rd.
St. Peters, MO 63376
(314)928-2900
Fax: (314)928-2900
E-mail: score01@mail.win.org

SCORE Office (Springfield)
620 S. Glenstone, Ste. 110
Springfield, MO 65802-3200
(417)864-7670
Fax: (417)864-4108

SCORE office (Southeast Kansas)
1206 W. First St.
Webb City, MO 64870
(417)673-3984

Montana

SCORE Office (Billings)
815 S. 27th St.
Billings, MT 59101
(406)245-4111

SCORE Office (Bozeman)
1205 E. Main St.
Bozeman, MT 59715
(406)586-5421

SCORE Office (Butte)
1000 George St.
Butte, MT 59701
(406)723-3177

SCORE Office (Great Falls)
710 First Ave. N
Great Falls, MT 59401
(406)761-4434
E-mail: scoregtf@in.tch.com

SCORE Office (Havre, Montana)
518 First St.
Havre, MT 59501
(406)265-4383

SCORE Office (Helena)
Federal Bldg.
301 S. Park
Helena, MT 59626-0054
(406)441-1081

SCORE Office (Kalispell)
2 Main St.
Kalispell, MT 59901
(406)756-5271
Fax: (406)752-6665

SCORE Office (Missoula)
723 Ronan
Missoula, MT 59806
(406)327-8806
E-mail: score@safeshop.com
Website: http://missoula.bigsky.net/
score/

Nebraska

SCORE Office (Columbus)
Columbus, NE 68601
(402)564-2769

SCORE Office (Fremont)
92 W. 5th St.
Fremont, NE 68025
(402)721-2641

SCORE Office (Hastings)
Hastings, NE 68901
(402)463-3447

SCORE Office (Lincoln)
8800 O St.
Lincoln, NE 68520
(402)437-2409

SCORE Office (Panhandle)
150549 CR 30
Minatare, NE 69356
(308)632-2133
Website: http://www.tandt.com/
SCORE

SCORE Office (Norfolk)
3209 S. 48th Ave.
Norfolk, NE 68106
(402)564-2769

SCORE Office (North Platte)
3301 W. 2nd St.
North Platte, NE 69101
(308)532-4466

SCORE Office (Omaha)
11145 Mill Valley Rd.
Omaha, NE 68154
(402)221-3606
Fax: (402)221-3680
E-mail: infoctr@ne.uswest.net
Website: http://www.tandt.com/score/

Nevada

SCORE Office (Incline Village)
969 Tahoe Blvd.
Incline Village, NV 89451
(702)831-7327
Fax: (702)832-1605

SCORE Office (Carson City)
301 E. Stewart
PO Box 7527
Las Vegas, NV 89125
(702)388-6104

SCORE Office (Las Vegas)
300 Las Vegas Blvd. S, Ste. 1100
Las Vegas, NV 89101
(702)388-6104

SCORE Office (Northern Nevada)
SBDC, College of Business
Administration
Univ. of Nevada
Reno, NV 89557-0100
(702)784-4436
Fax: (702)784-4337

New Hampshire

SCORE Office (North Country)
PO Box 34

Berlin, NH 03570
(603)752-1090

SCORE Office (Concord)
143 N. Main St., Rm. 202A
PO Box 1258
Concord, NH 03301
(603)225-1400
Fax: (603)225-1409

SCORE Office (Dover)
299 Central Ave.
Dover, NH 03820
(603)742-2218
Fax: (603)749-6317

SCORE Office (Monadnock)
34 Mechanic St.
Keene, NH 03431-3421
(603)352-0320

SCORE Office (Lakes Region)
67 Water St., Ste. 105
Laconia, NH 03246
(603)524-9168

SCORE Office (Upper Valley)
Citizens Bank Bldg., Rm. 310
20 W. Park St.
Lebanon, NH 03766
(603)448-3491
Fax: (603)448-1908
E-mail: billt@valley.net
Website: http://www.valley.net/~score/

SCORE Office (Merrimack Valley)
275 Chestnut St., Rm. 618
Manchester, NH 03103
(603)666-7561
Fax: (603)666-7925

SCORE Office (Mt. Washington Valley)
PO Box 1066
North Conway, NH 03818
(603)383-0800

SCORE Office (Seacoast)
195 Commerce Way, Unit-A
Portsmouth, NH 03801-3251
(603)433-0575

New Jersey

SCORE Office (Somerset)
Paritan Valley Community College,
Rte. 28
Branchburg, NJ 08807
(908)218-8874
E-mail: nj-score@grizbiz.com.
Website: http://www.nj-score.org/

SCORE Office (Chester)
5 Old Mill Rd.
Chester, NJ 07930
(908)879-7080

SCORE Office (Greater Princeton)
4 A George Washington Dr.
Cranbury, NJ 08512
(609)520-1776

SCORE Office (Freehold)
36 W. Main St.
Freehold, NJ 07728
(908)462-3030
Fax: (908)462-2123

SCORE Office (North West)
Picantinny Innovation Ctr.
3159 Schrader Rd.
Hamburg, NJ 07419
(973)209-8525
Fax: (973)209-7252
E-mail: nj-score@grizbiz.com
Website: http://www.nj-score.org/

SCORE Office (Monmouth)
765 Newman Springs Rd.
Lincroft, NJ 07738
(908)224-2573
E-mail: nj-score@grizbiz.com
Website: http://www.nj-score.org/

SCORE Office (Manalapan)
125 Symmes Dr.
Manalapan, NJ 07726
(908)431-7220

SCORE Office (Jersey City)
2 Gateway Ctr., 4th Fl.
Newark, NJ 07102
(973)645-3982
Fax: (973)645-2375

SCORE Office (Newark)
2 Gateway Center, 15th Fl.
Newark, NJ 07102-5553
(973)645-3982
Fax: (973)645-2375
E-mail: nj-score@grizbiz.com
Website: http://www.nj-score.org

SCORE Office (Bergen County)
327 E. Ridgewood Ave.
Paramus, NJ 07652
(201)599-6090
E-mail: nj-score@grizbiz.com
Website: http://www.nj-score.org/

SCORE Office (Pennsauken)
4900 Rte. 70

Pennsauken, NJ 08109
(609)486-3421

SCORE Office (Southern New Jersey)
4900 Rte. 70
Pennsauken, NJ 08109
(609)486-3421
E-mail: nj-score@grizbiz.com
Website: http://www.nj-score.org/

SCORE Office (Greater Princeton)
216 Rockingham Row
Princeton Forrestal Village
Princeton, NJ 08540
(609)520-1776
Fax: (609)520-9107
E-mail: nj-score@grizbiz.com
Website: http://www.nj-score.org/

SCORE Office (Shrewsbury)
Hwy. 35
Shrewsbury, NJ 07702
(908)842-5995
Fax: (908)219-6140

SCORE Office (Ocean County)
33 Washington St.
Toms River, NJ 08754
(732)505-6033
E-mail: nj-score@grizbiz.com
Website: http://www.nj-score.org/

SCORE Office (Wall)
2700 Allaire Rd.
Wall, NJ 07719
(908)449-8877

SCORE Office (Wayne)
2055 Hamburg Tpke.
Wayne, NJ 07470
(201)831-7788
Fax: (201)831-9112

New Mexico

SCORE Office (Albuquerque)
525 Buena Vista, SE
Albuquerque, NM 87106
(505)272-7999
Fax: (505)272-7963

SCORE Office (Las Cruces)
Loretto Towne Center
505 S. Main St., Ste. 125
Las Cruces, NM 88001
(505)523-5627
Fax: (505)524-2101
E-mail: score.397@zianet.com

SCORE Office (Roswell)
Federal Bldg., Rm. 237

Roswell, NM 88201
(505)625-2112
Fax: (505)623-2545

SCORE Office (Santa Fe)
Montoya Federal Bldg.
120 Federal Place, Rm. 307
Santa Fe, NM 87501
(505)988-6302
Fax: (505)988-6300

New York

SCORE Office (Northeast)
1 Computer Dr. S
Albany, NY 12205
(518)446-1118
Fax: (518)446-1228

SCORE Office (Auburn)
30 South St.
PO Box 675
Auburn, NY 13021
(315)252-7291

SCORE Office (South Tier Binghamton)
Metro Center, 2nd Fl.
49 Court St.
PO Box 995
Binghamton, NY 13902
(607)772-8860

SCORE Office (Queens County City)
12055 Queens Blvd., Rm. 333
Borough Hall, NY 11424
(718)263-8961

SCORE Office (Buffalo)
Federal Bldg., Rm. 1311
111 W. Huron St.
Buffalo, NY 14202
(716)551-4301
Website: http://www2.pcom.net/score/buf45.html

SCORE Office (Canandaigua)
Chamber of Commerce Bldg.
113 S. Main St.
Canandaigua, NY 14424
(716)394-4400
Fax: (716)394-4546

SCORE Office (Chemung)
333 E. Water St., 4th Fl.
Elmira, NY 14901
(607)734-3358

SCORE Office (Geneva)
Chamber of Commerce Bldg.
PO Box 587

Geneva, NY 14456
(315)789-1776
Fax: (315)789-3993

SCORE Office (Glens Falls)
84 Broad St.
Glens Falls, NY 12801
(518)798-8463
Fax: (518)745-1433

SCORE Office (Orange County)
40 Matthews St.
Goshen, NY 10924
(914)294-8080
Fax: (914)294-6121

SCORE Office (Huntington Area)
151 W. Carver St.
Huntington, NY 11743
(516)423-6100

SCORE Office (Tompkins County)
904 E. Shore Dr.
Ithaca, NY 14850
(607)273-7080

SCORE Office (Long Island City)
120-55 Queens Blvd.
Jamaica, NY 11424
(718)263-8961
Fax: (718)263-9032

SCORE Office (Chatauqua)
101 W. 5th St.
Jamestown, NY 14701
(716)484-1103

SCORE Office (Westchester)
2 Caradon Ln.
Katonah, NY 10536
(914)948-3907
Fax: (914)948-4645
E-mail: score@w-w-w.com
Website: http://w-w-w.com/score/

SCORE Office (Queens County)
Queens Borough Hall
120-55 Queens Blvd. Rm. 333
Kew Gardens, NY 11424
(718)263-8961
Fax: (718)263-9032

SCORE Office (Brookhaven)
3233 Rte. 112
Medford, NY 11763
(516)451-6563
Fax: (516)451-6925

SCORE Office (Melville)
35 Pinelawn Rd., Rm. 207-W
Melville, NY 11747
(516)454-0771

SCORE Office (Nassau County)
400 County Seat Dr., No. 140
Mineola, NY 11501
(516)571-3303
E-mail: Counse1998@aol.com
Website: http://members.aol.com/Counse1998/Default.htm

SCORE Office (Mt. Vernon)
4 N. 7th Ave.
Mt. Vernon, NY 10550
(914)667-7500

SCORE Office (New York)
26 Federal Plz., Rm. 3100
New York, NY 10278
(212)264-4507
Fax: (212)264-4963
E-mail: score1000@erols.com
Website: http://users.erols.com/score-nyc/

SCORE Office (Newburgh)
47 Grand St.
Newburgh, NY 12550
(914)562-5100

SCORE Office (Owego)
188 Front St.
Owego, NY 13827
(607)687-2020

SCORE Office (Peekskill)
1 S. Division St.
Peekskill, NY 10566
(914)737-3600
Fax: (914)737-0541

SCORE Office (Penn Yan)
2375 Rte. 14A
Penn Yan, NY 14527
(315)536-3111

SCORE Office (Dutchess)
110 Main St.
Poughkeepsie, NY 12601
(914)454-1700

SCORE Office (Rochester)
601 Keating Federal Bldg., Rm. 410
100 State St.
Rochester, NY 14614
(716)263-6473
Fax: (716)263-3146
Website: http://www.ggw.org/score/

SCORE Office (Saranac Lake)
30 Main St.
Saranac Lake, NY 12983
(315)448-0415

SCORE Office (Suffolk)
286 Main St.
Setauket, NY 11733
(516)751-3886

SCORE Office (Staten Island)
130 Bay St.
Staten Island, NY 10301
(718)727-1221

SCORE Office (Ulster)
Clinton Bldg., Rm. 107
Stone Ridge, NY 12484
(914)687-5035
Fax: (914)687-5015
Website: http://www.scoreulster.org/

SCORE Office (Syracuse)
401 S. Salina, 5th Fl.
Syracuse, NY 13202
(315)471-9393

SCORE Office (Utica)
SUNY Institute of Technology, Route 12
Utica, NY 13504-3050
(315)792-7553

SCORE Office (Watertown)
518 Davidson St.
Watertown, NY 13601
(315)788-1200
Fax: (315)788-8251

North Carolina

SCORE office (Asheboro)
317 E. Dixie Dr.
Asheboro, NC 27203
(336)626-2626
Fax: (336)626-7077

SCORE Office (Asheville)
Federal Bldg., Rm. 259
151 Patton
Asheville, NC 28801-5770
(828)271-4786
Fax: (828)271-4009

SCORE Office (Chapel Hill)
104 S. Estes Dr.
PO Box 2897
Chapel Hill, NC 27514
(919)967-7075

SCORE Office (Coastal Plains)
PO Box 2897
Chapel Hill, NC 27515
(919)967-7075
Fax: (919)968-6874

SCORE Office (Charlotte)
200 N. College St., Ste. A-2015

Charlotte, NC 28202
(704)344-6576
Fax: (704)344-6769
E-mail: CharlotteSCORE47@AOL.com
Website: http://www.charweb.org/
business/score/

SCORE Office (Durham)
411 W. Chapel Hill St.
Durham, NC 27707
(919)541-2171

SCORE Office (Gastonia)
PO Box 2168
Gastonia, NC 28053
(704)864-2621
Fax: (704)854-8723

SCORE Office (Greensboro)
400 W. Market St., Ste. 103
Greensboro, NC 27401-2241
(910)333-5399

SCORE Office (Henderson)
PO Box 917
Henderson, NC 27536
(919)492-2061
Fax: (919)430-0460

SCORE Office (Hendersonville)
Federal Bldg., Rm. 108
W. 4th Ave. & Church St.
Hendersonville, NC 28792
(828)693-8702
E-mail: score@circle.net
Website: http://www.wncguide.com/
score/Welcome.html

SCORE Office (Unifour)
PO Box 1828
Hickory, NC 28603
(704)328-6111

SCORE Office (High Point)
1101 N. Main St.
High Point, NC 27262
(336)882-8625
Fax: (336)889-9499

SCORE Office (Outer Banks)
Collington Rd. and Mustain
Kill Devil Hills, NC 27948
(252)441-8144

SCORE Office (Down East)
312 S. Front St., Ste. 6
New Bern, NC 28560
(252)633-6688
Fax: (252)633-9608

SCORE Office (Kinston)
PO Box 95

New Bern, NC 28561
(919)633-6688

SCORE Office (Raleigh)
Century Post Office Bldg., Ste. 306
300 Federal St. Mall
Raleigh, NC 27601
(919)856-4739
E-mail: jendres@ibm.net
Website: http://www.intrex.net/score96/
score96.htm

SCORE Office (Sanford)
1801 Nash St.
Sanford, NC 27330
(919)774-6442
Fax: (919)776-8739

SCORE Office (Sandhills Area)
1480 Hwy. 15-501
PO Box 458
Southern Pines, NC 28387
(910)692-3926

SCORE Office (Wilmington)
Corps of Engineers Bldg.
96 Darlington Ave., Ste. 207
Wilmington, NC 28403
(910)815-4576
Fax: (910)815-4658

North Dakota

SCORE Office
(Bismarck-Mandan)
700 E. Main Ave., 2nd Fl.
PO Box 5509
Bismarck, ND 58506-5509
(701)250-4303

SCORE Office (Fargo)
657 2nd Ave., Rm. 225
Fargo, ND 58108-3083
(701)239-5677

SCORE Office (Upper Red River)
4275 Technology Dr., Rm. 156
Grand Forks, ND 58202-8372
(701)777-3051

SCORE Office (Minot)
100 1st St. SW
Minot, ND 58701-3846
(701)852-6883
Fax: (701)852-6905

Ohio

SCORE Office (Akron)
1 Cascade Plz., 7th Fl.
Akron, OH 44308

(330)379-3163
Fax: (330)379-3164

SCORE Office (Ashland)
Gill Center
47 W. Main St.
Ashland, OH 44805
(419)281-4584

SCORE Office (Canton)
116 Cleveland Ave. NW, Ste. 601
Canton, OH 44702-1720
(330)453-6047

SCORE Office (Chillicothe)
165 S. Paint St.
Chillicothe, OH 45601
(614)772-4530

SCORE Office (Cincinnati)
Ameritrust Bldg., Rm. 850
525 Vine St.
Cincinnati, OH 45202
(513)684-2812
Fax: (513)684-3251
Website: http://www.score.
chapter34.org/

SCORE Office (Cleveland)
Eaton Center, Ste. 620
1100 Superior Ave.
Cleveland, OH 44114-2507
(216)522-4194
Fax: (216)522-4844

SCORE Office (Columbus)
2 Nationwide Plz., Ste. 1400
Columbus, OH 43215-2542
(614)469-2357
Fax: (614)469-2391
E-mail: info@scorecolumbus.org
Website: http://www.scorecolumbus.org/

SCORE Office (Dayton)
Dayton Federal Bldg., Rm. 505
200 W. Second St.
Dayton, OH 45402-1430
(513)225-2887
Fax: (513)225-7667

SCORE Office (Defiance)
615 W. 3rd St.
PO Box 130
Defiance, OH 43512
(419)782-7946

SCORE Office (Findlay)
123 E. Main Cross St.
PO Box 923
Findlay, OH 45840
(419)422-3314

SCORE Office (Lima)
147 N. Main St.
Lima, OH 45801
(419)222-6045
Fax: (419)229-0266

SCORE Office (Mansfield)
55 N. Mulberry St.
Mansfield, OH 44902
(419)522-3211

SCORE Office (Marietta)
Thomas Hall
Marietta, OH 45750
(614)373-0268

SCORE Office (Medina)
County Administrative Bldg.
144 N. Broadway
Medina, OH 44256
(216)764-8650

SCORE Office (Licking County)
50 W. Locust St.
Newark, OH 43055
(614)345-7458

SCORE Office (Salem)
2491 State Rte. 45 S
Salem, OH 44460
(216)332-0361

SCORE Office (Tiffin)
62 S. Washington St.
Tiffin, OH 44883
(419)447-4141
Fax: (419)447-5141

SCORE Office (Toledo)
608 Madison Ave, Ste. 910
Toledo, OH 43624
(419)259-7598
Fax: (419)259-6460

SCORE Office (Heart of Ohio)
377 W. Liberty St.
Wooster, OH 44691
(330)262-5735
Fax: (330)262-5745

SCORE Office (Youngstown)
306 Williamson Hall
Youngstown, OH 44555
(330)746-2687

Oklahoma

SCORE Office (Anadarko)
PO Box 366
Anadarko, OK 73005
(405)247-6651

SCORE Office (Ardmore)
410 W. Main
Ardmore, OK 73401
(580)226-2620

SCORE Office (Northeast Oklahoma)
210 S. Main
Grove, OK 74344
(918)787-2796
Fax: (918)787-2796
E-mail: Score595@greencis.net

SCORE Office (Lawton)
4500 W. Lee Blvd., Bldg. 100, Ste. 107
Lawton, OK 73505
(580)353-8727
Fax: (580)250-5677

SCORE Office (Oklahoma City)
210 Park Ave., No. 1300
Oklahoma City, OK 73102
(405)231-5163
Fax: (405)231-4876
E-mail: score212@usa.net

SCORE Office (Stillwater)
439 S. Main
Stillwater, OK 74074
(405)372-5573
Fax: (405)372-4316

SCORE Office (Tulsa)
616 S. Boston, Ste. 406
Tulsa, OK 74119
(918)581-7462
Fax: (918)581-6908
Website: http://www.ionet.net/~tulscore/

Oregon

SCORE Office (Bend)
63085 N. Hwy. 97
Bend, OR 97701
(541)923-2849
Fax: (541)330-6900

SCORE Office (Willamette)
1401 Willamette St.
PO Box 1107
Eugene, OR 97401-4003
(541)465-6600
Fax: (541)484-4942

SCORE Office (Florence)
3149 Oak St.
Florence, OR 97439
(503)997-8444
Fax: (503)997-8448

SCORE Office (Southern Oregon)
33 N. Central Ave., Ste. 216

Medford, OR 97501
(541)776-4220
E-mail: pgr134f@prodigy.com

SCORE Office (Portland)
1515 SW 5th Ave., Ste. 1050
Portland, OR 97201
(503)326-3441
Fax: (503)326-2808
E-mail: gr134@prodigy.com

SCORE Office (Salem)
416 State St. (corner of Liberty)
Salem, OR 97301
(503)370-2896

Pennsylvania

SCORE Office (Altoona-Blair)
1212 12th Ave.
Altoona, PA 16601-3493
(814)943-8151

SCORE Office (Lehigh Valley)
Rauch Bldg. 37
Lehigh University
621 Taylor St.
Bethlehem, PA 18015
(610)758-4496
Fax: (610)758-5205

SCORE Office (Butler County)
100 N. Main St.
PO Box 1082
Butler, PA 16003
(412)283-2222
Fax: (412)283-0224

SCORE Office (Harrisburg)
4211 Trindle Rd.
Camp Hill, PA 17011
(717)761-4304
Fax: (717)761-4315

SCORE Office (Cumberland Valley)
75 S. 2nd St.
Chambersburg, PA 17201
(717)264-2935

SCORE Office (Monroe County-Stroudsburg)
556 Main St.
East Stroudsburg, PA 18301
(717)421-4433

SCORE Office (Erie)
120 W. 9th St.
Erie, PA 16501
(814)871-5650
Fax: (814)871-7530

SCORE Office (Bucks County)
409 Hood Blvd.
Fairless Hills, PA 19030
(215)943-8850
Fax: (215)943-7404

SCORE Office (Hanover)
146 Broadway
Hanover, PA 17331
(717)637-6130
Fax: (717)637-9127

SCORE Office (Harrisburg)
100 Chestnut, Ste. 309
Harrisburg, PA 17101
(717)782-3874

SCORE Office (East Montgomery County)
Baederwood Shopping Center
1653 The Fairways, Ste. 204
Jenkintown, PA 19046
(215)885-3027

SCORE Office (Kittanning)
2 Butler Rd.
Kittanning, PA 16201
(412)543-1305
Fax: (412)543-6206

SCORE Office (Lancaster)
118 W. Chestnut St.
Lancaster, PA 17603
(717)397-3092

SCORE Office (Westmoreland County)
300 Fraser Purchase Rd.
Latrobe, PA 15650-2690
(412)539-7505
Fax: (412)539-1850

SCORE Office (Lebanon)
252 N. 8th St.
PO Box 899
Lebanon, PA 17042-0899
(717)273-3727
Fax: (717)273-7940

SCORE Office (Lewistown)
3 W. Monument Sq., Ste. 204
Lewistown, PA 17044
(717)248-6713
Fax: (717)248-6714

SCORE Office (Delaware County)
602 E. Baltimore Pike
Media, PA 19063
(610)565-3677
Fax: (610)565-1606

SCORE Office (Milton Area)
112 S. Front St.
Milton, PA 17847

(717)742-7341
Fax: (717)792-2008

SCORE Office (Mon-Valley)
435 Donner Ave.
Monessen, PA 15062
(412)684-4277
Fax: (412)684-7688

SCORE Office (Monroeville)
William Penn Plaza
2790 Mosside Blvd., Ste. 295
Monroeville, PA 15146
(412)856-0622
Fax: (412)856-1030

SCORE Office (Airport Area)
986 Brodhead Rd.
Moon Township, PA 15108-2398
(412)264-6270
Fax: (412)264-1575

SCORE Office (Northeast)
8601 E. Roosevelt Blvd.
Philadelphia, PA 19152
(215)332-3400
Fax: (215)332-6050

SCORE Office (Philadelphia)
1315 Walnut St., Ste. 500
Philadelphia, PA 19107
(215)790-5050
Fax: (215)790-5057
E-mail: score46@bellatlantic.net
Website: http://www.pgweb.net/score46/

SCORE Office (Pittsburgh)
1000 Liberty Ave., Rm. 1122
Pittsburgh, PA 15222
(412)395-6560
Fax: (412)395-6562

SCORE Office (Tri-County)
801 N. Charlotte St.
Pottstown, PA 19464
(610)327-2673

SCORE Office (Reading)
601 Penn St.
Reading, PA 19601
(610)376-3497

SCORE Office (Scranton)
Oppenheim Bldg.
116 N. Washington Ave., Ste. 650
Scranton, PA 18503
(717)347-4611
Fax: (717)347-4611

SCORE Office (Central Pennsylvania)
200 Innovation Blvd., Ste. 242-B
State College, PA 16803

(814)234-9415
Fax: (814)238-9686
Website: http://countrystore.org/
business/score.htm

SCORE Office (Monroe-Stroudsburg)
556 Main St.
Stroudsburg, PA 18360
(717)421-4433

SCORE Office (Uniontown)
Federal Bldg.
Pittsburg St.
PO Box 2065 DTS
Uniontown, PA 15401
(412)437-4222
E-mail: uniontownscore@lcsys.net

SCORE Office (Warren County)
315 2nd Ave.
Warren, PA 16365
(814)723-9017

SCORE Office (Waynesboro)
323 E. Main St.
Waynesboro, PA 17268
(717)762-7123
Fax: (717)962-7124

SCORE Office (Chester County)
Government Service Center, Ste. 281
601 Westtown Rd.
West Chester, PA 19382-4538
(610)344-6910
Fax: (610)344-6919
E-mail: score@locke.ccil.org

SCORE Office (Wilkes-Barre)
7 N. Wilkes-Barre Blvd.
Wilkes Barre, PA 18702-5241
(717)826-6502
Fax: (717)826-6287

SCORE Office (North Central Pennsylvania)
240 W. 3rd St., Rm. 227
PO Box 725
Williamsport, PA 17703
(717)322-3720
Fax: (717)322-1607
E-mail: score234@mail.csrlink.net
Website: http://www.lycoming.org/score/

SCORE Office (York)
Cyber Center
2101 Pennsylvania Ave.
York, PA 17404
(717)845-8830
Fax: (717)854-9333

Puerto Rico

SCORE Office (Puerto Rico & Virgin Islands)
PO Box 12383-96
San Juan, PR 00914-0383
(787)726-8040
Fax: (787)726-8135

Rhode Island

SCORE Office (Barrington)
281 County Rd.
Barrington, RI 02806
(401)247-1920
Fax: (401)247-3763

SCORE Office (Woonsocket)
640 Washington Hwy.
Lincoln, RI 02865
(401)334-1000
Fax: (401)334-1009

SCORE Office (Wickford)
8045 Post Rd.
North Kingstown, RI 02852
(401)295-5566
Fax: (401)295-8987

SCORE Office (J.G.E. Knight)
380 Westminster St.
Providence, RI 02903
(401)528-4571
Fax: (401)528-4539
Website: http://www.riscore.org

SCORE Office (Warwick)
3288 Post Rd.
Warwick, RI 02886
(401)732-1100
Fax: (401)732-1101

SCORE Office (Westerly)
74 Post Rd.
Westerly, RI 02891
(401)596-7761
800-732-7636
Fax: (401)596-2190

South Carolina

SCORE Office (Aiken)
PO Box 892
Aiken, SC 29802
(803)641-1111
800-542-4536
Fax: (803)641-4174

SCORE Office (Anderson)
Anderson Mall
3130 N. Main St.

Anderson, SC 29621
(864)224-0453

SCORE Office (Coastal)
284 King St.
Charleston, SC 29401
(803)727-4778
Fax: (803)853-2529

SCORE Office (Midlands)
Strom Thurmond Bldg., Rm. 358
1835 Assembly St., Rm 358
Columbia, SC 29201
(803)765-5131
Fax: (803)765-5962
Website: http://www.scoremidlands.org/

SCORE Office (Piedmont)
Federal Bldg., Rm. B-02
300 E. Washington St.
Greenville, SC 29601
(864)271-3638

SCORE Office (Greenwood)
PO Drawer 1467
Greenwood, SC 29648
(864)223-8357

SCORE Office (Hilton Head Island)
52 Savannah Trail
Hilton Head, SC 29926
(803)785-7107
Fax: (803)785-7110

SCORE Office (Grand Strand)
937 Broadway
Myrtle Beach, SC 29577
(803)918-1079
Fax: (803)918-1083
E-mail: score381@aol.com

SCORE Office (Spartanburg)
PO Box 1636
Spartanburg, SC 29304
(864)594-5000
Fax: (864)594-5055

South Dakota

SCORE Office (West River)
Rushmore Plz. Civic Ctr.
444 Mount Rushmore Rd., No. 209
Rapid City, SD 57701
(605)394-5311
E-mail: score@gwtc.net

SCORE Office (Sioux Falls)
First Financial Center
110 S. Phillips Ave., Ste. 200
Sioux Falls, SD 57104-6727

(605)330-4231
Fax: (605)330-4231

Tennessee

SCORE Office (Chattanooga)
Federal Bldg., Rm. 26
900 Georgia Ave.
Chattanooga, TN 37402
(423)752-5190
Fax: (423)752-5335

SCORE Office (Cleveland)
PO Box 2275
Cleveland, TN 37320
(423)472-6587
Fax: (423)472-2019

SCORE Office (Upper Cumberland Center)
1225 S. Willow Ave.
Cookeville, TN 38501
(615)432-4111
Fax: (615)432-6010

SCORE Office (Unicoi County)
PO Box 713
Erwin, TN 37650
(423)743-3000
Fax: (423)743-0942

SCORE Office (Greeneville)
115 Academy St.
Greeneville, TN 37743
(423)638-4111
Fax: (423)638-5345

SCORE Office (Jackson)
194 Auditorium St.
Jackson, TN 38301
(901)423-2200

SCORE Office (Northeast Tennessee)
1st Tennessee Bank Bldg.
2710 S. Roan St., Ste. 584
Johnson City, TN 37601
(423)929-7686
Fax: (423)461-8052

SCORE Office (Kingsport)
151 E. Main St.
Kingsport, TN 37662
(423)392-8805

SCORE Office (Greater Knoxville)
Farragot Bldg., Ste. 224
530 S. Gay St.
Knoxville, TN 37902
(423)545-4203
E-mail: scoreknox@ntown.com
Website: http://www.scoreknox.org/

SCORE Office (Maryville)
201 S. Washington St.
Maryville, TN 37804-5728
(423)983-2241
800-525-6834
Fax: (423)984-1386

SCORE Office (Memphis)
Federal Bldg., Ste. 390
167 N. Main St.
Memphis, TN 38103
(901)544-3588

SCORE Office (Nashville)
50 Vantage Way, Ste. 201
Nashville, TN 37228-1500
(615)736-7621

Texas

SCORE Office (Abilene)
2106 Federal Post Office and Court Bldg.
Abilene, TX 79601
(915)677-1857

SCORE Office (Austin)
2501 S. Congress
Austin, TX 78701
(512)442-7235
Fax: (512)442-7528

SCORE Office (Golden Triangle)
450 Boyd St.
Beaumont, TX 77704
(409)838-6581
Fax: (409)833-6718

SCORE Office (Brownsville)
3505 Boca Chica Blvd., Ste. 305
Brownsville, TX 78521
(210)541-4508

SCORE Office (Brazos Valley)
3000 Briarcrest, Ste. 302
Bryan, TX 77802
(409)776-8876
E-mail: 102633.2612@compuserve.com

SCORE Office (Cleburne)
Watergarden Pl., 9th Fl., Ste. 400
Cleburne, TX 76031
(817)871-6002

SCORE Office (Corpus Christi)
651 Upper North Broadway, Ste. 654
Corpus Christi, TX 78477
(512)888-4322
Fax: (512)888-3418

SCORE Office (Dallas)
6260 E. Mockingbird
Dallas, TX 75214-2619

(214)828-2471
Fax: (214)821-8033

SCORE Office (El Paso)
10 Civic Center Plaza
El Paso, TX 79901
(915)534-0541
Fax: (915)534-0513

SCORE Office (Bedford)
100 E. 15th St., Ste. 400
Ft. Worth, TX 76102
(817)871-6002

SCORE Office (Ft. Worth)
100 E. 15th St., No. 24
Ft. Worth, TX 76102
(817)871-6002
Fax: (817)871-6031
E-mail: fwbac@onramp.net

SCORE Office (Garland)
2734 W. Kingsley Rd.
Garland, TX 75041
(214)271-9224

SCORE Office (Granbury Chamber of Commerce)
416 S. Morgan
Granbury, TX 76048
(817)573-1622
Fax: (817)573-0805

SCORE Office (Lower Rio Grande Valley)
222 E. Van Buren, Ste. 500
Harlingen, TX 78550
(956)427-8533
Fax: (956)427-8537

SCORE Office (Houston)
9301 Southwest Fwy., Ste. 550
Houston, TX 77074
(713)773-6565
Fax: (713)773-6550

SCORE Office (Irving)
3333 N. MacArthur Blvd., Ste. 100
Irving, TX 75062
(214)252-8484
Fax: (214)252-6710

SCORE Office (Lubbock)
1205 Texas Ave., Rm. 411D
Lubbock, TX 79401
(806)472-7462
Fax: (806)472-7487

SCORE Office (Midland)
Post Office Annex
200 E. Wall St., Rm. P121
Midland, TX 79701
(915)687-2649

SCORE Office (Orange)
1012 Green Ave.
Orange, TX 77630-5620
(409)883-3536
800-528-4906
Fax: (409)886-3247

SCORE Office (Plano)
1200 E. 15th St.
PO Drawer 940287
Plano, TX 75094-0287
(214)424-7547
Fax: (214)422-5182

SCORE Office (Port Arthur)
4749 Twin City Hwy., Ste. 300
Port Arthur, TX 77642
(409)963-1107
Fax: (409)963-3322

SCORE Office (Richardson)
411 Belle Grove
Richardson, TX 75080
(214)234-4141
800-777-8001
Fax: (214)680-9103

SCORE Office (San Antonio)
Federal Bldg., Rm. A527
727 E. Durango
San Antonio, TX 78206
(210)472-5931
Fax: (210)472-5935

SCORE Office (Texarkana State College)
819 State Line Ave.
Texarkana, TX 75501
(903)792-7191
Fax: (903)793-4304

SCORE Office (East Texas)
RTDC
1530 SSW Loop 323, Ste. 100
Tyler, TX 75701
(903)510-2975
Fax: (903)510-2978

SCORE Office (Waco)
401 Franklin Ave.
Waco, TX 76701
(817)754-8898
Fax: (817)756-0776
Website: http://www.brc-waco.com/

SCORE Office (Wichita Falls)
Hamilton Bldg.
900 8th St.
Wichita Falls, TX 76307
(940)723-2741
Fax: (940)723-8773

Utah

SCORE Office (Northern Utah)
160 N. Main
Logan, UT 84321
(435)746-2269

SCORE Office (Ogden)
1701 E. Windsor Dr.
Ogden, UT 84604
(801)629-8613
E-mail: score158@netscape.net

SCORE Office (Central Utah)
1071 E. Windsor Dr.
Provo, UT 84604
(801)373-8660

SCORE Office (Southern Utah)
225 South 700 East
St. George, UT 84770
(435)652-7751

SCORE Office (Salt Lake)
310 S Main St.
Salt Lake City, UT 84101
(801)746-2269
Fax: (801)746-2273

Vermont

SCORE Office (Champlain Valley)
Winston Prouty Federal Bldg.
11 Lincoln St., Rm. 106
Essex Junction, VT 05452
(802)951-6762

SCORE Office (Montpelier)
87 State St., Rm. 205
PO Box 605
Montpelier, VT 05601
(802)828-4422
Fax: (802)828-4485

SCORE Office (Marble Valley)
256 N. Main St.
Rutland, VT 05701-2413
(802)773-9147

SCORE Office (Northeast Kingdom)
20 Main St.
PO Box 904
St. Johnsbury, VT 05819
(802)748-5101

Virgin Islands

SCORE Office (St. Croix)
United Plaza Shopping Center
PO Box 4010, Christiansted
St. Croix, VI 00822
(809)778-5380

SCORE Office (St. Thomas-St. John)
Federal Bldg., Rm. 21
Veterans Dr.
St. Thomas, VI 00801
(809)774-8530

Virginia

SCORE Office (Arlington)
2009 N. 14th St., Ste. 111
Arlington, VA 22201
(703)525-2400

SCORE Office (Blacksburg)
141 Jackson St.
Blacksburg, VA 24060
(540)552-4061

SCORE Office (Bristol)
20 Volunteer Pkwy.
Bristol, VA 24203
(540)989-4850

SCORE Office (Central Virginia)
1001 E. Market St., Ste. 101
Charlottesville, VA 22902
(804)295-6712
Fax: (804)295-7066

SCORE Office (Alleghany Satellite)
241 W. Main St.
Covington, VA 24426
(540)962-2178
Fax: (540)962-2179

SCORE Office (Central Fairfax)
3975 University Dr., Ste. 350
Fairfax, VA 22030
(703)591-2450

SCORE Office (Falls Church)
PO Box 491
Falls Church, VA 22040
(703)532-1050
Fax: (703)237-7904

SCORE Office (Glenns)
Glenns Campus
Box 287
Glenns, VA 23149
(804)693-9650

SCORE Office (Peninsula)
6 Manhattan Sq.
PO Box 7269
Hampton, VA 23666
(757)766-2000
Fax: (757)865-0339
E-mail: score100@seva.net

SCORE Office (Tri-Cities)
108 N. Main St.

Hopewell, VA 23860
(804)458-5536

SCORE Office (Lynchburg)
Federal Bldg.
1100 Main St.
Lynchburg, VA 24504-1714
(804)846-3235

SCORE Office (Greater Prince William)
8963 Center St
Manassas, VA 20110
(703)368-4813
Fax: (703)368-4733

SCORE Office (Martinsvile)
115 Broad St.
Martinsville, VA 24112-0709
(540)632-6401
Fax: (540)632-5059

SCORE Office (Hampton Roads)
Federal Bldg., Rm. 737
200 Grandby St.
Norfolk, VA 23510
(757)441-3733
Fax: (757)441-3733
E-mail: scorehr60@juno.com

SCORE Office (Norfolk)
Federal Bldg., Rm. 737
200 Granby St.
Norfolk, VA 23510
(757)441-3733
Fax: (757)441-3733

SCORE Office (Virginia Beach)
Chamber of Commerce
200 Grandby St., Rm 737
Norfolk, VA 23510
(804)441-3733

SCORE Office (Radford)
1126 Norwood St.
Radford, VA 24141
(540)639-2202

SCORE Office (Richmond)
Federal Bldg.
400 N. 8th St., Ste. 1150
PO Box 10126
Richmond, VA 23240-0126
(804)771-2400
Fax: (804)771-8018
E-mail: scorechapter12@yahoo.com
Website: http://www.cvco.org/score/

SCORE Office (Roanoke)
Federal Bldg., Rm. 716
250 Franklin Rd.
Roanoke, VA 24011

(540)857-2834
Fax: (540)857-2043
E-mail: scorerva@juno.com
Website: http://hometown.aol.com/
scorerv/Index.html

SCORE Office (Fairfax)
8391 Old Courthouse Rd., Ste. 300
Vienna, VA 22182
(703)749-0400

SCORE Office (Greater Vienna)
513 Maple Ave. West
Vienna, VA 22180
(703)281-1333
Fax: (703)242-1482

SCORE Office (Shenandoah Valley)
301 W. Main St.
Waynesboro, VA 22980
(540)949-8203
Fax: (540)949-7740
E-mail: score427@intelos.net

SCORE Office (Williamsburg)
201 Penniman Rd.
Williamsburg, VA 23185
(757)229-6511
E-mail: wacc@williamsburgcc.com

SCORE Office (Northern Virginia)
1360 S. Pleasant Valley Rd.
Winchester, VA 22601
(540)662-4118

Washington

SCORE Office (Gray's Harbor)
506 Duffy St.
Aberdeen, WA 98520
(360)532-1924
Fax: (360)533-7945

SCORE Office (Bellingham)
101 E. Holly St.
Bellingham, WA 98225
(360)676-3307

SCORE Office (Everett)
2702 Hoyt Ave.
Everett, WA 98201-3556
(206)259-8000

SCORE Office (Gig Harbor)
3125 Judson St.
Gig Harbor, WA 98335
(206)851-6865

SCORE Office (Kennewick)
PO Box 6986
Kennewick, WA 99336
(509)736-0510

SCORE Office (Puyallup)
322 2nd St. SW
PO Box 1298
Puyallup, WA 98371
(206)845-6755
Fax: (206)848-6164

SCORE Office (Seattle)
1200 6th Ave., Ste. 1700
Seattle, WA 98101
(206)553-7320
Fax: (206)553-7044
E-mail: score55@aol.com
Website: http://www.scn.org/civic/score-
online/index55.html

SCORE Office (Spokane)
801 W. Riverside Ave., No. 240
Spokane, WA 99201
(509)353-2820
Fax: (509)353-2600
E-mail: score@dmi.net
Website: http://www.dmi.net/score/

SCORE Office (Clover Park)
PO Box 1933
Tacoma, WA 98401-1933
(206)627-2175

SCORE Office (Tacoma)
1101 Pacific Ave.
Tacoma, WA 98402
(253)274-1288
Fax: (253)274-1289

SCORE Office (Fort Vancouver)
1701 Broadway, S-1
Vancouver, WA 98663
(360)699-1079

SCORE Office (Walla Walla)
500 Tausick Way
Walla Walla, WA 99362
(509)527-4681

SCORE Office (Mid-Columbia)
1113 S. 14th Ave.
Yakima, WA 98907
(509)574-4944
Fax: (509)574-2943
Website: http://www.ellensburg.com/
~score/

West Virginia

SCORE Office (Charleston)
1116 Smith St.
Charleston, WV 25301
(304)347-5463
E-mail: score256@juno.com

Organizations, Agencies, & Consultants

SCORE Office (Virginia Street)
1116 Smith St., Ste. 302
Charleston, WV 25301
(304)347-5463

SCORE Office (Marion County)
PO Box 208
Fairmont, WV 26555-0208
(304)363-0486

SCORE Office (Upper Monongahela Valley)
1000 Technology Dr., Ste. 1111
Fairmont, WV 26555
(304)363-0486
E-mail: score537@hotmail.com

SCORE Office (Huntington)
1101 6th Ave., Ste. 220
Huntington, WV 25701-2309
(304)523-4092

SCORE Office (Wheeling)
1310 Market St.
Wheeling, WV 26003
(304)233-2575
Fax: (304)233-1320

Wisconsin

SCORE Office (Fox Cities)
227 S. Walnut St.
Appleton, WI 54913
(920)734-7101
Fax: (920)734-7161

SCORE Office (Beloit)
136 W. Grand Ave., Ste. 100
PO Box 717
Beloit, WI 53511
(608)365-8835
Fax: (608)365-9170

SCORE Office (Eau Claire)
Federal Bldg., Rm. B11
510 S. Barstow St.
Eau Claire, WI 54701
(715)834-1573
E-mail: score@ecol.net
Website: http://www.ecol.net/~score/

SCORE Office (Fond du Lac)
207 N. Main St.
Fond du Lac, WI 54935
(414)921-9500
Fax: (414)921-9559

SCORE Office (Green Bay)
835 Potts Ave.
Green Bay, WI 54304
(414)496-8930
Fax: (414)496-6009

SCORE Office (Janesville)
20 S. Main St., Ste. 11
PO Box 8008
Janesville, WI 53547
(608)757-3160
Fax: (608)757-3170

SCORE Office (La Crosse)
712 Main St.
La Crosse, WI 54602-0219
(608)784-4880

SCORE Office (Madison)
505 S. Rosa Rd.
Madison, WI 53719
(608)441-2820

SCORE Office (Manitowoc)
1515 Memorial Dr.
PO Box 903
Manitowoc, WI 54221-0903
(414)684-5575
Fax: (414)684-1915

SCORE Office (Milwaukee)
310 W. Wisconsin Ave., Ste. 425
Milwaukee, WI 53203
(414)297-3942
Fax: (414)297-1377

SCORE Office (Central Wisconsin)
1224 Lindbergh Ave.
Stevens Point, WI 54481
(715)344-7729

SCORE Office (Superior)
Superior Business Center Inc.
1423 N. 8th St.
Superior, WI 54880
(715)394-7388
Fax: (715)393-7414

SCORE Office (Waukesha)
223 Wisconsin Ave.
Waukesha, WI 53186-4926
(414)542-4249

SCORE Office (Wausau)
300 3rd St., Ste. 200
Wausau, WI 54402-6190
(715)845-6231

SCORE Office (Wisconsin Rapids)
2240 Kingston Rd.
Wisconsin Rapids, WI 54494
(715)423-1830

Wyoming

SCORE Office (Casper)
Federal Bldg., No. 2215
100 East B St.

Casper, WY 82602
(307)261-6529
Fax: (307)261-6530

Venture capital & financing companies
This section contains a listing of financing and loan companies in the United States and Canada. These listing are arranged alphabetically by country, then by state or province, then by city, then by organization name.

Canada

Alberta

Launchworks Inc.
1902J 11th St., S.E.
Calgary, AB, Canada T2G 3G2
(403)269-1119
Fax: (403)269-1141
Website: http://www.launchworks.com

Native Venture Capital Company, Inc.
21 Artist View Point, Box 7
Site 25, RR 12
Calgary, AB, Canada T3E 6W3
(903)208-5380

Miralta Capital Inc.
4445 Calgary Trail South
888 Terrace Plaza Alberta
Edmonton, AB, Canada T6H 5R7
(780)438-3535
Fax: (780)438-3129

Vencap Equities Alberta Ltd.
10180-101st St., Ste. 1980
Edmonton, AB, Canada T5J 3S4
(403)420-1171
Fax: (403)429-2541

British Columbia

Discovery Capital
5th Fl., 1199 West Hastings
Vancouver, BC, Canada V6E 3T5
(604)683-3000
Fax: (604)662-3457
E-mail: info@discoverycapital.com
Website: http://www.discoverycapital.com

Greenstone Venture Partners
1177 West Hastings St.
Ste. 400
Vancouver, BC, Canada V6E 2K3
(604)717-1977
Fax: (604)717-1976
Website: http://www.greenstonevc.com

Growthworks Capital
2600-1055 West Georgia St.
Box 11170 Royal Centre
Vancouver, BC, Canada V6E 3R5
(604)895-7259
Fax: (604)669-7605
Website: http://www.wofund.com

MDS Discovery Venture Management, Inc.
555 W. Eighth Ave., Ste. 305
Vancouver, BC, Canada V5Z 1C6
(604)872-8464
Fax: (604)872-2977
E-mail: info@mds-ventures.com

Ventures West Management Inc.
1285 W. Pender St., Ste. 280
Vancouver, BC, Canada V6E 4B1
(604)688-9495
Fax: (604)687-2145
Website: http://www.ventureswest.com

Nova Scotia

ACF Equity Atlantic Inc.
Purdy's Wharf Tower II
Ste. 2106
Halifax, NS, Canada B3J 3R7
(902)421-1965
Fax: (902)421-1808

Montgomerie, Huck & Co.
146 Bluenose Dr.
PO Box 538
Lunenburg, NS, Canada B0J 2C0
(902)634-7125
Fax: (902)634-7130

Ontario

IPS Industrial Promotion Services Ltd.
60 Columbia Way, Ste. 720
Markham, ON, Canada L3R 0C9
(905)475-9400
Fax: (905)475-5003

Betwin Investments Inc.
Box 23110
Sault Ste. Marie, ON, Canada P6A 6W6
(705)253-0744
Fax: (705)253-0744

Bailey & Company, Inc.
594 Spadina Ave.
Toronto, ON, Canada M5S 2H4
(416)921-6930
Fax: (416)925-4670

BCE Capital
200 Bay St.

South Tower, Ste. 3120
Toronto, ON, Canada M5J 2J2
(416)815-0078
Fax: (416)941-1073
Website: http://www.bcecapital.com

Castlehill Ventures
55 University Ave., Ste. 500
Toronto, ON, Canada M5J 2H7
(416)862-8574
Fax: (416)862-8875

CCFL Mezzanine Partners of Canada
70 University Ave.
Ste. 1450
Toronto, ON, Canada M5J 2M4
(416)977-1450
Fax: (416)977-6764
E-mail: info@ccfl.com
Website: http://www.ccfl.com

Celtic House International
100 Simcoe St., Ste. 100
Toronto, ON, Canada M5H 3G2
(416)542-2436
Fax: (416)542-2435
Website: http://www.celtic-house.com

Clairvest Group Inc.
22 St. Clair Ave. East
Ste. 1700
Toronto, ON, Canada M4T 2S3
(416)925-9270
Fax: (416)925-5753

Crosbie & Co., Inc.
One First Canadian Place
9th Fl.
PO Box 116
Toronto, ON, Canada M5X 1A4
(416)362-7726
Fax: (416)362-3447
E-mail: info@crosbieco.com
Website: http://www.crosbieco.com

Drug Royalty Corp.
Eight King St. East
Ste. 202
Toronto, ON, Canada M5C 1B5
(416)863-1865
Fax: (416)863-5161

Grieve, Horner, Brown & Asculai
8 King St. E, Ste. 1704
Toronto, ON, Canada M5C 1B5
(416)362-7668
Fax: (416)362-7660

Jefferson Partners
77 King St. West
Ste. 4010

PO Box 136
Toronto, ON, Canada M5K 1H1
(416)367-1533
Fax: (416)367-5827
Website: http://www.jefferson.com

J.L. Albright Venture Partners
Canada Trust Tower, 161 Bay St.
Ste. 4440
PO Box 215
Toronto, ON, Canada M5J 2S1
(416)367-2440
Fax: (416)367-4604
Website: http://www.jlaventures.com

McLean Watson Capital Inc.
One First Canadian Place
Ste. 1410
PO Box 129
Toronto, ON, Canada M5X 1A4
(416)363-2000
Fax: (416)363-2010
Website: http://www.mcleanwatson.com

Middlefield Capital Fund
One First Canadian Place
85th Fl.
PO Box 192
Toronto, ON, Canada M5X 1A6
(416)362-0714
Fax: (416)362-7925
Website: http://www.middlefield.com

Mosaic Venture Partners
24 Duncan St.
Ste. 300
Toronto, ON, Canada M5V 3M6
(416)597-8889
Fax: (416)597-2345

Onex Corp.
161 Bay St.
PO Box 700
Toronto, ON, Canada M5J 2S1
(416)362-7711
Fax: (416)362-5765

Penfund Partners Inc.
145 King St. West
Ste. 1920
Toronto, ON, Canada M5H 1J8
(416)865-0300
Fax: (416)364-6912
Website: http://www.penfund.com

Primaxis Technology Ventures Inc.
1 Richmond St. West, 8th Fl.
Toronto, ON, Canada M5H 3W4
(416)313-5210
Fax: (416)313-5218
Website: http://www.primaxis.com

Priveq Capital Funds
240 Duncan Mill Rd., Ste. 602
Toronto, ON, Canada M3B 3P1
(416)447-3330
Fax: (416)447-3331
E-mail: priveq@sympatico.ca

Roynat Ventures
40 King St. West, 26th Fl.
Toronto, ON, Canada M5H 1H1
(416)933-2667
Fax: (416)933-2783
Website: http://www.roynatcapital.com

Tera Capital Corp.
366 Adelaide St. East, Ste. 337
Toronto, ON, Canada M5A 3X9
(416)368-1024
Fax: (416)368-1427

Working Ventures Canadian Fund Inc.
250 Bloor St. East, Ste. 1600
Toronto, ON, Canada M4W 1E6
(416)934-7718
Fax: (416)929-0901
Website: http://www.workingventures.ca

Quebec

Altamira Capital Corp.
202 University
Niveau de Maisoneuve, Bur. 201
Montreal, QC, Canada H3A 2A5
(514)499-1656
Fax: (514)499-9570

Federal Business Development Bank
Venture Capital Division
Five Place Ville Marie, Ste. 600
Montreal, QC, Canada H3B 5E7
(514)283-1896
Fax: (514)283-5455

Hydro-Quebec Capitech Inc.
75 Boul, Rene Levesque Quest
Montreal, QC, Canada H2Z 1A4
(514)289-4783
Fax: (514)289-5420
Website: http://www.hqcapitech.com

Investissement Desjardins
2 complexe Desjardins
C.P. 760
Montreal, QC, Canada H5B 1B8
(514)281-7131
Fax: (514)281-7808
Website: http://www.desjardins.com/id

Marleau Lemire Inc.
One Place Ville-Marie, Ste. 3601
Montreal, QC, Canada H3B 3P2

(514)877-3800
Fax: (514)875-6415

Speirs Consultants Inc.
365 Stanstead
Montreal, QC, Canada H3R 1X5
(514)342-3858
Fax: (514)342-1977

Tecnocap Inc.
4028 Marlowe
Montreal, QC, Canada H4A 3M2
(514)483-6009
Fax: (514)483-6045
Website: http://www.technocap.com

Telsoft Ventures
1000, Rue de la Gauchetiere
Quest, 25eme Etage
Montreal, QC, Canada H3B 4W5
(514)397-8450
Fax: (514)397-8451

Saskatchewan

Saskatchewan Government Growth Fund
1801 Hamilton St., Ste. 1210
Canada Trust Tower
Regina, SK, Canada S4P 4B4
(306)787-2994
Fax: (306)787-2086

United states

Alabama

FHL Capital Corp.
600 20th Street North
Suite 350
Birmingham, AL 35203
(205)328-3098
Fax: (205)323-0001

Harbert Management Corp.
One Riverchase Pkwy. South
Birmingham, AL 35244
(205)987-5500
Fax: (205)987-5707
Website: http://www.harbert.net

Jefferson Capital Fund
PO Box 13129
Birmingham, AL 35213
(205)324-7709

Private Capital Corp.
100 Brookwood Pl., 4th Fl.
Birmingham, AL 35209
(205)879-2722
Fax: (205)879-5121

21st Century Health Ventures
One Health South Pkwy.
Birmingham, AL 35243
(256)268-6250
Fax: (256)970-8928

FJC Growth Capital Corp.
200 W. Side Sq., Ste. 340
Huntsville, AL 35801
(256)922-2918
Fax: (256)922-2909

Hickory Venture Capital Corp.
301 Washington St. NW
Suite 301
Huntsville, AL 35801
(256)539-1931
Fax: (256)539-5130
E-mail: hvcc@hvcc.com
Website: http://www.hvcc.com

Southeastern Technology Fund
7910 South Memorial Pkwy., Ste. F
Huntsville, AL 35802
(256)883-8711
Fax: (256)883-8558

Cordova Ventures
4121 Carmichael Rd., Ste. 301
Montgomery, AL 36106
(334)271-6011
Fax: (334)260-0120
Website: http://www.cordova
ventures.com

Small Business Clinic of Alabama/AG Bartholomew & Associates
PO Box 231074
Montgomery, AL 36123-1074
(334)284-3640

Arizona

Miller Capital Corp.
4909 E. McDowell Rd.
Phoenix, AZ 85008
(602)225-0504
Fax: (602)225-9024
Website: http://www.themiller
group.com

The Columbine Venture Funds
9449 North 90th St., Ste. 200
Scottsdale, AZ 85258
(602)661-9222
Fax: (602)661-6262

Koch Ventures
17767 N. Perimeter Dr., Ste. 101
Scottsdale, AZ 85255
(480)419-3600

Fax: (480)419-3606
Website: http://www.kochventures.com

McKee & Co.
7702 E. Doubletree Ranch Rd.
Suite 230
Scottsdale, AZ 85258
(480)368-0333
Fax: (480)607-7446

Merita Capital Ltd.
7350 E. Stetson Dr., Ste. 108-A
Scottsdale, AZ 85251
(480)947-8700
Fax: (480)947-8766

Valley Ventures / Arizona Growth Partners L.P.
6720 N. Scottsdale Rd., Ste. 208
Scottsdale, AZ 85253
(480)661-6600
Fax: (480)661-6262

Estreetcapital.com
660 South Mill Ave., Ste. 315
Tempe, AZ 85281
(480)968-8400
Fax: (480)968-8480
Website: http://www.estreetcapital.com

Coronado Venture Fund
PO Box 65420
Tucson, AZ 85728-5420
(520)577-3764
Fax: (520)299-8491

Arkansas

Arkansas Capital Corp.
225 South Pulaski St.
Little Rock, AR 72201
(501)374-9247
Fax: (501)374-9425
Website: http://www.arcapital.com

California

Sundance Venture Partners, L.P.
100 Clocktower Place, Ste. 130
Carmel, CA 93923
(831)625-6500
Fax: (831)625-6590

Westar Capital (Costa Mesa)
949 South Coast Dr., Ste. 650
Costa Mesa, CA 92626
(714)481-5160
Fax: (714)481-5166
E-mail: mailbox@westarcapital.com
Website: http://www.westarcapital.com

Alpine Technology Ventures
20300 Stevens Creek Boulevard, Ste. 495
Cupertino, CA 95014
(408)725-1810
Fax: (408)725-1207
Website: http://www.alpineventures.com

Bay Partners
10600 N. De Anza Blvd.
Cupertino, CA 95014-2031
(408)725-2444
Fax: (408)446-4502
Website: http://www.baypartners.com

Novus Ventures
20111 Stevens Creek Blvd., Ste. 130
Cupertino, CA 95014
(408)252-3900
Fax: (408)252-1713
Website: http://www.novusventures.com

Triune Capital
19925 Stevens Creek Blvd., Ste. 200
Cupertino, CA 95014
(310)284-6800
Fax: (310)284-3290

Acorn Ventures
268 Bush St., Ste. 2829
Daly City, CA 94014
(650)994-7801
Fax: (650)994-3305
Website: http://www.acornventures.com

Digital Media Campus
2221 Park Place
El Segundo, CA 90245
(310)426-8000
Fax: (310)426-8010
E-mail: info@thecampus.com
Website: http://www.digital
mediacampus.com

BankAmerica Ventures / BA Venture Partners
950 Tower Ln., Ste. 700
Foster City, CA 94404
(650)378-6000
Fax: (650)378-6040
Website: http://
www.baventurepartners.com

Starting Point Partners
666 Portofino Lane
Foster City, CA 94404
(650)722-1035
Website: http://www.startingpoint
partners.com

Opportunity Capital Partners
2201 Walnut Ave., Ste. 210

Fremont, CA 94538
(510)795-7000
Fax: (510)494-5439
Website: http://www.ocpcapital.com

Imperial Ventures Inc.
9920 S. La Cienega Boulevar, 14th Fl.
Inglewood, CA 90301
(310)417-5409
Fax: (310)338-6115

Ventana Global (Irvine)
18881 Von Karman Ave., Ste. 1150
Irvine, CA 92612
(949)476-2204
Fax: (949)752-0223
Website: http://www.ventanaglobal.com

Integrated Consortium Inc.
50 Ridgecrest Rd.
Kentfield, CA 94904
(415)925-0386
Fax: (415)461-2726

Enterprise Partners
979 Ivanhoe Ave., Ste. 550
La Jolla, CA 92037
(858)454-8833
Fax: (858)454-2489
Website: http://www.epvc.com

Domain Associates
28202 Cabot Rd., Ste. 200
Laguna Niguel, CA 92677
(949)347-2446
Fax: (949)347-9720
Website: http://www.domainvc.com

Cascade Communications Ventures
60 E. Sir Francis Drake Blvd., Ste. 300
Larkspur, CA 94939
(415)925-6500
Fax: (415)925-6501

Allegis Capital
One First St., Ste. Two
Los Altos, CA 94022
(650)917-5900
Fax: (650)917-5901
Website: http://www.allegiscapital.com

Aspen Ventures
1000 Fremont Ave., Ste. 200
Los Altos, CA 94024
(650)917-5670
Fax: (650)917-5677
Website: http://www.aspenventures.com

AVI Capital L.P.
1 First St., Ste. 2
Los Altos, CA 94022

(650)949-9862
Fax: (650)949-8510
Website: http://www.avicapital.com

Bastion Capital Corp.
1999 Avenue of the Stars, Ste. 2960
Los Angeles, CA 90067
(310)788-5700
Fax: (310)277-7582
E-mail: ga@bastioncapital.com
Website: http://www.bastioncapital.com

Davis Group
PO Box 69953
Los Angeles, CA 90069-0953
(310)659-6327
Fax: (310)659-6337

Developers Equity Corp.
1880 Century Park East, Ste. 211
Los Angeles, CA 90067
(213)277-0300

Far East Capital Corp.
350 S. Grand Ave., Ste. 4100
Los Angeles, CA 90071
(213)687-1361
Fax: (213)617-7939
E-mail: free@fareastnationalbank.com

Kline Hawkes & Co.
11726 San Vicente Blvd., Ste. 300
Los Angeles, CA 90049
(310)442-4700
Fax: (310)442-4707
Website: http://www.klinehawkes.com

Lawrence Financial Group
701 Teakwood
PO Box 491773
Los Angeles, CA 90049
(310)471-4060
Fax: (310)472-3155

Riordan Lewis & Haden
300 S. Grand Ave., 29th Fl.
Los Angeles, CA 90071
(213)229-8500
Fax: (213)229-8597

Union Venture Corp.
445 S. Figueroa St., 9th Fl.
Los Angeles, CA 90071
(213)236-4092
Fax: (213)236-6329

Wedbush Capital Partners
1000 Wilshire Blvd.
Los Angeles, CA 90017
(213)688-4545
Fax: (213)688-6642
Website: http://www.wedbush.com

Advent International Corp.
2180 Sand Hill Rd., Ste. 420
Menlo Park, CA 94025
(650)233-7500
Fax: (650)233-7515
Website: http://www.adventinter
national.com

Altos Ventures
2882 Sand Hill Rd., Ste. 100
Menlo Park, CA 94025
(650)234-9771
Fax: (650)233-9821
Website: http://www.altosvc.com

Applied Technology
1010 El Camino Real, Ste. 300
Menlo Park, CA 94025
(415)326-8622
Fax: (415)326-8163

APV Technology Partners
535 Middlefield, Ste. 150
Menlo Park, CA 94025
(650)327-7871
Fax: (650)327-7631
Website: http://www.apvtp.com

August Capital Management
2480 Sand Hill Rd., Ste. 101
Menlo Park, CA 94025
(650)234-9900
Fax: (650)234-9910
Website: http://www.augustcap.com

Baccharis Capital Inc.
2420 Sand Hill Rd., Ste. 100
Menlo Park, CA 94025
(650)324-6844
Fax: (650)854-3025

Benchmark Capital
2480 Sand Hill Rd., Ste. 200
Menlo Park, CA 94025
(650)854-8180
Fax: (650)854-8183
E-mail: info@benchmark.com
Website: http://www.benchmark.com

**Bessemer Venture Partners (Menlo
Park)**
535 Middlefield Rd., Ste. 245
Menlo Park, CA 94025
(650)853-7000
Fax: (650)853-7001
Website: http://www.bvp.com

The Cambria Group
1600 El Camino Real Rd., Ste. 155
Menlo Park, CA 94025
(650)329-8600

Fax: (650)329-8601
Website: http://www.cambriagroup.com

Canaan Partners
2884 Sand Hill Rd., Ste. 115
Menlo Park, CA 94025
(650)854-8092
Fax: (650)854-8127
Website: http://www.canaan.com

Capstone Ventures
3000 Sand Hill Rd., Bldg. One, Ste. 290
Menlo Park, CA 94025
(650)854-2523
Fax: (650)854-9010
Website: http://www.capstonevc.com

**Comdisco Venture Group (Silicon
Valley)**
3000 Sand Hill Rd., Bldg. 1, Ste. 155
Menlo Park, CA 94025
(650)854-9484
Fax: (650)854-4026

Commtech International
535 Middlefield Rd., Ste. 200
Menlo Park, CA 94025
(650)328-0190
Fax: (650)328-6442

Compass Technology Partners
1550 El Camino Real, Ste. 275
Menlo Park, CA 94025-4111
(650)322-7595
Fax: (650)322-0588
Website: http://www.compass
techpartners.com

Convergence Partners
3000 Sand Hill Rd., Ste. 235
Menlo Park, CA 94025
(650)854-3010
Fax: (650)854-3015
Website: http://www.conver
gencepartners.com

The Dakota Group
PO Box 1025
Menlo Park, CA 94025
(650)853-0600
Fax: (650)851-4899
E-mail: info@dakota.com

Delphi Ventures
3000 Sand Hill Rd.
Bldg. One, Ste. 135
Menlo Park, CA 94025
(650)854-9650
Fax: (650)854-2961
Website: http://www.delphiventures.com

El Dorado Ventures
2884 Sand Hill Rd., Ste. 121
Menlo Park, CA 94025
(650)854-1200
Fax: (650)854-1202
Website: http://www.eldorado
ventures.com

Glynn Ventures
3000 Sand Hill Rd., Bldg. 4, Ste. 235
Menlo Park, CA 94025
(650)854-2215

Indosuez Ventures
2180 Sand Hill Rd., Ste. 450
Menlo Park, CA 94025
(650)854-0587
Fax: (650)323-5561
Website: http://www.indosuez
ventures.com

Institutional Venture Partners
3000 Sand Hill Rd., Bldg. 2, Ste. 290
Menlo Park, CA 94025
(650)854-0132
Fax: (650)854-5762
Website: http://www.ivp.com

Interwest Partners (Menlo Park)
3000 Sand Hill Rd., Bldg. 3, Ste. 255
Menlo Park, CA 94025-7112
(650)854-8585
Fax: (650)854-4706
Website: http://www.interwest.com

Kleiner Perkins Caufield & Byers (Menlo Park)
2750 Sand Hill Rd.
Menlo Park, CA 94025
(650)233-2750
Fax: (650)233-0300
Website: http://www.kpcb.com

Magic Venture Capital LLC
1010 El Camino Real, Ste. 300
Menlo Park, CA 94025
(650)325-4149

Matrix Partners
2500 Sand Hill Rd., Ste. 113
Menlo Park, CA 94025
(650)854-3131
Fax: (650)854-3296
Website: http://www.matrixpartners.com

Mayfield Fund
2800 Sand Hill Rd.
Menlo Park, CA 94025
(650)854-5560
Fax: (650)854-5712
Website: http://www.mayfield.com

McCown De Leeuw and Co. (Menlo Park)
3000 Sand Hill Rd., Bldg. 3, Ste. 290
Menlo Park, CA 94025-7111
(650)854-6000
Fax: (650)854-0853
Website: http://www.mdcpartners.com

Menlo Ventures
3000 Sand Hill Rd., Bldg. 4, Ste. 100
Menlo Park, CA 94025
(650)854-8540
Fax: (650)854-7059
Website: http://www.menloventures.com

Merrill Pickard Anderson & Eyre
2480 Sand Hill Rd., Ste. 200
Menlo Park, CA 94025
(650)854-8600
Fax: (650)854-0345

New Enterprise Associates (Menlo Park)
2490 Sand Hill Rd.
Menlo Park, CA 94025
(650)854-9499
Fax: (650)854-9397
Website: http://www.nea.com

Onset Ventures
2400 Sand Hill Rd., Ste. 150
Menlo Park, CA 94025
(650)529-0700
Fax: (650)529-0777
Website: http://www.onset.com

Paragon Venture Partners
3000 Sand Hill Rd., Bldg. 1, Ste. 275
Menlo Park, CA 94025
(650)854-8000
Fax: (650)854-7260

Pathfinder Venture Capital Funds (Menlo Park)
3000 Sand Hill Rd., Bldg. 3, Ste. 255
Menlo Park, CA 94025
(650)854-0650
Fax: (650)854-4706

Rocket Ventures
3000 Sandhill Rd., Bldg. 1, Ste. 170
Menlo Park, CA 94025
(650)561-9100
Fax: (650)561-9183
Website: http://www.rocketventures.com

Sequoia Capital
3000 Sand Hill Rd., Bldg. 4, Ste. 280
Menlo Park, CA 94025
(650)854-3927
Fax: (650)854-2977

E-mail: sequoia@sequioacap.com
Website: http://www.sequoiacap.com

Sierra Ventures
3000 Sand Hill Rd., Bldg. 4, Ste. 210
Menlo Park, CA 94025
(650)854-1000
Fax: (650)854-5593
Website: http://www.sierraventures.com

Sigma Partners
2884 Sand Hill Rd., Ste. 121
Menlo Park, CA 94025-7022
(650)853-1700
Fax: (650)853-1717
E-mail: info@sigmapartners.com
Website: http://www.sigmapartners.com

Sprout Group (Menlo Park)
3000 Sand Hill Rd.
Bldg. 3, Ste. 170
Menlo Park, CA 94025
(650)234-2700
Fax: (650)234-2779
Website: http://www.sproutgroup.com

TA Associates (Menlo Park)
70 Willow Rd., Ste. 100
Menlo Park, CA 94025
(650)328-1210
Fax: (650)326-4933
Website: http://www.ta.com

Thompson Clive & Partners Ltd.
3000 Sand Hill Rd., Bldg. 1, Ste. 185
Menlo Park, CA 94025-7102
(650)854-0314
Fax: (650)854-0670
E-mail: mail@tcvc.com
Website: http://www.tcvc.com

Trinity Ventures Ltd.
3000 Sand Hill Rd., Bldg. 1, Ste. 240
Menlo Park, CA 94025
(650)854-9500
Fax: (650)854-9501
Website: http://www.trinityventures.com

U.S. Venture Partners
2180 Sand Hill Rd., Ste. 300
Menlo Park, CA 94025
(650)854-9080
Fax: (650)854-3018
Website: http://www.usvp.com

USVP-Schlein Marketing Fund
2180 Sand Hill Rd., Ste. 300
Menlo Park, CA 94025
(415)854-9080
Fax: (415)854-3018
Website: http://www.usvp.com

Venrock Associates
2494 Sand Hill Rd., Ste. 200
Menlo Park, CA 94025
(650)561-9580
Fax: (650)561-9180
Website: http://www.venrock.com

Brad Peery Capital Inc.
145 Chapel Pkwy.
Mill Valley, CA 94941
(415)389-0625
Fax: (415)389-1336

Dot Edu Ventures
650 Castro St., Ste. 270
Mountain View, CA 94041
(650)575-5638
Fax: (650)325-5247
Website: http://www.dotedu
ventures.com

Forrest, Binkley & Brown
840 Newport Ctr. Dr., Ste. 480
Newport Beach, CA 92660
(949)729-3222
Fax: (949)729-3226
Website: http://www.fbbvc.com

Marwit Capital LLC
180 Newport Center Dr., Ste. 200
Newport Beach, CA 92660
(949)640-6234
Fax: (949)720-8077
Website: http://www.marwit.com

Kaiser Permanente / National Venture Development
1800 Harrison St., 22nd Fl.
Oakland, CA 94612
(510)267-4010
Fax: (510)267-4036
Website: http://www.kpventures.com

Nu Capital Access Group, Ltd.
7677 Oakport St., Ste. 105
Oakland, CA 94621
(510)635-7345
Fax: (510)635-7068

Inman and Bowman
4 Orinda Way, Bldg. D, Ste. 150
Orinda, CA 94563
(510)253-1611
Fax: (510)253-9037

Accel Partners (San Francisco)
428 University Ave.
Palo Alto, CA 94301
(650)614-4800
Fax: (650)614-4880
Website: http://www.accel.com

Advanced Technology Ventures
485 Ramona St., Ste. 200
Palo Alto, CA 94301
(650)321-8601
Fax: (650)321-0934
Website: http://www.atvcapital.com

Anila Fund
400 Channing Ave.
Palo Alto, CA 94301
(650)833-5790
Fax: (650)833-0590
Website: http://www.anila.com

Asset Management Company Venture Capital
2275 E. Bayshore, Ste. 150
Palo Alto, CA 94303
(650)494-7400
Fax: (650)856-1826
E-mail: postmaster@assetman.com
Website: http://www.assetman.com

BancBoston Capital / BancBoston Ventures
435 Tasso St., Ste. 250
Palo Alto, CA 94305
(650)470-4100
Fax: (650)853-1425
Website: http://www.bancboston
capital.com

Charter Ventures
525 University Ave., Ste. 1400
Palo Alto, CA 94301
(650)325-6953
Fax: (650)325-4762
Website: http://www.charterventures.com

Communications Ventures
505 Hamilton Avenue, Ste. 305
Palo Alto, CA 94301
(650)325-9600
Fax: (650)325-9608
Website: http://www.comven.com

HMS Group
2468 Embarcadero Way
Palo Alto, CA 94303-3313
(650)856-9862
Fax: (650)856-9864

Jafco America Ventures, Inc.
505 Hamilton Ste. 310
Palto Alto, CA 94301
(650)463-8800
Fax: (650)463-8801
Website: http://www.jafco.com

New Vista Capital
540 Cowper St., Ste. 200

Palo Alto, CA 94301
(650)329-9333
Fax: (650)328-9434
E-mail: fgreene@nvcap.com
Website: http://www.nvcap.com

Norwest Equity Partners (Palo Alto)
245 Lytton Ave., Ste. 250
Palo Alto, CA 94301-1426
(650)321-8000
Fax: (650)321-8010
Website: http://www.norwestvp.com

Oak Investment Partners
525 University Ave., Ste. 1300
Palo Alto, CA 94301
(650)614-3700
Fax: (650)328-6345
Website: http://www.oakinv.com

Patricof & Co. Ventures, Inc. (Palo Alto)
2100 Geng Rd., Ste. 150
Palo Alto, CA 94303
(650)494-9944
Fax: (650)494-6751
Website: http://www.patricof.com

RWI Group
835 Page Mill Rd.
Palo Alto, CA 94304
(650)251-1800
Fax: (650)213-8660
Website: http://www.rwigroup.com

Summit Partners (Palo Alto)
499 Hamilton Ave., Ste. 200
Palo Alto, CA 94301
(650)321-1166
Fax: (650)321-1188
Website: http://www.summit
partners.com

Sutter Hill Ventures
755 Page Mill Rd., Ste. A-200
Palo Alto, CA 94304
(650)493-5600
Fax: (650)858-1854
E-mail: shv@shv.com

Vanguard Venture Partners
525 University Ave., Ste. 600
Palo Alto, CA 94301
(650)321-2900
Fax: (650)321-2902
Website: http://www.vanguard
ventures.com

Venture Growth Associates
2479 East Bayshore St., Ste. 710
Palo Alto, CA 94303

(650)855-9100
Fax: (650)855-9104

Worldview Technology Partners
435 Tasso St., Ste. 120
Palo Alto, CA 94301
(650)322-3800
Fax: (650)322-3880
Website: http://www.worldview.com

Draper, Fisher, Jurvetson / Draper Associates
400 Seaport Ct., Ste.250
Redwood City, CA 94063
(415)599-9000
Fax: (415)599-9726
Website: http://www.dfj.com

Gabriel Venture Partners
350 Marine Pkwy., Ste. 200
Redwood Shores, CA 94065
(650)551-5000
Fax: (650)551-5001
Website: http://www.gabrielvp.com

Hallador Venture Partners, L.L.C.
740 University Ave., Ste. 110
Sacramento, CA 95825-6710
(916)920-0191
Fax: (916)920-5188
E-mail: chris@hallador.com

Emerald Venture Group
12396 World Trade Dr., Ste. 116
San Diego, CA 92128
(858)451-1001
Fax: (858)451-1003
Website: http://www.emerald
venture.com

Forward Ventures
9255 Towne Centre Dr.
San Diego, CA 92121
(858)677-6077
Fax: (858)452-8799
E-mail: info@forwardventure.com
Website: http://www.forward
venture.com

Idanta Partners Ltd.
4660 La Jolla Village Dr., Ste. 850
San Diego, CA 92122
(619)452-9690
Fax: (619)452-2013
Website: http://www.idanta.com

Kingsbury Associates
3655 Nobel Dr., Ste. 490
San Diego, CA 92122
(858)677-0600
Fax: (858)677-0800

Kyocera International Inc.
Corporate Development
8611 Balboa Ave.
San Diego, CA 92123
(858)576-2600
Fax: (858)492-1456

Sorrento Associates, Inc.
4370 LaJolla Village Dr., Ste. 1040
San Diego, CA 92122
(619)452-3100
Fax: (619)452-7607
Website: http://www.sorrento
ventures.com

Western States Investment Group
9191 Towne Ctr. Dr., Ste. 310
San Diego, CA 92122
(619)678-0800
Fax: (619)678-0900

Aberdare Ventures
One Embarcadero Center, Ste. 4000
San Francisco, CA 94111
(415)392-7442
Fax: (415)392-4264
Website: http://www.aberdare.com

Acacia Venture Partners
101 California St., Ste. 3160
San Francisco, CA 94111
(415)433-4200
Fax: (415)433-4250
Website: http://www.acaciavp.com

Access Venture Partners
319 Laidley St.
San Francisco, CA 94131
(415)586-0132
Fax: (415)392-6310
Website: http://www.access
venturepartners.com

Alta Partners
One Embarcadero Center, Ste. 4050
San Francisco, CA 94111
(415)362-4022
Fax: (415)362-6178
E-mail: alta@altapartners.com
Website: http://www.altapartners.com

Bangert Dawes Reade Davis & Thom
220 Montgomery St., Ste. 424
San Francisco, CA 94104
(415)954-9900
Fax: (415)954-9901
E-mail: bdrdt@pacbell.net

Berkeley International Capital Corp.
650 California St., Ste. 2800
San Francisco, CA 94108-2609

(415)249-0450
Fax: (415)392-3929
Website: http://www.berkeleyvc.com

Blueprint Ventures LLC
456 Montgomery St., 22nd Fl.
San Francisco, CA 94104
(415)901-4000
Fax: (415)901-4035
Website: http://www.blue
printventures.com

Blumberg Capital Ventures
580 Howard St., Ste. 401
San Francisco, CA 94105
(415)905-5007
Fax: (415)357-5027
Website: http://www.blumberg-
capital.com

Burr, Egan, Deleage, and Co. (San Francisco)
1 Embarcadero Center, Ste. 4050
San Francisco, CA 94111
(415)362-4022
Fax: (415)362-6178

Burrill & Company
120 Montgomery St., Ste. 1370
San Francisco, CA 94104
(415)743-3160
Fax: (415)743-3161
Website: http://www.burrillandco.com

CMEA Ventures
235 Montgomery St., Ste. 920
San Francisco, CA 94401
(415)352-1520
Fax: (415)352-1524
Website: http://www.cmeaventures.com

Crocker Capital
1 Post St., Ste. 2500
San Francisco, CA 94101
(415)956-5250
Fax: (415)959-5710

Dominion Ventures, Inc.
44 Montgomery St., Ste. 4200
San Francisco, CA 94104
(415)362-4890
Fax: (415)394-9245

Dorset Capital
Pier 1
Bay 2
San Francisco, CA 94111
(415)398-7101
Fax: (415)398-7141
Website: http://www.dorsetcapital.com

Gatx Capital
Four Embarcadero Center, Ste. 2200
San Francisco, CA 94904
(415)955-3200
Fax: (415)955-3449

IMinds
135 Main St., Ste. 1350
San Francisco, CA 94105
(415)547-0000
Fax: (415)227-0300
Website: http://www.iminds.com

LF International Inc.
360 Post St., Ste. 705
San Francisco, CA 94108
(415)399-0110
Fax: (415)399-9222
Website: http://www.lfvc.com

Newbury Ventures
535 Pacific Ave., 2nd Fl.
San Francisco, CA 94133
(415)296-7408
Fax: (415)296-7416
Website: http://www.newburyven.com

Quest Ventures (San Francisco)
333 Bush St., Ste. 1750
San Francisco, CA 94104
(415)782-1414
Fax: (415)782-1415

Robertson-Stephens Co.
555 California St., Ste. 2600
San Francisco, CA 94104
(415)781-9700
Fax: (415)781-2556
Website: http://www.omegaad
ventures.com

Rosewood Capital, L.P.
One Maritime Plaza, Ste. 1330
San Francisco, CA 94111-3503
(415)362-5526
Fax: (415)362-1192
Website: http://www.rosewoodvc.com

Ticonderoga Capital Inc.
555 California St., No. 4950
San Francisco, CA 94104
(415)296-7900
Fax: (415)296-8956

21st Century Internet Venture Partners
Two South Park
2nd Floor
San Francisco, CA 94107
(415)512-1221
Fax: (415)512-2650
Website: http://www.21vc.com

VK Ventures
600 California St., Ste.1700
San Francisco, CA 94111
(415)391-5600
Fax: (415)397-2744

Walden Group of Venture Capital Funds
750 Battery St., Seventh Floor
San Francisco, CA 94111
(415)391-7225
Fax: (415)391-7262

Acer Technology Ventures
2641 Orchard Pkwy.
San Jose, CA 95134
(408)433-4945
Fax: (408)433-5230

Authosis
226 Airport Pkwy., Ste. 405
San Jose, CA 95110
(650)814-3603
Website: http://www.authosis.com

Western Technology Investment
2010 N. First St., Ste. 310
San Jose, CA 95131
(408)436-8577
Fax: (408)436-8625
E-mail: mktg@westerntech.com

Drysdale Enterprises
177 Bovet Rd., Ste. 600
San Mateo, CA 94402
(650)341-6336
Fax: (650)341-1329
E-mail: drysdale@aol.com

Greylock
2929 Campus Dr., Ste. 400
San Mateo, CA 94401
(650)493-5525
Fax: (650)493-5575
Website: http://www.greylock.com

Technology Funding
2000 Alameda de las Pulgas, Ste. 250
San Mateo, CA 94403
(415)345-2200
Fax: (415)345-1797

2M Invest Inc.
1875 S. Grant St.
Suite 750
San Mateo, CA 94402
(650)655-3765
Fax: (650)372-9107
E-mail: 2minfo@2minvest.com
Website: http://www.2minvest.com

Phoenix Growth Capital Corp.
2401 Kerner Blvd.
San Rafael, CA 94901
(415)485-4569
Fax: (415)485-4663

NextGen Partners LLC
1705 East Valley Rd.
Santa Barbara, CA 93108
(805)969-8540
Fax: (805)969-8542
Website: http://www.nextgen
partners.com

Denali Venture Capital
1925 Woodland Ave.
Santa Clara, CA 95050
(408)690-4838
Fax: (408)247-6979
E-mail: wael@denaliventurecapital.com
Website: http://www.denali
venturecapital.com

Dotcom Ventures LP
3945 Freedom Circle, Ste. 740
Santa Clara, CA 95045
(408)919-9855
Fax: (408)919-9857
Website: http://www.dotcom
venturesatl.com

Silicon Valley Bank
3003 Tasman
Santa Clara, CA 95054
(408)654-7400
Fax: (408)727-8728

Al Shugart International
920 41st Ave.
Santa Cruz, CA 95062
(831)479-7852
Fax: (831)479-7852
Website: http://www.alshugart.com

Leonard Mautner Associates
1434 Sixth St.
Santa Monica, CA 90401
(213)393-9788
Fax: (310)459-9918

Palomar Ventures
100 Wilshire Blvd., Ste. 450
Santa Monica, CA 90401
(310)260-6050
Fax: (310)656-4150
Website: http://www.palomar
ventures.com

Medicus Venture Partners
12930 Saratoga Ave., Ste. D8
Saratoga, CA 95070

(408)447-8600
Fax: (408)447-8599
Website: http://www.medicusvc.com

Redleaf Venture Management
14395 Saratoga Ave., Ste. 130
Saratoga, CA 95070
(408)868-0800
Fax: (408)868-0810
E-mail: nancy@redleaf.com
Website: http://www.redleaf.com

Artemis Ventures
207 Second St., Ste. E
3rd Fl.
Sausalito, CA 94965
(415)289-2500
Fax: (415)289-1789
Website: http://www.artemisventures.com

Deucalion Venture Partners
19501 Brooklime
Sonoma, CA 95476
(707)938-4974
Fax: (707)938-8921

Windward Ventures
PO Box 7688
Thousand Oaks, CA 91359-7688
(805)497-3332
Fax: (805)497-9331

National Investment Management, Inc.
2601 Airport Dr., Ste.210
Torrance, CA 90505
(310)784-7600
Fax: (310)784-7605

Southern California Ventures
406 Amapola Ave. Ste. 125
Torrance, CA 90501
(310)787-4381
Fax: (310)787-4382

Sandton Financial Group
21550 Oxnard St., Ste. 300
Woodland Hills, CA 91367
(818)702-9283

Woodside Fund
850 Woodside Dr.
Woodside, CA 94062
(650)368-5545
Fax: (650)368-2416
Website: http://www.woodsidefund.com

Colorado

Colorado Venture Management
Ste. 300
Boulder, CO 80301

(303)440-4055
Fax: (303)440-4636

Dean & Associates
4362 Apple Way
Boulder, CO 80301
Fax: (303)473-9900

Roser Ventures LLC
1105 Spruce St.
Boulder, CO 80302
(303)443-6436
Fax: (303)443-1885
Website: http://www.roserventures.com

Sequel Venture Partners
4430 Arapahoe Ave., Ste. 220
Boulder, CO 80303
(303)546-0400
Fax: (303)546-9728
E-mail: tom@sequelvc.com
Website: http://www.sequelvc.com

New Venture Resources
445C E. Cheyenne Mtn. Blvd.
Colorado Springs, CO 80906-4570
(719)598-9272
Fax: (719)598-9272

The Centennial Funds
1428 15th St.
Denver, CO 80202-1318
(303)405-7500
Fax: (303)405-7575
Website: http://www.centennial.com

Rocky Mountain Capital Partners
1125 17th St., Ste. 2260
Denver, CO 80202
(303)291-5200
Fax: (303)291-5327

Sandlot Capital LLC
600 South Cherry St., Ste. 525
Denver, CO 80246
(303)893-3400
Fax: (303)893-3403
Website: http://www.sandlotcapital.com

Wolf Ventures
50 South Steele St., Ste. 777
Denver, CO 80209
(303)321-4800
Fax: (303)321-4848
E-mail: businessplan@wolf
ventures.com
Website: http://www.wolfventures.com

The Columbine Venture Funds
5460 S. Quebec St., Ste. 270
Englewood, CO 80111

(303)694-3222
Fax: (303)694-9007

Investment Securities of Colorado, Inc.
4605 Denice Dr.
Englewood, CO 80111
(303)796-9192

Kinship Partners
6300 S. Syracuse Way, Ste. 484
Englewood, CO 80111
(303)694-0268
Fax: (303)694-1707
E-mail: block@vailsys.com

Boranco Management, L.L.C.
1528 Hillside Dr.
Fort Collins, CO 80524-1969
(970)221-2297
Fax: (970)221-4787

Aweida Ventures
890 West Cherry St., Ste. 220
Louisville, CO 80027
(303)664-9520
Fax: (303)664-9530
Website: http://www.aweida.com

Access Venture Partners
8787 Turnpike Dr., Ste. 260
Westminster, CO 80030
(303)426-8899
Fax: (303)426-8828

Medmax Ventures LP
1 Northwestern Dr., Ste. 203
Bloomfield, CT 06002
(860)286-2960
Fax: (860)286-9960

James B. Kobak & Co.
Four Mansfield Place
Darien, CT 06820
(203)656-3471
Fax: (203)655-2905

Orien Ventures
1 Post Rd.
Fairfield, CT 06430
(203)259-9933
Fax: (203)259-5288

ABP Acquisition Corporation
115 Maple Ave.
Greenwich, CT 06830
(203)625-8287
Fax: (203)447-6187

Catterton Partners
9 Greenwich Office Park
Greenwich, CT 06830
(203)629-4901

Fax: (203)629-4903
Website: http://www.cpequity.com

Consumer Venture Partners
3 Pickwick Plz.
Greenwich, CT 06830
(203)629-8800
Fax: (203)629-2019

Insurance Venture Partners
31 Brookside Dr., Ste. 211
Greenwich, CT 06830
(203)861-0030
Fax: (203)861-2745

The NTC Group
Three Pickwick Plaza
Ste. 200
Greenwich, CT 06830
(203)862-2800
Fax: (203)622-6538

Regulus International Capital Co., Inc.
140 Greenwich Ave.
Greenwich, CT 06830
(203)625-9700
Fax: (203)625-9706

Axiom Venture Partners
City Place II
185 Asylum St., 17th Fl.
Hartford, CT 06103
(860)548-7799
Fax: (860)548-7797
Website: http://www.axiomventures.com

Conning Capital Partners
City Place II
185 Asylum St.
Hartford, CT 06103-4105
(860)520-1289
Fax: (860)520-1299
E-mail: pe@conning.com
Website: http://www.conning.com

First New England Capital L.P.
100 Pearl St.
Hartford, CT 06103
(860)293-3333
Fax: (860)293-3338
E-mail: info@firstnewenglandcapital.com
Website: http://www.firstnewengland
capital.com

Northeast Ventures
One State St., Ste. 1720
Hartford, CT 06103
(860)547-1414
Fax: (860)246-8755

Windward Holdings
38 Sylvan Rd.
Madison, CT 06443
(203)245-6870
Fax: (203)245-6865

Advanced Materials Partners, Inc.
45 Pine St.
PO Box 1022
New Canaan, CT 06840
(203)966-6415
Fax: (203)966-8448
E-mail: wkb@amplink.com

RFE Investment Partners
36 Grove St.
New Canaan, CT 06840
(203)966-2800
Fax: (203)966-3109
Website: http://www.rfeip.com

Connecticut Innovations, Inc.
999 West St.
Rocky Hill, CT 06067
(860)563-5851
Fax: (860)563-4877
E-mail: pamela.hartley@ctin
novations.com
Website: http://www.ctinnovations.com

Canaan Partners
105 Rowayton Ave.
Rowayton, CT 06853
(203)855-0400
Fax: (203)854-9117
Website: http://www.canaan.com

Landmark Partners, Inc.
10 Mill Pond Ln.
Simsbury, CT 06070
(860)651-9760
Fax: (860)651-8890
Website: http://
www.landmarkpartners.com

Sweeney & Company
PO Box 567
Southport, CT 06490
(203)255-0220
Fax: (203)255-0220
E-mail: sweeney@connix.com

Baxter Associates, Inc.
PO Box 1333
Stamford, CT 06904
(203)323-3143
Fax: (203)348-0622

Beacon Partners Inc.
6 Landmark Sq., 4th Fl.
Stamford, CT 06901-2792

(203)359-5776
Fax: (203)359-5876

Collinson, Howe, and Lennox, LLC
1055 Washington Blvd., 5th Fl.
Stamford, CT 06901
(203)324-7700
Fax: (203)324-3636
E-mail: info@chlmedical.com
Website: http://www.chlmedical.com

Prime Capital Management Co.
550 West Ave.
Stamford, CT 06902
(203)964-0642
Fax: (203)964-0862

Saugatuck Capital Co.
1 Canterbury Green
Stamford, CT 06901
(203)348-6669
Fax: (203)324-6995
Website: http://www.sauga
tuckcapital.com

Soundview Financial Group Inc.
22 Gatehouse Rd.
Stamford, CT 06902
(203)462-7200
Fax: (203)462-7350
Website: http://www.sndv.com

TSG Ventures, L.L.C.
177 Broad St., 12th Fl.
Stamford, CT 06901
(203)406-1500
Fax: (203)406-1590

Whitney & Company
177 Broad St.
Stamford, CT 06901
(203)973-1400
Fax: (203)973-1422
Website: http://www.jhwhitney.com

Cullinane & Donnelly Venture Partners L.P.
970 Farmington Ave.
West Hartford, CT 06107
(860)521-7811

The Crestview Investment and Financial Group
431 Post Rd. E, Ste. 1
Westport, CT 06880-4403
(203)222-0333
Fax: (203)222-0000

Marketcorp Venture Associates, L.P. (MCV)
274 Riverside Ave.
Westport, CT 06880

(203)222-3030
Fax: (203)222-3033

Oak Investment Partners (Westport)
1 Gorham Island
Westport, CT 06880
(203)226-8346
Fax: (203)227-0372
Website: http://www.oakinv.com

Oxford Bioscience Partners
315 Post Rd. W
Westport, CT 06880-5200
(203)341-3300
Fax: (203)341-3309
Website: http://www.oxbio.com

Prince Ventures (Westport)
25 Ford Rd.
Westport, CT 06880
(203)227-8332
Fax: (203)226-5302

LTI Venture Leasing Corp.
221 Danbury Rd.
Wilton, CT 06897
(203)563-1100
Fax: (203)563-1111
Website: http://www.ltileasing.com

Delaware

Blue Rock Capital
5803 Kennett Pike, Ste. A
Wilmington, DE 19807
(302)426-0981
Fax: (302)426-0982
Website: http://www.bluerockcapital.com

District of Columbia

Allied Capital Corp.
1919 Pennsylvania Ave. NW
Washington, DC 20006-3434
(202)331-2444
Fax: (202)659-2053
Website: http://www.alliedcapital.com

Atlantic Coastal Ventures, L.P.
3101 South St. NW
Washington, DC 20007
(202)293-1166
Fax: (202)293-1181
Website: http://www.atlanticcv.com

Columbia Capital Group, Inc.
1660 L St. NW, Ste. 308
Washington, DC 20036
(202)775-8815
Fax: (202)223-0544

Core Capital Partners
901 15th St., NW
9th Fl.
Washington, DC 20005
(202)589-0090
Fax: (202)589-0091
Website: http://www.core-capital.com

Next Point Partners
701 Pennsylvania Ave. NW, Ste. 900
Washington, DC 20004
(202)661-8703
Fax: (202)434-7400
E-mail: mf@nextpoint.vc
Website: http://www.nextpointvc.com

Telecommunications Development Fund
2020 K. St. NW
Ste. 375
Washington, DC 20006
(202)293-8840
Fax: (202)293-8850
Website: http://www.tdfund.com

Wachtel & Co., Inc.
1101 4th St. NW
Washington, DC 20005-5680
(202)898-1144

Winslow Partners LLC
1300 Connecticut Ave. NW
Washington, DC 20036-1703
(202)530-5000
Fax: (202)530-5010
E-mail: winslow@winslowpartners.com

Women's Growth Capital Fund
1054 31st St., NW
Ste. 110
Washington, DC 20007
(202)342-1431
Fax: (202)341-1203
Website: http://www.wgcf.com

Sigma Capital Corp.
22668 Caravelle Circle
Boca Raton, FL 33433
(561)368-9783

North American Business Development Co., L.L.C.
111 East Las Olas Blvd.
Ft. Lauderdale, FL 33301
(305)463-0681
Fax: (305)527-0904
Website: http://www.northamericanfund.com

Chartwell Capital Management Co. Inc.
1 Independent Dr., Ste. 3120

Jacksonville, FL 32202
(904)355-3519
Fax: (904)353-5833
E-mail: info@chartwellcap.com

CEO Advisors
1061 Maitland Center Commons
Ste. 209
Maitland, FL 32751
(407)660-9327
Fax: (407)660-2109

Henry & Co.
8201 Peters Rd., Ste. 1000
Plantation, FL 33324
(954)797-7400

Avery Business Development Services
2506 St. Michel Ct.
Ponte Vedra, FL 32082
(904)285-6033

New South Ventures
5053 Ocean Blvd.
Sarasota, FL 34242
(941)358-6000
Fax: (941)358-6078
Website: http://www.newsouthventures.com

Venture Capital Management Corp.
PO Box 2626
Satellite Beach, FL 32937
(407)777-1969

Florida Capital Venture Ltd.
325 Florida Bank Plaza
100 W. Kennedy Blvd.
Tampa, FL 33602
(813)229-2294
Fax: (813)229-2028

Quantum Capital Partners
339 South Plant Ave.
Tampa, FL 33606
(813)250-1999
Fax: (813)250-1998
Website: http://www.quantumcapitalpartners.com

South Atlantic Venture Fund
614 W. Bay St.
Tampa, FL 33606-2704
(813)253-2500
Fax: (813)253-2360
E-mail: venture@southatlantic.com
Website: http://www.southatlantic.com

LM Capital Corp.
120 S. Olive, Ste. 400
West Palm Beach, FL 33401

(561)833-9700
Fax: (561)655-6587
Website: http://www.lmcapital
securities.com

Georgia

Venture First Associates
4811 Thornwood Dr.
Acworth, GA 30102
(770)928-3733
Fax: (770)928-6455

Alliance Technology Ventures
8995 Westside Pkwy., Ste. 200
Alpharetta, GA 30004
(678)336-2000
Fax: (678)336-2001
E-mail: info@atv.com
Website: http://www.atv.com

Cordova Ventures
2500 North Winds Pkwy., Ste. 475
Alpharetta, GA 30004
(678)942-0300
Fax: (678)942-0301
Website: http://www.cordovaventures.
com

**Advanced Technology Development
Fund**
1000 Abernathy, Ste. 1420
Atlanta, GA 30328-5614
(404)668-2333
Fax: (404)668-2333

CGW Southeast Partners
12 Piedmont Center, Ste. 210
Atlanta, GA 30305
(404)816-3255
Fax: (404)816-3258
Website: http://www.cgwlp.com

Cyberstarts
1900 Emery St., NW
3rd Fl.
Atlanta, GA 30318
(404)267-5000
Fax: (404)267-5200
Website: http://www.cyberstarts.com

EGL Holdings, Inc.
10 Piedmont Center, Ste. 412
Atlanta, GA 30305
(404)949-8300
Fax: (404)949-8311

Equity South
1790 The Lenox Bldg.
3399 Peachtree Rd. NE
Atlanta, GA 30326

(404)237-6222
Fax: (404)261-1578

Five Paces
3400 Peachtree Rd., Ste. 200
Atlanta, GA 30326
(404)439-8300
Fax: (404)439-8301
Website: http://www.fivepaces.com

Frontline Capital, Inc.
3475 Lenox Rd., Ste. 400
Atlanta, GA 30326
(404)240-7280
Fax: (404)240-7281

Fuqua Ventures LLC
1201 W. Peachtree St. NW, Ste. 5000
Atlanta, GA 30309
(404)815-4500
Fax: (404)815-4528
Website: http://www.fuquaventures.com

Noro-Moseley Partners
4200 Northside Pkwy., Bldg. 9
Atlanta, GA 30327
(404)233-1966
Fax: (404)239-9280
Website: http://www.noro-moseley.com

Renaissance Capital Corp.
34 Peachtree St. NW, Ste. 2230
Atlanta, GA 30303
(404)658-9061
Fax: (404)658-9064

River Capital, Inc.
Two Midtown Plaza
1360 Peachtree St. NE, Ste. 1430
Atlanta, GA 30309
(404)873-2166
Fax: (404)873-2158

State Street Bank & Trust Co.
3414 Peachtree Rd. NE, Ste. 1010
Atlanta, GA 30326
(404)364-9500
Fax: (404)261-4469

UPS Strategic Enterprise Fund
55 Glenlake Pkwy. NE
Atlanta, GA 30328
(404)828-8814
Fax: (404)828-8088
E-mail: jcacyce@ups.com
Website: http://www.ups.com/sef/
sef_home

Wachovia
191 Peachtree St. NE, 26th Fl.
Atlanta, GA 30303

(404)332-1000
Fax: (404)332-1392
Website: http://www.wachovia.com/wca

Brainworks Ventures
4243 Dunwoody Club Dr.
Chamblee, GA 30341
(770)239-7447

First Growth Capital Inc.
Best Western Plaza, Ste. 105
PO Box 815
Forsyth, GA 31029
(912)781-7131

Financial Capital Resources, Inc.
21 Eastbrook Bend, Ste. 116
Peachtree City, GA 30269
(404)487-6650

Hawaii

HMS Hawaii Management Partners
Davies Pacific Center
841 Bishop St., Ste. 860
Honolulu, HI 96813
(808)545-3755
Fax: (808)531-2611

Idaho

Sun Valley Ventures
160 Second St.
Ketchum, ID 83340
(208)726-5005
Fax: (208)726-5094

Illinois

Open Prairie Ventures
115 N. Neil St., Ste. 209
Champaign, IL 61820
(217)351-7000
Fax: (217)351-7051
E-mail: inquire@openprairie.com
Website: http://www.openprairie.com

ABN AMRO Private Equity
208 S. La Salle St., 10th Fl.
Chicago, IL 60604
(312)855-7079
Fax: (312)553-6648
Website: http://www.abnequity.com

Alpha Capital Partners, Ltd.
122 S. Michigan Ave., Ste. 1700
Chicago, IL 60603
(312)322-9800
Fax: (312)322-9808
E-mail: acp@alphacapital.com

Ameritech Development Corp.
30 S. Wacker Dr., 37th Fl.
Chicago, IL 60606
(312)750-5083
Fax: (312)609-0244

Apex Investment Partners
225 W. Washington, Ste. 1450
Chicago, IL 60606
(312)857-2800
Fax: (312)857-1800
E-mail: apex@apexvc.com
Website: http://www.apexvc.com

Arch Venture Partners
8725 W. Higgins Rd., Ste. 290
Chicago, IL 60631
(773)380-6600
Fax: (773)380-6606
Website: http://www.archventure.com

The Bank Funds
208 South LaSalle St., Ste. 1680
Chicago, IL 60604
(312)855-6020
Fax: (312)855-8910

Batterson Venture Partners
303 W. Madison St., Ste. 1110
Chicago, IL 60606-3309
(312)269-0300
Fax: (312)269-0021
Website: http://www.battersonvp.com

William Blair Capital Partners, L.L.C.
222 W. Adams St., Ste. 1300
Chicago, IL 60606
(312)364-8250
Fax: (312)236-1042
E-mail: privateequity@wmblair.com
Website: http://www.wmblair.com

Bluestar Ventures
208 South LaSalle St., Ste. 1020
Chicago, IL 60604
(312)384-5000
Fax: (312)384-5005
Website: http://www.bluestarventures.com

The Capital Strategy Management Co.
233 S. Wacker Dr.
Box 06334
Chicago, IL 60606
(312)444-1170

DN Partners
77 West Wacker Dr., Ste. 4550
Chicago, IL 60601
(312)332-7960
Fax: (312)332-7979

Dresner Capital Inc.
29 South LaSalle St., Ste. 310
Chicago, IL 60603
(312)726-3600
Fax: (312)726-7448

Eblast Ventures LLC
11 South LaSalle St., 5th Fl.
Chicago, IL 60603
(312)372-2600
Fax: (312)372-5621
Website: http://www.eblastventures.com

Essex Woodlands Health Ventures, L.P.
190 S. LaSalle St., Ste. 2800
Chicago, IL 60603
(312)444-6040
Fax: (312)444-6034
Website: http://www.essexwood
lands.com

First Analysis Venture Capital
233 S. Wacker Dr., Ste. 9500
Chicago, IL 60606
(312)258-1400
Fax: (312)258-0334
Website: http://www.firstanalysis.com

Frontenac Co.
135 S. LaSalle St., Ste.3800
Chicago, IL 60603
(312)368-0044
Fax: (312)368-9520
Website: http://www.frontenac.com

GTCR Golder Rauner, LLC
6100 Sears Tower
Chicago, IL 60606
(312)382-2200
Fax: (312)382-2201
Website: http://www.gtcr.com

High Street Capital LLC
311 South Wacker Dr., Ste. 4550
Chicago, IL 60606
(312)697-4990
Fax: (312)697-4994
Website: http://www.highstr.com

IEG Venture Management, Inc.
70 West Madison
Chicago, IL 60602
(312)644-0890
Fax: (312)454-0369
Website: http://www.iegventure.com

JK&B Capital
180 North Stetson, Ste. 4500
Chicago, IL 60601
(312)946-1200
Fax: (312)946-1103

E-mail: gspencer@jkbcapital.com
Website: http://www.jkbcapital.com

Kettle Partners L.P.
350 W. Hubbard, Ste. 350
Chicago, IL 60610
(312)329-9300
Fax: (312)527-4519
Website: http://www.kettlevc.com

Lake Shore Capital Partners
20 N. Wacker Dr., Ste. 2807
Chicago, IL 60606
(312)803-3536
Fax: (312)803-3534

LaSalle Capital Group Inc.
70 W. Madison St., Ste. 5710
Chicago, IL 60602
(312)236-7041
Fax: (312)236-0720

Linc Capital, Inc.
303 E. Wacker Pkwy., Ste. 1000
Chicago, IL 60601
(312)946-2670
Fax: (312)938-4290
E-mail: bdemars@linccap.com

Madison Dearborn Partners, Inc.
3 First National Plz., Ste. 3800
Chicago, IL 60602
(312)895-1000
Fax: (312)895-1001
E-mail: invest@mdcp.com
Website: http://www.mdcp.com

Mesirow Private Equity Investments Inc.
350 N. Clark St.
Chicago, IL 60610
(312)595-6950
Fax: (312)595-6211
Website: http://www.meisrow
financial.com

Mosaix Ventures LLC
1822 North Mohawk
Chicago, IL 60614
(312)274-0988
Fax: (312)274-0989
Website: http://www.mosaix
ventures.com

Nesbitt Burns
111 West Monroe St.
Chicago, IL 60603
(312)416-3855
Fax: (312)765-8000
Website: http://www.harrisbank.com

Polestar Capital, Inc.
180 N. Michigan Ave., Ste. 1905
Chicago, IL 60601
(312)984-9090
Fax: (312)984-9877
E-mail: wl@polestarvc.com
Website: http://www.polestarvc.com

Prince Ventures (Chicago)
10 S. Wacker Dr., Ste. 2575
Chicago, IL 60606-7407
(312)454-1408
Fax: (312)454-9125

Prism Capital
444 N. Michigan Ave.
Chicago, IL 60611
(312)464-7900
Fax: (312)464-7915
Website: http://www.prismfund.com

Third Coast Capital
900 N. Franklin St., Ste. 700
Chicago, IL 60610
(312)337-3303
Fax: (312)337-2567
E-mail: manic@earthlink.com
Website: http://www.third
coastcapital.com

Thoma Cressey Equity Partners
4460 Sears Tower, 92nd Fl.
233 S. Wacker Dr.
Chicago, IL 60606
(312)777-4444
Fax: (312)777-4445
Website: http://www.thomacressey.com

Tribune Ventures
435 N. Michigan Ave., Ste. 600
Chicago, IL 60611
(312)527-8797
Fax: (312)222-5993
Website: http://www.tribuneventures.com

Wind Point Partners (Chicago)
676 N. Michigan Ave., Ste. 330
Chicago, IL 60611
(312)649-4000
Website: http://www.wppartners.com

Marquette Venture Partners
520 Lake Cook Rd., Ste. 450
Deerfield, IL 60015
(847)940-1700
Fax: (847)940-1724
Website: http://www.marquette
ventures.com

Duchossois Investments Limited, LLC
845 Larch Ave.
Elmhurst, IL 60126

(630)530-6105
Fax: (630)993-8644
Website: http://www.duchtec.com

Evanston Business Investment Corp.
1840 Oak Ave.
Evanston, IL 60201
(847)866-1840
Fax: (847)866-1808
E-mail: t-parkinson@nwu.com
Website: http://www.ebic.com

Inroads Capital Partners L.P.
1603 Orrington Ave., Ste. 2050
Evanston, IL 60201-3841
(847)864-2000
Fax: (847)864-9692

The Cerulean Fund/WGC Enterprises
1701 E. Lake Ave., Ste. 170
Glenview, IL 60025
(847)657-8002
Fax: (847)657-8168

Ventana Financial Resources, Inc.
249 Market Sq.
Lake Forest, IL 60045
(847)234-3434

Beecken, Petty & Co.
901 Warrenville Rd., Ste. 205
Lisle, IL 60532
(630)435-0300
Fax: (630)435-0370
E-mail: hep@bpcompany.com
Website: http://www.bpcompany.com

Allstate Private Equity
3075 Sanders Rd., Ste. G5D
Northbrook, IL 60062-7127
(847)402-8247
Fax: (847)402-0880

KB Partners
1101 Skokie Blvd., Ste. 260
Northbrook, IL 60062-2856
(847)714-0444
Fax: (847)714-0445
E-mail: keith@kbpartners.com
Website: http://www.kbpartners.com

Transcap Associates Inc.
900 Skokie Blvd., Ste. 210
Northbrook, IL 60062
(847)753-9600
Fax: (847)753-9090

**Graystone Venture Partners, L.L.C. /
Portage Venture Partners**
One Northfield Plaza, Ste. 530
Northfield, IL 60093

(847)446-9460
Fax: (847)446-9470
Website: http://www.portage
ventures.com

Motorola Inc.
1303 E. Algonquin Rd.
Schaumburg, IL 60196-1065
(847)576-4929
Fax: (847)538-2250
Website: http://www.mot.com/mne

Indiana

Irwin Ventures LLC
500 Washington St.
Columbus, IN 47202
(812)373-1434
Fax: (812)376-1709
Website: http://www.irwinventures.com

Cambridge Venture Partners
4181 East 96th St., Ste. 200
Indianapolis, IN 46240
(317)814-6192
Fax: (317)944-9815

CID Equity Partners
One American Square, Ste. 2850
Box 82074
Indianapolis, IN 46282
(317)269-2350
Fax: (317)269-2355
Website: http://www.cidequity.com

Gazelle Techventures
6325 Digital Way, Ste. 460
Indianapolis, IN 46278
(317)275-6800
Fax: (317)275-1101
Website: http://www.gazellevc.com

Monument Advisors Inc.
Bank One Center/Circle
111 Monument Circle, Ste. 600
Indianapolis, IN 46204-5172
(317)656-5065
Fax: (317)656-5060
Website: http://www.monumentadv.com

MWV Capital Partners
201 N. Illinois St., Ste. 300
Indianapolis, IN 46204
(317)237-2323
Fax: (317)237-2325
Website: http://www.mwvcapital.com

First Source Capital Corp.
100 North Michigan St.
PO Box 1602
South Bend, IN 46601

(219)235-2180
Fax: (219)235-2227

Iowa

Allsop Venture Partners
118 Third Ave. SE, Ste. 837
Cedar Rapids, IA 52401
(319)368-6675
Fax: (319)363-9515

**InvestAmerica Investment
Advisors, Inc.**
101 2nd St. SE, Ste. 800
Cedar Rapids, IA 52401
(319)363-8249
Fax: (319)363-9683

Pappajohn Capital Resources
2116 Financial Center
Des Moines, IA 50309
(515)244-5746
Fax: (515)244-2346
Website: http://www.pappajohn.com

**Berthel Fisher & Company Planning
Inc.**
701 Tama St.
PO Box 609
Marion, IA 52302
(319)497-5700
Fax: (319)497-4244

Kansas

Enterprise Merchant Bank
7400 West 110th St., Ste. 560
Overland Park, KS 66210
(913)327-8500
Fax: (913)327-8505

**Kansas Venture Capital, Inc. (Overland
Park)**
6700 Antioch Plz., Ste. 460
Overland Park, KS 66204
(913)262-7117
Fax: (913)262-3509
E-mail: jdalton@kvci.com

Child Health Investment Corp.
6803 W. 64th St., Ste. 208
Shawnee Mission, KS 66202
(913)262-1436
Fax: (913)262-1575
Website: http://www.chca.com

Kansas Technology Enterprise Corp.
214 SW 6th, 1st Fl.
Topeka, KS 66603-3719
(785)296-5272
Fax: (785)296-1160

E-mail: ktec@ktec.com
Website: http://www.ktec.com

Kentucky

Kentucky Highlands Investment Corp.
362 Old Whitley Rd.
London, KY 40741
(606)864-5175
Fax: (606)864-5194
Website: http://www.khic.org

Chrysalis Ventures, L.L.C.
1850 National City Tower
Louisville, KY 40202
(502)583-7644
Fax: (502)583-7648
E-mail: bobsany@chrysalisventures.com
Website: http://www.chrysalis
ventures.com

Humana Venture Capital
500 West Main St.
Louisville, KY 40202
(502)580-3922
Fax: (502)580-2051
E-mail: gemont@humana.com
George Emont, Director

Summit Capital Group, Inc.
6510 Glenridge Park Pl., Ste. 8
Louisville, KY 40222
(502)332-2700

Louisiana

Bank One Equity Investors, Inc.
451 Florida St.
Baton Rouge, LA 70801
(504)332-4421
Fax: (504)332-7377

Advantage Capital Partners
LLE Tower
909 Poydras St., Ste. 2230
New Orleans, LA 70112
(504)522-4850
Fax: (504)522-4950
Website: http://www.advantagecap.com

Maine

CEI Ventures / Coastal Ventures LP
2 Portland Fish Pier, Ste. 201
Portland, ME 04101
(207)772-5356
Fax: (207)772-5503
Website: http://www.ceiventures.com

Commwealth Bioventures, Inc.
4 Milk St.
Portland, ME 04101

(207)780-0904
Fax: (207)780-0913

Maryland

Annapolis Ventures LLC
151 West St., Ste. 302
Annapolis, MD 21401
(443)482-9555
Fax: (443)482-9565
Website: http://www.annapolis
ventures.com

Delmag Ventures
220 Wardour Dr.
Annapolis, MD 21401
(410)267-8196
Fax: (410)267-8017
Website: http://www.delmag
ventures.com

Abell Venture Fund
111 S. Calvert St., Ste. 2300
Baltimore, MD 21202
(410)547-1300
Fax: (410)539-6579
Website: http://www.abell.org

ABS Ventures (Baltimore)
1 South St., Ste. 2150
Baltimore, MD 21202
(410)895-3895
Fax: (410)895-3899
Website: http://www.absventures.com

Anthem Capital, L.P.
16 S. Calvert St., Ste. 800
Baltimore, MD 21202-1305
(410)625-1510
Fax: (410)625-1735
Website: http://www.anthemcapital.com

Catalyst Ventures
1119 St. Paul St.
Baltimore, MD 21202
(410)244-0123
Fax: (410)752-7721

Maryland Venture Capital Trust
217 E. Redwood St., Ste. 2200
Baltimore, MD 21202
(410)767-6361
Fax: (410)333-6931

New Enterprise Associates (Baltimore)
1119 St. Paul St.
Baltimore, MD 21202
(410)244-0115
Fax: (410)752-7721
Website: http://www.nea.com

T. Rowe Price Threshold Partnerships
100 E. Pratt St., 8th Fl.
Baltimore, MD 21202
(410)345-2000
Fax: (410)345-2800

Spring Capital Partners
16 W. Madison St.
Baltimore, MD 21201
(410)685-8000
Fax: (410)727-1436
E-mail: mailbox@springcap.com

Arete Corporation
3 Bethesda Metro Ctr., Ste. 770
Bethesda, MD 20814
(301)657-6268
Fax: (301)657-6254
Website: http://www.arete-
microgen.com

Embryon Capital
7903 Sleaford Place
Bethesda, MD 20814
(301)656-6837
Fax: (301)656-8056

Potomac Ventures
7920 Norfolk Ave., Ste. 1100
Bethesda, MD 20814
(301)215-9240
Website: http://www.potomac
ventures.com

Toucan Capital Corp.
3 Bethesda Metro Center, Ste. 700
Bethesda, MD 20814
(301)961-1970
Fax: (301)961-1969
Website: http://www.toucancapital.com

Kinetic Ventures LLC
2 Wisconsin Cir., Ste. 620
Chevy Chase, MD 20815
(301)652-8066
Fax: (301)652-8310
Website: http://www.kineticventures.com

Boulder Ventures Ltd.
4750 Owings Mills Blvd.
Owings Mills, MD 21117
(410)998-3114
Fax: (410)356-5492
Website: http://www.boulderventures.com

Grotech Capital Group
9690 Deereco Rd., Ste. 800
Timonium, MD 21093
(410)560-2000
Fax: (410)560-1910
Website: http://www.grotech.com

Massachusetts

Adams, Harkness & Hill, Inc.
60 State St.
Boston, MA 02109
(617)371-3900

Advent International
75 State St., 29th Fl.
Boston, MA 02109
(617)951-9400
Fax: (617)951-0566
Website: http://www.adventiner
national.com

American Research and Development
30 Federal St.
Boston, MA 02110-2508
(617)423-7500
Fax: (617)423-9655

Ascent Venture Partners
255 State St., 5th Fl.
Boston, MA 02109
(617)270-9400
Fax: (617)270-9401
E-mail: info@ascentvp.com
Website: http://www.ascentvp.com

Atlas Venture
222 Berkeley St.
Boston, MA 02116
(617)488-2200
Fax: (617)859-9292
Website: http://www.atlasventure.com

Axxon Capital
28 State St., 37th Fl.
Boston, MA 02109
(617)722-0980
Fax: (617)557-6014
Website: http://www.axxoncapital.com

BancBoston Capital/BancBoston Ventures
175 Federal St., 10th Fl.
Boston, MA 02110
(617)434-2509
Fax: (617)434-6175
Website: http://
www.bancbostoncapital.com

Boston Capital Ventures
Old City Hall
45 School St.
Boston, MA 02108
(617)227-6550
Fax: (617)227-3847
E-mail: info@bcv.com
Website: http://www.bcv.com

Boston Financial & Equity Corp.
20 Overland St.
PO Box 15071
Boston, MA 02215
(617)267-2900
Fax: (617)437-7601
E-mail: debbie@bfec.com

Boston Millennia Partners
30 Rowes Wharf
Boston, MA 02110
(617)428-5150
Fax: (617)428-5160
Website: http://www.millennia
partners.com

Bristol Investment Trust
842A Beacon St.
Boston, MA 02215-3199
(617)566-5212
Fax: (617)267-0932

Brook Venture Management LLC
50 Federal St., 5th Fl.
Boston, MA 02110
(617)451-8989
Fax: (617)451-2369
Website: http://www.brookventure.com

Burr, Egan, Deleage, and Co. (Boston)
200 Clarendon St., Ste. 3800
Boston, MA 02116
(617)262-7770
Fax: (617)262-9779

Cambridge/Samsung Partners
One Exeter Plaza
Ninth Fl.
Boston, MA 02116
(617)262-4440
Fax: (617)262-5562

Chestnut Street Partners, Inc.
75 State St., Ste. 2500
Boston, MA 02109
(617)345-7220
Fax: (617)345-7201
E-mail: chestnut@chestnutp.com

Claflin Capital Management, Inc.
10 Liberty Sq., Ste. 300
Boston, MA 02109
(617)426-6505
Fax: (617)482-0016
Website: http://www.claflincapital.com

Copley Venture Partners
99 Summer St., Ste. 1720
Boston, MA 02110
(617)737-1253
Fax: (617)439-0699

Corning Capital / Corning Technology Ventures
121 High Street, Ste. 400
Boston, MA 02110
(617)338-2656
Fax: (617)261-3864
Website: http://www.corningventures.com

Downer & Co.
211 Congress St.
Boston, MA 02110
(617)482-6200
Fax: (617)482-6201
E-mail: cdowner@downer.com
Website: http://www.downer.com

Fidelity Ventures
82 Devonshire St.
Boston, MA 02109
(617)563-6370
Fax: (617)476-9023
Website: http://www.fidelityventures.com

Greylock Management Corp. (Boston)
1 Federal St.
Boston, MA 02110-2065
(617)423-5525
Fax: (617)482-0059

Gryphon Ventures
222 Berkeley St., Ste.1600
Boston, MA 02116
(617)267-9191
Fax: (617)267-4293
E-mail: all@gryphoninc.com

Halpern, Denny & Co.
500 Boylston St.
Boston, MA 02116
(617)536-6602
Fax: (617)536-8535

Harbourvest Partners, LLC
1 Financial Center, 44th Fl.
Boston, MA 02111
(617)348-3707
Fax: (617)350-0305
Website: http://www.hvpllc.com

Highland Capital Partners
2 International Pl.
Boston, MA 02110
(617)981-1500
Fax: (617)531-1550
E-mail: info@hcp.com
Website: http://www.hcp.com

Lee Munder Venture Partners
John Hancock Tower T-53
200 Clarendon St.
Boston, MA 02103

(617)380-5600
Fax: (617)380-5601
Website: http://www.leemunder.com

M/C Venture Partners
75 State St., Ste. 2500
Boston, MA 02109
(617)345-7200
Fax: (617)345-7201
Website: http://www.mcventure
partners.com

Massachusetts Capital Resources Co.
420 Boylston St.
Boston, MA 02116
(617)536-3900
Fax: (617)536-7930

Massachusetts Technology Development Corp. (MTDC)
148 State St.
Boston, MA 02109
(617)723-4920
Fax: (617)723-5983
E-mail: jhodgman@mtdc.com
Website: http://www.mtdc.com

New England Partners
One Boston Place, Ste. 2100
Boston, MA 02108
(617)624-8400
Fax: (617)624-8999
Website: http://www.nepartners.com

North Hill Ventures
Ten Post Office Square
11th Fl.
Boston, MA 02109
(617)788-2112
Fax: (617)788-2152
Website: http://www.northhill
ventures.com

OneLiberty Ventures
150 Cambridge Park Dr.
Boston, MA 02140
(617)492-7280
Fax: (617)492-7290
Website: http://www.oneliberty.com

Schroder Ventures
Life Sciences
60 State St., Ste. 3650
Boston, MA 02109
(617)367-8100
Fax: (617)367-1590
Website: http://www.shroderventures.com

Shawmut Capital Partners
75 Federal St., 18th Fl.
Boston, MA 02110

(617)368-4900
Fax: (617)368-4910
Website: http://www.shawmutcapital.com

Solstice Capital LLC
15 Broad St., 3rd Fl.
Boston, MA 02109
(617)523-7733
Fax: (617)523-5827
E-mail: solticecapital@solcap.com

Spectrum Equity Investors
One International Pl., 29th Fl.
Boston, MA 02110
(617)464-4600
Fax: (617)464-4601
Website: http://www.spectrumequity.com

Spray Venture Partners
One Walnut St.
Boston, MA 02108
(617)305-4140
Fax: (617)305-4144
Website: http://www.sprayventure.com

The Still River Fund
100 Federal St., 29th Fl.
Boston, MA 02110
(617)348-2327
Fax: (617)348-2371
Website: http://www.stillriverfund.com

Summit Partners
600 Atlantic Ave., Ste. 2800
Boston, MA 02210-2227
(617)824-1000
Fax: (617)824-1159
Website: http://www.summitpartners.com

TA Associates, Inc. (Boston)
High Street Tower
125 High St., Ste. 2500
Boston, MA 02110
(617)574-6700
Fax: (617)574-6728
Website: http://www.ta.com

TVM Techno Venture Management
101 Arch St., Ste. 1950
Boston, MA 02110
(617)345-9320
Fax: (617)345-9377
E-mail: info@tvmvc.com
Website: http://www.tvmvc.com

UNC Ventures
64 Burough St.
Boston, MA 02130-4017
(617)482-7070
Fax: (617)522-2176

Venture Investment Management Company (VIMAC)
177 Milk St.
Boston, MA 02190-3410
(617)292-3300
Fax: (617)292-7979
E-mail: bzeisig@vimac.com
Website: http://www.vimac.com

MDT Advisers, Inc.
125 Cambridge Park Dr.
Cambridge, MA 02140-2314
(617)234-2200
Fax: (617)234-2210
Website: http://www.mdtai.com

TTC Ventures
One Main St., 6th Fl.
Cambridge, MA 02142
(617)528-3137
Fax: (617)577-1715
E-mail: info@ttcventures.com

Zero Stage Capital Co. Inc.
101 Main St., 17th Fl.
Cambridge, MA 02142
(617)876-5355
Fax: (617)876-1248
Website: http://www.zerostage.com

Atlantic Capital
164 Cushing Hwy.
Cohasset, MA 02025
(617)383-9449
Fax: (617)383-6040
E-mail: info@atlanticcap.com
Website: http://www.atlanticcap.com

Seacoast Capital Partners
55 Ferncroft Rd.
Danvers, MA 01923
(978)750-1300
Fax: (978)750-1301
E-mail: gdeli@seacoastcapital.com
Website: http://www.seacoast
capital.com

Sage Management Group
44 South Street
PO Box 2026
East Dennis, MA 02641
(508)385-7172
Fax: (508)385-7272
E-mail: sagemgt@capecod.net

Applied Technology
1 Cranberry Hill
Lexington, MA 02421-7397
(617)862-8622
Fax: (617)862-8367

Royalty Capital Management
5 Downing Rd.
Lexington, MA 02421-6918
(781)861-8490

Argo Global Capital
210 Broadway, Ste. 101
Lynnfield, MA 01940
(781)592-5250
Fax: (781)592-5230
Website: http://www.gsmcapital.com

Industry Ventures
6 Bayne Lane
Newburyport, MA 01950
(978)499-7606
Fax: (978)499-0686
Website: http://
www.industryventures.com

Softbank Capital Partners
10 Langley Rd., Ste. 202
Newton Center, MA 02459
(617)928-9300
Fax: (617)928-9305
E-mail: clax@bvc.com

Advanced Technology Ventures (Boston)
281 Winter St., Ste. 350
Waltham, MA 02451
(781)290-0707
Fax: (781)684-0045
E-mail: info@atvcapital.com
Website: http://www.atvcapital.com

Castile Ventures
890 Winter St., Ste. 140
Waltham, MA 02451
(781)890-0060
Fax: (781)890-0065
Website: http://www.castileventures.com

Charles River Ventures
1000 Winter St., Ste. 3300
Waltham, MA 02451
(781)487-7060
Fax: (781)487-7065
Website: http://www.crv.com

Comdisco Venture Group (Waltham)
Totton Pond Office Center
400-1 Totten Pond Rd.
Waltham, MA 02451
(617)672-0250
Fax: (617)398-8099

Marconi Ventures
890 Winter St., Ste. 310
Waltham, MA 02451
(781)839-7177

Fax: (781)522-7477
Website: http://www.marconi.com

Matrix Partners
Bay Colony Corporate Center
1000 Winter St., Ste.4500
Waltham, MA 02451
(781)890-2244
Fax: (781)890-2288
Website: http://www.matrix
partners.com

North Bridge Venture Partners
950 Winter St. Ste. 4600
Waltham, MA 02451
(781)290-0004
Fax: (781)290-0999
E-mail: eta@nbvp.com

Polaris Venture Partners
Bay Colony Corporate Ctr.
1000 Winter St., Ste. 3500
Waltham, MA 02451
(781)290-0770
Fax: (781)290-0880
E-mail: partners@polarisventures.com
Website: http://www.polar
isventures.com

Seaflower Ventures
Bay Colony Corporate Ctr.
1000 Winter St. Ste. 1000
Waltham, MA 02451
(781)466-9552
Fax: (781)466-9553
E-mail: moot@seaflower.com
Website: http://www.seaflower.com

Ampersand Ventures
55 William St., Ste. 240
Wellesley, MA 02481
(617)239-0700
Fax: (617)239-0824
E-mail: info@ampersandventures.com
Website: http://www.ampersand
ventures.com

Battery Ventures (Boston)
20 William St., Ste. 200
Wellesley, MA 02481
(781)577-1000
Fax: (781)577-1001
Website: http://www.battery.com

Commonwealth Capital Ventures, L.P.
20 William St., Ste.225
Wellesley, MA 02481
(781)237-7373
Fax: (781)235-8627
Website: http://www.ccvlp.com

Fowler, Anthony & Company
20 Walnut St.
Wellesley, MA 02481
(781)237-4201
Fax: (781)237-7718

Gemini Investors
20 William St.
Wellesley, MA 02481
(781)237-7001
Fax: (781)237-7233

Grove Street Advisors Inc.
20 William St., Ste. 230
Wellesley, MA 02481
(781)263-6100
Fax: (781)263-6101
Website: http://www.groves
treetadvisors.com

Mees Pierson Investeringsmaat B.V.
20 William St., Ste. 210
Wellesley, MA 02482
(781)239-7600
Fax: (781)239-0377

Norwest Equity Partners
40 William St., Ste. 305
Wellesley, MA 02481-3902
(781)237-5870
Fax: (781)237-6270
Website: http://www.norwestvp.com

Bessemer Venture Partners (Wellesley Hills)
83 Walnut St.
Wellesley Hills, MA 02481
(781)237-6050
Fax: (781)235-7576
E-mail: travis@bvpny.com
Website: http://www.bvp.com

Venture Capital Fund of New England
20 Walnut St., Ste. 120
Wellesley Hills, MA 02481-2175
(781)239-8262
Fax: (781)239-8263

Prism Venture Partners
100 Lowder Brook Dr., Ste. 2500
Westwood, MA 02090
(781)302-4000
Fax: (781)302-4040
E-mail: dwbaum@prismventure.com

Palmer Partners LP
200 Unicorn Park Dr.
Woburn, MA 01801
(781)933-5445
Fax: (781)933-0698

Michigan

Arbor Partners, L.L.C.
130 South First St.
Ann Arbor, MI 48104
(734)668-9000
Fax: (734)669-4195
Website: http://www.arborpartners.com

EDF Ventures
425 N. Main St.
Ann Arbor, MI 48104
(734)663-3213
Fax: (734)663-7358
E-mail: edf@edfvc.com
Website: http://www.edfvc.com

White Pines Management, L.L.C.
2401 Plymouth Rd., Ste. B
Ann Arbor, MI 48105
(734)747-9401
Fax: (734)747-9704
E-mail: ibund@whitepines.com
Website: http://www.whitepines.com

Wellmax, Inc.
3541 Bendway Blvd., Ste. 100
Bloomfield Hills, MI 48301
(248)646-3554
Fax: (248)646-6220

Venture Funding, Ltd.
Fisher Bldg.
3011 West Grand Blvd., Ste. 321
Detroit, MI 48202
(313)871-3606
Fax: (313)873-4935

Investcare Partners L.P. / GMA Capital LLC
32330 W. Twelve Mile Rd.
Farmington Hills, MI 48334
(248)489-9000
Fax: (248)489-8819
E-mail: gma@gmacapital.com
Website: http://www.gmacapital.com

Liberty Bidco Investment Corp.
30833 Northwestern Highway, Ste. 211
Farmington Hills, MI 48334
(248)626-6070
Fax: (248)626-6072

Seaflower Ventures
5170 Nicholson Rd.
PO Box 474
Fowlerville, MI 48836
(517)223-3335
Fax: (517)223-3337
E-mail: gibbons@seaflower.com
Website: http://www.seaflower.com

Ralph Wilson Equity Fund LLC
15400 E. Jefferson Ave.
Gross Pointe Park, MI 48230
(313)821-9122
Fax: (313)821-9101
Website: http://www.Ralph
WilsonEquityFund.com
J. Skip Simms, President

Minnesota

Development Corp. of Austin
1900 Eighth Ave., NW
Austin, MN 55912
(507)433-0346
Fax: (507)433-0361
E-mail: dca@smig.net
Website: http://www.spamtownusa.com

Northeast Ventures Corp.
802 Alworth Bldg.
Duluth, MN 55802
(218)722-9915
Fax: (218)722-9871

Medical Innovation Partners, Inc.
6450 City West Pkwy.
Eden Prairie, MN 55344-3245
(612)828-9616
Fax: (612)828-9596

St. Paul Venture Capital, Inc.
10400 Vicking Dr., Ste. 550
Eden Prairie, MN 55344
(612)995-7474
Fax: (612)995-7475
Website: http://www.stpaulvc.com

Cherry Tree Investments, Inc.
7601 France Ave. S, Ste. 150
Edina, MN 55435
(612)893-9012
Fax: (612)893-9036
Website: http://www.cherrytree.com

Shared Ventures, Inc.
6550 York Ave. S
Edina, MN 55435
(612)925-3411

Sherpa Partners LLC
5050 Lincoln Dr., Ste. 490
Edina, MN 55436
(952)942-1070
Fax: (952)942-1071
Website: http://www.sherpapartners.com

Affinity Capital Management
901 Marquette Ave., Ste. 1810
Minneapolis, MN 55402
(612)252-9900

Fax: (612)252-9911
Website: http://www.affinitycapital.com

Artesian Capital
1700 Foshay Tower
821 Marquette Ave.
Minneapolis, MN 55402
(612)334-5600
Fax: (612)334-5601
E-mail: artesian@artesian.com

Coral Ventures
60 S. 6th St., Ste. 3510
Minneapolis, MN 55402
(612)335-8666
Fax: (612)335-8668
Website: http://www.coralventures.com

Crescendo Venture Management, L.L.C.
800 LaSalle Ave., Ste. 2250
Minneapolis, MN 55402
(612)607-2800
Fax: (612)607-2801
Website: http://www.crescendo
ventures.com

Gideon Hixon Venture
1900 Foshay Tower
821 Marquette Ave.
Minneapolis, MN 55402
(612)904-2314
Fax: (612)204-0913

Norwest Equity Partners
3600 IDS Center
80 S. 8th St.
Minneapolis, MN 55402
(612)215-1600
Fax: (612)215-1601
Website: http://www.norwestvp.com

Oak Investment Partners (Minneapolis)
4550 Norwest Center
90 S. 7th St.
Minneapolis, MN 55402
(612)339-9322
Fax: (612)337-8017
Website: http://www.oakinv.com

Pathfinder Venture Capital Funds (Minneapolis)
7300 Metro Blvd., Ste. 585
Minneapolis, MN 55439
(612)835-1121
Fax: (612)835-8389
E-mail: jahrens620@aol.com

U.S. Bancorp Piper Jaffray Ventures, Inc.
800 Nicollet Mall, Ste. 800
Minneapolis, MN 55402

(612)303-5686
Fax: (612)303-1350
Website: http://www.paperjaffrey
ventures.com

The Food Fund, Ltd. Partnership
5720 Smatana Dr., Ste. 300
Minnetonka, MN 55343
(612)939-3950
Fax: (612)939-8106

Mayo Medical Ventures
200 First St. SW
Rochester, MN 55905
(507)266-4586
Fax: (507)284-5410
Website: http://www.mayo.edu

Missouri

Bankers Capital Corp.
3100 Gillham Rd.
Kansas City, MO 64109
(816)531-1600
Fax: (816)531-1334

Capital for Business, Inc. (Kansas City)
1000 Walnut St., 18th Fl.
Kansas City, MO 64106
(816)234-2357
Fax: (816)234-2952
Website: http://
www.capitalforbusiness.com

De Vries & Co. Inc.
800 West 47th St.
Kansas City, MO 64112
(816)756-0055
Fax: (816)756-0061

InvestAmerica Venture Group Inc. (Kansas City)
Commerce Tower
911 Main St., Ste. 2424
Kansas City, MO 64105
(816)842-0114
Fax: (816)471-7339

Kansas City Equity Partners
233 W. 47th St.
Kansas City, MO 64112
(816)960-1771
Fax: (816)960-1777
Website: http://www.kcep.com

Bome Investors, Inc.
8000 Maryland Ave., Ste. 1190
St. Louis, MO 63105
(314)721-5707
Fax: (314)721-5135

Website: http://www.gateway
ventures.com

Capital for Business, Inc. (St. Louis)
11 S. Meramac St., Ste. 1430
St. Louis, MO 63105
(314)746-7427
Fax: (314)746-8739
Website: http://www.capitalfor
business.com

Crown Capital Corp.
540 Maryville Centre Dr., Ste. 120
Saint Louis, MO 63141
(314)576-1201
Fax: (314)576-1525
Website: http://www.crown-
cap.com

Gateway Associates L.P.
8000 Maryland Ave., Ste. 1190
St. Louis, MO 63105
(314)721-5707
Fax: (314)721-5135

Harbison Corp.
8112 Maryland Ave., Ste. 250
Saint Louis, MO 63105
(314)727-8200
Fax: (314)727-0249

Heartland Capital Fund, Ltd.
PO Box 642117
Omaha, NE 68154
(402)778-5124
Fax: (402)445-2370
Website: http://www.heartland
capitalfund.com

Odin Capital Group
1625 Farnam St., Ste. 700
Omaha, NE 68102
(402)346-6200
Fax: (402)342-9311
Website: http://www.odincapital.com

Nevada

Edge Capital Investment Co. LLC
1350 E. Flamingo Rd., Ste. 3000
Las Vegas, NV 89119
(702)438-3343
E-mail: info@edgecapital.net
Website: http://www.edgecapital.net

The Benefit Capital Companies Inc.
PO Box 542
Logandale, NV 89021
(702)398-3222
Fax: (702)398-3700

Millennium Three Venture Group LLC
6880 South McCarran Blvd., Ste. A-11
Reno, NV 89509
(775)954-2020
Fax: (775)954-2023
Website: http://www.m3vg.com

New Jersey

Alan I. Goldman & Associates
497 Ridgewood Ave.
Glen Ridge, NJ 07028
(973)857-5680
Fax: (973)509-8856

CS Capital Partners LLC
328 Second St., Ste. 200
Lakewood, NJ 08701
(732)901-1111
Fax: (212)202-5071
Website: http://www.cs-capital.com

Edison Venture Fund
1009 Lenox Dr., Ste. 4
Lawrenceville, NJ 08648
(609)896-1900
Fax: (609)896-0066
E-mail: info@edisonventure.com
Website: http://www.edisonventure.com

Tappan Zee Capital Corp. (New Jersey)
201 Lower Notch Rd.
PO Box 416
Little Falls, NJ 07424
(973)256-8280
Fax: (973)256-2841

The CIT Group/Venture Capital, Inc.
650 CIT Dr.
Livingston, NJ 07039
(973)740-5429
Fax: (973)740-5555
Website: http://www.cit.com

Capital Express, L.L.C.
1100 Valleybrook Ave.
Lyndhurst, NJ 07071
(201)438-8228
Fax: (201)438-5131
E-mail: niles@capitalexpress.com
Website: http://www.capitalexpress.com

Westford Technology Ventures, L.P.
17 Academy St.
Newark, NJ 07102
(973)624-2131
Fax: (973)624-2008

Accel Partners
1 Palmer Sq.
Princeton, NJ 08542

(609)683-4500
Fax: (609)683-4880
Website: http://www.accel.com

Cardinal Partners
221 Nassau St.
Princeton, NJ 08542
(609)924-6452
Fax: (609)683-0174
Website: http://www.cardinal
healthpartners.com

Domain Associates L.L.C.
One Palmer Sq., Ste. 515
Princeton, NJ 08542
(609)683-5656
Fax: (609)683-9789
Website: http://www.domainvc.com

Johnston Associates, Inc.
181 Cherry Valley Rd.
Princeton, NJ 08540
(609)924-3131
Fax: (609)683-7524
E-mail: jaincorp@aol.com

Kemper Ventures
Princeton Forrestal Village
155 Village Blvd.
Princeton, NJ 08540
(609)936-3035
Fax: (609)936-3051

Penny Lane Parnters
One Palmer Sq., Ste. 309
Princeton, NJ 08542
(609)497-4646
Fax: (609)497-0611

Early Stage Enterprises L.P.
995 Route 518
Skillman, NJ 08558
(609)921-8896
Fax: (609)921-8703
Website: http://www.esevc.com

MBW Management Inc.
1 Springfield Ave.
Summit, NJ 07901
(908)273-4060
Fax: (908)273-4430

BCI Advisors, Inc.
Glenpointe Center W.
Teaneck, NJ 07666
(201)836-3900
Fax: (201)836-6368
E-mail: info@bciadvisors.com
Website: http://www.bci
partners.com

**Demuth, Folger & Wetherill / DFW
Capital Partners**
Glenpointe Center E., 5th Fl.
300 Frank W. Burr Blvd.
Teaneck, NJ 07666
(201)836-2233
Fax: (201)836-5666
Website: http://www.dfwcapital.com

First Princeton Capital Corp.
189 Berdan Ave., No. 131
Wayne, NJ 07470-3233
(973)278-3233
Fax: (973)278-4290
Website: http://www.lytellcatt.net

Edelson Technology Partners
300 Tice Blvd.
Woodcliff Lake, NJ 07675
(201)930-9898
Fax: (201)930-8899
Website: http://www.edelsontech.com

New Mexico

Bruce F. Glaspell & Associates
10400 Academy Rd. NE, Ste. 313
Albuquerque, NM 87111
(505)292-4505
Fax: (505)292-4258

High Desert Ventures, Inc.
6101 Imparata St. NE, Ste. 1721
Albuquerque, NM 87111
(505)797-3330
Fax: (505)338-5147

New Business Capital Fund, Ltd.
5805 Torreon NE
Albuquerque, NM 87109
(505)822-8445

SBC Ventures
10400 Academy Rd. NE, Ste. 313
Albuquerque, NM 87111
(505)292-4505
Fax: (505)292-4528

Technology Ventures Corp.
1155 University Blvd. SE
Albuquerque, NM 87106
(505)246-2882
Fax: (505)246-2891

New York

**New York State Science & Technology
Foundation**
**Small Business Technology Investment
Fund**
99 Washington Ave., Ste. 1731
Albany, NY 12210

(518)473-9741
Fax: (518)473-6876

Rand Capital Corp.
2200 Rand Bldg.
Buffalo, NY 14203
(716)853-0802
Fax: (716)854-8480
Website: http://www.randcapital.com

Seed Capital Partners
620 Main St.
Buffalo, NY 14202
(716)845-7520
Fax: (716)845-7539
Website: http://www.seedcp.com

Coleman Venture Group
5909 Northern Blvd.
PO Box 224
East Norwich, NY 11732
(516)626-3642
Fax: (516)626-9722

Vega Capital Corp.
45 Knollwood Rd.
Elmsford, NY 10523
(914)345-9500
Fax: (914)345-9505

Herbert Young Securities, Inc.
98 Cuttermill Rd.
Great Neck, NY 11021
(516)487-8300
Fax: (516)487-8319

Sterling/Carl Marks Capital, Inc.
175 Great Neck Rd., Ste. 408
Great Neck, NY 11021
(516)482-7374
Fax: (516)487-0781
E-mail: stercrlmar@aol.com
Website: http://www.serling
carlmarks.com

Impex Venture Management Co.
PO Box 1570
Green Island, NY 12183
(518)271-8008
Fax: (518)271-9101

Corporate Venture Partners L.P.
200 Sunset Park
Ithaca, NY 14850
(607)257-6323
Fax: (607)257-6128

Arthur P. Gould & Co.
One Wilshire Dr.
Lake Success, NY 11020
(516)773-3000
Fax: (516)773-3289

Dauphin Capital Partners
108 Forest Ave.
Locust Valley, NY 11560
(516)759-3339
Fax: (516)759-3322
Website: http://www.dauphincapital.com

550 Digital Media Ventures
555 Madison Ave., 10th Fl.
New York, NY 10022
Website: http://www.550dmv.com

Aberlyn Capital Management Co., Inc.
500 Fifth Ave.
New York, NY 10110
(212)391-7750
Fax: (212)391-7762

Adler & Company
342 Madison Ave., Ste. 807
New York, NY 10173
(212)599-2535
Fax: (212)599-2526

Alimansky Capital Group, Inc.
605 Madison Ave., Ste. 300
New York, NY 10022-1901
(212)832-7300
Fax: (212)832-7338

Allegra Partners
515 Madison Ave., 29th Fl.
New York, NY 10022
(212)826-9080
Fax: (212)759-2561

The Argentum Group
The Chyrsler Bldg.
405 Lexington Ave.
New York, NY 10174
(212)949-6262
Fax: (212)949-8294
Website: http://www.argentum
group.com

Axavision Inc.
14 Wall St., 26th Fl.
New York, NY 10005
(212)619-4000
Fax: (212)619-7202

Bedford Capital Corp.
18 East 48th St., Ste. 1800
New York, NY 10017
(212)688-5700
Fax: (212)754-4699
E-mail: info@bedfordnyc.com
Website: http://www.bedfordnyc.com

Bloom & Co.
950 Third Ave.

New York, NY 10022
(212)838-1858
Fax: (212)838-1843

Bristol Capital Management
300 Park Ave., 17th Fl.
New York, NY 10022
(212)572-6306
Fax: (212)705-4292

**Citicorp Venture Capital Ltd.
(New York City)**
399 Park Ave., 14th Fl.
Zone 4
New York, NY 10043
(212)559-1127
Fax: (212)888-2940

CM Equity Partners
135 E. 57th St.
New York, NY 10022
(212)909-8428
Fax: (212)980-2630

Cohen & Co., L.L.C.
800 Third Ave.
New York, NY 10022
(212)317-2250
Fax: (212)317-2255
E-mail: nlcohen@aol.com

Cornerstone Equity Investors, L.L.C.
717 5th Ave., Ste. 1100
New York, NY 10022
(212)753-0901
Fax: (212)826-6798
Website: http://www.cornerstone-
equity.com

CW Group, Inc.
1041 3rd Ave., 2nd fl.
New York, NY 10021
(212)308-5266
Fax: (212)644-0354
Website: http://www.cwventures.com

DH Blair Investment Banking Corp.
44 Wall St., 2nd Fl.
New York, NY 10005
(212)495-5000
Fax: (212)269-1438

Dresdner Kleinwort Capital
75 Wall St.
New York, NY 10005
(212)429-3131
Fax: (212)429-3139
Website: http://www.dresdnerkb.com

East River Ventures, L.P.
645 Madison Ave., 22nd Fl.

New York, NY 10022
(212)644-2322
Fax: (212)644-5498

Easton Hunt Capital Partners
641 Lexington Ave., 21st Fl.
New York, NY 10017
(212)702-0950
Fax: (212)702-0952
Website: http://www.eastoncapital.com

Elk Associates Funding Corp.
747 3rd Ave., Ste. 4C
New York, NY 10017
(212)355-2449
Fax: (212)759-3338

EOS Partners, L.P.
320 Park Ave., 22nd Fl.
New York, NY 10022
(212)832-5800
Fax: (212)832-5815
E-mail: mfirst@eospartners.com
Website: http://www.eospartners.com

Euclid Partners
45 Rockefeller Plaza, Ste. 3240
New York, NY 10111
(212)218-6880
Fax: (212)218-6877
E-mail: graham@euclidpartners.com
Website: http://www.euclidpartners.com

Evergreen Capital Partners, Inc.
150 East 58th St.
New York, NY 10155
(212)813-0758
Fax: (212)813-0754

Exeter Capital L.P.
10 E. 53rd St.
New York, NY 10022
(212)872-1172
Fax: (212)872-1198
E-mail: exeter@usa.net

Financial Technology Research Corp.
518 Broadway
Penthouse
New York, NY 10012
(212)625-9100
Fax: (212)431-0300
E-mail: fintek@financier.com

4C Ventures
237 Park Ave., Ste. 801
New York, NY 10017
(212)692-3680
Fax: (212)692-3685
Website: http://www.4cventures.com

Fusient Ventures
99 Park Ave., 20th Fl.
New York, NY 10016
(212)972-8999
Fax: (212)972-9876
E-mail: info@fusient.com
Website: http://www.fusient.com

Generation Capital Partners
551 Fifth Ave., Ste. 3100
New York, NY 10176
(212)450-8507
Fax: (212)450-8550
Website: http://www.genpartners.com

Golub Associates, Inc.
555 Madison Ave.
New York, NY 10022
(212)750-6060
Fax: (212)750-5505

Hambro America Biosciences Inc.
650 Madison Ave., 21st Floor
New York, NY 10022
(212)223-7400
Fax: (212)223-0305

Hanover Capital Corp.
505 Park Ave., 15th Fl.
New York, NY 10022
(212)755-1222
Fax: (212)935-1787

Harvest Partners, Inc.
280 Park Ave, 33rd Fl.
New York, NY 10017
(212)559-6300
Fax: (212)812-0100
Website: http://www.harvpart.com

Holding Capital Group, Inc.
10 E. 53rd St., 30th Fl.
New York, NY 10022
(212)486-6670
Fax: (212)486-0843

Hudson Venture Partners
660 Madison Ave., 14th Fl.
New York, NY 10021-8405
(212)644-9797
Fax: (212)644-7430
Website: http://www.hudsonptr.com

IBJS Capital Corp.
1 State St., 9th Fl.
New York, NY 10004
(212)858-2018
Fax: (212)858-2768

InterEquity Capital Partners, L.P.
220 5th Ave.
New York, NY 10001

(212)779-2022
Fax: (212)779-2103
Website: http://www.interequity-capital.com

The Jordan Edmiston Group Inc.
150 East 52nd St., 18th Fl.
New York, NY 10022
(212)754-0710
Fax: (212)754-0337

Josephberg, Grosz and Co., Inc.
633 3rd Ave., 13th Fl.
New York, NY 10017
(212)974-9926
Fax: (212)397-5832

J.P. Morgan Capital Corp.
60 Wall St.
New York, NY 10260-0060
(212)648-9000
Fax: (212)648-5002
Website: http://www.jpmorgan.com

The Lambda Funds
380 Lexington Ave., 54th Fl.
New York, NY 10168
(212)682-3454
Fax: (212)682-9231

Lepercq Capital Management Inc.
1675 Broadway
New York, NY 10019
(212)698-0795
Fax: (212)262-0155

Loeb Partners Corp.
61 Broadway, Ste. 2400
New York, NY 10006
(212)483-7000
Fax: (212)574-2001

Madison Investment Partners
660 Madison Ave.
New York, NY 10021
(212)223-2600
Fax: (212)223-8208

MC Capital Inc.
520 Madison Ave., 16th Fl.
New York, NY 10022
(212)644-0841
Fax: (212)644-2926

**McCown, De Leeuw and Co.
(New York)**
65 E. 55th St., 36th Fl.
New York, NY 10022
(212)355-5500
Fax: (212)355-6283
Website: http://www.mdcpartners.com

Morgan Stanley Venture Partners
1221 Avenue of the Americas, 33rd Fl.
New York, NY 10020
(212)762-7900
Fax: (212)762-8424
E-mail: msventures@ms.com
Website: http://www.msvp.com

Nazem and Co.
645 Madison Ave., 12th Fl.
New York, NY 10022
(212)371-7900
Fax: (212)371-2150

Needham Capital Management, L.L.C.
445 Park Ave.
New York, NY 10022
(212)371-8300
Fax: (212)705-0299
Website: http://www.needhamco.com

Norwood Venture Corp.
1430 Broadway, Ste. 1607
New York, NY 10018
(212)869-5075
Fax: (212)869-5331
E-mail: nvc@mail.idt.net
Website: http://www.norven.com

Noveltek Venture Corp.
521 Fifth Ave., Ste. 1700
New York, NY 10175
(212)286-1963

Paribas Principal, Inc.
787 7th Ave.
New York, NY 10019
(212)841-2005
Fax: (212)841-3558

**Patricof & Co. Ventures, Inc.
(New York)**
445 Park Ave.
New York, NY 10022
(212)753-6300
Fax: (212)319-6155
Website: http://www.patricof.com

The Platinum Group, Inc.
350 Fifth Ave, Ste. 7113
New York, NY 10118
(212)736-4300
Fax: (212)736-6086
Website: http://www.platinumgroup.com

Pomona Capital
780 Third Ave., 28th Fl.
New York, NY 10017
(212)593-3639
Fax: (212)593-3987
Website: http://www.pomonacapital.com

Prospect Street Ventures
10 East 40th St., 44th Fl.
New York, NY 10016
(212)448-0702
Fax: (212)448-9652
E-mail: wkohler@prospectstreet.com
Website: http://www.prospectstreet.com

Regent Capital Management
505 Park Ave., Ste. 1700
New York, NY 10022
(212)735-9900
Fax: (212)735-9908

Rothschild Ventures, Inc.
1251 Avenue of the Americas, 51st Fl.
New York, NY 10020
(212)403-3500
Fax: (212)403-3652
Website: http://www.nmrothschild.com

Sandler Capital Management
767 Fifth Ave., 45th Fl.
New York, NY 10153
(212)754-8100
Fax: (212)826-0280

Siguler Guff & Company
630 Fifth Ave., 16th Fl.
New York, NY 10111
(212)332-5100
Fax: (212)332-5120

Spencer Trask Ventures Inc.
535 Madison Ave.
New York, NY 10022
(212)355-5565
Fax: (212)751-3362
Website: http://www.spencertrask.com

Sprout Group (New York City)
277 Park Ave.
New York, NY 10172
(212)892-3600
Fax: (212)892-3444
E-mail: info@sproutgroup.com
Website: http://www.sproutgroup.com

US Trust Private Equity
114 W.47th St.
New York, NY 10036
(212)852-3949
Fax: (212)852-3759
Website: http://www.ustrust.com/
privateequity

Vencon Management Inc.
301 West 53rd St., Ste. 10F
New York, NY 10019
(212)581-8787
Fax: (212)397-4126
Website: http://www.venconinc.com

Venrock Associates
30 Rockefeller Plaza, Ste. 5508
New York, NY 10112
(212)649-5600
Fax: (212)649-5788
Website: http://www.venrock.com

Venture Capital Fund of America, Inc.
509 Madison Ave., Ste. 812
New York, NY 10022
(212)838-5577
Fax: (212)838-7614
E-mail: mail@vcfa.com
Website: http://www.vcfa.com

Venture Opportunities Corp.
150 E. 58th St.
New York, NY 10155
(212)832-3737
Fax: (212)980-6603

Warburg Pincus Ventures, Inc.
466 Lexington Ave., 11th Fl.
New York, NY 10017
(212)878-9309
Fax: (212)878-9200
Website: http://www.warburgpincus.com

Wasserstein, Perella & Co. Inc.
31 W. 52nd St., 27th Fl.
New York, NY 10019
(212)702-5691
Fax: (212)969-7879

Welsh, Carson, Anderson, & Stowe
320 Park Ave., Ste. 2500
New York, NY 10022-6815
(212)893-9500
Fax: (212)893-9575

Whitney and Co. (New York)
630 Fifth Ave. Ste. 3225
New York, NY 10111
(212)332-2400
Fax: (212)332-2422
Website: http://www.jhwitney.com

Winthrop Ventures
74 Trinity Place, Ste. 600
New York, NY 10006
(212)422-0100

The Pittsford Group
8 Lodge Pole Rd.
Pittsford, NY 14534
(716)223-3523

Genesee Funding
70 Linden Oaks, 3rd Fl.
Rochester, NY 14625
(716)383-5550
Fax: (716)383-5305

Gabelli Multimedia Partners
One Corporate Center
Rye, NY 10580
(914)921-5395
Fax: (914)921-5031

Stamford Financial
108 Main St.
Stamford, NY 12167
(607)652-3311
Fax: (607)652-6301
Website: http://www.stamford
financial.com

Northwood Ventures LLC
485 Underhill Blvd., Ste. 205
Syosset, NY 11791
(516)364-5544
Fax: (516)364-0879
E-mail: northwood@northwood.com
Website: http://www.north
woodventures.com

Exponential Business Development Co.
216 Walton St.
Syracuse, NY 13202-1227
(315)474-4500
Fax: (315)474-4682
E-mail: dirksonn@aol.com
Website: http://www.exponential-ny.com

Onondaga Venture Capital Fund Inc.
714 State Tower Bldg.
Syracuse, NY 13202
(315)478-0157
Fax: (315)478-0158

Bessemer Venture Partners (Westbury)
1400 Old Country Rd., Ste. 109
Westbury, NY 11590
(516)997-2300
Fax: (516)997-2371
E-mail: bob@bvpny.com
Website: http://www.bvp.com

Ovation Capital Partners
120 Bloomingdale Rd., 4th Fl.
White Plains, NY 10605
(914)258-0011
Fax: (914)684-0848
Website: http://www.ovation
capital.com

North Carolina

Carolinas Capital Investment Corp.
1408 Biltmore Dr.
Charlotte, NC 28207
(704)375-3888
Fax: (704)375-6226

First Union Capital Partners
1st Union Center, 12th Fl.
301 S. College St.
Charlotte, NC 28288-0732
(704)383-0000
Fax: (704)374-6711
Website: http://www.fucp.com

Frontier Capital LLC
525 North Tryon St., Ste. 1700
Charlotte, NC 28202
(704)414-2880
Fax: (704)414-2881
Website: http://www.frontierfunds.com

Kitty Hawk Capital
2700 Coltsgate Rd., Ste. 202
Charlotte, NC 28211
(704)362-3909
Fax: (704)362-2774
Website: http://www.kittyhawk
capital.com

Piedmont Venture Partners
One Morrocroft Centre
6805 Morisson Blvd., Ste. 380
Charlotte, NC 28211
(704)731-5200
Fax: (704)365-9733
Website: http://www.piedmontvp.com

Ruddick Investment Co.
1800 Two First Union Center
Charlotte, NC 28282
(704)372-5404
Fax: (704)372-6409

The Shelton Companies Inc.
3600 One First Union Center
301 S. College St.
Charlotte, NC 28202
(704)348-2200
Fax: (704)348-2260

Wakefield Group
1110 E. Morehead St.
PO Box 36329
Charlotte, NC 28236
(704)372-0355
Fax: (704)372-8216
Website: http://www.wakefiel
dgroup.com

Aurora Funds, Inc.
2525 Meridian Pkwy., Ste. 220
Durham, NC 27713
(919)484-0400
Fax: (919)484-0444
Website: http://www.aurora
funds.com

Intersouth Partners
3211 Shannon Rd., Ste. 610
Durham, NC 27707
(919)493-6640
Fax: (919)493-6649
E-mail: info@intersouth.com
Website: http://www.intersouth.com

Geneva Merchant Banking Partners
PO Box 21962
Greensboro, NC 27420
(336)275-7002
Fax: (336)275-9155
Website: http://www.geneva
merchantbank.com

The North Carolina Enterprise Fund, L.P.
3600 Glenwood Ave., Ste. 107
Raleigh, NC 27612
(919)781-2691
Fax: (919)783-9195
Website: http://www.ncef.com

Ohio

Senmend Medical Ventures
4445 Lake Forest Dr., Ste. 600
Cincinnati, OH 45242
(513)563-3264
Fax: (513)563-3261

The Walnut Group
312 Walnut St., Ste. 1151
Cincinnati, OH 45202
(513)651-3300
Fax: (513)929-4441
Website: http://www.thewal
nutgroup.com

Brantley Venture Partners
20600 Chagrin Blvd., Ste. 1150
Cleveland, OH 44122
(216)283-4800
Fax: (216)283-5324

Clarion Capital Corp.
1801 E. 9th St., Ste. 1120
Cleveland, OH 44114
(216)687-1096
Fax: (216)694-3545

Crystal Internet Venture Fund, L.P.
1120 Chester Ave., Ste. 418
Cleveland, OH 44114
(216)263-5515
Fax: (216)263-5518
E-mail: jf@crystalventure.com
Website: http://www.crystal
venture.com

Key Equity Capital Corp.
127 Public Sq., 28th Fl.
Cleveland, OH 44114
(216)689-3000
Fax: (216)689-3204
Website: http://www.keybank.com

Morgenthaler Ventures
Terminal Tower
50 Public Square, Ste. 2700
Cleveland, OH 44113
(216)416-7500
Fax: (216)416-7501
Website: http://www.morgenthaler.com

National City Equity Partners Inc.
1965 E. 6th St.
Cleveland, OH 44114
(216)575-2491
Fax: (216)575-9965
E-mail: nccap@aol.com
Website: http://www.nccapital.com

Primus Venture Partners, Inc.
5900 LanderBrook Dr., Ste. 2000
Cleveland, OH 44124-4020
(440)684-7300
Fax: (440)684-7342
E-mail: info@primusventure.com
Website: http://www.primusventure.com

Banc One Capital Partners (Columbus)
150 East Gay St., 24th Fl.
Columbus, OH 43215
(614)217-1100
Fax: (614)217-1217

Battelle Venture Partners
505 King Ave.
Columbus, OH 43201
(614)424-7005
Fax: (614)424-4874

Ohio Partners
62 E. Board St., 3rd Fl.
Columbus, OH 43215
(614)621-1210
Fax: (614)621-1240

Capital Technology Group, L.L.C.
400 Metro Place North, Ste. 300
Dublin, OH 43017
(614)792-6066
Fax: (614)792-6036
E-mail: info@capitaltech.com
Website: http://www.capitaltech.com

Northwest Ohio Venture Fund
4159 Holland-Sylvania R., Ste. 202
Toledo, OH 43623
(419)824-8144

Fax: (419)882-2035
E-mail: bwalsh@novf.com

Oklahoma

Moore & Associates
1000 W. Wilshire Blvd., Ste. 370
Oklahoma City, OK 73116
(405)842-3660
Fax: (405)842-3763

Chisholm Private Capital Partners
100 West 5th St., Ste. 805
Tulsa, OK 74103
(918)584-0440
Fax: (918)584-0441
Website: http://www.chisholmvc.com

Davis, Tuttle Venture Partners (Tulsa)
320 S. Boston, Ste. 1000
Tulsa, OK 74103-3703
(918)584-7272
Fax: (918)582-3404
Website: http://www.davistuttle.com

RBC Ventures
2627 E. 21st St.
Tulsa, OK 74114
(918)744-5607
Fax: (918)743-8630

Oregon

Utah Ventures II LP
10700 SW Beaverton-Hillsdale Hwy.,
Ste. 548
Beaverton, OR 97005
(503)574-4125
E-mail: adishlip@uven.com
Website: http://www.uven.com

Orien Ventures
14523 SW Westlake Dr.
Lake Oswego, OR 97035
(503)699-1680
Fax: (503)699-1681

OVP Venture Partners (Lake Oswego)
340 Oswego Pointe Dr., Ste. 200
Lake Oswego, OR 97034
(503)697-8766
Fax: (503)697-8863
E-mail: info@ovp.com
Website: http://www.ovp.com

Oregon Resource and Technology Development Fund
4370 NE Halsey St., Ste. 233
Portland, OR 97213-1566
(503)282-4462
Fax: (503)282-2976

Shaw Venture Partners
400 SW 6th Ave., Ste. 1100
Portland, OR 97204-1636
(503)228-4884
Fax: (503)227-2471
Website: http://www.shawventures.com

Pennsylvania

Mid-Atlantic Venture Funds
125 Goodman Dr.
Bethlehem, PA 18015
(610)865-6550
Fax: (610)865-6427
Website: http://www.mavf.com

Newspring Ventures
100 W. Elm St., Ste. 101
Conshohocken, PA 19428
(610)567-2380
Fax: (610)567-2388
Website: http://www.news
printventures.com

Patricof & Co. Ventures, Inc.
455 S. Gulph Rd., Ste. 410
King of Prussia, PA 19406
(610)265-0286
Fax: (610)265-4959
Website: http://www.patricof.com

Loyalhanna Venture Fund
527 Cedar Way, Ste. 104
Oakmont, PA 15139
(412)820-7035
Fax: (412)820-7036

Innovest Group Inc.
2000 Market St., Ste. 1400
Philadelphia, PA 19103
(215)564-3960
Fax: (215)569-3272

Keystone Venture Capital Management Co.
1601 Market St., Ste. 2500
Philadelphia, PA 19103
(215)241-1200
Fax: (215)241-1211
Website: http://www.keystonevc.com

Liberty Venture Partners
2005 Market St., Ste. 200
Philadelphia, PA 19103
(215)282-4484
Fax: (215)282-4485
E-mail: info@libertyvp.com
Website: http://www.libertyvp.com

Penn Janney Fund, Inc.
1801 Market St., 11th Fl.
Philadelphia, PA 19103

(215)665-4447
Fax: (215)557-0820

Philadelphia Ventures, Inc.
The Bellevue
200 S. Broad St.
Philadelphia, PA 19102
(215)732-4445
Fax: (215)732-4644

Birchmere Ventures Inc.
2000 Technology Dr.
Pittsburgh, PA 15219-3109
(412)803-8000
Fax: (412)687-8139
Website: http://www.birchmerevc.com

CEO Venture Fund
2000 Technology Dr., Ste. 160
Pittsburgh, PA 15219-3109
(412)687-3451
Fax: (412)687-8139
E-mail: ceofund@aol.com
Website: http://www.ceoventure
fund.com

Innovation Works Inc.
2000 Technology Dr., Ste. 250
Pittsburgh, PA 15219
(412)681-1520
Fax: (412)681-2625
Website: http://www.innovation
works.org

Keystone Minority Capital Fund L.P.
1801 Centre Ave., Ste. 201
Williams Sq.
Pittsburgh, PA 15219
(412)338-2230
Fax: (412)338-2224

Mellon Ventures, Inc.
One Mellon Bank Ctr., Rm. 3500
Pittsburgh, PA 15258
(412)236-3594
Fax: (412)236-3593
Website: http://www.mellon
ventures.com

Pennsylvania Growth Fund
5850 Ellsworth Ave., Ste. 303
Pittsburgh, PA 15232
(412)661-1000
Fax: (412)361-0676

Point Venture Partners
The Century Bldg.
130 Seventh St., 7th Fl.
Pittsburgh, PA 15222
(412)261-1966
Fax: (412)261-1718

Cross Atlantic Capital Partners
5 Radnor Corporate Center, Ste. 555
Radnor, PA 19087
(610)995-2650
Fax: (610)971-2062
Website: http://www.xacp.com

Meridian Venture Partners (Radnor)
The Radnor Court Bldg., Ste. 140
259 Radnor-Chester Rd.
Radnor, PA 19087
(610)254-2999
Fax: (610)254-2996
E-mail: mvpart@ix.netcom.com

TDH
919 Conestoga Rd., Bldg. 1, Ste. 301
Rosemont, PA 19010
(610)526-9970
Fax: (610)526-9971

Adams Capital Management
500 Blackburn Ave.
Sewickley, PA 15143
(412)749-9454
Fax: (412)749-9459
Website: http://www.acm.com

S.R. One, Ltd.
Four Tower Bridge
200 Barr Harbor Dr., Ste. 250
W. Conshohocken, PA 19428
(610)567-1000
Fax: (610)567-1039

Greater Philadelphia Venture Capital Corp.
351 East Conestoga Rd.
Wayne, PA 19087
(610)688-6829
Fax: (610)254-8958

PA Early Stage
435 Devon Park Dr., Bldg. 500, Ste. 510
Wayne, PA 19087
(610)293-4075
Fax: (610)254-4240
Website: http://www.paearlystage.com

The Sandhurst Venture Fund, L.P.
351 E. Constoga Rd.
Wayne, PA 19087
(610)254-8900
Fax: (610)254-8958

TL Ventures
700 Bldg.
435 Devon Park Dr.
Wayne, PA 19087-1990
(610)975-3765
Fax: (610)254-4210
Website: http://www.tlventures.com

Rockhill Ventures, Inc.
100 Front St., Ste. 1350
West Conshohocken, PA 19428
(610)940-0300
Fax: (610)940-0301

Puerto Rico

Advent-Morro Equity Partners
Banco Popular Bldg.
206 Tetuan St., Ste. 903
San Juan, PR 00902
(787)725-5285
Fax: (787)721-1735

North America Investment Corp.
Mercantil Plaza, Ste. 813
PO Box 191831
San Juan, PR 00919
(787)754-6178
Fax: (787)754-6181

Rhode Island

Manchester Humphreys, Inc.
40 Westminster St., Ste. 900
Providence, RI 02903
(401)454-0400
Fax: (401)454-0403

Navis Partners
50 Kennedy Plaza, 12th Fl.
Providence, RI 02903
(401)278-6770
Fax: (401)278-6387
Website: http://www.navis
partners.com

South Carolina

Capital Insights, L.L.C.
PO Box 27162
Greenville, SC 29616-2162
(864)242-6832
Fax: (864)242-6755
E-mail: jwarner@capitalinsights.com
Website: http://www.capitalin
sights.com

Transamerica Mezzanine Financing
7 N. Laurens St., Ste. 603
Greenville, SC 29601
(864)232-6198
Fax: (864)241-4444

Tennessee

Valley Capital Corp.
Krystal Bldg.
100 W. Martin Luther King Blvd.,
Ste. 212

Chattanooga, TN 37402
(423)265-1557
Fax: (423)265-1588

Coleman Swenson Booth Inc.
237 2nd Ave. S
Franklin, TN 37064-2649
(615)791-9462
Fax: (615)791-9636
Website: http://
www.colemanswenson.com

Capital Services & Resources, Inc.
5159 Wheelis Dr., Ste. 106
Memphis, TN 38117
(901)761-2156
Fax: (907)767-0060

Paradigm Capital Partners LLC
6410 Poplar Ave., Ste. 395
Memphis, TN 38119
(901)682-6060
Fax: (901)328-3061

SSM Ventures
845 Crossover Ln., Ste. 140
Memphis, TN 38117
(901)767-1131
Fax: (901)767-1135
Website: http://www.ssm
ventures.com

Capital Across America L.P.
501 Union St., Ste. 201
Nashville, TN 37219
(615)254-1414
Fax: (615)254-1856
Website: http://
www.capitalacrossamerica.com

Equitas L.P.
2000 Glen Echo Rd., Ste. 101
PO Box 158838
Nashville, TN 37215-8838
(615)383-8673
Fax: (615)383-8693

Massey Burch Capital Corp.
One Burton Hills Blvd., Ste. 350
Nashville, TN 37215
(615)665-3221
Fax: (615)665-3240
E-mail: tcalton@masseyburch.com
Website: http://www.masseyburch.com

Nelson Capital Corp.
3401 West End Ave., Ste. 300
Nashville, TN 37203
(615)292-8787
Fax: (615)385-3150

Texas

Phillips-Smith Specialty Retail Group
5080 Spectrum Dr., Ste. 805 W
Addison, TX 75001
(972)387-0725
Fax: (972)458-2560
E-mail: pssrg@aol.com
Website: http://www.phillips-smith.com

Austin Ventures, L.P.
701 Brazos St., Ste. 1400
Austin, TX 78701
(512)485-1900
Fax: (512)476-3952
E-mail: info@ausven.com
Website: http://www.austinventures.com

The Capital Network
3925 West Braker Lane, Ste. 406
Austin, TX 78759-5321
(512)305-0826
Fax: (512)305-0836

Techxas Ventures LLC
5000 Plaza on the Lake
Austin, TX 78746
(512)343-0118
Fax: (512)343-1879
E-mail: bruce@techxas.com
Website: http://www.techxas.com

Alliance Financial of Houston
218 Heather Ln.
Conroe, TX 77385-9013
(936)447-3300
Fax: (936)447-4222

Amerimark Capital Corp.
1111 W. Mockingbird, Ste. 1111
Dallas, TX 75247
(214)638-7878
Fax: (214)638-7612
E-mail: amerimark@amcapital.com
Website: http://www.amcapital.com

AMT Venture Partners / AMT Capital Ltd.
5220 Spring Valley Rd., Ste. 600
Dallas, TX 75240
(214)905-9757
Fax: (214)905-9761
Website: http://www.amtcapital.com

Arkoma Venture Partners
5950 Berkshire Lane, Ste. 1400
Dallas, TX 75225
(214)739-3515
Fax: (214)739-3572
E-mail: joelf@arkomavp.com

Capital Southwest Corp.
12900 Preston Rd., Ste. 700
Dallas, TX 75230
(972)233-8242
Fax: (972)233-7362
Website: http://
www.capitalsouthwest.com

Dali, Hook Partners
One Lincoln Center, Ste. 1550
5400 LBJ Freeway
Dallas, TX 75240
(972)991-5457
Fax: (972)991-5458
E-mail: dhook@hookpartners.com
Website: http://www.hookpartners.com

HO2 Partners
Two Galleria Tower
13455 Noel Rd., Ste. 1670
Dallas, TX 75240
(972)702-1144
Fax: (972)702-8234
Website: http://www.ho2.com

Interwest Partners (Dallas)
2 Galleria Tower
13455 Noel Rd., Ste. 1670
Dallas, TX 75240
(972)392-7279
Fax: (972)490-6348
Website: http://www.interwest.com

Kahala Investments, Inc.
8214 Westchester Dr., Ste. 715
Dallas, TX 75225
(214)987-0077
Fax: (214)987-2332

MESBIC Ventures Holding Co.
2435 North Central Expressway, Ste. 200
Dallas, TX 75080
(972)991-1597
Fax: (972)991-4770
Website: http://www.mvhc.com

North Texas MESBIC, Inc.
9500 Forest Lane, Ste. 430
Dallas, TX 75243
(214)221-3565
Fax: (214)221-3566

Richard Jaffe & Company, Inc,
7318 Royal Cir.
Dallas, TX 75230
(214)265-9397
Fax: (214)739-1845

Sevin Rosen Management Co.
13455 Noel Rd., Ste. 1670
Dallas, TX 75240

(972)702-1100
Fax: (972)702-1103
E-mail: info@srfunds.com
Website: http://www.srfunds.com

Stratford Capital Partners, L.P.
300 Crescent Ct., Ste. 500
Dallas, TX 75201
(214)740-7377
Fax: (214)720-7393
E-mail: stratcap@hmtf.com

Sunwestern Investment Group
12221 Merit Dr., Ste. 935
Dallas, TX 75251
(972)239-5650
Fax: (972)701-0024

Wingate Partners
750 N. St. Paul St., Ste. 1200
Dallas, TX 75201
(214)720-1313
Fax: (214)871-8799

Buena Venture Associates
201 Main St., 32nd Fl.
Fort Worth, TX 76102
(817)339-7400
Fax: (817)390-8408
Website: http://www.buenaventure.com

The Catalyst Group
3 Riverway, Ste. 770
Houston, TX 77056
(713)623-8133
Fax: (713)623-0473
E-mail: herman@thecatalystgroup.net
Website: http://www.thecatalyst
group.net

Cureton & Co., Inc.
1100 Louisiana, Ste. 3250
Houston, TX 77002
(713)658-9806
Fax: (713)658-0476

Davis, Tuttle Venture Partners (Dallas)
8 Greenway Plaza, Ste. 1020
Houston, TX 77046
(713)993-0440
Fax: (713)621-2297
Website: http://www.davistuttle.com

Houston Partners
401 Louisiana, 8th Fl.
Houston, TX 77002
(713)222-8600
Fax: (713)222-8932

Southwest Venture Group
10878 Westheimer, Ste. 178

Houston, TX 77042
(713)827-8947
(713)461-1470

AM Fund
4600 Post Oak Place, Ste. 100
Houston, TX 77027
(713)627-9111
Fax: (713)627-9119

Ventex Management, Inc.
3417 Milam St.
Houston, TX 77002-9531
(713)659-7870
Fax: (713)659-7855

MBA Venture Group
1004 Olde Town Rd., Ste. 102
Irving, TX 75061
(972)986-6703

First Capital Group Management Co.
750 East Mulberry St., Ste. 305
PO Box 15616
San Antonio, TX 78212
(210)736-4233
Fax: (210)736-5449

The Southwest Venture Partnerships
16414 San Pedro, Ste. 345
San Antonio, TX 78232
(210)402-1200
Fax: (210)402-1221
E-mail: swvp@aol.com

Medtech International Inc.
1742 Carriageway
Sugarland, TX 77478
(713)980-8474
Fax: (713)980-6343

Utah

First Security Business Investment Corp.
15 East 100 South, Ste. 100
Salt Lake City, UT 84111
(801)246-5737
Fax: (801)246-5740

Utah Ventures II, L.P.
423 Wakara Way, Ste. 206
Salt Lake City, UT 84108
(801)583-5922
Fax: (801)583-4105
Website: http://www.uven.com

Wasatch Venture Corp.
1 S. Main St., Ste. 1400
Salt Lake City, UT 84133
(801)524-8939

Fax: (801)524-8941
E-mail: mail@wasatchvc.com

Vermont

North Atlantic Capital Corp.
76 Saint Paul St., Ste. 600
Burlington, VT 05401
(802)658-7820
Fax: (802)658-5757
Website: http://www.north
atlanticcapital.com

Green Mountain Advisors Inc.
PO Box 1230
Quechee, VT 05059
(802)296-7800
Fax: (802)296-6012
Website: http://www.gmtcap.com

Virginia

Oxford Financial Services Corp.
Alexandria, VA 22314
(703)519-4900
Fax: (703)519-4910
E-mail: oxford133@aol.com

Continental SBIC
4141 N. Henderson Rd.
Arlington, VA 22203
(703)527-5200
Fax: (703)527-3700

Novak Biddle Venture Partners
1750 Tysons Blvd., Ste. 1190
McLean, VA 22102
(703)847-3770
Fax: (703)847-3771
E-mail: roger@novakbiddle.com
Website: http://www.novakbiddle.com

Spacevest
11911 Freedom Dr., Ste. 500
Reston, VA 20190
(703)904-9800
Fax: (703)904-0571
E-mail: spacevest@spacevest.com
Website: http://www.spacevest.com

Virginia Capital
1801 Libbie Ave., Ste. 201
Richmond, VA 23226
(804)648-4802
Fax: (804)648-4809
E-mail: webmaster@vacapital.com
Website: http://www.vacapital.com

Calvert Social Venture Partners
402 Maple Ave. W
Vienna, VA 22180

(703)255-4930
Fax: (703)255-4931
E-mail: calven2000@aol.com

Fairfax Partners
8000 Towers Crescent Dr., Ste. 940
Vienna, VA 22182
(703)847-9486
Fax: (703)847-0911

Global Internet Ventures
8150 Leesburg Pike, Ste. 1210
Vienna, VA 22182
(703)442-3300
Fax: (703)442-3388
Website: http://www.givinc.com

Walnut Capital Corp. (Vienna)
8000 Towers Crescent Dr., Ste. 1070
Vienna, VA 22182
(703)448-3771
Fax: (703)448-7751

Washington

Encompass Ventures
777 108th Ave. NE, Ste. 2300
Bellevue, WA 98004
(425)486-3900
Fax: (425)486-3901
E-mail: info@evpartners.com
Website: http://www.encom
passventures.com

Fluke Venture Partners
11400 SE Sixth St., Ste. 230
Bellevue, WA 98004
(425)453-4590
Fax: (425)453-4675
E-mail: gabelein@flukeventures.com
Website: http://www.flukeventures.com

Pacific Northwest Partners SBIC, L.P.
15352 SE 53rd St.
Bellevue, WA 98006
(425)455-9967
Fax: (425)455-9404

Materia Venture Associates, L.P.
3435 Carillon Pointe
Kirkland, WA 98033-7354
(425)822-4100
Fax: (425)827-4086

OVP Venture Partners (Kirkland)
2420 Carillon Pt.
Kirkland, WA 98033
(425)889-9192
Fax: (425)889-0152
E-mail: info@ovp.com
Website: http://www.ovp.com

Digital Partners
999 3rd Ave., Ste. 1610
Seattle, WA 98104
(206)405-3607
Fax: (206)405-3617
Website: http://www.digitalpartners.com

Frazier & Company
601 Union St., Ste. 3300
Seattle, WA 98101
(206)621-7200
Fax: (206)621-1848
E-mail: jon@frazierco.com

Kirlan Venture Capital, Inc.
221 First Ave. W, Ste. 108
Seattle, WA 98119-4223
(206)281-8610
Fax: (206)285-3451
Website: http://www.kirlanventure.com

Phoenix Partners
1000 2nd Ave., Ste. 3600
Seattle, WA 98104
(206)624-8968
Fax: (206)624-1907

Voyager Capital
800 5th St., Ste. 4100
Seattle, WA 98103
(206)470-1180
Fax: (206)470-1185
E-mail: info@voyagercap.com
Website: http://www.voyagercap.com

Northwest Venture Associates
221 N. Wall St., Ste. 628
Spokane, WA 99201
(509)747-0728
Fax: (509)747-0758
Website: http://www.nwva.com

Wisconsin

Venture Investors Management, L.L.C.
University Research Park
505 S. Rosa Rd.
Madison, WI 53719
(608)441-2700
Fax: (608)441-2727
E-mail: roger@ventureinvestors.com
Website: http://www.venture
investers.com

Capital Investments, Inc.
1009 West Glen Oaks Lane, Ste. 103
Mequon, WI 53092
(414)241-0303
Fax: (414)241-8451
Website: http://
www.capitalinvestmentsinc.com

Future Value Venture, Inc.
2745 N. Martin Luther King
Dr., Ste. 204
Milwaukee, WI 53212-2300
(414)264-2252
Fax: (414)264-2253
E-mail: fvvventures@aol.com
William Beckett, President

Lubar and Co., Inc.
700 N. Water St., Ste. 1200
Milwaukee, WI 53202
(414)291-9000
Fax: (414)291-9061

GCI
20875 Crossroads Cir., Ste. 100
Waukesha, WI 53186
(262)798-5080
Fax: (262)798-5087

Glossary of Small Business Terms

Absolute liability
Liability that is incurred due to product defects or negligent actions. Manufacturers or retail establishments are held responsible, even though the defect or action may not have been intentional or negligent.

ACE
See Active Corps of Executives

Accident and health benefits
Benefits offered to employees and their families in order to offset the costs associated with accidental death, accidental injury, or sickness.

Account statement
A record of transactions, including payments, new debt, and deposits, incurred during a defined period of time.

Accounting system
System capturing the costs of all employees and/or machinery included in business expenses.

Accounts payable
See Trade credit

Accounts receivable
Unpaid accounts which arise from unsettled claims and transactions from the sale of a company's products or services to its customers.

Active Corps of Executives (ACE)
A group of volunteers for a management assistance program of the U.S. Small Business Administration; volunteers provide one-on-one counseling and teach workshops and seminars for small firms.

ADA
See Americans with Disabilities Act

Adaptation
The process whereby an invention is modified to meet the needs of users.

Adaptive engineering
The process whereby an invention is modified to meet the manufacturing and commercial requirements of a targeted market.

Adverse selection
The tendency for higher-risk individuals to purchase health care and more comprehensive plans, resulting in increased costs.

Advertising
A marketing tool used to capture public attention and influence purchasing decisions for a product or service. Utilizes various forms of media to generate consumer response, such as flyers, magazines, newspapers, radio, and television.

Age discrimination
The denial of the rights and privileges of employment based solely on the age of an individual.

Agency costs
Costs incurred to insure that the lender or investor maintains control over assets while allowing the borrower or entrepreneur to use them. Monitoring and information costs are the two major types of agency costs.

Agribusiness
The production and sale of commodities and products from the commercial farming industry.

America Online
An online service which is accessible by computer modem. The service features Internet access, bulletin boards, online periodicals, electronic mail, and other services for subscribers.

Americans with Disabilities Act (ADA)
Law designed to ensure equal access and opportunity to handicapped persons.

Annual report
Yearly financial report prepared by a business that adheres to the requirements set forth by the Securities and Exchange Commission (SEC).

Antitrust immunity
Exemption from prosecution under antitrust laws. In the transportation industry, firms with antitrust immunity are permitted under certain conditions to set schedules and sometimes prices for the public benefit.

Applied research
Scientific study targeted for use in a product or process.

Asians
A minority category used by the U.S. Bureau of the Census to represent a diverse group that includes Aleuts, Eskimos, American Indians, Asian Indians, Chinese, Japanese, Koreans, Vietnamese, Filipinos, Hawaiians, and other Pacific Islanders.

Assets
Anything of value owned by a company.

Audit
The verification of accounting records and business procedures conducted by an outside accounting service.

Average cost
Total production costs divided by the quantity produced.

Balance Sheet
A financial statement listing the total assets and liabilities of a company at a given time.

Bankruptcy
The condition in which a business cannot meet its debt obligations and petitions a federal district court either for reorganization of its debts (Chapter 11) or for liquidation of its assets (Chapter 7).

Basic research
Theoretical scientific exploration not targeted to application.

Basket clause
A provision specifying the amount of public pension funds that may be placed in investments not included on a state's legal list (see separate citation).

BBS
See Bulletin Board Service

BDC
See Business development corporation

Benefit
Various services, such as health care, flextime, day care, insurance, and vacation, offered to employees as part of a hiring package. Typically subsidized in whole or in part by the business.

BIDCO
See Business and industrial development company

Billing cycle
A system designed to evenly distribute customer billing throughout the month, preventing clerical backlogs.

Birth
See Business birth

Blue chip security
A low-risk, low-yield security representing an interest in a very stable company.

Blue sky laws
A general term that denotes various states' laws regulating securities.

Bond
A written instrument executed by a bidder or contractor (the principal) and a second party (the surety or sureties) to assure fulfillment of the principal's obligations to a third party (the obligee or government) identified in the bond. If the principal's obligations are not met, the bond assures payment to the extent stipulated of any loss sustained by the obligee.

Bonding requirements
Terms contained in a bond (see separate citation).

Bonus
An amount of money paid to an employee as a reward for achieving certain business goals or objectives.

Brainstorming
A group session where employees contribute their ideas for solving a problem or meeting a company objective without fear of retribution or ridicule.

Brand name
The part of a brand, trademark, or service mark that can be spoken. It can be a word, letter, or group of words or letters.

Bridge financing
A short-term loan made in expectation of intermediateterm or long-term financing. Can be used when a company plans to go public in the near future.

Broker
One who matches resources available for innovation with those who need them.

Budget
An estimate of the spending necessary to complete a project or offer a service in comparison to cash-on-hand and expected earnings for the coming year, with an emphasis on cost control.

Bulletin Board Service (BBS)
An online service enabling users to communicate with each other about specific topics.

Business and industrial development company (BIDCO)
A private, for-profit financing corporation chartered by the state to provide both equity and long-term debt capital to small business owners (see separate citations for equity and debt capital).

Business birth
The formation of a new establishment or enterprise. The appearance of a new establishment or enterprise in the Small Business Data Base (see separate citation).

Business conditions
Outside factors that can affect the financial performance of a business.

Business contractions
The number of establishments that have decreased in employment during a specified time.

Business cycle
A period of economic recession and recovery. These cycles vary in duration.

Business death
The voluntary or involuntary closure of a firm or establishment. The disappearance of an establishment or enterprise from the Small Business Data Base (see separate citation).

Business development corporation (BDC)
A business financing agency, usually composed of the financial institutions in an area or state, organized to

assist in financing businesses unable to obtain assistance through normal channels; the risk is spread among various members of the business development corporation, and interest rates may vary somewhat from those charged by member institutions. A venture capital firm in which shares of ownership are publicly held and to which the Investment Act of 1940 applies.

Business dissolution
For enumeration purposes, the absence of a business that was present in the prior time period from any current record.

Business entry
See Business birth

Business ethics
Moral values and principles espoused by members of the business community as a guide to fair and honest business practices.

Business exit
See Business death

Business expansions
The number of establishments that added employees during a specified time.

Business failure
Closure of a business causing a loss to at least one creditor.

Business format franchising
The purchase of the name, trademark, and an ongoing business plan of the parent corporation or franchisor by the franchisee.

Business license
A legal authorization issued by municipal and state governments and required for business operations.

Business name
Enterprises must register their business names with local governments usually on a "doing business as" (DBA) form. (This name is sometimes referred to as a "fictional name.") The procedure is part of the business licensing process and prevents any other business from using that same name for a similar business in the same locality.

Business norms
See Financial ratios

Business permit
See Business license

Business plan
A document that spells out a company's expected course of action for a specified period, usually including a detailed listing and analysis of risks and uncertainties. For the small business, it should examine the proposed products, the market, the industry, the management policies, the marketing policies, production needs, and financial needs. Frequently, it is used as a prospectus for potential investors and lenders.

Business proposal
See Business plan

Business service firm
An establishment primarily engaged in rendering services to other business organizations on a fee or contract basis.

Business start
For enumeration purposes, a business with a name or similar designation that did not exist in a prior time period.

Cafeteria plan
See Flexible benefit plan

Capacity
Level of a firm's, industry's, or nation's output corresponding to full practical utilization of available resources.

Capital
Assets less liabilities, representing the ownership interest in a business. A stock of accumulated goods, especially at a specified time and in contrast to income received during a specified time period. Accumulated goods devoted to production. Accumulated possessions calculated to bring income.

Capital expenditure
Expenses incurred by a business for improvements that will depreciate over time.

Capital gain
The monetary difference between the purchase price and the selling price of capital. Capital gains are taxed at a rate of 28% by the federal government.

Capital intensity
The relative importance of capital in the production process, usually expressed as the ratio of capital to labor but also sometimes as the ratio of capital to output.

Capital resource
The equipment, facilities and labor used to create products and services.

Caribbean Basin Initiative
An interdisciplinary program to support commerce among the businesses in the nations of the Caribbean Basin and the United States. Agencies involved include: the Agency for International Development, the U.S. Small Business Administration, the International Trade Administration of the U.S. Department of Commerce, and various private sector groups.

Catastrophic care
Medical and other services for acute and long-term illnesses that cost more than insurance coverage limits or that cost the amount most families may be expected to pay with their own resources.

CDC
See Certified development corporation

CD-ROM
Compact disc with read-only memory used to store large amounts of digitized data.

Certified development corporation (CDC)
A local area or statewide corporation or authority (for profit or nonprofit) that packages U.S. Small Business Administration (SBA), bank, state, and/or private money into financial assistance for existing business capital improvements. The SBA holds the second lien on its maximum share of 40 percent involvement. Each state has at least one certified development corporation. This program is called the SBA 504 Program.

Certified lenders
Banks that participate in the SBA guaranteed loan program (see separate citation). Such banks must have a good track record with the U.S. Small Business Administration (SBA) and must agree to certain conditions set forth by the agency. In return, the SBA agrees to process any guaranteed loan application within three business days.

Champion
An advocate for the development of an innovation.

Channel of distribution
The means used to transport merchandise from the manufacturer to the consumer.

Chapter 7 of the 1978 Bankruptcy Act
Provides for a court-appointed trustee who is responsible for liquidating a company's assets in order to settle outstanding debts.

Chapter 11 of the 1978 Bankruptcy Act
Allows the business owners to retain control of the company while working with their creditors to reorganize their finances and establish better business practices to prevent liquidation of assets.

Closely held corporation
A corporation in which the shares are held by a few persons, usually officers, employees, or others close to the management; these shares are rarely offered to the public.

Code of Federal Regulations
Codification of general and permanent rules of the federal government published in the Federal Register.

Code sharing
See Computer code sharing

Coinsurance
Upon meeting the deductible payment, health insurance participants may be required to make additional health care cost-sharing payments. Coinsurance is a payment of a fixed percentage of the cost of each service; copayment is usually a fixed amount to be paid with each service.

Collateral
Securities, evidence of deposit, or other property pledged by a borrower to secure repayment of a loan.

Collective ratemaking
The establishment of uniform charges for services by a group of businesses in the same industry.

Commercial insurance plan
See Underwriting

Commercial loans
Short-term renewable loans used to finance specific capital needs of a business.

Commercialization
The final stage of the innovation process, including production and distribution.

Common stock
The most frequently used instrument for purchasing ownership in private or public companies. Common stock generally carries the right to vote on certain corporate actions and may pay dividends, although it rarely does in venture investments. In liquidation, common stockholders are the last to share in the proceeds from the sale of a corporation's assets; bondholders and preferred shareholders have priority. Common stock is often used in firstround start-up financing.

Community development corporation
A corporation established to develop economic programs for a community and, in most cases, to provide financial support for such development.

Competitor
A business whose product or service is marketed for the same purpose/use and to the same consumer group as the product or service of another.

Computer code sharing
An arrangement whereby flights of a regional airline are identified by the two-letter code of a major carrier in the computer reservation system to help direct passengers to new regional carriers.

Consignment
A merchandising agreement, usually referring to secondhand shops, where the dealer pays the owner of an item a percentage of the profit when the item is sold.

Consortium
A coalition of organizations such as banks and corporations for ventures requiring large capital resources.

Consultant
An individual that is paid by a business to provide advice and expertise in a particular area.

Consumer price index
A measure of the fluctuation in prices between two points in time.

Consumer research
Research conducted by a business to obtain information about existing or potential consumer markets.

Glossary

Continuation coverage
Health coverage offered for a specified period of time to employees who leave their jobs and to their widows, divorced spouses, or dependents.

Contractions
See Business contractions

Convertible preferred stock
A class of stock that pays a reasonable dividend and is convertible into common stock (see separate citation). Generally the convertible feature may only be exercised after being held for a stated period of time. This arrangement is usually considered second-round financing when a company needs equity to maintain its cash flow.

Convertible securities
A feature of certain bonds, debentures, or preferred stocks that allows them to be exchanged by the owner for another class of securities at a future date and in accordance with any other terms of the issue.

Copayment
See Coinsurance

Copyright
A legal form of protection available to creators and authors to safeguard their works from unlawful use or claim of ownership by others. Copyrights may be acquired for works of art, sculpture, music, and published or unpublished manuscripts. All copyrights should be registered at the Copyright Office of the Library of Congress.

Corporate financial ratios
The relationship between key figures found in a company's financial statement expressed as a numeric value. Used to evaluate risk and company performance. Also known as Financial averages, Operating ratios, and Business ratios.

Corporation
A legal entity, chartered by a state or the federal government, recognized as a separate entity having its own rights, privileges, and liabilities distinct from those of its members.

Cost containment
Actions taken by employers and insurers to curtail rising health care costs; for example, increasing employee cost sharing (see separate citation), requiring second opinions, or preadmission screening.

Cost sharing
The requirement that health care consumers contribute to their own medical care costs through deductibles and coinsurance (see separate citations). Cost sharing does not include the amounts paid in premiums. It is used to control utilization of services; for example, requiring a fixed amount to be paid with each health care service.

Cottage industry
Businesses based in the home in which the family members are the labor force and family-owned equipment is used to process the goods.

Credit Rating
A letter or number calculated by an organization (such as Dun & Bradstreet) to represent the ability and disposition of a business to meet its financial obligations.

Customer service
Various techniques used to ensure the satisfaction of a customer.

Cyclical peak
The upper turning point in a business cycle.

Cyclical trough
The lower turning point in a business cycle.

DBA
See Business name

Death
See Business death

Debenture
A certificate given as acknowledgment of a debt (see separate citation) secured by the general credit of the issuing corporation. A bond, usually without security, issued by a corporation and sometimes convertible to common stock.

Debt
Something owed by one person to another. Financing in which a company receives capital that must be repaid; no ownership is transferred.

Debt capital
Business financing that normally requires periodic interest payments and repayment of the principal within a specified time.

Debt financing
See Debt capital

Debt securities
Loans such as bonds and notes that provide a specified rate of return for a specified period of time.

Deductible
A set amount that an individual must pay before any benefits are received.

Demand shock absorbers
A term used to describe the role that some small firms play by expanding their output levels to accommodate a transient surge in demand.

Demographics
Statistics on various markets, including age, income, and education, used to target specific products or services to appropriate consumer groups.

Demonstration
Showing that a product or process has been modified sufficiently to meet the needs of users.

Deregulation
The lifting of government restrictions; for example, the lifting of government restrictions on the entry of new businesses, the expansion of services, and the setting of prices in particular industries.

Desktop Publishing
Using personal computers and specialized software to produce camera-ready copy for publications.

Disaster loans
Various types of physical and economic assistance available to individuals and businesses through the U.S. Small Business Administration (SBA). This is the only SBA loan program available for residential purposes.

Discrimination
The denial of the rights and privileges of employment based on factors such as age, race, religion, or gender.

Diseconomies of scale
The condition in which the costs of production increase faster than the volume of production.

Dissolution
See Business dissolution

Distribution
Delivering a product or process to the user.

Distributor
One who delivers merchandise to the user.

Diversified company
A company whose products and services are used by several different markets.

Doing business as (DBA)
See Business name

Dow Jones
An information services company that publishes the Wall Street Journal and other sources of financial information.

Dow Jones Industrial Average
An indicator of stock market performance.

Earned income
A tax term that refers to wages and salaries earned by the recipient, as opposed to monies earned through interest and dividends.

Economic efficiency
The use of productive resources to the fullest practical extent in the provision of the set of goods and services that is most preferred by purchasers in the economy.

Economic indicators
Statistics used to express the state of the economy. These include the length of the average work week, the rate of unemployment, and stock prices.

Economically disadvantaged
See Socially and economically disadvantaged

Economies of scale
See Scale economies

EEOC
See Equal Employment Opportunity Commission

8(a) Program
A program authorized by the Small Business Act that directs federal contracts to small businesses owned and

operated by socially and economically disadvantaged individuals.

Electronic mail (e-mail)
The electronic transmission of mail via phone lines.

E-mail
See Electronic mail

Employee leasing
A contract by which employers arrange to have their workers hired by a leasing company and then leased back to them for a management fee. The leasing company typically assumes the administrative burden of payroll and provides a benefit package to the workers.

Employee tenure
The length of time an employee works for a particular employer.

Employer identification number
The business equivalent of a social security number. Assigned by the U.S. Internal Revenue Service.

Enterprise
An aggregation of all establishments owned by a parent company. An enterprise may consist of a single, independent establishment or include subsidiaries and other branches under the same ownership and control.

Enterprise zone
A designated area, usually found in inner cities and other areas with significant unemployment, where businesses receive tax credits and other incentives to entice them to establish operations there.

Entrepreneur
A person who takes the risk of organizing and operating a new business venture.

Entry
See Business entry

Equal Employment Opportunity Commission (EEOC)
A federal agency that ensures nondiscrimination in the hiring and firing practices of a business.

Equal opportunity employer
An employer who adheres to the standards set by the Equal Employment Opportunity Commission (see separate citation).

Equity
The ownership interest. Financing in which partial or total ownership of a company is surrendered in exchange for capital. An investor's financial return comes from dividend payments and from growth in the net worth of the business.

Equity capital
See Equity; Equity midrisk venture capital

Equity financing
See Equity; Equity midrisk venture capital

Equity midrisk venture capital
An unsecured investment in a company. Usually a purchase of ownership interest in a company that occurs in the later stages of a company's development.

Equity partnership
A limited partnership arrangement for providing start-up and seed capital to businesses.

Equity securities
See Equity

Equity-type
Debt financing subordinated to conventional debt.

Establishment
A single-location business unit that may be independent (a single-establishment enterprise) or owned by a parent enterprise.

Establishment and Enterprise Microdata File
See U.S. Establishment and Enterprise Microdata File

Establishment birth
See Business birth

Establishment Longitudinal Microdata File
See U.S. Establishment Longitudinal Microdata File

Ethics
See Business ethics

Evaluation
Determining the potential success of translating an invention into a product or process.

Exit
See Business exit

Experience rating
See Underwriting

Export
A product sold outside of the country.

Export license
A general or specific license granted by the U.S. Department of Commerce required of anyone wishing to export goods. Some restricted articles need approval from the U.S. Departments of State, Defense, or Energy.

Failure
See Business failure

Fair share agreement
An agreement reached between a franchisor and a minority business organization to extend business ownership to minorities by either reducing the amount of capital required or by setting aside certain marketing areas for minority business owners.

Feasibility study
A study to determine the likelihood that a proposed product or development will fulfill the objectives of a particular investor.

Federal Trade Commission (FTC)
Federal agency that promotes free enterprise and competition within the U.S.

Federal Trade Mark Act of 1946
See Lanham Act

Fictional name
See Business name

Fiduciary
An individual or group that hold assets in trust for a beneficiary.

Financial analysis
The techniques used to determine money needs in a business. Techniques include ratio analysis, calculation of return on investment, guides for measuring profitability, and break-even analysis to determine ultimate success.

Financial intermediary
A financial institution that acts as the intermediary between borrowers and lenders. Banks, savings and loan associations, finance companies, and venture capital companies are major financial intermediaries in the United States.

Financial ratios
See Corporate financial ratios; Industry financial ratios

Financial statement
A written record of business finances, including balance sheets and profit and loss statements.

Financing
See First-stage financing; Second-stage financing; Thirdstage financing

First-stage financing
Financing provided to companies that have expended their initial capital, and require funds to start full-scale manufacturing and sales. Also known as First-round financing.

Fiscal year
Any twelve-month period used by businesses for accounting purposes.

504 Program
See Certified development corporation

Flexible benefit plan
A plan that offers a choice among cash and/or qualified benefits such as group term life insurance, accident and health insurance, group legal services, dependent care assistance, and vacations.

FOB
See Free on board

Format franchising
See Business format franchising; Franchising

401(k) plan
A financial plan where employees contribute a percentage of their earnings to a fund that is invested in stocks, bonds, or money markets for the purpose of saving money for retirement.

Four Ps
Marketing terms referring to Product, Price, Place, and Promotion.

Franchising
A form of licensing by which the owner-the franchisor- distributes or markets a product, method, or service through affiliated dealers called franchisees. The product, method, or service being marketed is identified by a brand name, and the franchisor

maintains control over the marketing methods employed. The franchisee is often given exclusive access to a defined geographic area.

Free on board (FOB)
A pricing term indicating that the quoted price includes the cost of loading goods into transport vessels at a specified place.

Frictional unemployment
See Unemployment

FTC
See Federal Trade Commission

Fulfillment
The systems necessary for accurate delivery of an ordered item, including subscriptions and direct marketing.

Full-time workers
Generally, those who work a regular schedule of more than 35 hours per week.

Garment registration number
A number that must appear on every garment sold in the U.S. to indicate the manufacturer of the garment, which may or may not be the same as the label under which the garment is sold. The U.S. Federal Trade Commission assigns and regulates garment registration numbers.

Gatekeeper
A key contact point for entry into a network.

GDP
See Gross domestic product

General obligation bond
A municipal bond secured by the taxing power of the municipality. The Tax Reform Act of 1986 limits the purposes for which such bonds may be issued and establishes volume limits on the extent of their issuance.

GNP
See Gross national product

Good Housekeeping Seal
Seal appearing on products that signifies the fulfillment of the standards set by the Good Housekeeping Institute to protect consumer interests.

Goods sector
All businesses producing tangible goods, including agriculture, mining, construction, and manufacturing businesses.

GPO
See Gross product originating

Gross domestic product (GDP)
The part of the nation's gross national product (see separate citation) generated by private business using resources from within the country.

Gross national product (GNP)
The most comprehensive single measure of aggregate economic output. Represents the market value of the total output of goods and services produced by a nation's economy.

Gross product originating (GPO)
A measure of business output estimated from the income or production side using employee compensation, profit income, net interest, capital consumption, and indirect business taxes.

HAL
See Handicapped assistance loan program

Handicapped assistance loan program (HAL)
Low-interest direct loan program through the U.S. Small Business Administration (SBA) for handicapped persons. The SBA requires that these persons demonstrate that their disability is such that it is impossible for them to secure employment, thus making it necessary to go into their own business to make a living.

Health maintenance organization (HMO)
Organization of physicians and other health care professionals that provides health services to subscribers and their dependents on a prepaid basis.

Health provider
An individual or institution that gives medical care. Under Medicare, an institutional provider is a hospital, skilled nursing facility, home health agency, or provider of certain physical therapy services.

Hispanic
A person of Cuban, Mexican, Puerto Rican, Latin American (Central or South American), European Spanish, or other Spanish-speaking origin or ancestry.

HMO
See Health maintenance organization

Home-based business
A business with an operating address that is also a residential address (usually the residential address of the proprietor).

Hub-and-spoke system
A system in which flights of an airline from many different cities (the spokes) converge at a single airport (the hub). After allowing passengers sufficient time to make connections, planes then depart for different cities.

Human Resources Management
A business program designed to oversee recruiting, pay, benefits, and other issues related to the company's work force, including planning to determine the optimal use of labor to increase production, thereby increasing profit.

Idea
An original concept for a new product or process.

Import
Products produced outside the country in which they are consumed.

Income
Money or its equivalent, earned or accrued, resulting from the sale of goods and services.

Income statement
A financial statement that lists the profits and losses of a company at a given time.

Incorporation
The filing of a certificate of incorporation with a state's secretary of state, thereby limiting the business owner's liability.

Incubator
A facility designed to encourage entrepreneurship and minimize obstacles to new business formation and growth, particularly for high-technology firms, by housing a number of fledgling enterprises that share an array of services, such as meeting areas, secretarial services, accounting, research library, on-site financial and management counseling, and word processing facilities.

Independent contractor
An individual considered self-employed (see separate citation) and responsible for paying Social Security taxes and income taxes on earnings.

Indirect health coverage
Health insurance obtained through another individual's health care plan; for example, a spouse's employersponsored plan.

Industrial development authority
The financial arm of a state or other political subdivision established for the purpose of financing economic development in an area, usually through loans to nonprofit organizations, which in turn provide facilities for manufacturing and other industrial operations.

Industry financial ratios
Corporate financial ratios averaged for a specified industry. These are used for comparison purposes and reveal industry trends and identify differences between the performance of a specific company and the performance of its industry. Also known as Industrial averages, Industry ratios, Financial averages, and Business or Industrial norms.

Inflation
Increases in volume of currency and credit, generally resulting in a sharp and continuing rise in price levels.

Informal capital
Financing from informal, unorganized sources; includes informal debt capital such as trade credit or loans from friends and relatives and equity capital from informal investors.

Initial public offering (IPO)
A corporation's first offering of stock to the public.

Innovation
The introduction of a new idea into the marketplace in the form of a new product or service or an improvement in organization or process.

Intellectual property
Any idea or work that can be considered proprietary in nature and is thus protected from infringement by others.

Internal capital
Debt or equity financing obtained from the owner or through retained business earnings.

Internet
A government-designed computer network that contains large amounts of information and is accessible through various vendors for a fee.

Intrapreneurship
The state of employing entrepreneurial principles to nonentrepreneurial situations.

Invention
The tangible form of a technological idea, which could include a laboratory prototype, drawings, formulas, etc.

IPO
See Initial public offering

Job description
The duties and responsibilities required in a particular position.

Job tenure
A period of time during which an individual is continuously employed in the same job.

Joint marketing agreements
Agreements between regional and major airlines, often involving the coordination of flight schedules, fares, and baggage transfer. These agreements help regional carriers operate at lower cost.

Joint venture
Venture in which two or more people combine efforts in a particular business enterprise, usually a single transaction or a limited activity, and agree to share the profits and losses jointly or in proportion to their contributions.

Keogh plan
Designed for self-employed persons and unincorporated businesses as a tax-deferred pension account.

Labor force
Civilians considered eligible for employment who are also willing and able to work.

Labor force participation rate
The civilian labor force as a percentage of the civilian population.

Labor intensity
The relative importance of labor in the production process, usually measured as the capital-labor ratio; i.e., the ratio of units of capital (typically, dollars of tangible assets) to the number of employees. The higher the capital-labor ratio exhibited by a firm or industry, the lower the capital intensity of that firm or industry is said to be.

Labor surplus area
An area in which there exists a high unemployment rate. In procurement (see separate citation), extra points are given to firms in counties that are designated a labor surplus area; this information is requested on procurement bid sheets.

Labor union
An organization of similarly-skilled workers who collectively bargain with management over the conditions of employment.

Laboratory prototype
See Prototype

LAN
See Local Area Network

Lanham Act
Refers to the Federal Trade Mark Act of 1946. Protects registered trademarks, trade names, and other service marks used in commerce.

Large business-dominated industry
Industry in which a minimum of 60 percent of employment or sales is in firms with more than 500 workers.

LBO
See Leveraged buy-out

Leader pricing
A reduction in the price of a good or service in order to generate more sales of that good or service.

Legal list
A list of securities selected by a state in which certain institutions and fiduciaries (such as pension funds, insurance companies, and banks) may invest. Securities not on the list are not eligible for investment. Legal lists typically restrict investments to high quality securities meeting certain specifications. Generally, investment is

limited to U.S. securities and investment-grade blue chip securities (see separate citation).

Leveraged buy-out (LBO)
The purchase of a business or a division of a corporation through a highly leveraged financing package.

Liability
An obligation or duty to perform a service or an act. Also defined as money owed.

License
A legal agreement granting to another the right to use a technological innovation.

Limited partnerships
See Venture capital limited partnerships

Liquidity
The ability to convert a security into cash promptly.

Loans
See Commercial loans; Disaster loans; SBA direct loans; SBA guaranteed loans; SBA special lending institution categories Local Area Network (LAN) Computer networks contained within a single building or small area; used to facilitate the sharing of information.

Local development corporation
An organization, usually made up of local citizens of a community, designed to improve the economy of the area by inducing business and industry to locate and expand there. A local development corporation establishes a capability to finance local growth.

Long-haul rates
Rates charged by a transporter in which the distance traveled is more than 800 miles.

Long-term debt
An obligation that matures in a period that exceeds five years.

Low-grade bond
A corporate bond that is rated below investment grade by the major rating agencies (Standard and Poor's, Moody's).

Macro-efficiency
Efficiency as it pertains to the operation of markets and market systems.

Managed care
A cost-effective health care program initiated by employers whereby low-cost health care is made available to the employees in return for exclusive patronage to program doctors.

Management Assistance Programs
See SBA Management Assistance Programs

Management and technical assistance
A term used by many programs to mean business (as opposed to technological) assistance.

Mandated benefits
Specific treatments, providers, or individuals required by law to be included in commercial health plans.

Market evaluation
The use of market information to determine the sales potential of a specific product or process.

Market failure
The situation in which the workings of a competitive market do not produce the best results from the point of view of the entire society.

Market information
Data of any type that can be used for market evaluation, which could include demographic data, technology forecasting, regulatory changes, etc.

Market research
A systematic collection, analysis, and reporting of data about the market and its preferences, opinions, trends, and plans; used for corporate decision-making.

Market share
In a particular market, the percentage of sales of a specific product.

Marketing
Promotion of goods or services through various media.

Master Establishment List (MEL)
A list of firms in the United States developed by the U.S. Small Business Administration; firms can be selected by industry, region, state, standard metropolitan statistical area (see separate citation), county, and zip code.

Maturity
The date upon which the principal or stated value of a bond or other indebtedness becomes due and payable.

Medicaid (Title XIX)
A federally aided, state-operated and administered program that provides medical benefits for certain low income persons in need of health and medical care who are eligible for one of the government's welfare cash payment programs, including the aged, the blind, the disabled, and members of families with dependent children where one parent is absent, incapacitated, or unemployed.

Medicare (Title XVIII)
A nationwide health insurance program for disabled and aged persons. Health insurance is available to insured persons without regard to income. Monies from payroll taxes cover hospital insurance and monies from general revenues and beneficiary premiums pay for supplementary medical insurance.

MEL
See Master Establishment List

MESBIC
See Minority enterprise small business investment corporation

MET
See Multiple employer trust

Metropolitan statistical area (MSA)
A means used by the government to define large population centers that may transverse different governmental jurisdictions. For example, the Washington, D.C. MSA includes the District of Columbia and contiguous parts of Maryland and Virginia because all of these geopolitical areas comprise one population and economic operating unit.

Mezzanine financing
See Third-stage financing

Micro-efficiency
Efficiency as it pertains to the operation of individual firms.

Microdata
Information on the characteristics of an individual business firm.

Mid-term debt
An obligation that matures within one to five years.

Midrisk venture capital
See Equity midrisk venture capital

Minimum premium plan
A combination approach to funding an insurance plan aimed primarily at premium tax savings. The employer self-funds a fixed percentage of estimated monthly claims and the insurance company insures the excess.

Minimum wage
The lowest hourly wage allowed by the federal government.

Minority Business Development Agency
Contracts with private firms throughout the nation to sponsor Minority Business Development Centers which provide minority firms with advice and technical assistance on a fee basis.

Minority Enterprise Small Business Investment Corporation (MESBIC)
A federally funded private venture capital firm licensed by the U.S. Small Business Administration to provide capital to minority-owned businesses (see separate citation).

Minority-owned business
Businesses owned by those who are socially or economically disadvantaged (see separate citation).

Mom and Pop business
A small store or enterprise having limited capital, principally employing family members.

Moonlighter
A wage-and-salary worker with a side business.

MSA
See Metropolitan statistical area

Multi-employer plan
A health plan to which more than one employer is required to contribute and that may be maintained through a collective bargaining agreement and required to meet standards prescribed by the U.S. Department of Labor.

Multi-level marketing
A system of selling in which you sign up other people to assist you and they, in turn, recruit others to help them. Some entrepreneurs have built successful

companies on this concept because the main focus of their activities is their product and product sales.

Multimedia
The use of several types of media to promote a product or service. Also, refers to the use of several different types of media (sight, sound, pictures, text) in a CD-ROM (see separate citation) product.

Multiple employer trust (MET)
A self-funded benefit plan generally geared toward small employers sharing a common interest.

NAFTA
See North American Free Trade Agreement

NASDAQ
See National Association of Securities Dealers Automated Quotations

National Association of Securities Dealers Automated Quotations
Provides price quotes on over-the-counter securities as well as securities listed on the New York Stock Exchange.

National income
Aggregate earnings of labor and property arising from the production of goods and services in a nation's economy.

Net assets
See Net worth

Net income
The amount remaining from earnings and profits after all expenses and costs have been met or deducted. Also known as Net earnings.

Net profit
Money earned after production and overhead expenses (see separate citations) have been deducted.

Net worth
The difference between a company's total assets and its total liabilities.

Network
A chain of interconnected individuals or organizations sharing information and/or services.

New York Stock Exchange (NYSE)
The oldest stock exchange in the U.S. Allows for trading in stocks, bonds, warrants, options, and rights that meet listing requirements.

Niche
A career or business for which a person is well-suited. Also, a product which fulfills one need of a particular market segment, often with little or no competition.

Nodes
One workstation in a network, either local area or wide area (see separate citations).

Nonbank bank
A bank that either accepts deposits or makes loans, but not both. Used to create many new branch banks.

Noncompetitive awards
A method of contracting whereby the federal government negotiates with only one contractor to supply a product or service.

Nonmember bank
A state-regulated bank that does not belong to the federal bank system.

Nonprofit
An organization that has no shareholders, does not distribute profits, and is without federal and state tax liabilities.

Norms
See Financial ratios

North American Free Trade Agreement (NAFTA)
Passed in 1993, NAFTA eliminates trade barriers among businesses in the U.S., Canada, and Mexico.

NYSE
See New York Stock Exchange

Occupational Safety & Health Administration (OSHA)
Federal agency that regulates health and safety standards within the workplace.

Optimal firm size
The business size at which the production cost per unit of output (average cost) is, in the long run, at its minimum.

Glossary

Organizational chart
A hierarchical chart tracking the chain of command within an organization.

OSHA
See Occupational Safety & Health Administration

Overhead
Expenses, such as employee benefits and building utilities, incurred by a business that are unrelated to the actual product or service sold.

Owner's capital
Debt or equity funds provided by the owner(s) of a business; sources of owner's capital are personal savings, sales of assets, or loans from financial institutions.

P & L
See Profit and loss statement

Part-time workers
Normally, those who work less than 35 hours per week. The Tax Reform Act indicated that part-time workers who work less than 17.5 hours per week may be excluded from health plans for purposes of complying with federal nondiscrimination rules.

Part-year workers
Those who work less than 50 weeks per year.

Partnership
Two or more parties who enter into a legal relationship to conduct business for profit. Defined by the U.S. Internal Revenue Code as joint ventures, syndicates, groups, pools, and other associations of two or more persons organized for profit that are not specifically classified in the IRS code as corporations or proprietorships.

Patent
A grant made by the government assuring an inventor the sole right to make, use, and sell an invention for a period of 17 years.

PC
See Professional corporation

Peak
See Cyclical peak

Pension
A series of payments made monthly, semiannually, annually, or at other specified intervals during the lifetime of the pensioner for distribution upon retirement. The term is sometimes used to denote the portion of the retirement allowance financed by the employer's contributions.

Pension fund
A fund established to provide for the payment of pension benefits; the collective contributions made by all of the parties to the pension plan.

Performance appraisal
An established set of objective criteria, based on job description and requirements, that is used to evaluate the performance of an employee in a specific job.

Permit
See Business license

Plan
See Business plan

Pooling
An arrangement for employers to achieve efficiencies and lower health costs by joining together to purchase group health insurance or self-insurance.

PPO
See Preferred provider organization

Preferred lenders program
See SBA special lending institution categories

Preferred provider organization (PPO)
A contractual arrangement with a health care services organization that agrees to discount its health care rates in return for faster payment and/or a patient base.

Premiums
The amount of money paid to an insurer for health insurance under a policy. The premium is generally paid periodically (e.g., monthly), and often is split between the employer and the employee. Unlike deductibles and coinsurance or copayments, premiums are paid for coverage whether or not benefits are actually used.

Prime-age workers
Employees 25 to 54 years of age.

Prime contract
A contract awarded directly by the U.S. Federal Government.

Private company
See Closely held corporation

Private placement
A method of raising capital by offering for sale an investment or business to a small group of investors (generally avoiding registration with the Securities and Exchange Commission or state securities registration agencies). Also known as Private financing or Private offering.

Pro forma
The use of hypothetical figures in financial statements to represent future expenditures, debts, and other potential financial expenses.

Proactive
Taking the initiative to solve problems and anticipate future events before they happen, instead of reacting to an already existing problem or waiting for a difficult situation to occur.

Procurement
A contract from an agency of the federal government for goods or services from a small business.

Prodigy
An online service which is accessible by computer modem. The service features Internet access, bulletin boards, online periodicals, electronic mail, and other services for subscribers.

Product development
The stage of the innovation process where research is translated into a product or process through evaluation, adaptation, and demonstration.

Product franchising
An arrangement for a franchisee to use the name and to produce the product line of the franchisor or parent corporation.

Production
The manufacture of a product.

Production prototype
See Prototype

Productivity
A measurement of the number of goods produced during a specific amount of time.

Professional corporation (PC)
Organized by members of a profession such as medicine, dentistry, or law for the purpose of conducting their professional activities as a corporation. Liability of a member or shareholder is limited in the same manner as in a business corporation.

Profit and loss statement (P & L)
The summary of the incomes (total revenues) and costs of a company's operation during a specific period of time. Also known as Income and expense statement.

Proposal
See Business plan

Proprietorship
The most common legal form of business ownership; about 85 percent of all small businesses are proprietorships. The liability of the owner is unlimited in this form of ownership.

Prospective payment system
A cost-containment measure included in the Social Security Amendments of 1983 whereby Medicare payments to hospitals are based on established prices, rather than on cost reimbursement.

Prototype
A model that demonstrates the validity of the concept of an invention (laboratory prototype); a model that meets the needs of the manufacturing process and the user (production prototype).

Prudent investor rule or standard
A legal doctrine that requires fiduciaries to make investments using the prudence, diligence, and intelligence that would be used by a prudent person in making similar investments. Because fiduciaries make investments on behalf of third-party beneficiaries, the standard results in very conservative investments. Until recently, most state regulations required the fiduciary to apply this standard to each investment. Newer, more progressive regulations permit fiduciaries to apply this standard to the portfolio taken as a whole, thereby allowing a fiduciary to balance a portfolio with higher-yield, higher-risk investments. In states with more progressive regulations, practically every type of security is eligible for inclusion in the portfolio of investments made by a fiduciary, provided

that the portfolio investments, in their totality, are those of a prudent person.

Public equity markets
Organized markets for trading in equity shares such as common stocks, preferred stocks, and warrants. Includes markets for both regularly traded and nonregularly traded securities.

Public offering
General solicitation for participation in an investment opportunity. Interstate public offerings are supervised by the U.S. Securities and Exchange Commission (see separate citation).

Quality control
The process by which a product is checked and tested to ensure consistent standards of high quality.

Rate of return
The yield obtained on a security or other investment based on its purchase price or its current market price. The total rate of return is current income plus or minus capital appreciation or depreciation.

Real property
Includes the land and all that is contained on it.

Realignment
See Resource realignment

Recession
Contraction of economic activity occurring between the peak and trough (see separate citations) of a business cycle.

Regulated market
A market in which the government controls the forces of supply and demand, such as who may enter and what price may be charged.

Regulation D
A vehicle by which small businesses make small offerings and private placements of securities with limited disclosure requirements. It was designed to ease the burdens imposed on small businesses utilizing this method of capital formation.

Regulatory Flexibility Act
An act requiring federal agencies to evaluate the impact of their regulations on small businesses before the regulations are issued and to consider less burdensome alternatives.

Research
The initial stage of the innovation process, which includes idea generation and invention.

Research and development financing
A tax-advantaged partnership set up to finance product development for start-ups as well as more mature companies.

Resource mobility
The ease with which labor and capital move from firm to firm or from industry to industry.

Resource realignment
The adjustment of productive resources to interindustry changes in demand.

Resources
The sources of support or help in the innovation process, including sources of financing, technical evaluation, market evaluation, management and business assistance, etc.

Retained business earnings
Business profits that are retained by the business rather than being distributed to the shareholders as dividends.

Revolving credit
An agreement with a lending institution for an amount of money, which cannot exceed a set maximum, over a specified period of time. Each time the borrower repays a portion of the loan, the amount of the repayment may be borrowed yet again.

Risk capital
See Venture capital

Risk management
The act of identifying potential sources of financial loss and taking action to minimize their negative impact.

Routing
The sequence of steps necessary to complete a product during production.

S corporations
See Sub chapter S corporations

Glossary

SBA
See Small Business Administration

SBA direct loans
Loans made directly by the U.S. Small Business Administration (SBA); monies come from funds appropriated specifically for this purpose. In general, SBA direct loans carry interest rates slightly lower than those in the private financial markets and are available only to applicants unable to secure private financing or an SBA guaranteed loan.

SBA 504 Program
See Certified development corporation

SBA guaranteed loans
Loans made by lending institutions in which the U.S. Small Business Administration (SBA) will pay a prior agreed-upon percentage of the outstanding principal in the event the borrower of the loan defaults. The terms of the loan and the interest rate are negotiated between theborrower and the lending institution, within set parameters.

SBA loans
See Disaster loans; SBA direct loans; SBA guaranteed loans; SBA special lending institution categories

SBA Management Assistance Programs
Classes, workshops, counseling, and publications offered by the U.S. Small Business Administration.

SBA special lending institution categories
U.S. Small Business Administration (SBA) loan program in which the SBA promises certified banks a 72-hour turnaround period in giving its approval for a loan, and in which preferred lenders in a pilot program are allowed to write SBA loans without seeking prior SBA approval.

SBDB
See Small Business Data Base

SBDC
See Small business development centers

SBI
See Small business institutes program

SBIC
See Small business investment corporation

SBIR Program
See Small Business Innovation Development Act of 1982

Scale economies
The decline of the production cost per unit of output (average cost) as the volume of output increases.

Scale efficiency
The reduction in unit cost available to a firm when producing at a higher output volume.

SCORE
See Service Corps of Retired Executives

SEC
See Securities and Exchange Commission

SECA
See Self-Employment Contributions Act

Second-stage financing
Working capital for the initial expansion of a company that is producing, shipping, and has growing accounts receivable and inventories. Also known as Second-round financing.

Secondary market
A market established for the purchase and sale of outstanding securities following their initial distribution.

Secondary worker
Any worker in a family other than the person who is the primary source of income for the family.

Secondhand capital
Previously used and subsequently resold capital equipment (e.g., buildings and machinery).

Securities and Exchange Commission (SEC)
Federal agency charged with regulating the trade of securities to prevent unethical practices in the investor market.

Securitized debt
A marketing technique that converts long-term loans to marketable securities.

Seed capital
Venture financing provided in the early stages of the innovation process, usually during product development.

Self-employed person
One who works for a profit or fees in his or her own business, profession, or trade, or who operates a farm.

Self-Employment Contributions Act (SECA)
Federal law that governs the self-employment tax (see separate citation).

Self-employment income
Income covered by Social Security if a business earns a net income of at least $400.00 during the year. Taxes are paid on earnings that exceed $400.00.

Self-employment retirement plan
See Keogh plan

Self-employment tax
Required tax imposed on self-employed individuals for the provision of Social Security and Medicare. The tax must be paid quarterly with estimated income tax statements.

Self-funding
A health benefit plan in which a firm uses its own funds to pay claims, rather than transferring the financial risks of paying claims to an outside insurer in exchange for premium payments.

Service Corps of Retired Executives (SCORE)
Volunteers for the SBA Management Assistance Program who provide one-on-one counseling and teach workshops and seminars for small firms.

Service firm
See Business service firm

Service sector
Broadly defined, all U.S. industries that produce intangibles, including the five major industry divisions of transportation, communications, and utilities; wholesale trade; retail trade; finance, insurance, and real estate; and services.

Set asides
See Small business set asides

Short-haul service
A type of transportation service in which the transporter supplies service between cities where the maximum distance is no more than 200 miles.

Short-term debt
An obligation that matures in one year.

SIC codes
See Standard Industrial Classification codes

Single-establishment enterprise
See Establishment

Small business
An enterprise that is independently owned and operated, is not dominant in its field, and employs fewer than 500 people. For SBA purposes, the U.S. Small Business Administration (SBA) considers various other factors (such as gross annual sales) in determining size of a business.

Small Business Administration (SBA)
An independent federal agency that provides assistance with loans, management, and advocating interests before other federal agencies.

Small Business Data Base
A collection of microdata (see separate citation) files on individual firms developed and maintained by the U.S. Small Business Administration.

Small business development centers (SBDC)
Centers that provide support services to small businesses, such as individual counseling, SBA advice, seminars and conferences, and other learning center activities. Most services are free of charge, or available at minimal cost.

Small business development corporation
See Certified development corporation

Small business-dominated industry
Industry in which a minimum of 60 percent of employment or sales is in firms with fewer than 500 employees.

Small Business Innovation Development Act of 1982
Federal statute requiring federal agencies with large extramural research and development budgets to allocate a certain percentage of these funds to small research and development firms. The program, called the Small Business Innovation Research (SBIR) Program, is designed to stimulate technological innovation and make greater use of small businesses in meeting national innovation needs.

Small business institutes (SBI) program
Cooperative arrangements made by U.S. Small Business Administration district offices and local colleges and

universities to provide small business firms with graduate students to counsel them without charge.

Small business investment corporation (SBIC)
A privately owned company licensed and funded through the U.S. Small Business Administration and private sector sources to provide equity or debt capital to small businesses.

Small business set asides
Procurement (see separate citation) opportunities required by law to be on all contracts under $10,000 or a certain percentage of an agency's total procurement expenditure.

Smaller firms
For U.S. Department of Commerce purposes, those firms not included in the Fortune 1000.

SMSA
See Metropolitan statistical area

Socially and economically disadvantaged
Individuals who have been subjected to racial or ethnic prejudice or cultural bias without regard to their qualities as individuals, and whose abilities to compete are impaired because of diminished opportunities to obtain capital and credit.

Sole proprietorship
An unincorporated, one-owner business, farm, or professional practice.

Special lending institution categories
See SBA special lending institution categories

Standard Industrial Classification (SIC) codes
Four-digit codes established by the U.S. Federal Government to categorize businesses by type of economic activity; the first two digits correspond to major groups such as construction and manufacturing, while the last two digits correspond to subgroups such as home construction or highway construction.

Standard metropolitan statistical area (SMSA)
See Metropolitan statistical area

Start-up
A new business, at the earliest stages of development and financing.

Start-up costs
Costs incurred before a business can commence operations.

Start-up financing
Financing provided to companies that have either completed product development and initial marketing or have been in business for less than one year but have not yet sold their product commercially.

Stock
A certificate of equity ownership in a business.

Stop-loss coverage
Insurance for a self-insured plan that reimburses the company for any losses it might incur in its health claims beyond a specified amount.

Strategic planning
Projected growth and development of a business to establish a guiding direction for the future. Also used to determine which market segments to explore for optimal sales of products or services.

Structural unemployment
See Unemployment

Sub chapter S corporations
Corporations that are considered noncorporate for tax purposes but legally remain corporations.

Subcontract
A contract between a prime contractor and a subcontractor, or between subcontractors, to furnish supplies or services for performance of a prime contract (see separate citation) or a subcontract.

Surety bonds
Bonds providing reimbursement to an individual, company, or the government if a firm fails to complete a contract. The U.S. Small Business Administration guarantees surety bonds in a program much like the SBA guaranteed loan program (see separate citation).

Swing loan
See Bridge financing

Target market
The clients or customers sought for a business' product or service.

Glossary

Targeted Jobs Tax Credit
Federal legislation enacted in 1978 that provides a tax credit to an employer who hires structurally unemployed individuals.

Tax number
A number assigned to a business by a state revenue department that enables the business to buy goods without paying sales tax.

Taxable bonds
An interest-bearing certificate of public or private indebtedness. Bonds are issued by public agencies to finance economic development.

Technical assistance
See Management and technical assistance

Technical evaluation
Assessment of technological feasibility.

Technology
The method in which a firm combines and utilizes labor and capital resources to produce goods or services; the application of science for commercial or industrial purposes.

Technology transfer
The movement of information about a technology or intellectual property from one party to another for use.

Tenure
See Employee tenure

Term
The length of time for which a loan is made.

Terms of a note
The conditions or limits of a note; includes the interest rate per annum, the due date, and transferability and convertibility features, if any.

Third-party administrator
An outside company responsible for handling claims and performing administrative tasks associated with health insurance plan maintenance.

Third-stage financing
Financing provided for the major expansion of a company whose sales volume is increasing and that is breaking even or profitable. These funds are used for further plant expansion, marketing, working capital,

or development of an improved product. Also known as Third-round or Mezzanine financing.

Time deposit
A bank deposit that cannot be withdrawn before a specified future time.

Time management
Skills and scheduling techniques used to maximize productivity.

Trade credit
Credit extended by suppliers of raw materials or finished products. In an accounting statement, trade credit is referred to as "accounts payable."

Trade name
The name under which a company conducts business, or by which its business, goods, or services are identified. It may or may not be registered as a trademark.

Trade periodical
A publication with a specific focus on one or more aspects of business and industry.

Trade secret
Competitive advantage gained by a business through the use of a unique manufacturing process or formula.

Trade show
An exhibition of goods or services used in a particular industry. Typically held in exhibition centers where exhibitors rent space to display their merchandise.

Trademark
A graphic symbol, device, or slogan that identifies a business. A business has property rights to its trademark from the inception of its use, but it is still prudent to register all trademarks with the Trademark Office of the U.S. Department of Commerce.

Translation
See Product development

Treasury bills
Investment tender issued by the Federal Reserve Bank in amounts of $10,000 that mature in 91 to 182 days.

Treasury bonds
Long-term notes with maturity dates of not less than seven and not more than twenty-five years.

Treasury notes
Short-term notes maturing in less than seven years.

Trend
A statistical measurement used to track changes that occur over time.

Trough
See Cyclical trough

UCC
See Uniform Commercial Code

UL
See Underwriters Laboratories

Underwriters Laboratories (UL)
One of several private firms that tests products and processes to determine their safety. Although various firms can provide this kind of testing service, many local and insurance codes specify UL certification.

Underwriting
A process by which an insurer determines whether or not and on what basis it will accept an application for insurance. In an experience-rated plan, premiums are based on a firm's or group's past claims; factors other than prior claims are used for community-rated or manually rated plans.

Unfair competition
Refers to business practices, usually unethical, such as using unlicensed products, pirating merchandise, or misleading the public through false advertising, which give the offending business an unequitable advantage over others.

Unfunded accrued liability
The excess of total liabilities, both present and prospective, over present and prospective assets.

Unemployment
The joblessness of individuals who are willing to work, who are legally and physically able to work, and who are seeking work. Unemployment may represent the temporary joblessness of a worker between jobs (frictional unemployment) or the joblessness of a worker whose skills are not suitable for jobs available in the labor market (structural unemployment).

Uniform Commercial Code (UCC)
A code of laws governing commercial transactions across the U.S., except Louisiana. Their purpose is to bring uniformity to financial transactions.

Uniform product code (UPC symbol)
A computer-readable label comprised of ten digits and stripes that encodes what a product is and how much it costs. The first five digits are assigned by the Uniform Product Code Council, and the last five digits by the individual manufacturer.

Unit cost
See Average cost

UPC symbol
See Uniform product code

U.S. Establishment and Enterprise Microdata (USEEM) File
A cross-sectional database containing information on employment, sales, and location for individual enterprises and establishments with employees that have a Dun & Bradstreet credit rating.

U.S. Establishment Longitudinal Microdata (USELM) File
A database containing longitudinally linked sample microdata on establishments drawn from the U.S. Establishment and Enterprise Microdata file (see separate citation).

U.S. Small Business Administration 504 Program
See Certified development corporation

USEEM
See U.S. Establishment and Enterprise Microdata File

USELM
See U.S. Establishment Longitudinal Microdata File

VCN
See Venture capital network

Venture capital
Money used to support new or unusual business ventures that exhibit above-average growth rates, significant potential for market expansion, and are in need of additional financing to sustain growth or further research and development; equity or equity-type financing traditionally provided at the

commercialization stage, increasingly available prior to commercialization.

Venture capital company

A company organized to provide seed capital to a business in its formation stage, or in its first or second stage of expansion. Funding is obtained through public or private pension funds, commercial banks and bank holding companies, small business investment corporations licensed by the U.S. Small Business Administration, private venture capital firms, insurance companies, investment management companies, bank trust departments, industrial companies seeking to diversify their investment, and investment bankers acting as intermediaries for other investors or directly investing on their own behalf.

Venture capital limited partnerships

Designed for business development, these partnerships are an institutional mechanism for providing capital for young, technology-oriented businesses. The investors' money is pooled and invested in money market assets until venture investments have been selected. The general partners are experienced investment managers who select and invest the equity and debt securities of firms with high growth potential and the ability to go public in the near future.

Venture capital network (VCN)

A computer database that matches investors with entrepreneurs.

WAN

See Wide Area Network

Wide Area Network (WAN)

Computer networks linking systems throughout a state or around the world in order to facilitate the sharing of information.

Withholding

Federal, state, social security, and unemployment taxes withheld by the employer from employees' wages; employers are liable for these taxes and the corporate umbrella and bankruptcy will not exonerate an employer from paying back payroll withholding. Employers should escrow these funds in a separate account and disperse them quarterly to withholding authorities.

Workers' compensation

A state-mandated form of insurance covering workers injured in job-related accidents. In some states, the state is the insurer; in other states, insurance must be acquired from commercial insurance firms. Insurance rates are based on a number of factors, including salaries, firm history, and risk of occupation.

Working capital

Refers to a firm's short-term investment of current assets, including cash, short-term securities, accounts receivable, and inventories.

Yield

The rate of income returned on an investment, expressed as a percentage. Income yield is obtained by dividing the current dollar income by the current market price of the security. Net yield or yield to maturity is the current income yield minus any premium above par or plus any discount from par in purchase price, with the adjustment spread over the period from the date of purchase to the date of maturity.

Index

Listings in this index are arranged alphabetically by business plan type, then alphabetically by business plan name. Users are provided with the volume number in which the plan appears.

Index

Index